The
Sunday Telegraph
Cookbook

Marika Hanbury Tenison

The
Sunday Telegraph
Cookbook

Illustrated by Ursula Sieger
Photographs by Bob Croxford

GRANADA
London Toronto Sydney New York

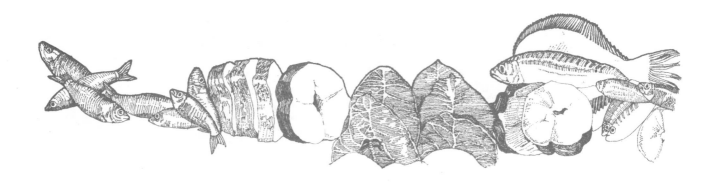

Granada Publishing Limited
Frogmore, St Albans, Herts AL2 2NF
and
3 Upper James Street, London W1R 4BP
Suite 405, 4th Floor, 866 United Nations Plaza, New York, NY 10017, USA
117 York Street, Sydney, NSW 2000, Australia
100 Skyway Avenue, Rexdale, Ontario M9W 3A6, Canada
PO Box 84165, Greenside, 2034 Johannesburg, South Africa
61 Beach Road, Auckland, New Zealand

Published by Granada Publishing 1980

Copyright © Marika Hanbury Tenison 1980

ISBN 0 246 11127 5

Filmset by Keyspools Ltd, Golborne, Lancashire
Printed in Great Britain by W. S. Cowell Limited, Ipswich

Granada ®
Granada Publishing ®

Contents

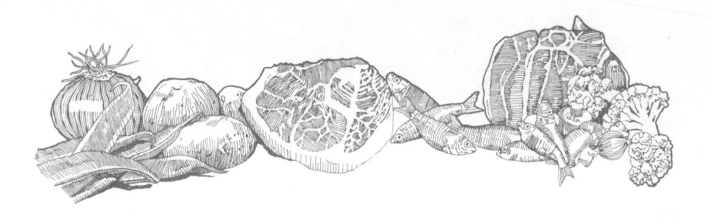

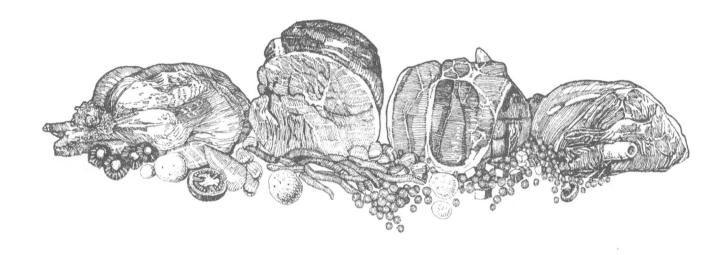

To Winifred Jackson, Eileen, Anthea Hall and everyone else on the *Sunday Telegraph*, with thanks

Preface

1966: I had been married seven years, moved to a remote farm on Bodmin Moor in Cornwall with my explorer husband Robin, had achieved a daughter who was six and decided, like so many wives of my generation, that I needed a job. I had no qualifications, had left school under a cloud at fourteen and had a distinct spelling block. I could, however, cook and I had always wanted to write.

I was lucky – I wrote a children's book about a princess and a unicorn and although it has never been published it caused enough interest for a publisher to be persuaded I should write a cookery book on deep freezing. I worked for eighteen months on a local newspaper, writing a cookery column for £1 a week and then, through sheer misrepresentation, persuaded the magazine *Nova* to give me a job as their cookery editor, where I struggled tearfully to produce a page of bright food ideas for *avant garde* women who didn't want to cook anyway.

Then I heard by chance that the Cookery Editor of the *Sunday Telegraph*, Jean Robertson, was leaving. I leapt on a train to London and appeared in the office of the Women's Page. I knew that as a potential journalist, one should have a cuttings book, and as my cuttings were on the meagre side I compensated by putting them in

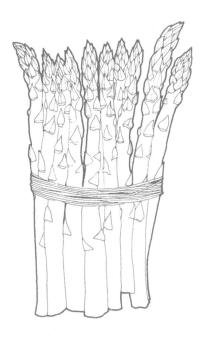

the largest, most garish and expensive scrap-book I could find. This I proudly presented to Winifred Jackson. It was so large that unfortunately she couldn't actually open it in the space she had between her desk and the wall and she dryly suggested I should confine myself to smaller books in the future. To my amazement she gave me the chance to write three trial pieces for the pages and, without ever having been officially taken on, I found myself writing weekly for the paper and going through all the nightmares experienced by anyone who has to produce the goods to a deadline week after week and month after month right through the year. I loved every minute of it.

Twelve years later I am still writing for the *Sunday Telegraph* and I still get as much of a kick out of seeing my name on the page as I did in those first nerve-racking weeks. I no longer have to take the train to London on a Thursday morning in order to read through and check my column in the proofs but we are still in constant touch and the many letters I get from readers still give me just as much pleasure as they did in my first few years.

People always ask me how I manage to think up something to say week after week. My problem is that I have *too* much to say; so many ideas that they would fill a page each week with no trouble at all, so many new ideas to share, so many old recipes to revive and so many new trends in food to talk about and ideas of my own to develop that I could all too easily become a sub-editor's most unpopular contributor. Fashions in food, like fashions in clothes, are always changing, prices are always rising and adjustments having to be made and every single day I make some discovery working in my kitchen that I feel must be shared.

Winifred Jackson became not only my editor but also an exceptional friend. She taught me how to write for a newspaper, how to present my thoughts reasonably logically and she dealt kindly with my wilder flights of fancy such as deciding it would be fun to present recipes in verse or the occasion when I felt, for a change, it would be a good idea to produce egg recipes in egg-shaped print.

My ideas for the cookery column are based on essentials. Food should be seasonal, attention should be paid to cost as prices steadily rise; the quality of cooking should be high but great attention should be paid to its timing as everyone becomes more and more busy; recipes from other countries should be included and my recipes should, above all, be easy to understand, easy to follow and reliable. When I travel abroad my taste buds tingle for new experiences, and when I am at home as much time is spent in my kitchen, trying out new recipes and experimenting with food, as it is at my desk. I

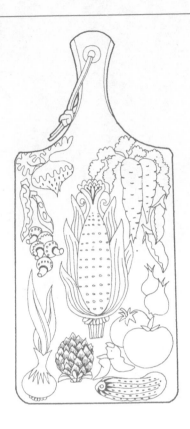

developed a kitchen garden and herb garden so that I learnt about growing as well as cooking vegetables and fruit, and I visited butchers, fishermen and fishmongers so that I could learn more about the source and preparation of raw ingredients.

I also wrote books. *Deep-Freeze Cookery* was swiftly followed by *Soups and Hors d'Oeuvres* (soon to be re-issued as *Soups and Starters*), *Left Over for Tomorrow*, *Deep-Freeze Sense*, *The Best of British Cooking*, *Eat Well and Stay Slim*, *Recipes from a Country Kitchen* and *New Fish Cookery*. I travelled for the *Sunday Telegraph* to Portugal, France and Spain and to areas of Britain concerned with the production of food; I went over factories, visited food shops and attended press conferences where new ideas and products were launched and I read through just about every cookery book that was produced. All the time my knowledge, my delight and my interest in all the many aspects of good food, good cooking and the economics of cooking grew and goes on growing.

This book includes a selection of some of the recipes I produced during the past twelve years. All of them have been tested by me in my kitchen and by the many readers who liked them enough to try them out. It is not a book of *haute cuisine* but rather a collection of recipes which I feel fit in with our life style today and will stand up to the rigours of time and be used again and again in the years to come.

Note that *either* imperial *or* metric measurements should be used for each recipe, never both.

Marika Hanbury Tenison

Acknowledgements

As a cookery and food writer I receive enormous help from manufacturers of kitchen equipment and suppliers of food and I would like to thank all those who have helped me in the past and particularly to mention those who supplied equipment for the photographs in this book, including: Dartington Glass; Ekco Heating & Appliances; I.C.T.C.; Calor Gas Limited; Kennick International; Le Creuset; Divertimenti; Magimix.

Soups

Whatever the soup you plan to make I cannot emphasise too highly the argument for using home-made stock. Of course stock cubes are a boon, and marvellous when you do not happen to have any home-made stock handy. You can use chicken or beef stock cubes, or substitute a can of consommé or commercially packaged soup as the basis of a home-made concoction. But in the end there will always be a faint, underlying flavour from the manufactured product, and a uniformity of taste which never appears when a home-made stock is used. I also use stock cubes in order to intensify the flavour of stock which is a little on the thin side and which I have not got time to boil in order to reduce it. Always remember when using a cube to allow for the salt in it when seasoning.

Home-made stocks are surprisingly simple to produce and they have the definite advantage of using up scraps, bones and vegetable trimmings which might otherwise be thrown away. You can make them very inexpensively in a large 'slow cook' pot or a pressure cooker, and with modern deep-freeze equipment and techniques they can easily be stored for future use, with none of the one-time problems of boiling every day in order to keep it from going off.

Giving a recipe for home-made stock is not really feasible because the whole joy of these liquids is that, since they are made from an assortment of ingredients as available, and since these ingredients will never be quite the same, the flavour of the finished stock will always be an individual one. For reference, however, here is a list of potential ingredients, a basic recipe and some 'tricks of the trade' for good stock making.

1. If you want a richly coloured brown stock brown the bones and onions in a little oil before adding the other ingredients. Tomato skins, onion skins and mushroom peelings will also help to add colour.

2. The ingredients in your stock pan must always be covered (any rising above the surface of the water are apt to dry and develop an 'off' flavour).

3. Once the stock has come to the boil lower the heat and leave the stock to simmer fairly briskly (bubbles should just be breaking the surface all the time) for up to four hours.

4. Strain your stock through a very fine sieve (you can also re-strain it through a piece of muslin), leave to cool and then chill until the fat forms a skin over the surface and can easily be removed. If you are in a hurry the fat can be soaked up with paper towels.

5. If you want to intensify the flavour return the strained, skimmed stock to a clean pan, bring it to the boil and boil over a high heat until it is reduced and the strength intensified.

Ingredients for Chicken Stock

Chicken bones from a raw or cooked carcass (break up the carcass before adding it)
Chicken giblets
Onions and onion skins
Carrots and carrot peelings
Turnip
Celery stalks and leaves
Bouquet garni of parsley stalks, sage, thyme and bay leaves
A little lemon peel
Salt and black peppercorns
Tomato skins

These are not all essential ingredients but those which you might have available.

Combine all ingredients (having browned the chicken carcass if required), cover with cold water, bring to the boil and simmer, covered, for 2–4 hours. Strain through a fine sieve or muslin, leave to cool and then refrigerate until the fat has formed a solid crust over the surface. Remove fat, return to a clean pan and boil until the required strength is reached.

The stock can be poured into polythene containers and then frozen. Concentrated stock (well reduced) can be frozen in ice cube trays.

Ingredients for Meat Stock

Beef marrow bones from the butcher
*Lamb bones and trimmings with the fat
   removed*
*A small quantity of shin beef for flavouring
   and colour*
Onions and onion skins
Tomatoes and tomato skins
Mushroom stalks and peelings
Carrots and carrot peelings
Celery stalks and leaves
Turnip
*Bouquet garni of parsley stalks, oregano,
   thyme and bay leaves*
Salt and black peppercorns
Pinch of allspice
Red or white wine

These are not all essential ingredients but those which you might have available.

Brown the bones and onions in a little dripping or oil. Add the remaining ingredients, cover with water and any leftover wine, bring to the boil, cover and simmer for 3–4 hours. Strain the stock through a fine sieve, leave to cool and refrigerate until the fat forms a crust on the surface. Remove the fat, return the stock to a clean pan and boil until the required strength is reached. Freeze in the same way as chicken stock.

Extra flavouring can be given by adding some tomato purée, Worcestershire or soya sauce or some mushroom ketchup.

Other Stock-making Ingredients

*Water from cooked vegetables (except from
   cabbage family)*
The trimmings from beans and peas
Ham bones
Bacon rinds
The core and seeds of green or red peppers
Lemon and orange peel

Fish Stock

Fishmongers will usually give you fish bones for nothing and it is certainly worth while taking home the bones of any fish that you may have had filleted by your fishmonger. Fish stock is simple to make and takes far less time than a meat stock. By using the stock for cooking your fish in, or for incorporating into sauces, you will achieve a far better overall flavour for your fish soups and fish dishes.

Place the bones in a saucepan, add some sliced onion, carrot and celery, a piece of lemon peel and any leftover white wine. Pour in enough water to cover the ingredients, season with salt and pepper, add a bouquet garni, bring to the boil and simmer for 30 minutes. Strain the stock through a very fine sieve or a piece of muslin.

This stock, too, can be frozen for future use.

Jellied Soups

Cold jellied soups are delicious in the summer but they must be well jelled and not 'slurpy'. The jelly is usually produced by using raw beef marrow bones or poultry carcass, but extra jellifying ingredients can be added in the form of veal bones or pig's trotters when you are making the stock. If the consistency of your soup is not thick enough dissolve a little gelatine in some hot water and stock and add it to the soup.

Soups in General

Four major points should be considered when making soups: colour, texture, flavour and temperature.

1. The colour of your soup should be fresh and bright; muddy coloured or wishy-washy looking soups will never taste any better than they look. Tomato purée will enrich the colour of a brown soup and green soups can be helped along by a few drops of green vegetable colouring.
2. Thick soups should be really thick and satisfying; thicken them with egg yolks beaten with cream, mashed potato, a roux of flour mixed with softened butter, or with cream. Thin soups should be light, sparkling and elegant; thin by adding wine or more stock.
3. The flavour of soup is, of course, all-important. The first hint of this flavour (in a hot soup) should be a rich and satisfying aroma which rises from the bowl as the soup is put in front of you. If your soup is not well flavoured enough add stock cubes if necessary, herbs, spices, tomato purée, mushroom ketchup, etc., a little at a time until the desired strength is reached.

   On the whole cold soups are more subtle than hot soups. Their flavour should be delicate, and usually the addition of a little lemon juice will not only heighten the taste of the ingredients but also add that pleasant 'zip' that is so much a part of summer eating.
4. The temperature a soup is served at is almost as important as the flavour. Nothing is worse than a hot soup which is served tepid. Not only will the flavour be impaired but any fat still remaining in the soup will rise to the surface. Serve soup really piping hot and always pour into well-heated bowls.

   It also follows that the colder cold soups are served the better will be their flavour. Chill the soup thoroughly in the refrigerator before serving it, chill your soup bowls in the refrigerator as well and, if the weather is really hot, add one or two ice cubes when serving.

Soup Accompaniments

Nothing is easier to dress up than a soup. Add a little finely chopped parsley, chives or celery leaves at the last minute before serving and you add an instant touch of sophistication.

Swirl a tablespoon of cream into each serving and sprinkle just a pinch of cayenne over that to produce a simple dramatic effect. Or cover some thin slices of French bread with grated cheese, float one in each serving and then brown quickly under a hot grill to make a really hearty winter soup. Soups can also be garnished with slices of lemon or orange, chopped watercress or even a whole marigold flower head.

To add extra interest to your soups you can float small croutons (diced squares of crisply fried bread) on the top of the soup. Accompany them with piping hot bread rolls, crisp French bread and butter, thin slices of brown buttered bread or delicious hot pita, the Greek bread now widely available in supermarkets.

Soups as a Main Course

I find a rich meat and vegetable or vegetable soup makes an excellent main course family meal. Serve the soup with hot toast and some pâté, or with slices of bread topped with tomatoes and grated cheese and baked in the oven, and follow it with fresh fruit and cheese to have an admirable meal which is quick to produce and which all the family will enjoy.

Iced Tomato Soup with Prawns

Serves 6

1 large onion
1 clove garlic
675 g (1½ lb) tomatoes
1 tablespoon olive oil
1 tablespoon flour
1·2 litres (2 pints) strong chicken stock
1 teaspoon sugar
Juice of ½ lemon
1 teaspoon white wine vinegar
Pinch of marjoram and celery salt
1 bay leaf
Salt and freshly ground black pepper
100 g (4 oz) peeled prawns
½ cucumber
1 tablespoon finely chopped chives
150 ml (5 fl oz) carton single cream
1 sprig fresh tarragon or lemon thyme

Finely chop the onion and crush the garlic clove. Roughly chop the tomatoes. Heat the olive oil in a saucepan, add the onions and garlic and cook over a low heat until soft and transparent. Add the flour and mix well. Gradually add 300 ml (½ pint) stock, stirring continually until the mixture is smooth. Mix in the tomatoes, sugar, lemon juice, vinegar, marjoram, celery salt and bay leaf and season with salt and pepper. Cover and simmer gently for 20 minutes. Add the remaining stock and simmer for a further 30 minutes. Remove the bay leaf, rub the soup through a sieve and refrigerate for at least two hours or until cold.

Finely chop the prawns, peel the cucumber and cut the flesh into small dice. Add the prawns, cucumber and half the chives to the soup and blend in the cream. Check seasoning and top with finely chopped tarragon or lemon thyme leaves. Garnish with the remaining chives.

Iced Haddock Soup

100 g (4 oz) smoked haddock
600 ml (1 pint) milk
Two 150 g (5 oz) cartons yoghurt
4–5 tablespoons finely chopped pickled
    cucumber
2 tablespoons finely chopped chives
¾ tablespoon grated onion
1 teaspoon lemon juice
Pepper
Red caviar or finely chopped red pepper
    garnish (optional)

Serves 4

An unusual summer soup with a delicious smoky flavour. This can be served hot, but take care not to let the soup boil as it will curdle. The soup may need a little extra milk for thinning.

Poach the haddock gently in the milk until soft. Drain off the milk and flake the fish (make sure you remove any bones). When the milk has cooled skim off any fat from the surface and mix in the yoghurt.

Add the cucumber to the milk and yoghurt with the fish, chives, grated onion and lemon juice. Season with a little pepper and chill well.

A spoonful of red caviar or finely chopped red pepper on top of each serving turns this soup into something really special.

Gazpacho

400 g (14 oz) can tomato juice
2 tomatoes, skinned and chopped
1 large cucumber, peeled and chopped
2 green peppers, deseeded and chopped
1 small shallot, chopped
Salt
1 large clove garlic, crushed
2 teaspoons paprika
1 teaspoon cumin seeds
3 tablespoons wine vinegar
1 tablespoon olive oil

Serves 6

This ice-cold soup originated in Andalusia and is popular throughout Spain during the long hot summer–not least with foreign visitors. It should be made in a big bowl, since any that remains is always welcome for another meal, but must be covered to prevent everything else in the refrigerator from acquiring its piquant flavour.

Pour the tomato juice into a large bowl, together with water measured by filling the empty can four times. If you have a blender you can save time by using it to chop the vegetables in some of the liquid–but be careful to stop before reducing them to a purée. With the amounts given it will be necessary to put the vegetables through the blender in batches.

Put all the chopped vegetables into the bowl with the liquid. Use of a blender results in a white foam, which must be removed with a spoon before seasoning. Add a little salt, the crushed or minutely chopped garlic, and the paprika first mixed in a little water. Pound the cumin seeds in a mortar and add to the soup with the vinegar. Cover and put in the refrigerator to cool. Just before serving add the tablespoon of olive oil, stirring well.

Many recipes for gazpacho include breadcrumbs, which are sometimes served separately in restaurants. But ordinary breadcrumbs form a glutinous mass in the soup and in my opinion are best left out.

Iced Strawberry Soup

225 g (8 oz) strawberries
600 ml (1 pint) strong chicken stock, or water
  and stock cubes
Salt, pepper and ½ teaspoon ginger
150 g (5 oz) carton yoghurt
1 tablespoon finely chopped fresh mint

Serves 6

This is one of my special secrets and always a spectacular success.

Purée the strawberries until smooth, combine them in a saucepan with stock and season with salt, pepper and ginger. Simmer for five minutes and leave to cool. Beat in the yoghurt and refrigerate until really icy cold. Sprinkle with mint before serving.

Iced Cucumber and Mint Soup

2 medium cucumbers, peeled and chopped
300 ml (½ pint) water
1 small onion, peeled and thinly sliced
Salt and white pepper
2 tablespoons flour
450 ml (¾ pint) chicken stock, or water and
  stock cube
2 bay leaves
Juice of ½ lemon
150 g (5 oz) carton yoghurt
3 mint leaves
Thin slices of lemon

Serves 4–6

Combine the cucumber, water and onion in a saucepan. Season with salt and pepper, bring to the boil, cover and simmer until the cucumber is soft. Purée in liquidiser or through a fine food mill or sieve and return to a clean saucepan.

Add enough chicken stock to the flour to make a thin, smooth paste. Blend in remaining stock and add to the purée with the bay leaves and lemon juice. Bring slowly to the boil, stirring continuously, and simmer gently for two minutes. Remove the bay leaves and leave to cool. Blend in yoghurt and mint leaves; check seasoning and refrigerate for at least two hours before serving. Garnish with thin slices of lemon.

Chilled Curried Avocado Soup

2 teaspoons curry powder
1·2 litres (2 pints) chicken stock, or water
  and 3 stock cubes
2 ripe avocado pears
2 tablespoons lemon juice
Salt
200 ml (7½ fl oz) double cream
Thin slices of lemon

Serves 6

Heat the curry powder in four tablespoons of the stock over a low heat, stirring until the powder dissolves. Remove from the heat and cool.

Peel and halve the avocados and remove stones. Sprinkle the flesh with lemon juice and rub through a fine sieve. Add 300 ml (½ pint) of the stock and beat until smooth (this can be done in a liquidiser). Blend in remaining stock and curry mixture and season with a little salt.

Stir in the cream and chill well before serving garnished with thin slices of lemon.

Avocado Soup with Prawns

Serves 4

1 large ripe avocado pear
Juice of ½ lemon
450 ml (¾ pint) cold chicken stock
2 tablespoons yoghurt
2 tablespoons milk
4 tablespoons single cream
1 teaspoon grated raw onion
Salt, white pepper and Tabasco sauce
100 g (4 oz) peeled prawns
1 tablespoon very finely chopped chives

A delicious way to start a meal: smooth, velvety and very subtle.

Peel and halve the avocado and remove stone. Mash the flesh with a fork and blend in the lemon juice, stock, yoghurt, milk, cream and onion. Purée the mixture through a fine sieve or food mill or in liquidiser. Season with salt, pepper and a hint of Tabasco.

Divide the prawns between four soup bowls. Pour over the avocado soup, top with chopped chives and chill before serving.

Patio Soup

Serves 6

450 ml (¾ pint) chicken stock or canned
    consommé
2 ripe avocado pears
Juice of ½ lemon
150 ml (5 fl oz) single cream
150 ml (5 fl oz) soured cream or yoghurt
100 g (4 oz) peeled prawns
½ teaspoon finely grated raw onion
½ teaspoon finely chopped mint
Salt and freshly ground black pepper
6 fresh mint leaves to garnish

Beautiful to look at, cool and sophisticated to taste. Chill the soup bowls as well as the soup to make sure it is served icy cold.

If the stock is home made make sure it is free from all particles of fat as these ruin the taste of a cold soup.

Mash the avocados with a fork and beat in the lemon juice, stock or consommé, cream and sour cream or yoghurt. Purée the mixture until absolutely smooth in a liquidiser or food mill. Roughly chop the prawns and add them to the soup with the onion and chopped mint. Season with salt and pepper, mix well and pour into individual soup bowls. Refrigerate for at least an hour and garnish each bowl with a mint leaf.

Iced Borsch

Serves 4

450 g (1 lb) raw beetroot
2 carrots
1 onion
1·2 litres (2 pints) strong beef stock
1 teaspoon white wine vinegar
Salt and pepper
50 g (2 oz) ham
4 tablespoons sour cream
1 tablespoon finely chopped chives

Peel the beetroot and chop into small pieces. Peel and finely chop the carrots and onion. Simmer all the vegetables in the stock until they are tender and the soup is deep red; strain through a fine sieve. Add the vinegar and season with salt and pepper. Chill well.

Cut the ham into thin strips and add to the soup. Garnish each serving with a spoonful of sour cream mixed with finely chopped chives.

This soup can also be served hot.

Apple Vichyssoise

Serves 8–10

5 large cooking apples
3·5 litres (6 pints) chicken stock
600 ml (1 pint) double cream, chilled
Salt to taste
Sugar to taste
Fresh lemon juice to taste
1 apple cut in fine julienne strips and mixed
  with lemon juice

Peel and core the apples, cut into small pieces and cook in stock until tender. Pass through a sieve or blender and chill. Add cream, salt, sugar and lemon juice; mix well. Adjust seasoning with sugar and salt. Sprinkle the apple julienne on top.

Marika's Onion and Parsley Soup

Serves 4

1 very large onion
50 g (2 oz) butter
1½ tablespoons flour
450 ml (¾ pint) chicken stock, or water and
  1 stock cube
300 ml (½ pint) milk
3 tablespoons finely chopped parsley
Salt and white pepper
2–3 tablespoons cream
1 egg yolk

Peel and finely chop the onion. Melt the butter in a saucepan, add the onion and cook gently over a low heat, stirring to prevent browning, until soft and transparent. Add the flour and mix well. Gradually blend in the stock, stirring continuously until the soup is slightly thickened and comes to the boil. Lower the heat, add the milk and parsley, season with salt and pepper and simmer for 20 minutes.

Beat the egg yolk with the cream, add a couple of spoonfuls of the hot soup and mix well, then add to the soup, stirring in with a wire whisk and on no account allowing the soup to boil.

Serve with hot crusty bread.

Cream of Onion Soup

Serves 4

3 large onions
40 g (1½ oz) butter
1 tablespoon flour
1 litre (1¾ pints) chicken stock, or water and
  stock cubes
Salt, pepper and a pinch of nutmeg
2 egg yolks
150 ml (5 fl oz) double cream
2 tablespoons finely chopped parsley

Peel and very thinly slice the onions and divide into rings. Heat the butter in a large saucepan, add the onions and cook over a low heat, without browning, until soft and transparent. Add the flour and mix lightly. Gradually blend in the stock, stirring continually until the soup is smooth and slightly thickened. Season with salt, pepper and nutmeg, bring to the boil and simmer gently for 20 minutes.

Beat the egg yolks with the cream and add to the soup, stirring continually, over a low heat, for five minutes—*do not boil*. Divide the parsley between four soup bowls, pour over the hot soup and serve at once.

Kitchen Stove Soup

1 small turnip
1 large onion
2 sticks celery
2 carrots
50 g (2 oz) small button mushrooms
1 small can sweetcorn
2 chipolata sausages
1 tablespoon dripping
1½ tablespoons tomato purée
¼ teaspoon turmeric
1·8 litres (3 pints) stock
Salt and freshly ground black pepper
2 tablespoons finely chopped parsley
Slices of white bread
Butter
25 g (1 oz) Cheddar cheese, finely grated
Paprika pepper

Serves 6

Don't worry if you haven't the exact ingredients listed here; use what you have to hand instead.

Peel the turnip and cut into small dice. Peel and finely chop the onion. Trim off leaves and tough fibres from the celery and thinly slice stalks. Peel the carrots and cut into small dice. Very thinly slice the mushrooms. Drain the sweetcorn.

Cook the sausages over medium heat, without pricking, in the dripping until well browned and cooked through. Remove from pan and leave to cool. Add the turnip, carrots, onion and celery to the pan and cook over a low heat, stirring to prevent sticking, until the onion is soft and transparent.

Remove the vegetables with a slotted spoon to a large saucepan, stir in tomato purée, turmeric and stock, mix well and season. Bring to the boil and simmer gently until the vegetables are almost cooked.

Add the sweetcorn and mushrooms, and sausages cut into thin slices; cook for a further three minutes. Mix in the parsley and check seasoning.

Cut twelve 5 cm (2 in) rounds from the bread, spread with butter and cover with grated cheese. Sprinkle with paprika.

Pour the soup into heat-proof earthenware bowls, float circles of bread on top and put under a hot grill until the cheese has melted.

Midnight Soup

2 thin rashers bacon
2 onions
2 tomatoes
15 g (½ oz) butter
2 tablespoons finely chopped canned pimento
25 g (1 oz) flour
2 teaspoons paprika pepper
750 ml (1¼ pints) chicken stock, or water and
    stock cubes
Pinch of dried marjoram and dill weed
Salt and freshly ground black pepper
1 teaspoon sugar

Serves 4

Well-flavoured vegetable soups like this are surprisingly quick to prepare.

Remove rinds and finely chop the bacon rashers. Peel and finely chop the onions. Cover the tomatoes with boiling water for one minute, slide off skins and chop flesh. Melt the butter in a large saucepan. Add the bacon, onions, tomatoes and pimento and cook over a low heat for five minutes, stirring to prevent sticking. Add the flour and paprika and mix well. Gradually blend in the stock, stirring over a high heat until the soup comes to the boil and is smooth. Add the herbs, season with salt and pepper and mix in the sugar. Cover and simmer for about 20 minutes.

Natalia Polonski's Soup Sensation

1 cucumber
3 tomatoes
2 cloves garlic
450 ml ($\frac{3}{4}$ pint) water
1 chicken stock cube
1 tablespoon tomato purée
15 g ($\frac{1}{2}$ oz) gelatine powder
Juice of $\frac{1}{2}$ lemon
Freshly ground black pepper
150 ml (5 fl oz) carton soured cream
175 g (6 oz) peeled prawns
Cayenne pepper

Serves 6

When I first experimented with this soup I found it so fabulous that we had it three nights running as a starter without losing our enthusiasm for the sparkling summer taste.

Peel and grate the cucumber. Peel the tomatoes (cover with boiling water for two minutes and slide off the skins), remove tough cores and finely chop the flesh. Squeeze the garlic through a garlic press or crush with a knife blade. Combine the water, stock cube and tomato purée in a saucepan, bring to the boil and simmer for five minutes, stirring occasionally. Remove from the heat, add the gelatine and stir until melted. Leave to cool, then mix in the cucumber, tomato, garlic and lemon juice; season with pepper.

Refrigerate until lightly set. Mix up gently with a fork and spoon into individual bowls, leaving a hole in the centre of each one. Fill the holes with soured cream and top with prawns. Sprinkle over a small pinch of cayenne and serve well chilled.

Pea Soup

450 g (1 lb) dried yellow peas
2 onions
2 cloves garlic
2 carrots
1 stick celery
1 ham bone
Scant 2·5 litres (4 pints) stock; water will do
    but a light stock is better
Freshly ground black pepper
2 cloves
1 bay leaf

Serves 6

When times were really hard soup was often the only dish of the day, and if a housewife could get hold of a ham bone, pea soup was considered to be a veritable feast. Any shop that sells ham off the bone will sell the bone when carving is finished, and it is surprising how much meat one can get off that scraggy object.

Soak the peas for 12 hours or overnight. Peel and chop the onions, garlic and carrots. Chop the celery. Drain the peas, combine with the vegetables in a saucepan with the ham bone and stock or water. Season with pepper and add the cloves and bay leaf. Bring to the boil, cover and simmer for about 1$\frac{1}{2}$ hours or until the peas are absolutely tender.

Remove the ham bone and discard the cloves and bay leaf. Purée the soup through a fine sieve or food mill (do not liquidise as this will make it too thick). Remove any meat still sticking to the bone and cut it into thin strips. Return the soup to a clean pan, thin if necessary with water and check seasoning. Heat through and serve with fried bread croutons.

Smoky Pea Soup

1 medium onion
4 smoked bacon rashers
40 g (1½ oz) butter
225 g (8 oz) frozen peas
1·2 litres (2 pints) water
1 chicken stock cube
1 teaspoon sugar
Salt, pepper and a pinch of nutmeg
1 egg yolk
4–5 tablespoons single cream

Serves 4

Frozen peas are ideal for using in this warming and nourishing soup.

Peel and finely chop the onion. Remove the rinds and finely chop bacon. Cook onion and bacon gently in the butter until the onions are transparent. Add the peas, water, stock cube and sugar; season with salt, pepper and nutmeg. Bring to the boil and simmer gently for 20 minutes.

Purée the soup in a liquidiser or through a food mill and return to a clean pan. Beat the egg yolk with the cream, add to the soup and heat through without boiling, stirring well until the soup is piping hot and slightly thickened. Serve at once.

Maidenwell Pea Soup

2 rashers smoked bacon
15 g (½ oz) butter
1 small onion, finely chopped
1 carrot, finely chopped
450 g (1 lb) frozen peas
2 teaspoons lemon juice
Pinch of mixed dried herbs
Pinch of sugar
300 ml (½ pint) water
2 chicken stock cubes
450 ml (¾ pint) milk

Serves 6

Discard rind and finely chop the bacon. Melt the butter, add the onion, carrot and bacon and cook gently for ten minutes. Add peas, lemon juice, herbs, sugar, water and stock cubes; bring to the boil, cover and simmer for 20 minutes.

Purée the soup in a liquidiser or through a fine food mill or sieve. Return the soup to a clean pan, add the milk, check for seasoning and heat through. If the soup is too thick add some extra milk.

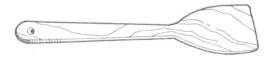

Broad Bean Soup

1 small onion
40 g (1½ oz) butter
900 ml (1½ pints) chicken stock
¼ teaspoon sugar
Salt and freshly ground black pepper
¼ teaspoon chopped savory
350 g (12 oz) shelled broad beans
4–5 tablespoons double cream

Serves 4–5

Peel and finely chop the onion. Heat the butter in a saucepan, add the onion and cook over low heat until soft and transparent. Add the stock, sugar, a pinch of salt and the savory. Bring to the boil, add the beans and cook until they are quite tender.

Remove and skin about a dozen beans for garnishing and purée the remainder in a sieve, food mill or liquidiser. Return the purée to a clean pan, heat through, season with salt and pepper and blend in the cream before serving.

Curly Cabbage and Apple Soup

Serves 6

350 g (12 oz) Savoy cabbage
1 large onion
1 medium cooking apple
1 tablespoon dripping or lard
1 teaspoon curry powder
1·2 litres (2 pints) good stock, or water and
    stock cubes
150 ml (5 fl oz) carton soured cream
Salt and pepper

This has an unusual and memorable flavour and goes well with fried bread croutons.

Shred the cabbage. Peel and chop the onion; peel, core and chop the cooking apple. Heat the fat in a large saucepan, add the cabbage, onion and apple and cook over a medium heat, without browning, for three minutes. Mix in the curry powder and add the stock. Mix well and bring to the boil. Lower the heat, cover and simmer gently for 30 minutes. Purée the soup through a sieve, a food mill or in a liquidiser and return to a clean pan.

Heat the soup through, season with salt and pepper if necessary and pour into hot soup bowls. Add a spoonful of soured cream, lightly seasoned, to each bowl just before serving.

Cooper's Soup

Serves 6

1 small white cabbage
3 Bramley apples
2 large onions
1 clove garlic
50 g (2 oz) butter
1 teaspoon sugar
1·8 litres (3 pints) chicken stock
Salt and freshly ground black pepper
3 thin rashers streaky bacon
2 tablespoons single cream

An inexpensive and warming soup from the cider area of the West Country. Serve it with a sprinkling of crispy chopped bacon over the top and some piping hot French bread and you have almost a meal in itself.

Remove core and shred the cabbage leaves. Peel, core and chop the apples. Peel and finely chop the onions. Crush the garlic. Melt the butter in a large heavy pan, add the onions and garlic and cook over a low heat for two minutes without browning. Add the apples and cabbage and continue to cook over a low heat, stirring continuously until all the butter has been absorbed. Mix in the sugar, pour over the stock and bring to the boil. Season with salt and pepper, cover and simmer for about 20 minutes or until the cabbage is soft but not mushy. Purée the soup through a sieve, a food mill or in a liquidiser.

Fry the bacon until crisp without using extra fat. Drain on kitchen paper, cut off the rinds with scissors and crumble the rashers. Return the soup to a clean pan, heat through, add the cream and check seasoning.

Pour the soup into heated bowls and sprinkle over the bacon just before serving.

Carrot and Tomato Soup

675 g (1½ lb) carrots
1 large potato
1 large onion
40 g (1½ oz) butter
1·2 litres (2 pints) stock
425 g (15 oz) can tomatoes
½ teaspoon oregano
1 bay leaf
Salt and pepper
150 ml (5 fl oz) single cream or top of milk
1 tablespoon finely chopped parsley or chives

Serves 6

Peel and chop the carrots and the potato; peel and finely chop the onion. Melt the butter in a large heavy saucepan, add the prepared vegetables and cook over a gentle heat until the butter is absorbed.

Add the stock, tomatoes, oregano and bay leaf and season with salt and pepper. Bring to the boil and simmer for 30 minutes or until the vegetables are tender. Remove the bay leaf and purée the soup in an electric liquidiser or through a fine sieve or food mill.

Return to a clean pan and blend in the cream. Heat through and check seasoning. Pour into heated bowls and garnish with the chives or parsley.

Harvest Moon Soup

450 g (1 lb) carton yoghurt
600 ml (1 pint) tomato juice
Pinch of oregano
1 teaspoon lemon juice
½ cucumber
175 g (6 oz) peeled prawns
1 tablespoon grated onion
Salt and pepper
Thin slices of lemon
Lettuce

Serves 4–5

You know that amazing colour which the moon sometimes turns at harvest time? This soup is a somewhat similar red. The flavouring is very subtle and goes well with hot garlic bread.

Combine the yoghurt, tomato juice, oregano and lemon juice and mix well. Peel and halve the cucumber and scoop out the seeds. Finely chop the flesh, sprinkle with a little salt and leave to stand for half an hour. Drain off excess liquid and dry on kitchen paper.

Add the prawns, cucumber and grated onion to the soup, mix well and season with salt and pepper. Serve chilled in bowls with a thin slice of lemon and a little shredded lettuce floating on top.

Minestrone

100 g (4 oz) streaky bacon
2 courgettes
4 sticks celery
450 g (1 lb) new potatoes
2 carrots
2 small onions
1 clove garlic
225 g (8 oz) young peas in the pod, or
    mange-tout peas
225 g (8 oz) tomatoes
1·8 litres (3 pints) light stock
Pinch of sage and marjoram
Sprig of parsley
Salt and pepper
50 g (2 oz) Parmesan cheese, grated

Finely chop the bacon. Thinly slice the courgettes and celery. Peel potatoes and carrots and cut into small dice. Peel and finely chop the onions and garlic clove. Trim off the ends of the pea pods. Peel and roughly chop the tomatoes.

Heat the stock to boiling point. Add the bacon, celery, carrots and potatoes and simmer for 30 minutes. Add all the remaining ingredients except the cheese, season with salt and pepper and simmer slowly for a further 30–45 minutes. Stir in the cheese just before serving.

Tomato Soup with Ham

1 onion
1 tablespoon olive or vegetable oil
425 g (15 oz) can tomatoes
50 g (2 oz) cooked ham
1 standard can tomato soup
1 chicken stock cube
1 teaspoon white wine vinegar
¼ teaspoon sage
¼ teaspoon oregano
Few drops Worcestershire sauce
Salt and freshly ground black pepper
3 tablespoons single cream

Peel and finely chop the onion. Heat the olive oil in a large pan, add the onion and cook over a low heat until soft and transparent. Purée the tinned tomatoes through a food mill or a sieve. Finely chop the ham.

Add the tomato soup, puréed tomatoes, chicken stock cube, vinegar and herbs to the onions, bring to the boil and simmer gently for 20 minutes. Add the Worcestershire sauce, season with a little salt and pepper and mix in the ham. Blend in the cream and heat through without boiling.

Serve the soup with small croutons of fried bread.

Country Mushroom Soup

100 g (4 oz) firm button mushrooms
1 small onion
50 g (2 oz) butter
1½ tablespoons flour
600 ml (1 pint) milk
300 ml (½ pint) good stock, or water and
　　stock cube
150 ml (5 fl oz) carton soured cream
Salt and cayenne pepper

Serves 4

Even the simplest recipe can be made exciting by a little added garnishing: sour cream, for instance, cheaper and with more flavour than plain cream, gives a smooth and interesting finish to vegetable soups.

Thinly slice the mushrooms. Peel and very finely chop the onion. Heat a quarter of the butter in a frying pan and cook the mushrooms over a low heat, shaking the pan frequently, until all the butter has been absorbed.

Melt the remaining butter in a saucepan, add the onion and cook over a low heat until soft and transparent. Stir in the flour, mix well and gradually blend in the milk, stirring continually until the mixture is thickened and smooth. Add the stock, bring to the boil and simmer for 15 minutes. Add the mushrooms and simmer for a further ten minutes.

Remove from the heat, blend in the soured cream and season with salt and a pinch of cayenne pepper.

Country Vegetable Soup

1 onion
1 clove garlic
350 g (12 oz) new potatoes
225 g (8 oz) courgettes
1 green or red pepper
100 g (4 oz) green beans
50 g (2 oz) cooked ham
50 g (2 oz) bacon fat
1·8 litres (3 pints) good stock, or water and
　　stock cubes
1 tablespoon tomato purée
Salt and freshly ground black pepper
Pinch of paprika pepper
1 bay leaf
100 g (4 oz) peas
1 tablespoon chives

Serves 6

Peel and very finely chop the onion. Peel and crush the garlic. Scrape and finely dice the potatoes. Finely dice the courgettes and green pepper (discarding the core and seeds). Cut the beans into 2·5 cm (1 in) lengths and chop the ham.

Heat the bacon fat in a large saucepan, add the onion and garlic and cook over a medium heat for a few minutes until the onion is pale golden. Add the potatoes and pepper and continue to cook over a low heat for five minutes. Add the courgettes, cook for one minute and pour over the stock. Blend in the tomato purée, season with salt, pepper and a pinch of paprika, add the bay leaf, cover and simmer for 20 minutes.

Add the beans, peas and chives and simmer for a further ten minutes. Check seasoning, remove the bay leaf and stir in the ham just before serving.

Lentil Soup

Serves 6

225 g (8 oz) lentils
2 onions
2 leeks
25 g (1 oz) butter
1 tablespoon olive oil
1·5 litres (2½ pints) water
½ teaspoon white wine vinegar
Salt and freshly ground black pepper
150 g (5 oz) carton yoghurt

Rinse the lentils, place in a bowl, cover generously with water and leave to soak overnight. Drain well.

Peel and finely chop the onions. Finely slice the white part of the leeks (use the green tops in a stock pot). Melt the butter with the oil in a large saucepan over a low heat. Add the onions and leeks and cook gently until the onions are soft and transparent. Add the lentils, mix well and pour over the water and vinegar. Season with salt and pepper, bring to the boil, cover and simmer gently for about 1½ hours until lentils are soft.

Purée through a sieve, a food mill or in a liquidiser. Check seasoning and serve with a spoonful of yoghurt in each bowl.

For extra flavour sprinkle with thin rashers of bacon, crisply fried and crumbled into small pieces.

Celery and Watercress Soup

Serves 4–6

1 head celery
1 small onion
2 rashers bacon
1 bunch watercress
1 teaspoon curry powder
1·2 litres (2 pints) stock, or water and stock
    cubes
Pinch of celery salt
Salt and freshly ground black pepper
1 teaspoon lemon juice
2 tablespoons double cream (optional)

Wash the celery, trim off the leaves (keep these in the refrigerator in a polythene bag and use in your next stock pot) and cut the stalks into thin slices. Thinly slice the onion; remove rind and finely chop the bacon; wash and chop the watercress. Put the bacon in a saucepan and cook over a low heat to extract the fat for 3–4 minutes. Add the celery and onion and continue to cook gently until they are soft and transparent. Add the watercress, mix in the curry powder and pour over the stock. Bring to the boil, stirring all the time, reduce the heat, season, add the lemon juice and simmer for 20 minutes.

Purée the soup in a liquidiser or through a fine food mill or sieve and return to a clean pan. Heat through, check seasoning and, if you have some handy, stir in two tablespoons of thick cream just before serving.

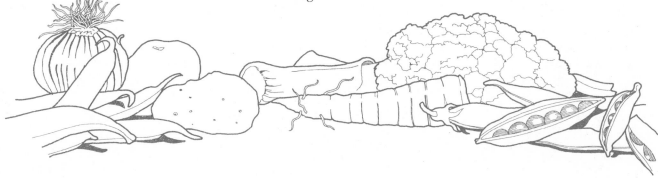

Green Pepper Soup

350 g (12 oz) green peppers
1 parsnip
1 onion
2 rashers fat bacon
150 ml ($\frac{1}{4}$ pint) white wine
600 ml (1 pint) stock
1 bay leaf
150 ml ($\frac{1}{4}$ pint) Jersey milk or thin cream
Salt and pepper

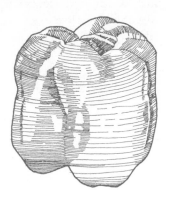

Serves 4

This soup is a warming first course, and also delicious chilled.

Remove the cores and seeds from the green peppers and roughly chop the flesh. Finely chop one tablespoon of this and reserve for garnishing. Peel and chop the parsnip and onion. Remove rinds and finely chop the bacon.

Cook the bacon gently in a saucepan for three minutes. Add the peppers, parsnip and onion and cook in the bacon fat, stirring every now and then to prevent sticking or browning, for a further five minutes. Add wine, stock and bay leaf, bring to the boil and simmer gently until the vegetables are tender–about 20 minutes.

Remove the bay leaf and purée the soup through a food mill or in a liquidiser and return to a clean pan. Add the milk or cream and heat through without boiling. Check seasoning and stir in the reserved green pepper before serving.

Potato Soup with Orange

900 g (2 lb) potatoes
1 large onion
15 g ($\frac{1}{2}$ oz) butter
1·2 litres (2 pints) well-flavoured stock
1 bay leaf
Rind of $\frac{1}{2}$ orange
Salt and white pepper
2 tablespoons double cream

Serves 5–6

A small quantity of orange peel adds an interesting flavour to many soups.

Boil the potatoes until tender and drain well; mash until smooth. Peel and finely chop the onion and cook over a low heat in the butter until soft and transparent. Add the stock and bay leaf, bring to the boil and simmer gently for ten minutes. Add the mashed potatoes and cook for a further ten minutes.

Pare off the rind from the orange half and cut into very thin strips. Plunge these into boiling water for five minutes and drain well. Remove the bay leaf and pass the soup through a fine sieve. Return to a clean pan and season with salt and pepper. Blend in the cream and heat through. Pour into heated bowls and scatter orange strips over the top.

Satin Soup with Almonds

900 g (2 lb) Jerusalem artichokes
1 tablespoon lemon juice
2 small onions
2 sticks celery
40 g (1½ oz) butter
1·2 litres (2 pints) chicken stock, or water and stock cubes
1 tablespoon grated Parmesan cheese
300 ml (10 fl oz) single cream
Salt, freshly ground black pepper and a pinch of nutmeg
40 g (1½ oz) flaked almonds

Serves 4

Peel the artichokes, dropping them into cold water to which the lemon juice has been added (peeled artichokes have a tendency to go brown and the lemon juice will prevent this). Drain well and cut into thick slices. Peel and roughly chop onions. Slice the celery, having removed green leaves. Heat the butter in a heavy saucepan, add the artichokes, onions and celery and cook over a low heat, stirring continuously to prevent browning, for five minutes until the onion is soft and transparent. Add the stock, bring to the boil and simmer for 20 minutes.

Purée the soup in a food mill, fine sieve or liquidiser and return to a clean pan. Stir in the cheese and cook over low heat until it has melted. Add the cream, season with salt, pepper and nutmeg and heat through without boiling.

Toast the almonds under a hot grill for 1½ minutes or until crisp and golden. Sprinkle over the soup just before serving.

Bacon and Cabbage Soup

100 g (4 oz) bacon rashers
275 g (10 oz) cabbage
1 small onion
600 ml (1 pint) stock, or water and 1½ stock cubes
Pepper and a pinch of nutmeg
25 g (1 oz) bacon fat
1 heaped tablespoon flour
450 ml (¾ pint) milk

Serves 4

A useful soup which is almost a meal in its own right. After a steaming bowl of this, served with hot rolls, the most anyone could possibly wish for would be some fresh fruit or cheese to round off the meal.

Trim off rinds and chop the bacon into small pieces. Finely shred the cabbage and finely chop the onion.

Place the bacon rinds in a saucepan over a low heat and cook until fat has melted. Remove rinds, add the onion to the fat and cook over a medium heat until transparent. Add the cabbage and cook for a further two minutes. Pour over the stock, add bacon, season with pepper and nutmeg, bring to the boil and simmer for ten minutes.

Melt the bacon fat in a clean pan. Add the flour and mix well. Gradually blend in the milk, stirring continuously until thick and smooth. Mix in the soup, bring to the boil and simmer for a few minutes. Check seasoning before serving.

Pheasant Soup with Curried Croutons

½ uncooked pheasant
2 onions
2 carrots
1 stick celery
1 tablespoon bacon fat or dripping
2 sprigs parsley
2 sage leaves
1 sprig thyme
1 chicken stock cube
Salt and freshly ground black pepper
½ teaspoon allspice
2 thick slices white bread
Lard or dripping
1 teaspoon lemon juice
½ teaspoon curry powder
2 tablespoons sherry
1 tablespoon finely chopped parsley

Serves 6

Cut off flesh from the breast and outside tender part of the leg and reserve. Break up the carcass. Quarter but do not peel the onions. Wash and roughly chop the carrots. Roughly chop the celery.

Heat the bacon fat or dripping in a large heavy pan. Add the carcass and cook over a high heat until lightly browned on all sides and fat absorbed. Add the vegetables, herbs and chicken stock cube and pour over a scant 2·5 litres (4 pints) water. Season with salt, pepper and allspice, bring to the boil, cover and simmer gently for 3 hours.

Strain the soup through a sieve and then through muslin; leave until cool. Refrigerate until any fat forms a layer on the top and can be neatly removed.

Remove any skin from the reserved pheasant meat and cut the flesh into very small dice. Reheat the cleared soup, add diced pheasant and cook for about 20 minutes or until the meat is tender.

Remove bread crusts and cut slices into small square croutons. Heat lard or dripping in a frying pan, add the bread cubes and cook over a high heat, shaking to prevent burning, until golden brown on all sides. Sprinkle over the lemon juice and curry powder, toss well and drain on crumpled kitchen paper.

Add the sherry and chopped parsley to the soup, taste for seasoning and serve very hot with the croutons in a separate bowl.

Chicken and Lemon Soup

1 small onion
20 g (¾ oz) butter
Scant tablespoon flour
900 ml (1½ pints) strong chicken stock
Juice of 1 lemon
2 egg yolks
4 tablespoons cream
Salt and freshly ground black pepper
Fresh parsley to garnish

Serves 4

A soup combining warmth, goodness and flavour with the pick-you-up quality of a strong whisky and soda but none of the after-effects.

Peel and finely chop the onion. Melt the butter in a medium-large saucepan, add the onion and cook over a low heat, without burning, until transparent. Add the flour, mix well and gradually blend in the chicken stock, stirring continuously until the mixture is smooth. Add the lemon juice, bring to the boil and simmer gently for ten minutes. Strain the soup through a fine sieve.

Beat the egg yolks and cream together until smooth. Add the soup, a little at a time, and whisk it into the egg/cream liaison. Return to a clean saucepan and heat gently, stirring continuously, until hot through. *Do not boil.* Add salt and pepper if necessary and sprinkle a little finely chopped parsley over the top before serving.

Giblet Soup

Serves 6

1 large onion
40 g (1½ oz) butter
675 g (1½ lb) giblets
1.5 litres (2½ pints) water
1 stock cube
1 teaspoon salt
5 peppercorns
Bouquet garni
2 tablespoons redcurrant jelly
2 tablespoons whisky

Peel and chop the onion. Melt the butter in a large pan, add the onion and giblets and cook over a medium high heat for 10 minutes, stirring to prevent sticking. Add the water, stock cube, salt, peppercorns, bouquet garni and redcurrant jelly. Bring to the boil and simmer for two hours.

Strain, cool and remove all excess fat. Cut meat from the giblets into small pieces and add to the soup. Check seasoning and add the whisky before serving.

Corn and Bacon Chowder

Serves 4

100 g (4 oz) streaky bacon
2 green peppers
1 large onion
2 sticks celery
2 tomatoes
100 g (4 oz) frozen peas
900 ml (1½ pints) milk
350 g (12 oz) can sweetcorn
2 bay leaves
2 tablespoons cornflour
Salt and freshly ground black pepper
100 g (4 oz) grated Cheddar cheese
1 tablespoon chopped parsley

Chowders are associated with American cookery, but the word actually derives from the French *chaudière*, a large iron pot in which soups were made.

Remove rinds and cut the bacon into small pieces. Remove core and seeds of green peppers and chop the flesh. Peel and chop onion. Thinly slice celery and finely chop leaves. Peel tomatoes, remove core and seeds and chop the flesh. Cook the peas until tender.

Fry the bacon in large heavy pan without extra fat, over medium high heat, until the fat has melted and the bacon is crisp. Remove from the pan, add the onion, celery and pepper to the fat and cook until the onion is transparent. Add the milk, sweetcorn, tomatoes and bay leaves. Bring to simmering point, stir in cornflour (mixed to a smooth paste with water), and cook, stirring, until the soup has thickened. Season with salt and pepper.

Cover and cook for five minutes. Remove bay leaves, add the grated cheese, peas and parsley and stir well. Scatter some cooked bacon over each bowl before serving.

Serve with cream crackers that have been spread with a little butter and then baked in a hot oven until crisp and hot.

Beef Broth with Vegetables

225 g (8 oz) shin beef
1½ tablespoons bacon fat or dripping
1·2 litres (2 pints) stock
Salt and freshly ground black pepper
1 large onion
1 large carrot
100 g (4 oz) turnip
1 stick celery
Pinch of allspice
1 tablespoon tomato purée
Finely chopped parsley

Serves 4

In this soup an extra-rich flavouring is given by the addition of a little shin beef.

Cut the meat into thin slices and then into very thin strips about 1 cm (½ in) long. Melt ½ tablespoon of the fat in a heavy saucepan, add the meat and cook over a high heat until browned on all sides. Add the stock, bring to the boil, season with salt and pepper, cover and simmer for 45 minutes.

Peel and finely chop the onion. Peel the carrot and turnip and cut into small dice. Finely chop the celery.

Melt the remaining dripping in a heavy pan. Add the vegetables and cook over a low heat, stirring frequently, until the onions are soft and transparent. Add the stock and meat, allspice and tomato purée, bring to the boil and simmer for a further 45 minutes or until the meat is really tender (this will depend to some extent on how finely the meat is cut). Sprinkle the soup with parsley before serving.

Beef Broth with Dumplings

225 g (8 oz) shin beef
1·2 litres (2 pints) vegetable or beef stock
Salt and white pepper
Small pinch of mixed herbs
1 onion
1 carrot
1 small turnip
1 stick celery
1 oz (25 g) dripping
100 g (4 oz) self-raising flour
50 g (2 oz) shredded suet
1½ tablespoons finely chopped parsley

Serves 4–6

Dumplings may be a rather old-fashioned ingredient but add great body to main course soups and give them an added interest.

Very finely chop the meat, having removed any tough sinews. Combine meat and stock in a saucepan, bring to the boil and skim off any scum from surface. Season with salt and pepper, add mixed herbs, cover and simmer for about 45 minutes.

Peel and finely chop the onion. Peel and dice the carrot and turnip; thinly chop celery. Melt the dripping in saucepan, add the vegetables and cook over medium heat, stirring to prevent browning, for three minutes. Add the vegetables to the meat and stock, return to the boil, cover and simmer for 40 minutes.

To make the dumplings: combine flour and suet, season with salt and pepper, add ½ tablespoon of the parsley and mix well. Add enough cold water to form a stiff dough, and, using floured hands, form the mixture into small balls. Add to the soup and continue to simmer for a further 20 minutes or until the dumplings rise to the surface.

Sprinkle the soup with parsley before serving.

Fish Soup

Serves 4–5

450 g (1 lb) cod or coley fillet
1 small mackerel, filleted
1 small onion
1 leek
1 clove garlic
1 medium potato
½ cucumber
2 tablespoons olive oil
15 g (½ oz) butter
900 ml (1½ pints) chicken stock
425 g (15 oz) can tomatoes
Salt and freshly ground black pepper
Few drops Tabasco sauce
100 g (4 oz) peeled prawns
1 tablespoon very finely chopped parsley

Cut the cod and mackerel into small bite-sized pieces. Peel and finely chop the onion. Thinly slice the leek including the green top. Peel and crush the garlic clove. Peel and finely dice the potato and cucumber.

Combine the oil and butter in a heavy pan. Add the onion, leek, garlic and potato and cook over a low heat without browning until the onion is transparent and the fat absorbed. Add the cod and mackerel and pour over the stock. Add the tomatoes puréed through a sieve, a food mill or a liquidiser. Season with salt, pepper and Tabasco, bring to the boil and simmer gently for about 15 minutes until the fish is just cooked but not mushy.

Add the cucumber, prawns and parsley, check seasoning and heat through before serving.

Crab Soup

Serves 6

15 g (½ oz) butter
2 teaspoons flour
900 ml (1½ pints) milk
8 oz crab meat (mixed brown and white meat)
½ teaspoon grated raw onion
½ teaspoon Worcestershire sauce
Salt and white pepper
Pinch of mace
150 ml (5 fl oz) double cream
2 hard-boiled eggs
5 tablespoons sherry
1 tablespoon finely chopped parsley
Paprika pepper

The best New Orleans soup recipes call for 'she' crabs; but bearing in mind the Sex Discrimination Act I thought it would be better not to make a distinction.

Melt the butter in a heavy pan or the top of a double saucepan. Add the flour and mix well. Gradually blend in the milk, stirring continuously over low heat until smooth. Add the crab meat, raw onion and Worcestershire sauce; season with salt, pepper and mace. Cook over low heat, without boiling, for 20 minutes. Beat the cream until stiff.

Shell the hard-boiled eggs, rub the yolks through a coarse sieve and finely chop the whites. Place whites and yolks in the bottom of six hot soup bowls.

Blend the sherry with the soup and pour into the soup bowls. Top with a dollop of whipped cream sprinkled with parsley and a tiny pinch of paprika. Serve at once.

First Courses

I suppose it is not surprising that, since one of the cookery books I wrote was all about soups and hors-d'oeuvres (otherwise known as 'starters') I should be particularly fond of first courses of all sorts. In fact one of my fantasies is to spend an evening at my favourite restaurants in London, not going through their menus but merely having a favourite first course at each. I also find that often when I am looking at restaurant menus what I actually want is a first course followed by another first course, and I am always delighted to find an establishment that does not object to this.

First courses are, of course, versatile. If a soup is rich and hearty you can happily serve it as the main course of a meal with crisp French bread, cheese and, perhaps, pickles. In the same way many hors-d'oeuvres can be increased in proportion and served as a light dinner, or summer main meal, and very delicious they can be.

So what are first courses? As far as I am concerned they are titillating concoctions, designed to excite the appetite by their appearance and taste. They must be light, they should be colourful and attractive to look at and, in most cases, it is a distinct advantage if they can be cooked in advance, especially if you are entertaining. Egg, fish, vegetable and some meat-based dishes come into this category

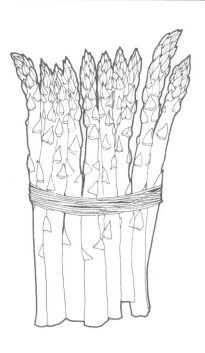

and so do pâtés, terrines and some savoury mousses. There are savoury-filled pastry cases, savoury pancakes and any number of exciting and inexpensive vegetable dishes, and the great delight about most of them is that they take little time to prepare and to cook.

Since first courses are really designed to ease you into a meal and to excite the appetite the question of appearance is extra important. These dishes must both appear, and taste, fresh. They respond to careful garnishing and attractive serving and they fall down completely if they look dull or dreary. Garnishing can be simple and need never be expensive, but it is surprising how much difference a twist of thinly sliced lemon or a thin twist of lemon peel, a scattering of very finely chopped parsley, chives or celery leaves, a bed of watercress or shredded lettuce, chopped red pepper or tinned pimento, or a lattice-work topping of anchovy fillets can make to a dish.

Temperature is also important. If a dish is prepared in advance but is to be served hot then it must be absolutely piping hot, and care must be taken with dishes which are to be finished under a grill to make sure that the whole dish is hot and not just the topping. In the same way cold dishes must be served really cold. I despair, for instance, at the number of restaurants which serve dishes like prawn cocktail at room temperature–they should certainly be well chilled and, if possible, they should even be served in glasses with a delicious frosting on the outside (to achieve this put the glasses or goblets containing the cocktails into the deep-freeze for five minutes before serving them).

Another matter of importance when considering this whole question of 'the first course' is the place it is going to take in the pattern of the whole meal. It is disastrous to present a rich, red-coloured first course before a rich, red-coloured main course, with both of them relying heavily on tomato paste to provide the basic flavouring. First courses should provide a contrast to the rest of the meal and this is something to bear very much in mind when planning a menu.

The weather should also provide a guide-line as to suitable dishes to serve at the beginning of a meal. The hotter the weather the cooler and lighter your first course should be (unless you are preparing a highly spiced, chilli-flavoured dish, when the opposite should apply) and the colder the weather the heavier you can afford to be. On the whole, if I am going to be serving a hot main course then I find it easier and more popular to provide a cold first course and vice versa.

A few last points. There should be a fineness about your first course dishes–if ingredients are to be finely chopped, grated or shredded, then they should be just that, and servings should be on the small rather than the large side (with second helpings available for those who want them). Seasoning should be delicate and subtle rather than overpowering and freshness is the thing to remember above all. The hor-d'oeuvres nightmare of my life is a dull and colourless selection of mini-dishes wheeled into a restaurant dining room on a trolley. My delight is to be offered a wide selection of dishes to choose from as a first course, which sparkle, glow like jewels and taste just as good as they look.

Cool and Easy Melons

Serves 4

4 small ripe melons
½ cucumber
½ teaspoon curry powder
1 tablespoon lemon juice
3 tablespoons olive oil
Salt and freshly ground black pepper

Cut a thin slice off the top of the melons. Scoop out the seeds, spoon out the flesh and cut into small dice. Peel the cucumber and cut the flesh into small dice. Combine the melon and cucumber in bowl.

Combine the curry powder, lemon juice and oil and heat gently over low flame, stirring continually until the curry powder has dissolved. Cool, pour over the melon and cucumber, mix lightly and season with salt and pepper.

Fill the melon shells with this mixture, replace the tops and chill for at least two hours.

Guacamole

Serves 4

2 ripe tomatoes
1 clove garlic
1 small onion
1 large or 2 small avocado pears
1 tablespoon finely chopped celery
2 teaspoons very finely chopped parsley
2 teaspoons lemon juice
Drop of Tabasco sauce
Salt and freshly ground black pepper

An exciting pâté or dip of avocado.

Peel the tomatoes, discard core and seeds and finely chop the flesh. Crush the garlic; peel and very finely chop the onion or grate it through the coarse side of a grater. Peel the avocado, remove stone and mash the flesh with a fork until smooth. Combine all the ingredients, mix well and season with salt and ground black pepper.

Pile in a serving dish, chill and serve with hot toast or hot cream crackers. Guacamole can also be served as a dip with crisp sticks of raw carrot, celery and green pepper or it can be served in whole green peppers with a slice cut from the top and the core and seeds removed.

Seafood Cocktail with Parsley Dressing

1 crisp lettuce heart
225 g (8 oz) frozen prawns, thawed
2 large ripe tomatoes
Two 150 ml (5 fl oz) cartons soured cream
2–3 tablespoons finely chopped parsley
2 tablespoons finely chopped dill-pickled
    cucumber
Salt and freshly ground black pepper
Lemon slices to garnish

Serves 4–5

Here is a refreshing sauce that makes a few frozen prawns into a first-rate starter. Choose your frozen prawns carefully by examining the package before you buy them. They should be reasonably large, a bright pink, separated, and with no sign of frosting inside the package. Thaw them as slowly as possible in the refrigerator.

Very finely shred the lettuce heart and divide between four or five goblets. Divide up the prawns and place on top of the lettuce. Drop the tomatoes into boiling water for two minutes, slip off skins, remove core and seeds and very finely chop the flesh.

Mix the tomato with the sour cream, parsley and dill-pickled cucumber, season with salt and pepper and mix well. Pour this dressing over the prawns and refrigerate for at least one hour before serving with a slice of lemon and thin slices of buttered brown bread.

Prawn Cocktail with Apple

1 small onion
1 small clove garlic
25 g (1 oz) butter
1 teaspoon curry powder
225 g (8 oz) can tomatoes
Salt, freshly ground black pepper and a pinch
    of cayenne
175 g (6 oz) peeled prawns
4 crisp lettuce leaves
300 ml (½ pint) mayonnaise
2 tablespoons sour cream
2 crisp eating apples
Lemon slices to garnish

Serves 4

Peel and finely chop the onion. Peel and crush the garlic. Heat the butter in a saucepan, add the onion and garlic and cook over a low heat until the onion is soft and transparent. Add the curry powder and mix well. Mix in the tomatoes, season with salt, pepper and cayenne and cook over a medium heat for 15 minutes. Remove from the heat, mix in the prawns and leave to cool.

Shred the lettuce leaves and divide them between four glass goblets. Blend the mayonnaise and cream into the cooled tomato mixture and check the seasoning. Peel, core and dice the apples and fold them into the cocktail. Spoon the cocktail over the lettuce leaves, garnish with slices of lemon and serve well chilled with slices of buttered brown bread.

Shrimps in Butter

2 cloves garlic
100 g (4 oz) butter
450 g (1 lb) English shrimps
Juice of ½ lemon
Freshly ground black pepper

Serves 6

Press the garlic through a garlic press or crush with the blade of a knife. Heat the butter in a saucepan, add the garlic and shrimps and cook gently for 15–20 minutes. Add the lemon juice and season with plenty of pepper.

Serve at once with hot toast.

Smoked Salmon Mousse with Cucumber

100 g (4 oz) smoked salmon
1 lemon
1 teaspoon French Dijon mustard
2 egg yolks
150 ml (¼ pint) olive oil
½ teaspoon green peppercorns
¾ envelope (¾ tablespoon) powdered gelatine
2 tablespoons warm water
2 egg whites
150 ml (¼ pint) double cream
1 cucumber
Salt
1 teaspoon vinegar
Paprika pepper

Serves 6

Smoked salmon is expensive so this is a dish for a very special occasion. You can sometimes buy the trimmings from smoked salmon or you could use smoked mackerel instead but there are times when only the very best will do.

Roughly chop the smoked salmon. Pare the rind from the lemon removing all the white membrane. Using a small, sharp knife cut the segments from the lemon; remove the pips. In a food processor or electric blender purée the smoked salmon until smooth. Remove the salmon and combine the lemon and mustard in the processor/blender with egg yolks and process until smooth. With the motor running gradually add the oil in a very thin stream and process until the mixture becomes the texture of a light mayonnaise. Add the smoked salmon and the peppercorns, crushed with a fork, and process until well mixed. Soak the gelatine in the warm water until dissolved. Add the gelatine to the salmon mixture and process to mix.

Turn the mixture into a mixing bowl. Whip the egg whites until stiff. Whip the cream until stiff. Lightly fold the cream and egg whites into the salmon mayonnaise and spoon into six dampened moulds. Chill in the refrigerator until set firm.

Peel and coarsely grate the cucumber. Place the cucumber in a colander, sprinkle with salt and vinegar and leave to 'sweat' for 30 minutes. Press out excess moisture and pat dry with kitchen paper. Turn out the moulds, sprinkle with a little paprika and surround with cucumber.

Kamano Miko (Pickled Smoked Salmon)

175 g (6 oz) smoked salmon trimmings
2 bunches spring onions
4–6 tomatoes
150 ml (¼ pint) vinegar
150 ml (¼ pint) water
2 teaspoons sugar
½ teaspoon ground dried red chillies

Serves 6

Remove any hard dry edges of smoked salmon and cut the rest into thin strips. Cut about 1 cm (½ in) off the green tops of the spring onions and trim the stems. Thinly slice each onion lengthwise. Peel and thinly slice tomatoes.

Combine the vinegar, water, sugar and ground chillies in a saucepan and bring to the boil. Arrange layers of tomato, onion and smoked salmon in a glass serving dish, pour over the hot vinegar mixture, cover and refrigerate for at least eight hours before serving with thin slices of buttered brown bread.

Cape Horn Salad

1½ tablespoons lemon juice
2 large ripe eating pears
100 g (4 oz) black grapes
100 g (4 oz) seedless green grapes
2 Kiwi fruit
4 anchovy fillets
2 tablespoons olive or sunflower oil
½ teaspoon dry English mustard
1 teaspoon honey
Salt and freshly ground black pepper
2 teaspoons finely chopped parsley
2 teaspoons finely chopped chives

Serves 4

A salad of pears, grapes and Kiwi fruit in a sweet/sharp dressing. For a hot summer's evening this tasty, cool and refreshing fruit starter is hard to beat. Kiwi fruit (also called Chinese Gooseberries) can now be found in most good greengrocers during their season which is usually around May and June and September to November.

Place lemon juice in a bowl. Peel and halve pears and carefully scoop out the core with a teaspoon, and place the pear halves in the lemon juice. Peel, halve and remove the pips from the black grapes. Remove the green grapes from their stems. Peel and thinly slice the Kiwi fruit. Drain off and reserve the lemon juice from the pears and arrange the pear halves cut side up on four small serving plates. Fill the scooped out centres with the grapes, surround with slices of Kiwi fruit and top with an anchovy fillet.

Combine reserved lemon juice, oil, mustard and honey and mix well. Season with salt and pepper, mix in the herbs and pour over the filled pears. Serve well chilled.

Charlestown Salata

2 slices white bread, crusts removed
Two 175 g (6 oz) smoked mackerel
200 ml (7½ fl oz) olive oil
Juice of ¼ lemon
1 teaspoon grated raw onion
1 clove garlic
1 tablespoon sour cream
Salt and freshly ground black pepper

Serves 6

Made in the manner of the delicious Greek taramasalata, this can also be used as a sandwich filling. Serve it in a mound on crisp lettuce leaves; garnish with olives and accompany with plenty of hot toast.

Dip the bread in warm water to soften it. Squeeze out all excess water. Remove the skin from the mackerel and fillet the fish, removing all the bones. Pound the flesh until smooth in a pestle and mortar. Add the bread and continue to pound to a smooth paste (this can be done in a liquidiser). Gradually beat in the oil, as for mayonnaise, so that the mixture emulsifies. After half the oil has been used beat in the remainder with the lemon juice. The mixture should be smooth, creamy and thick.

Add the grated onion, crushed garlic and sour cream. Season with salt and pepper, mix well and chill before serving.

Velvet Lady

Serves 4–5

3 medium parsnips
Juice of ½ lemon
4 sticks celery
300 ml (½ pint) mayonnaise
2 tablespoons cream
Salt and pepper
100 g (4 oz) peeled prawns
Cayenne pepper

Peel the parsnips and cut into 2·5 cm (1 in) long matchstick strips. Boil in salted water to which the lemon juice has been added for about 15 minutes or until just tender, but not mushy. Drain, plunge into cold water, drain again and pat dry. Cut the celery into matchstick strips of the same length as parsnips. Very finely chop 2 teaspoons of leaves from the celery tops for garnish.

Combine the mayonnaise with cream, season with salt and pepper if necessary and mix well. Add parsnips, celery sticks and prawns and mix lightly. Pile on to a serving dish, sprinkle with a pinch of cayenne pepper and the celery leaves and chill well before serving with thin slices of buttered brown bread.

Melons with Anchovies

Serves 4

2 ripe Ogen melons
1 can anchovy fillets
Milk
Juice of ½ lemon

For a dinner party, serve this starter with a well-chilled dry sherry.

Cut each melon in half and remove the seeds. Drain off the oil from the anchovies, cover the fillets with milk and leave them to soak for ten minutes to remove excess salt. Drain off the milk, pat the fillets dry with kitchen paper and cut each fillet in half along the centre.

Scoop out the melon flesh with a ball scoop. Return half of the melon balls to the melon shell and top with the remaining balls, each wrapped in half an anchovy fillet. Sprinkle over the lemon juice, wrap in foil and refrigerate for at least one hour before serving.

Avocado with Crab

Serves 4

2 large ripe avocado pears
Juice of ½ lemon
150 ml (¼ pint) home-made mayonnaise
Few drops Tabasco sauce
Few drops Worcestershire sauce
100 g (4 oz) mixed dark and white crab meat
50 g (2 oz) chopped walnuts
Small jar black caviar (Danish lumpfish roe)
Small jar red caviar

A rich, exotic first course. The crushed red roe from a fresh crab can be used in the place of the caviar.

Halve the avocados and remove stones. Scoop out the flesh and mash or purée with the lemon juice. Mix in the mayonnaise, flavour with a few drops of Tabasco and Worcestershire sauce and fold in the crab and walnuts. Pile the mixture into the avocado shells and sprinkle with a little red and black caviar. Chill well before serving.

Prawn and Cucumber Jelly

½ cucumber
2 red peppers
Juice of ½ lemon
1 teaspoon gelatine
Two 300 g (10 oz) cans jellied consommé
1 tablespoon medium dry sherry
225 g (8 oz) peeled prawns
150 ml (¼ pint) home-made mayonnaise
2 tablespoons double cream
1 teaspoon horseradish sauce
Few drops Tabasco sauce
Salt and pepper
Lettuce leaves

Serves 4

Serve this either as a starter, or as the main course for a light summer lunch.

Peel the cucumber and grate it coarsely. Put it into a sieve or colander, sprinkle with a little salt and leave to drain for 20 minutes. Lightly pat dry with kitchen paper. Remove core and seeds of red peppers and very finely chop the flesh.

Combine lemon juice and gelatine with a little of the consommé. Heat over a low flame until the gelatine has melted. Remove from the heat and mix in the remaining consommé and the sherry.

Pour a little of the consommé into a ring mould that has been rinsed in cold water. Chill the mould in the refrigerator until the jelly has set. Spread half the prawns over the set jelly and pour over enough consommé to cover. Return to the refrigerator until set.

Combine the cucumber and peppers and spread over the set prawns and jelly. Pour over enough consommé to cover and leave to set once more. Finish with a layer of prawns and the remaining consommé. Refrigerate for at least one hour.

Combine the mayonnaise with the cream and horseradish. Flavour with a few drops of Tabasco and with salt and pepper if necessary. Mix well.

Dip the mould quickly into very hot water and turn out on to a serving dish. Fill the centre with the mayonnaise and surround with crisp lettuce leaves.

Marinated Kipper

2 kippers
4 spring onions
2 tablespoons olive oil
1 tablespoon lemon juice
Freshly ground black pepper
150 ml (5 fl oz) double cream
1 teaspoon horseradish sauce
1 lettuce
Cayenne pepper

Serves 4

Using a small sharp knife and working as neatly as you can, remove backbone and skin from the kippers and cut the fillets into very thin slices. Put these into a dish. Clean the spring onions and finely chop, including stalks. Combine the olive oil and lemon juice and season with pepper. Add the spring onions, pour the dressing over the kippers and mix lightly. Refrigerate for at least an hour.

Whip the cream until stiff and mix in the horseradish. Arrange lettuce leaves on four plates, top with marinated kipper and then with a spoonful of horseradish cream. Sprinkle the cream with a little cayenne and serve chilled with hot toast or thin slices of buttered brown bread.

Chicken and Tomato Aspic

450 ml (¾ pint) tomato juice
½ teaspoon finely chopped tarragon
2 teaspoons lemon juice
Salt and pepper
25 g (1 oz) gelatine
350–450 g (12–16 oz) cooked chicken
1 green pepper
½ cucumber
1 bunch watercress
Vinaigrette dressing

Serves 3–4

Heat the tomato juice in a saucepan, add tarragon and lemon juice, bring to the boil and simmer for five minutes. Season with salt and pepper and strain through a fine sieve. Dissolve the gelatine in the hot liquid and leave in a cool place until the jelly begins to thicken.

Cut the chicken into small dice. Remove seeds and core from the green pepper and finely chop the flesh. Peel and chop the cucumber. Fold chicken, pepper and cucumber into the partially set jelly, pour into a ring mould and put in the refrigerator to set firm.

Turn out the jellied mould and fill the centre with watercress dipped into vinaigrette dressing.

Tomato Ice-Cream

1 clove garlic
1 sprig mint
150 ml (5 fl oz) double cream
600 ml (1 pint) basic tomato purée (p.163)
300 ml (½ pint) mayonnaise
2 teaspoons lemon juice
1 tablespoon tomato paste
Salt and pepper

Serves 6

Serve this unusual dish as a first course with hot crackers, or as an accompaniment to grilled fish.

Crush the garlic with a fork or squeeze through a garlic press. Very finely chop the mint. Whip the cream until thickened but not stiff. Combine the tomato purée, garlic, mayonnaise, mint, lemon juice, tomato paste and seasoning; mix really well.

Lightly blend in the whipped cream, pour into an ice-making tray and leave to freeze in the refrigerator. When the ice-cream is about half frozen through beat well to break up ice crystals, return to the refrigerator and leave until solid.

Paddington Cheese Ice-Cream

225 g (8 oz) ripe Brie
100 g (4 oz) cream cheese
2 tablespoons milk
¼ teaspoon cayenne pepper
Pinch of celery salt
2 tablespoons finely chopped chives
Paprika pepper

Serves 4

Mash the Brie with a fork until smooth and blend in the cream cheese and milk (this can be done in a liquidiser). Season with the cayenne pepper and celery salt and mix in the chives. Put in a small round bowl and freeze until solid in the freezing compartment of the refrigerator.

Dip the bowl into hot water, turn out the ice-cream and sprinkle with a little paprika. Return to the freezing compartment until 20 minutes before serving; then place it on one of the top refrigerator shelves to allow it to breathe and soften.

Serve the ice-cream with hot salted biscuits and crisp radishes.

Brandade de Morue

675 g (1½ lb) salt cod
2 cloves garlic
Juice of ½ lemon
200 ml (7½ fl oz) olive oil
200 ml (7½ fl oz) double cream
4 slices white bread
Extra oil for frying
8 black olives
1 tablespoon finely chopped parsley

Serves 4–5

In France this dish is considered to be a labour of love and certainly when I have made it the traditional way, by hand, pounding the cooked fish in a mortar, adding the olive oil, drop by drop, I have found it the most satisfying and therapeutic of jobs. Time however being all too frequently at a premium, I am giving a recipe which cheats by using a liquidiser for the hard work.

In Languedoc and Provence *brandade* is usually served as an hors-d'oeuvre, but it makes a fabulous lunch and supper dish too, served warm and accompanied by leaf spinach flavoured with nutmeg and tossed in butter. For a party I serve it cold with a tomato mousse and a mousse made from sorrel, and it is one of my most successful starters.

Soak the cod for 24 hours, changing the water three times. Pat dry, put in a saucepan, cover with clean cold water and bring slowly to the boil. Simmer very gently for about 20 minutes or until the flesh can be flaked from the bones (it is important not to overcook). Drain and, while the fish is still warm, remove all the bones and skin and flake the flesh.

Combine the fish, crushed garlic and lemon juice in a liquidiser, turning the setting low if possible, and add the oil in a slow steady stream–the resulting mixture should be thick and pulpy, not a smooth purée.

Transfer the mixture to a clean saucepan and heat gently, gradually beating in the cream until it has all been absorbed.

Remove crusts and cut the bread into triangles; fry them in a little oil until golden brown.

Serve the brandade in a shallow dish, garnished with the fried bread, olives and chopped parsley. Serve warm or cold, but not hot.

Stuffed Baked Artichokes

4 globe artichokes
1 clove garlic
1 onion
2 sticks celery
4 anchovy fillets
4 tablespoons fresh white breadcrumbs
1 tablespoon finely chopped parsley
25 g (1 oz) finely grated Parmesan cheese
Salt and freshly ground black pepper
300 ml (½ pint) stock, or water and stock
  cube
4 tablespoons olive oil
Melted butter

Serves 4

Trim the artichokes and blanch them in boiling salted water for five minutes. Drain well.

Crush the garlic clove. Peel and very finely chop the onion. Pass the celery sticks through the fine blades of a mincing machine. Drain off the oil from the anchovy fillets and chop them very finely. Combine the breadcrumbs, garlic, onion, celery, anchovies, parsley and cheese and mix well. Season the mixture with salt and pepper and gently push the stuffing down between the leaves of the artichokes. Stand them in a baking dish.

Add enough boiling stock to come 1 cm (½ in) up the sides of the artichokes. Pour over the olive oil, cover with tinfoil and bake in a moderate oven (180°C, 350°F, Reg. 4) for an hour or until tender. Remove to a heated serving dish and serve hot with melted butter handed separately.

Aubergine Salad

2 large ripe aubergines
1 clove garlic
Salt and freshly ground black pepper
3 tablespoons olive oil
Juice of ½ lemon
¼ raw onion, finely grated
3 teaspoons very finely chopped parsley
Lettuce leaves

Serves 4

Bake the aubergines in a hot oven or under a medium hot grill until the skins are black and the flesh soft–about 15–20 minutes. Remove the skins and pound the warm flesh in a mortar with the crushed garlic and a seasoning of salt and pepper.

When a smooth paste has been formed and the flesh is cold add the olive oil, a little at a time, beating with a spoon until the mixture emulsifies. Beat in the lemon juice, fold in the onion and parsley and check the seasoning.

Pile on to a bed of crisp lettuce leaves and chill for at least 30 minutes. Serve with hot toast and an accompanying dish of thin sticks of celery, raw carrots and black olives.

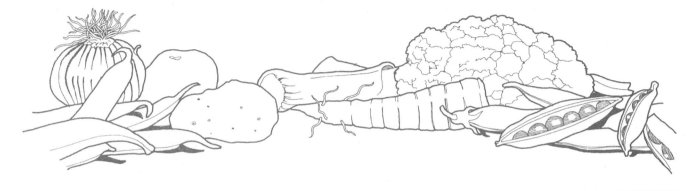

Aubergine Fritters

Serves 4

100 g (4 oz) plain flour
Pinch of salt
1 tablespoon olive oil
1 egg, beaten
200 ml (7½ fl oz) water
2 aubergines
Vegetable oil for deep-frying
Freshly ground black pepper
Lemon wedges

Sieve the flour into a basin with the salt. Add the olive oil and the egg and beat well until the mixture is smooth. Beat in the water and finish with a wire whisk to remove any lumps. Leave the batter to rest for 1–1½ hours.

Thinly slice the aubergines and pat dry on kitchen paper. Dip in batter at once and fry in hot oil until golden brown. Remove from the oil with a slotted spoon and drain on crumpled kitchen paper. The fritters can be kept crisp in a medium-hot oven whilst a second batch is being fried. Never try to fry too many at the same time.

Sprinkle the fritters with pepper and serve them, as soon as possible, with wedges of lemon on the side.

Broad Bean Hors-d'Oeuvre

Serves 4

450 g (1 lb) small shelled broad beans
3 rashers streaky bacon
100 g (4 oz) garlic sausage or Frankfurter sausages
3 tablespoons olive oil
½ teaspoon French Dijon mustard
1 tablespoon white wine vinegar
Salt and freshly ground black pepper
1 tablespoon finely chopped parsley
1 tablespoon finely chopped chives or spring onion tops

Cook the beans in boiling salted water for about 15 minutes until just tender. Drain well and leave to cool.

Fry the bacon, without extra fat, over medium heat until crisp. Drain well on kitchen paper, remove rinds and crumble the rashers. Cut the garlic sausage into small cubes.

Combine the olive oil, mustard and vinegar and mix well. Season with salt and pepper and mix in the parsley and chives. Add the bacon, beans and sausage. Turn into a serving dish and refrigerate for at least an hour before serving.

Mushrooms Circe

Serves 4

225 g (8 oz) firm button mushrooms
150 ml (5 fl oz) double cream
1 teaspoon lemon juice
1 tablespoon finely chopped chives
1 tablespoon finely chopped mint
Salt and a pinch of paprika pepper
4 lettuce leaves, finely chopped
25 g (1 oz) slivered blanched almonds

Top-quality mushrooms should need neither cleaning nor peeling. If they are dusty or dirty wash gently in cold water and pat dry on kitchen paper.

Whip the cream lightly until thick but not stiff. Add the lemon juice, chives and mint and season well with salt and paprika. Cut the mushrooms into wafer-thin slices and fold them into the cream. Arrange on four plates with a garnish of chopped lettuce.

Toast the almonds under a hot grill until golden brown. Leave to cool and sprinkle over the mushrooms before serving.

Ignazia's Stuffed Tomatoes

8 large firm tomatoes
2 tablespoons smoked cod's roe
1 tablespoon thick cream
1 small can tuna fish
4 hard-boiled eggs
1 teaspoon oregano
Salt and freshly ground black pepper

Serves 4

These make an attractive and delicious first course for either lunch or dinner. Choose large, firm tomatoes and use the smooth cod's roe which can be bought in jars from most fishmonger's or delicatessen shops.

Cut a slice off the top of each tomato; scoop out the inside without damaging the skin and discard the core. Mix the tomato pulp with the cod's roe and blend in the cream.

Drain the tuna and flake the flesh finely; rub the hard-boiled eggs through a coarse sieve. Add tuna and eggs to the tomato mixture with the oregano and season with salt and pepper, going easy on the salt. Fill the tomato cases and refrigerate for at least an hour before serving.

Chicken Liver Pâté

450 g (1 lb) chicken livers
75 g (3 oz) fat bacon
4 anchovy fillets
225 g (8 oz) sausage-meat
40 g (1½ oz) flour
3 eggs
150 ml (5 fl oz) double cream
3 tablespoons dry vermouth
Pinch of marjoram, ginger and mace
Salt and freshly ground black pepper
1 clove garlic
4 spring onions
100 g (4 oz) firm button mushrooms

Serves 6–8

Chicken liver pâté can often be too smooth and bland for my taste, so in this recipe I mince the ingredients coarsely, and add chopped spring onions and sliced button mushrooms. The pâté is undeniably rich, yet surprisingly light, and can be served either as a first course, with thick slices of white toast, or as a main course with salad and new potatoes. It will keep for up to five days in the refrigerator.

Remove any membrane from the chicken livers and pass them through the coarse blades of a mincing machine with the bacon and anchovies. In a large bowl, combine the minced ingredients with sausage-meat, flour, eggs, cream, vermouth and herbs. Season with salt and pepper and mix well.

Crush the garlic, finely chop the spring onions and very thinly slice the mushrooms. Fold lightly into the pâté and turn into a well-greased loaf tin.

Place the tin in a roasting pan half-full of hot water, cover with foil and bake in a slow oven (160°C, 325°F, Reg. 3) for two hours. Leave to cool in the tin and refrigerate overnight.

High-Flying Pheasant Pâté

1 pheasant
450 g (1 lb) fat belly pork
3 thick rashers fat bacon
225 g (8 oz) pig's liver
2 cloves garlic
6 juniper berries
Salt and freshly ground black pepper
Pinch of mace, ginger and nutmeg
100 g (4 oz) lean ham
3 tablespoons cooking brandy
2 sprigs parsley
1 sprig marjoram
1 sprig thyme (lemon thyme if you grow it is
    best of all)
2 bay leaves
Parsley or aspic jelly squares to garnish

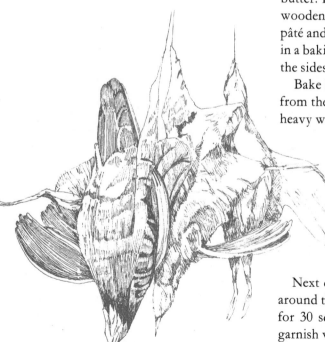

Serves 10 as a first course, 6 as a main course

If fresh herbs are unavailable use one of those dried bouquets in a muslin bag.

Using a sharp knife cut off all the pheasant's skin, reserving this for stock. Cut in half and reserve one half for soup. Cut the breast off the other half and set on one side. Cut off remaining meat from the leg and wing. Remove skin from the pork belly and roughly chop the flesh. Trim off rind from the bacon rashers. Mince twice (through the fine blades of a mincing machine) meat from pheasant leg and wing together with pig's liver, pork belly and bacon rashers, garlic cloves (peeled) and juniper berries.

Put the minced mixture in a bowl and season with plenty of salt and pepper. Add the spices and mix well with a wooden spoon, using a pounding movement until all ingredients are amalgamated and mixture is really smooth.

Cut the breast of pheasant and the ham into very small dice, add them to the minced ingredients with the brandy and mix lightly.

Generously grease a 1-litre (2-pint) earthenware terrine with butter. Pack in the mixture and press down firmly with the back of a wooden spoon. Place the fresh herbs or a bouquet garni on top of the pâté and wrap the dish tightly with tin foil to seal it on all sides. Place in a baking dish and pour in enough hot water to come two-thirds up the sides of the terrine.

Bake in a slow oven (160°C, 325°F, Reg. 3) for $1\frac{3}{4}$ hours. Remove from the baking dish, unwrap and weigh down with a flat plate and heavy weight. Leave to cool, then refrigerate overnight.

Next day remove the weight, run a knife dipped in boiling water around the inside of the terrine and dip the terrine into boiling water for 30 seconds. Turn on to a dish, trim up any untidy edges and garnish with sprigs of parsley or squares of aspic jelly.

Mousse of Pounded Chicken Livers

Serves 4–6

1 shallot
225 g (8 oz) chicken livers
75 g (3 oz) butter
1 tablespoon brandy
Pinch of thyme
Salt and freshly ground black pepper
4–5 tablespoons double cream
1 egg white

Peel and very finely chop the shallot. Remove any green patches or fibres from the chicken livers. Melt one third of the butter in a small pan, add the shallot and chicken livers and cook over a medium high heat for three minutes (the livers should remain pink on the inside).

Pound the livers in a pestle and mortar until smooth and blend in the brandy. Melt the remaining butter and whip into the livers. Add the thyme, season with salt and pepper and leave to cool and thicken. Beat the cream until stiff. Whip the egg white until stiff but not dry. Lightly fold the cream and egg white into the chicken liver mixture and turn the mousse into a terrine or earthenware pâté dish.

Chill before serving and accompany with plenty of thick white toast with the crusts removed.

Potted Mackerel

Serves 4

2 mackerel
1 tablespoon finely chopped onion
2 bay leaves
150 ml ($\frac{1}{4}$ pint) dry cider
2 anchovy fillets
100 g (4 oz) butter, softened
Freshly ground black pepper
Pinch of nutmeg, ginger, cayenne pepper and mace
Clarified butter

Serve this with hot toast as first course, or use as a sandwich filling.

Clean the mackerel and lay them side by side in an oven-proof dish just large enough to take them. Sprinkle over the chopped onion and top each fish with a bay leaf. Pour over the cider, cover tightly with foil and bake in a moderate oven (180°C, 350°F, Reg. 4) for 30 minutes until the fish are tender and the flesh falls off the bone.

Cool, drain off the liquid and remove the bay leaves. Skin the fish and remove all bones. Mince or very finely chop the anchovies.

Combine the mackerel, anchovies and softened butter and beat to a smooth paste with a wooden spoon. Season with pepper and spices. Pack tightly into an earthenware pot and pour over just enough clarified butter to cover the top completely.

Note: To clarify butter, heat it in a saucepan until foaming and then strain through muslin.

Potted Tongue and Ham

Serves 4

100 g (4 oz) ham
100 g (4 oz) tongue
Pinch of ginger, ground nutmeg, thyme and
    mace
175 g (6 oz) butter
Freshly ground black pepper

Put the ham and tongue twice through the coarse blades of a mincing machine. Powder the thyme by pounding it in a mortar with a pestle. Clarify the butter and, while it is still hot, mix with the meat, herbs and spices. Beat the mixture to smooth paste with a wooden spoon and season with pepper. Taste to see if salt is necessary–usually I find the saltiness of the meat is enough.

Pack the potted meat into small jars. If it is to be stored in the refrigerator or deep-freeze cover with extra clarified butter.

Note: To clarify butter heat it in a saucepan until foaming and then strain through muslin.

Cinderella Pâté

Serves 4

1 chicken liver
1 small onion or shallot
3 hard-boiled eggs
75 g (3 oz) butter
Pinch of mixed herbs
Salt and freshly ground black pepper
Pinch of cayenne
2 teaspoons medium dry sherry or brandy
Parsley to garnish

Cut out any green patches or fibres from the liver. Peel and finely chop the onion. Peel the hard-boiled eggs and very finely chop the whites and two of the yolks. Melt one third of the butter, add the onion and cook until soft and transparent. Add the liver and cook over medium heat until it is well browned on all sides but still just a little pink in the centre. Remove from the heat and pass through a sieve or food mill. Beat liver, onion, pan juices and herbs together until smooth.

Melt the remaining butter and blend into the liver mixture with a little salt, pepper and pinch of cayenne. Mix in the sherry or brandy and fold in the chopped egg. Shape into a mound on a serving dish and cover with the remaining egg yolk, rubbed through a coarse sieve. Garnish with fresh parsley and serve with hot toast and butter.

Avocados with Cottage Cheese

Serves 4

2 sticks celery
1 tablespoon lemon juice
225 g (8 oz) cottage cheese
Salt and paprika pepper
1 tablespoon very finely chopped onion
Small clove garlic (optional)
2 avocado pears

This makes a good lunch dish, as avocados are both nourishing and satisfying. Those you buy are usually on the under-ripe side, but they can be ripened by putting them in a brown paper bag and leaving in a warm dark place for a few days.

Cut off the leaves and any tough fibres from the celery and chop the stalks finely. Add lemon juice to the cottage cheese, season with salt and mix in the onion, celery and crushed garlic.

Halve the avocados and remove the stones. Pile the cottage cheese mixture on the halves and sprinkle with a little paprika pepper.

Oeufs Mollets Racine

24 young sorrel leaves
50 g (2 oz) ham
75 g (3 oz) butter
Salt and freshly ground black pepper
Pinch of nutmeg
4 eggs
1½ tablespoons flour
150 ml (¼ pint) milk
150 ml (5 fl oz) single cream
50 g (2 oz) finely grated Cheddar cheese

Serves 2

A useful starter to make in advance and whisk through the oven at the last minute.

Wash the sorrel leaves and cook in very little boiling water until tender. Drain well and chop. Cut the ham into very small dice. Melt 25 g (1 oz) of the butter, add the sorrel and ham and season with salt, pepper and nutmeg. Mix well and remove from the heat. Cook the eggs in boiling water for five minutes, plunge into cold water and carefully remove the shells. Melt the remaining butter, add the flour and mix well. Gradually add the milk, stirring continually over a medium heat until the sauce is thick and smooth. Lower the heat, mix in the cream without boiling, season with salt and pepper and cook over a low heat for three minutes, stirring.

Divide the sorrel mixture between four ramekin dishes, top each with an egg and spoon over the sauce. Sprinkle over the cheese and put into a hot oven (220°C, 425°F, Reg. 7) for long enough to heat through.

Hard-Boiled Eggs with Light Green Sauce

8 eggs
2 bunches watercress
40 g (1½ oz) butter
1 tablespoon flour
150 ml (¼ pint) milk
300 ml (10 fl oz) double cream
Salt and freshly ground black pepper
2 tomatoes

Serves 4

An alternative to egg mayonnaise: in this dish the hard-boiled eggs are served with a light, subtle sauce flavoured with watercress.

Hard-boil the eggs in boiling water for 6–8 minutes. Drop into cold water, peel off the shells and halve lengthwise. Arrange on a serving dish cut side down.

Remove tough stalks from one bunch of watercress and cook the leaves in boiling salted water for three minutes. Drain well and purée through a fine sieve. Leave to cool.

Melt the butter in a saucepan. Add the flour and mix well. Gradually blend in the milk, stirring continuously over a low heat until sauce is smooth but not too thick. Slowly add the cream and continue to stir for about one minute until hot through. Do not allow to boil. Remove from heat, beat in the watercress purée and season generously with salt and pepper.

Pour the sauce over the eggs and garnish with the remaining watercress and two tomatoes, peeled and thinly sliced. Refrigerate for at least an hour before serving.

Egg and Avocado Mayonnaise

8 eggs
2 avocado pears
1 tablespoon cream
1 clove garlic (optional)
Salt and pepper
1–2 lettuce hearts
200 ml (7½ fl oz) mayonnaise
4 anchovy fillets
A little lemon juice

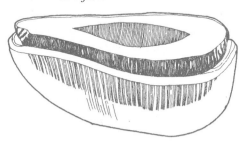

Serves 4

Egg mayonnaise is one of my favourite dishes but oh, dear, how it does vary. Properly made and attractively served it can be the most delicious of dishes. But with a couple of hard-boiled eggs slapped sloppily on a leaf or two of dried up lettuce, and bottled salad cream instead of home-made mayonnaise, it can be a disaster.

Hard-boil the eggs in boiling water for 6–8 minutes. Drop them into cold water, peel off shells and cut into halves lengthwise. Peel one of the avocados, discard the stone and mash the flesh in a bowl until smooth. Blend in the egg yolks, rubbed through a sieve, and the cream. Add the crushed garlic, season with salt and pepper and mix well.

Stuff the mixture into the egg whites and arrange the halves cut side down on a bed of shredded lettuce leaves. Coat the eggs generously with mayonnaise and garnish with anchovy fillets, neatly cut into two, and the second avocado, peeled, cut into thin slices and sprinkled with a little lemon juice to prevent it turning brown.

Christmas Jellied Eggs

4 eggs
½ clove garlic
Salt and pepper
1 small can pâté
1 can real turtle soup
1 tablespoon tomato purée
2 teaspoons lemon juice
1 tablespoon dry sherry
4 sprigs of tarragon
Tinned pimento to garnish

Serves 4

Poach the eggs until just set (please don't put vinegar in the poaching water; it ruins the taste and isn't necessary). Lift them from the pan with a slotted spoon to allow all excess water to drain off and slide on to a cold plate. Leave to cool and trim off any untidy edges with a circular pastry cutter.

Crush the garlic and blend it, with a little seasoning, into the pâté. Combine the turtle soup, tomato purée, lemon juice and sherry and heat until the tomato purée is dissolved.

Pour enough liquid into four ramekins to cover the bottom, place a sprig of tarragon in the centre of each one and leave to set firm. Cool the remaining liquid. Cover the jelly with a layer of pâté, place an egg in each dish and pour over the cooled liquid. Leave to set firm in the refrigerator or a very cool place and garnish with pieces of tinned pimento cut into leaf shapes and arranged to look like a poinsettia plant. Serve chilled with hot toast.

A selection of Hors-d'Oeuvre. From top to bottom left to right:
Broad Bean Hors-d'Oeuvre (p. 34), Avocado with Crab (p. 29), Christmas Jellied Eggs (p. 40),
High-Flying Pheasant Pâté (p. 36), Cape Horn Salad (p. 28), Kamano Miko (Pickled Smoked Salmon) (p. 27)

Cold Artichokes with Shrimp Mayonnaise

4 globe artichokes
1 onion
1 tablespoon white wine vinegar
1 teaspoon lemon juice
1 tablespoon tomato ketchup
200 ml (7½ fl oz) mayonnaise
100 g (4 oz) peeled prawns
2 spring onions
Salt and freshly ground black pepper

Serves 4

Trim the artichokes. Bring 2·5 cm (1 in) of water to the boil in a saucepan that is just large enough to take them all. Add the onion, peeled and finely chopped, and the vinegar. Place the artichokes upside down in the water, cover and cook over a medium heat for 30–45 minutes until tender. Drain well and leave to cool. Carefully pull out the centre leaves of the artichokes and remove the fibrous hairs from the centre.

Add the lemon juice and tomato ketchup to the mayonnaise and mix well. Roughly chop the prawns and finely slice the spring onions. Add them to the mayonnaise and season with salt and pepper. Fill the centre of the artichokes with the prawn mayonnaise and chill well before serving.

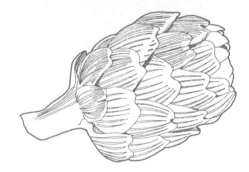

Anchovy and Mushroom Temptation

2 large onions
100 g (4 oz) button mushrooms
900 g (2 lb) potatoes
1 can anchovy fillets in oil
70 g (2½ oz) butter
200 ml (7½ fl oz) single cream
Pepper

8 small servings

This anchovy casserole can be made in advance and reheated.

Peel and thinly slice the onions and divide into rings. Thinly slice the mushrooms. Peel and thinly slice the potatoes. Remove the anchovies from the tin but reserve the oil. Melt 25 g (1 oz) of the butter in a saucepan, add the mushrooms and cook over a low heat for three minutes.

Arrange half the potatoes in a very well-buttered casserole. Cover with the onions, mushrooms and anchovies and top with remaining potatoes, seasoning the layers lightly with pepper. Pour over half the cream and all the anchovy oil, dot with the remaining butter and bake in a hot oven (220°C, 425°F, Reg. 7) for 45 minutes.

Pour over the remaining cream and continue to cook for a further ten minutes. Serve hot.

Barbecued Spare Ribs

Serves 4

900 g (2 lb) spare ribs of pork (American
　cut)
2 cloves garlic
1 large onion
2 tablespoons olive oil
3 tablespoons brown sugar
2 tablespoons malt vinegar
¼ teaspoon chilli powder
Pinch of sage
2 tablespoons tomato ketchup
Salt and freshly ground black pepper
150 ml (¼ pint) strong stock, or water and
　stock cube

A substantial first course which should be followed by a light main course.

Par-boil the spare ribs in boiling salted water for four minutes, drain well and pat dry on kitchen paper. Divide the ribs up by cutting between the bones with kitchen scissors. Crush the garlic. Peel and finely chop the onion.

Heat the olive oil in a saucepan, add the onion and garlic and cook over a medium heat until the onion is soft and transparent. Add the remaining ingredients, season with salt and pepper, bring to the boil and simmer for five minutes.

Place the spare ribs in a baking dish, brush with some of the sauce and cook in a moderately hot oven (190°C, 375°F, Reg. 5) for 30 minutes. Pour over the remaining sauce and cook for a further 45–60 minutes, basting frequently.

Transfer the spare ribs to a heated serving dish and serve the sauce separately after spooning off excess fat from the surface.

Fish

I have always had a sneaking feeling that all those Victorian and Edwardian nannies who maintained that one must eat one's fish because it was 'good for the brains' were right. It may have been my imagination but when recently I was working on a book of recipes for the unfamiliar fish which are appearing on the market at the moment, and we were eating fish at every meal, I noticed a marked increase in our general level of intelligence.

The great advantage of fish is that, on the whole, it needs very little preparation (since the nasty work is done by the fishmonger or before the fish reaches the slab) and a very short cooking time. Most forms of fish also provide the interested cook with an almost unlimited chance to practise or invent really exciting sauces to complement the somewhat bland flavours of most species, although the flavouring should never be so intense that the point of having fish at all is lost. Sauces should be subtle but well flavoured, light but full bodied, and the fish itself should never be overcooked.

Timing when cooking fish is a difficult thing to describe because it depends on so many factors: the thickness of the fish; its freshness (the fresher the fish the less it will need to be cooked); the length and also the type. The only sure way to tell whether fish is perfectly

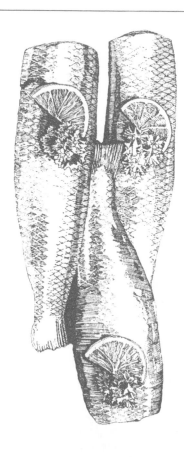

cooked is gently to pierce the skin and flesh with a fork. When the flesh is coming away from the bone or, in the case of fillets of fish, when it will flake away from the skin or just separate into flakes, the fish is ready.

Once cooked the fish should be served as soon as possible. If it *must* be kept waiting cover it with a piece of buttered greaseproof paper or foil, cover with an upside-down plate and keep warm in a very low oven.

In order to keep up with rising prices in these days of inflation there is more of an argument for keeping track of the fish world than there is in keeping up with food trends in almost any other department. Fish trends are changing. The cod has been so over fished that it is no longer inexpensive but extremely pricey. The same thing has happened to the herring, once a food of the poor and a fish treated by some with disdain. The answer is to turn to the lesser-known but equally delicious and relatively inexpensive fish now appearing on the market which provide very good value for money.

Keep an eye open for coley (a relation of the cod and equally good), pollock (another cod relation), huss, grey mullet, bass and bream. In the shellfish area try out crab, queens (miniature scallops), fresh scallops and mussels instead of the lobster which was once our birthright but which, sadly, is being swept up by the Continent. Monkfish is another delicious fish, though expensive, and on the cheaper side you can get a delicious meal from dabs (small flat fish which look like sole) and conger eel, which has a good robust white flesh.

One of my favourite fish is the mackerel, which has managed to retain its realistic price, is available for a good part of the year, and is a really delicious and well-flavoured food for both family meals and entertaining. The important thing about mackerel, however, is that it must be absolutely fresh or it should be forgotten about; the shorter the time from the sea to your table the better the taste will be. Like all fish mackerel, to be really fresh, must look shining, the eyes should be clear and the feel (if you have sufficient nerve to pick it up in the shop) should be supple and yet firm. Mackerel have rainbow tones in their scales and these should still be there when you buy them; if the fish are grey and dull avoid them. Cooked properly mackerel can provide an endless source of enjoyment for both first and main courses.

I have a lot of time for supermarkets, both for convenience and for their prices, but fish is a field in which you really want to see the product whole rather than to buy something wrapped up in a piece of transparent film. If you want to get really good fish and value for your

money then the best place to get it is from a good fishmonger, and the reason why there are not more good fishmongers around is because you, the customer, are not supporting them enough. It is a situation which there is still time to put right.

A good fishmonger will be prepared to tell you which fish you need to buy for your particular purpose, he will prepare the fish for you (do ask for the bones and head which he will be delighted to include and which provide excellent fish stock material) and he can help you to get really good value for money.

If you want to freeze your own fish make sure you buy them from a really reliable source. Prepare and fillet the fish before freezing, or cut them into steaks etc. (the bones and head can be frozen separately for making stock) and wrap each fillet slice or whole fish in clear film before freezing. The best source of fresh fish will be the fish market in your locality.

Grilled Fillets of Fish, Japanese Style

8 small fillets white fish (sole, plaice, whiting, haddock, etc.)
2 egg yolks
1 tablespoon sherry
Salt and freshly ground black pepper
Pinch of cayenne pepper

Serves 4

The Japanese have an unusual way of grilling fish with a glaze of egg yolks and rice wine which makes an exciting dish. This is an 'anglicised' version, with sherry instead of rice wine; any firm white fish fillets can be used. The coating gives a golden finish and imparts a delicate taste to the fish as well as sealing in the natural juices.

I serve this with individual bowls of rice into which a whole raw egg has been broken–very Japanese and absolutely delicious; each person seasons his rice with a little soya sauce, mixes it with a spoon or chopsticks and tops it with the pieces of fish.

Rub the fish fillets with salt and leave to stand for 15 minutes. Combine the egg yolks with the sherry and season with a little salt, pepper and a pinch of cayenne.

Arrange the fillets on a fireproof dish and brush them with half the egg mixture. Grill under a medium heat for five minutes, turn over, brush with the remaining glaze and continue to grill for a further five minutes until cooked through and golden brown.

Poached Fish with Parsley Lemon Sauce

Serves 2

1 carrot
1 small onion
1 stick celery
150 ml (¼ pint) white wine vinegar
1·2 litres (2 pints) water
½ bay leaf
Bouquet garni
½ teaspoon salt and six peppercorns
450 g (1 lb) filleted turbot, coley or pollock;
    or 675 g (1½ lb) white fish on the bone
1 lemon
4–5 tablespoons sour cream
2 tablespoons very finely chopped parsley
Salt and freshly ground black pepper

Peel and roughly chop the carrot. Peel and chop the onion. Chop the celery and leaves. Combine the vinegar, water, vegetables, bay leaf, bouquet garni, ½ teaspoon salt and peppercorns in a saucepan, bring to the boil and simmer for 30 minutes. Strain the liquid and return to a clean shallow pan.

Rub the fish with the cut half of the lemon. Bring the liquid to the boil, add the fish and simmer for 8–10 minutes until just tender. Transfer to a heated serving dish and keep warm.

Combine the sour cream and juice of the lemon in a saucepan, heat through without boiling and mix in the parsley. Season with salt and pepper, pour the sauce over the fish and serve at once.

Maidenwell Fish Pie

Serves 6–8

900 g (2 lb) coley, conger eel, pollock, etc.
2 onions
50 g (2 oz) butter
1½ tablespoons flour
450 ml (¾ pint) milk
6 anchovy fillets
½ teaspoon coriander
⅛ teaspoon grated nutmeg
⅛ teaspoon dill
Salt and freshly ground black pepper
450 g (1 lb) spinach
2 hard-boiled eggs
50 g (2 oz) Cheddar cheese
2 tablespoons finely chopped parsley

Steam the fish over boiling water until just cooked. Remove skin and flake the flesh. Peel and finely chop the onions. Melt the butter in a saucepan, add the onions and cook over a low heat until they are soft and yellow. Stir in the flour and gradually blend in the milk, stirring continuously over a medium heat until the sauce is thick and smooth.

Pound the anchovies, coriander, nutmeg and dill in a pestle and mortar until a smooth paste forms. Blend this paste into the sauce and season lightly with pepper.

Cook the spinach in a very little boiling, salted water until tender, drain well and roughly chop with kitchen scissors.

Add the fish and chopped hard-boiled eggs to the sauce and stir lightly to amalgamate the ingredients. Spread half the mixture over the bottom of a lightly greased baking dish, cover with spinach and spread over the remainder. Sprinkle over the cheese and bake in a moderate oven (180°C, 350°F, Reg. 4) for 20 minutes until the dish is hot through and the cheese is bubbling and a good golden yellow in colour. Serve sprinkled with parsley.

Curried Fish

Serves 4

1 small onion
1 clove garlic
½ green pepper
1 tablespoon oil
2 tablespoons Madras curry powder
1 tablespoon plain flour
425 g (15 oz) can tomatoes
450 ml (¾ pint) water
Grated rind and juice of ½ lemon
Salt and pepper
450 g (1 lb) cooked flaked white fish
  (haddock, coley, pollock, cod, etc.)

Peel and finely chop the onion and garlic. Remove core and seeds from the green pepper and chop the flesh. Heat the oil in a heavy saucepan. Add the onion, garlic and pepper and cook over a low heat until the onion is soft and transparent. Add the curry powder and flour, mix well and cook for one minute. Add the tomatoes, water, lemon rind and juice and bring to the boil, stirring well. Season with salt and pepper, cover and simmer for 25 minutes. Lightly mix in the fish and heat through.

Serve on a bed of fluffy rice with chutney and *popadums* on the side.

Fish and Prawn Chowder

Serves 6

100 g (4 oz) frozen prawns
2 leeks
4 thin rashers streaky bacon
450 g (1 lb) potatoes
15 g (½ oz) butter
1 tablespoon flour
300 ml (½ pint) chicken stock
600 ml (1 pint) milk
Salt and freshly ground black pepper
Pinch of mace
Bouquet garni (sprig of parsley and sage;
  2 bay leaves)
½ teaspoon saffron
675 g (1½ lb) coley or pollock
150 ml (5 fl oz) double cream
1 tablespoon finely chopped parsley or chives

A rich and nourishing fish chowder is more than just a first course. Served with hot French bread and followed by cheese and fruit it can make a perfect main course. Frozen fish is particularly suitable for these dishes where that evocative freshness of fish straight from the sea is not of paramount importance.

Thaw the frozen prawns. Clean the leeks and cut into thin slices. Remove rinds and chop the bacon finely. Peel the potatoes and dice.

Heat the butter, add the bacon and cook over a low heat for five minutes until the fat has oozed out. Add the leeks and potatoes and cook over low heat until leeks are transparent.

Add the flour, mix well and gradually blend in the stock and milk, stirring continuously over a high heat until thickened and smooth. Season with salt, pepper and pinch of mace. Add bouquet garni and simmer for 20 minutes.

Infuse the saffron in 2 tablespoons of boiling water for 15 minutes. Remove skin and any bones from the fish and cut the flesh into 1-cm (½-in) square cubes.

Strain the liquid saffron into the soup and add the fish. Simmer for about eight minutes or until the fish is nearly tender.

Add the prawns, bring to the boil and take off the heat. Stir in the cream. Pour the soup into a large tureen and sprinkle with parsley or chives.

Smoked Haddock with Spinach

675 g (1½ lb) smoked haddock
350 g (12 oz) packet frozen spinach
1 tablespoon olive oil
1 teaspoon lemon juice
Salt and freshly ground black pepper
2 firm ripe tomatoes
1 onion
15 g (½ oz) butter
4 tablespoons yoghurt
Pinch ground saffron

Serves 4

Steam the haddock over boiling water for about 15 minutes. Remove skin and bones and gently flake the fish. Cook the spinach in a little boiling water until tender and drain well. Add oil and lemon juice to the spinach, season with salt and pepper, toss lightly and arrange in a serving dish.

Drop the tomatoes into boiling water, leave for one minute, drain and slide off the skins. Remove core and seeds and chop the flesh. Peel and finely chop the onion and cook in the butter over a medium heat, without browning, until soft and pale gold. Add the tomatoes, season with salt and pepper and cook for three minutes. Blend in the yoghurt and saffron and heat through without boiling.

Arrange the flaked haddock over the spinach and spoon over the sauce. Heat through in a slow oven (160°C, 325°F, Reg. 3) for about ten minutes before serving.

Kedgeree Revival

450 g (1 lb) smoked haddock or smoked cod fillet
300 ml (½ pint) milk
225 g (8 oz) long-grain rice
2 hard-boiled eggs
1 large onion
50 g (2 oz) butter
1 egg
150 ml (5 fl oz) single cream
Freshly ground black pepper
Fresh parsley to garnish

Serves 4

Kedgeree used to be a breakfast dish in the good old days when some of our great-grandfathers ate four square meals a day. Nowadays it has become a light lunch or supper dish.

Lightly butter a large frying pan. Lay the smoked fish fillets, skin side down, in the pan and pour over the milk. Add enough water to cover the fish, bring gently to the boil, cover and simmer for 10–15 minutes until the fish is tender and will flake easily. Drain off the milk, remove any skin and bones and flake the fish.

Cook the rice in boiling, salted water until just tender. Drain and rinse through with cold water to remove excess starch. Drain well, spread on a plate and put into a slow oven for about 15 minutes to dry.

Roughly chop the hard-boiled eggs. Peel and chop onion. Melt the butter in a large frying pan over a low heat. Add the onion and cook slowly until soft and transparent. Add the rice and haddock and mix lightly until all the ingredients are hot through. Gently mix in the hard-boiled egg.

Combine the raw egg with the cream and mix until smooth. Add to the pan, season generously with pepper and mix lightly until the kedgeree is hot and creamy. Serve at once sprinkled with plenty of finely chopped parsley.

Chilled Kedgeree

Serves 6

900 g (2 lb) smoked haddock
600 ml (1 pint) milk
½ teaspoon tarragon
Juice of ½ lemon
300 ml (10 fl oz) double cream
Salt and pepper
350 g (12 oz) cooked rice
2 hard-boiled eggs

Poach the haddock in milk until tender. Drain off milk, remove skin from the fish and leave to cool. Flake the fish with a fork.

Soak the tarragon in the lemon juice for 15 minutes, add the cream, mix well and season with salt and pepper. Stir in the fish and rice and arrange in a serving dish. Garnish with quarters of hard-boiled egg.

Poached Fish with a Cheese and Cider Sauce

Serves 4

1 small carrot
1 small onion
1 stick celery
1 tablespoon cider vinegar
2 sprigs parsley
1 bay leaf
4 black peppercorns
1 teaspoon salt
1 slice lemon
600 ml (1 pint) water
450 ml (¾ pint) dry cider
675 g (1½ lb) white fish fillets (whiting is good)

Cheese and Cider Sauce

20 g (¾ oz) butter
1 heaped tablespoon flour
300 ml (½ pint) medium dry cider
50 g (2 oz) grated Cheddar cheese
Salt and white pepper
1 small red pepper
25 g (1 oz) grated Gruyère cheese
Paprika pepper

This dish can be served as a first course, or as a main course with mashed poatoes or rice and a crisp salad of Chinese cabbage, green peppers and fennel dressed with a vinaigrette made with garlic- or chilli-flavoured cider vinegar.

Peel and roughly chop the carrot and onion. Roughly chop the celery and leaves. Combine the carrot, onion, celery, cider vinegar, parsley, bay leaf, peppercorns, salt and lemon slice with the water and dry cider. Bring to the boil, simmer for 30 minutes and strain.

Return this court bouillon to a large shallow pan. Bring to simmering point, add the fish fillets, skin side down, and simmer for about 20 minutes without boiling until just tender. Drain, remove any dark skin and place the fillets in a lightly buttered serving dish.

Melt the butter in a saucepan. Add the flour and mix well. Gradually blend in the cider, stirring continuously over a medium heat until the sauce is thick and smooth. Lower the heat, stir in the Cheddar cheese and keep stirring until it has melted. Season with salt and pepper.

Remove core and seeds from the red pepper, cut the flesh into thin strips, blanch in boiling water for two minutes and drain.

Pour the cheese sauce over the fish, top with pepper strips and sprinkle over the Gruyère cheese. Shake over a little paprika pepper and reheat under a medium hot grill to brown the dish.

Cullen Skink

1 onion
675 g (1½ lb) smoked haddock fillets
900 ml (1½ pints) milk
225 g (8 oz) cooked potatoes mashed smooth
2 bay leaves
Salt, white pepper and nutmeg
150 ml (5 fl oz) single cream
1 tablespoon finely chopped parsley

Serves 4–6

A traditional Scottish recipe which I sometimes serve cold in the summer.

Peel and thinly slice the onion and divide into rings. Place the haddock fillets in a lightly greased baking dish, top them with onion rings and pour over just enough water to cover. Cover with foil and bake in a moderate oven (180°C, 350°F, Reg. 4) for about 20 minutes or until the fish is just tender. Drain off and reserve the liquid, discarding the onion. Remove skin from fish and gently flake the flesh.

Place the milk in a saucepan with the potato and heat, stirring continuously, until the mixture comes to the boil and is creamy smooth. Add the bay leaves and fish liquid and simmer for five minutes. Remove bay leaves, add the fish and season with salt, pepper and little ground nutmeg. Add the cream and heat through. Serve sprinkled with chopped parsley.

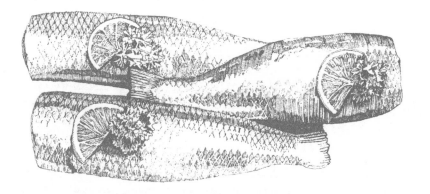

Curried Haddock

1 medium onion
25 g (1 oz) butter
1 teaspoon curry powder
1 tablespoon double cream
1 tablespoon milk
2 tablespoons mango chutney
100 g (4 oz) smoked haddock, cooked and
    flaked
4 slices bread
Oil or fat for frying
1 tablespoon finely chopped parsley

Serves 4

Peel and very finely chop the onion. Melt the butter in a saucepan, add the onion and cook over a low heat until soft and transparent. Add the curry powder, mix well and blend in the cream and milk. Simmer slowly for eight minutes without boiling.

Finely chop the mango chutney. Add it to the curry sauce with the haddock and heat through.

Remove the crusts from the bread and cut each slice in half. Fry the bread until golden brown on each side. Drain on kitchen paper and pile the curried haddock on top. Sprinkle with parsley before serving.

Stuffed Baked Herrings in Foil

4 large herrings
Juice of ½ lemon
Salt and freshly ground black pepper
1 shallot or small onion
175 g (6 oz) firm button mushrooms
50 g (2 oz) butter
¼ teaspoon lemon juice
Pinch of cayenne
2 tablespoons finely chopped parsley
1 tablespoon tomato purée

Serves 4

Mackerel can be used in the place of herrings.

Ask your fishmonger to remove the head, tail and backbone of the fish. Rub the insides with the juice of half a lemon, salt and pepper. Peel and very finely chop the shallot; very thinly slice the mushrooms. Melt the butter in a frying pan, add the shallot and cook over a moderate heat until soft. Add the mushrooms and cook for further 2–3 minutes. Mix in the ½ teaspoon lemon juice, cayenne, parsley and tomato purée. Season and simmer for five minutes.

Place each herring on a piece of lightly greased foil and spread stuffing on one side. Fold the foil over neatly and seal to make a parcel.

Bake in a moderate oven (180°C, 350°F, Reg. 4) for 20 minutes and serve in the foil parcels.

Mackerel Maître d'Hôtel

4 mackerel
2 teaspoons fish seasoning (celery salt, white
  pepper and paprika)
125 g (4½ oz) butter
Juice of 1 small lemon
2 tablespoons finely chopped parsley

Serves 4

Serve this beautifully simple dish with boiled rice.

Clean and wash the mackerel, leaving heads and tails on. Score through the skin, without cutting the flesh, on both sides at 1 cm (½ in) intervals. Rub skin and inside with fish seasoning. Heat the butter until foaming, add the fish and cook for ten minutes on each side over a high heat. Remove to a warm serving plate.

Add lemon juice to the cooking butter and mix well. Add parsley and pour this sauce over the mackerel.

Fried Mackerel

4 large mackerel fillets
Flour
Salt and pepper
Vegetable oil for frying
8 sprigs of parsley
Lemon wedges

Serves 4

Cut the mackerel in 6 mm (¼ in) thick strips across the centre of the fillets and toss the pieces in flour, well seasoned with salt and pepper.

Heat the oil until smoking in a deep pan and drop in the mackerel strips one by one so that they stay separate–don't fry too many pieces at a time. Cook the fish until golden brown. Remove with a slotted spoon and drain on kitchen paper. Keep cooked pieces hot while the rest are frying.

When all the fish is cooked drop whole sprigs of parsley in the fat and cook until crisp. Garnish the fried mackerel with the parsley and some lemon wedges and serve with a tartare or tomato sauce.

Grilled Plaice Fillets with Prawns

A little olive or vegetable oil
8 plaice fillets
Juice of 1 lemon
Salt and freshly ground black pepper
175 g (6 oz) peeled prawns
50 g (2 oz) finely grated cheese
Paprika pepper

Serves 4

Whiting fillets can be used instead of plaice.

Cover the grill pan with a sheet of foil lightly oiled with olive or vegetable oil. Arrange the fish fillets on the foil, brush them with lemon juice and a little oil and season with salt and pepper. Grill the fillets under a medium fast flame until cooked through.

Chop the prawns and spread them over the fillets. Top with grated cheese, sprinkle a pinch of paprika over each fillet and return to the grill for a few more minutes until the cheese has melted and is bubbling and golden brown.

Serve at once with salad or green vegetable.

Curried Fish (p. 47) served with chutney and fried popadums

Sea Bass in Wine and Orange Juice

2 medium sized sea bass
2 sprigs fennel or thyme or 2 bay leaves
Salt and freshly ground black pepper
4 tablespoons olive or vegetable oil
3 tablespoons dry white wine
Juice of ½ orange
8 black olives
4 thin slices of lemon
4 thin slices of orange

Serves 4

Sea bass is one of the most delicious of our fish and fortunately it is becoming easier to find these days. It is firm, well flavoured and can be surprisingly inexpensive. Choose fish that weigh around 675 g (1½ lb) and divide each fish into two to serve. With a bottle of good wine, a salad, fruit and cheese, what more could you want?

Grey mullet or whole whiting can be cooked in the same way.

Clean and scale the fish (your fishmonger will probably do this for you) and lay them in a lightly oiled fireproof serving dish. Place a sprig of fennel, or thyme, or 2 bay leaves inside each fish and season them inside and out with salt and freshly ground black pepper. Pour over the oil, white wine and orange juice and bake in a moderate oven (180°C, 350°F, Reg. 4), without covering, for 20 minutes.

Stone and thinly slice the olives, arrange the slices over the fish and continue to cook for a further five minutes. Arrange the slices of orange and lemon over the fish and serve at once.

Hot Baked Mackerel with Sharp Mustard Sauce

Six 175 g (6 oz) smoked mackerel
3 egg yolks
200 g (7 oz) butter
1 tablespoon French Dijon mustard
1 teaspoon tarragon
150 ml (5 fl oz) carton soured cream
Salt and pepper
Lemon wedges

Serves 6

An unusual main course with an exciting flavour. Serve with new, mashed or jacket potatoes and a green or mixed salad.

Wrap each fish in foil and bake in a moderately hot oven (200°C, 400°F, Reg. 6) for 15–20 minutes until hot through.

Beat the egg yolks and place them in the top of a double boiler over hot, not boiling, water with 100 g (4 oz) of the butter, softened. Cook, stirring continuously, until the mixture is thick enough to coat the back of a wooden spoon–about ten minutes. Remove from the heat and add the remaining butter, mustard and tarragon. Leave to stand for ten minutes. Blend in the soured cream and season with salt and pepper.

Unwrap the fish, arrange them on a serving dish and garnish with lemon wedges. Serve the sauce separately.

Note: occasionally a sauce like this, with a Hollandaise base, will separate and curdle. This usually happens if the sauce is made too quickly, and should be cured by beating in a teaspoon or two of boiling water.

Terrine of Salmon in Pastry Case

Serves 10–12

The filling:

About 750 g (1¾ lb) salmon
900 g (2 lb) white fish fillets (use haddock or
    hake etc., but not cod as its strong taste will
    overpower the salmon)
175 g (6 oz) white breadcrumbs
4 eggs, beaten
3 tablespoons double cream
Salt and freshly ground black pepper
Pinch of cayenne, nutmeg and mace
1 small onion
25 g (1 oz) mushrooms
40 g (1½ oz) butter
8 leaves sorrel or spinach
4 sprigs parsley
2 teaspoons dry sherry
1 small egg, beaten

The pastry:

350 g (12 oz) plain flour
½ teaspoon salt
150 ml (¼ pint) water
100 g (4 oz) lard

The fish stock:

Bones and skin of salmon and white fish
1 onion
1 sprig parsley
1 bay leaf
150 ml (¼ pint) dry white wine
150 ml (¼ pint) water
1½ teaspoons gelatine powder

Although this is a spectacular party dish, the base uses a relatively small amount of salmon. It is therefore a sensational way to stretch the salmon you have to buy or the piece you have left over from a large fish. The tail or head end are suitable enough for the recipe.

Some 19th-century cooks believed that salmon, like other game, should be hung before being cooked. I must admit I do not subscribe to the practice but I have noticed a salmon kept for a day or two in the refrigerator before cooking tends to be firmer of flesh than one cooked straight from the water, and its flavour is in no way impaired.

In this recipe the terrine of fish is cooked in a pastry case in order to ensure that all flavour and moisture are retained. Make the terrine in a cake tin with a removable bottom, or in a special hinged pie tin.

Slide a knife between skin and salmon and neatly remove the skin. Fillet the salmon by sliding a sharp knife along fish bones. Reserve skin and bones. Skin the white fillets and remove any bones. Reserve skin and bones. Mince the white fish twice through the fine blades of a mincing machine and pound with a wooden spoon in a bowl until smooth. Add 100 g (4 oz) of the breadcrumbs, the eggs and cream and continue to work until smooth and almost silky in texture. Season the mixture with salt, pepper and a pinch of cayenne, ground nutmeg and mace.

Peel and chop the onion and mince with the mushrooms. Melt one third of the butter in a saucepan, add the mushrooms and onions and cook over a low heat, stirring occasionally, for five minutes. Cook the sorrel or spinach with the parsley in a little boiling water for six minutes until soft. Drain well to remove all moisture and purée through a sieve or food mill.

Divide the white fish fillet mixture in half. Add the green purée and mushroom mixture to half the fish with the remaining breadcrumbs and mix until smooth (it should be a nice green colour. If it looks dull add a little green colouring). Cut the salmon flesh into matchstick strips about 6 mm (¼ in) thick and 2·5 cm (2 in) long.

Thoroughly grease a hinged pie tin of 2·5-litre (4-pint) capacity. Alternatively use a 2·5-litre (4-pint) cake tin with removable bottom.

Put the flour into a bowl and mix in the salt. Combine the water and lard in a saucepan, bring to the boil and cook until the lard has melted. Make a well in centre of the flour, pour in the hot liquid and mix well with a wooden spoon until ingredients are well blended. Turn the dough on to a floured board and knead lightly until smooth and firm.

Set aside one third of the pastry and thinly roll out the rest to a

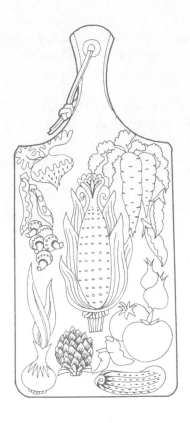

circle large enough to line the baking tin. The pastry is a bit difficult to handle but don't worry, you can even it out and patch up the holes later.

Line the tin with the pastry, pressing it into the bottom and sides with your fingertips to make an even thickness of about 3 mm ($\frac{1}{8}$ in).

Spoon half the green fish mixture into the bottom of the pastry case. Cover with one third of the salmon pieces, pressing in firmly. Spread over half the white fish mixture and press another one third of the salmon onto that. Cover with the remaining white fish, the salmon and, finally, the rest of the green mixture. Smooth down firmly with the back of a wooden spoon. Dot with the remaining butter and pour over the sherry.

Roll out the remaining pastry and cover the pie, dampening the edges with a little water. Pinch the edges firmly together, cut a small slit in the centre and decorate with pastry leaves stuck on with a little beaten egg. Brush over with beaten egg and bake in a hot oven (230°C, 450°F, Reg. 8) for 15 minutes, then cover the pie with a piece of dampened greaseproof paper and continue to bake for a further $1\frac{1}{4}$ hours in a moderate oven (180°C, 350°F, Reg. 4). Leave to cool in the tin and then chill for at least 6 hours.

Combine the fish bones and skin with an onion, peeled and quartered, a sprig of parsley and a bay leaf. Season with salt and pepper, add the wine and water, bring to the boil and simmer for 20 minutes. Strain the liquid through a fine sieve, add gelatine powder and stir until melted. Using a small funnel or jug, pour fish stock into the pie through the slit until as much liquid as possible has been absorbed. Return the pie to the refrigerator and chill for a further four hours.

To turn out run a knife dipped in hot water around the sides of the tin, or gently ease sides of a hinged tin apart. Serve cut into 1 cm ($\frac{1}{2}$ in) slices.

Stuffed Sprats

900 g (2 lb) sprats
1 small onion
75 g (3 oz) butter
50 g (2 oz) fresh white breadcrumbs
2 tablespoons finely chopped parsley
Juice of ½ lemon
Freshly ground black pepper
1 can anchovy fillets
Lemon wedges

Serves 6

When I was a child I used to watch old women filleting sprats with the lightning speed of years of experience. It is a job that takes patience but which, with a little practice, is no more of a chore than peeling potatoes.

Cut off the sprats' heads and tails. Use a sharp knife to cut a line down the belly and clean the fish under running water. Lay them on their backs and slide the knife under the backbone from the tail end, as close to the bones as possible. Stretch the fish by sliding the back of the knife firmly along its length.

Peel and very finely chop the onion. Melt one third of the butter in a saucepan, add the onion and cook over a low heat until soft and transparent. Add melted butter and onion to the breadcrumbs and parsley, pour in lemon juice, season with pepper and mix in the anchovies, cut into small pieces.

Spread a small amount of stuffing on each sprat and roll up neatly. Place in a lightly greased baking dish, dot with the remaining butter and bake in moderate oven (180°C, 350°F, Reg. 4) for 20 minutes. Serve garnished with lemon wedges.

Sprats in Batter

900 g (2 lb) sprats
100 g (4 oz) plain flour
Pinch of salt
1 tablespoon vegetable oil
5 tablespoons water
5 tablespoons pale ale
2 egg whites
Oil for deep-frying
12 sprigs parsley
Lemon wedges

Serves 6

Cooked in this way sprats can be served as a first course. Accompany them with thin slices of buttered brown bread.

Wash and dry the sprats but do not remove heads or tails and do not gut. Combine the flour, salt, vegetable oil, water and beer in a basin and beat until smooth with a rotary whisk. Beat the egg whites until stiff and fold them lightly into the batter mixture.

Dip the fish into the batter and fry in batches in very hot oil until crisp and golden brown. Drain on kitchen paper and keep warm while frying the remainder. Do not fry too many fish at a time.

Drop the parsley sprigs one by one into the hot oil and cook for just about one minute until crisp. Pile the sprats on to a serving dish and garnish with the parsley and with wedges of lemon.

Devilled Sprats with Piquant Sauce

Serves 4

100 g (4 oz) plain flour
½ teaspoon cayenne pepper
Salt and freshly ground black pepper
900 g (2 lb) sprats
Oil for deep-frying
150 ml (¼ pint) mayonnaise
4 tablespoons double or sour cream
1 teaspoon tomato purée
1 teaspoon finely chopped capers
1 teaspoon finely chopped dill-pickled cucumber
Few drops Tabasco and Worcestershire sauce
Lemon wedges

If there are any fish left over from this dish they are delicious served cold with a sharp vinaigrette dressing.

Mix the flour with the cayenne pepper and a little salt and pepper. Wash and dry the sprats but do not cut off heads or tails and do not gut. Roll them in the seasoned flour until they are well coated. Cook in batches in very hot oil until crisp and golden brown. Drain on kitchen paper and keep warm while the remainder are being cooked. Do not cook too many fish at one time.

Combine the mayonnaise and cream with the tomato purée, capers and dill-pickled cucumber. Add a few drops of Tabasco and Worcestershire sauce and mix well. Garnish the fish with lemon wedges and serve at once, handing the mayonnaise separately.

Piquant Whiting

Serves 4

4 medium whiting
1 shallot or small onion
2 bay leaves
Salt and freshly ground black pepper
Juice of 1 lemon
150 ml (¼ pint) white wine
150 ml (¼ pint) water
50 g (2 oz) butter
2 teaspoons finely chopped parsley

I have never really liked the fashion of serving whiting with the heads biting at their tails. As a child I used to feel so sorry for the fish I could not bear to look at them, let alone eat the poor things. They are good fish, however, for both flavour and texture, and this method of cooking them is well worth trying.

Remove heads and tails from the whiting, lay them flat and cut a couple of nicks through the backbones to prevent the fish curling up while cooking. Peel and finely chop the shallot or onion. Butter a shallow baking dish, lay the whiting in it, side by side, add the bay leaves and sprinkle over the shallot or onion. Season with salt and pepper, pour over the lemon juice, wine and water and dot with butter.

Bake the fish uncovered in a moderate oven (180°C, 350°F, Reg. 4) for 20 minutes, basting frequently, until they are beginning to flake from the backbone and most of the juices in the baking dish have been absorbed. Sprinkle with the chopped parsley and serve.

Stuffed Fillets of Whiting

Serves 4

1 small onion
50 g (2 oz) mushrooms
2 hard-boiled eggs
1 bacon rasher
25 g (1 oz) butter
3 tablespoons fresh white breadcrumbs
½ teaspoon lemon juice
1 tablespoon finely chopped parsley
Salt and freshly ground black pepper
2 tablespoons double cream
4 fresh whiting, filleted

Instead of whiting you can use herrings or mackerel for this dish.

Peel and very finely chop the onion. Finely chop the mushrooms and hard-boiled eggs. Remove rind and finely chop bacon. Heat the butter, add the onion, mushrooms and bacon and cook over a low heat until the onion is soft and transparent. Remove from heat and mix in the breadcrumbs, hard-boiled egg, lemon juice and parsley. Season with salt and pepper and bind with double cream.

Lightly butter a baking dish. Arrange half the fillets, skin side down, in the dish and spread them with the stuffing mixture. Top with remaining fillets, dot with a little extra butter and bake in a moderate oven (190°C, 375°F, Reg. 5) until tender; about 25 minutes.

Baked Crab

Serves 4

225 g (8 oz) firm button mushrooms
4 spring onions
25 g (1 oz) butter
25 g (1 oz) flour
300 ml (½ pint) milk
Salt and pepper
225 g (8 oz) fresh or frozen crab meat
4 tablespoons dry breadcrumbs
100 g (4 oz) grated Cheddar cheese

Thinly slice the mushrooms. Finely chop the spring onions. Melt the butter in a saucepan, add flour and mix well. Gradually blend in the milk, stirring continuously over a medium heat until the sauce comes to the boil and is thick and smooth. Season with salt and pepper and mix in the crab, mushrooms and onions.

Turn into a greased casserole or four scallop shells, sprinkle over the breadcrumbs and grated cheese and bake in a hot oven (230°C, 450°F, Reg. 8) for 20 minutes.

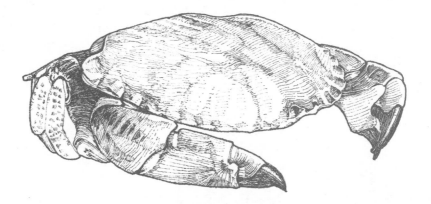

Mussels

Serves 4

2 litres (1½–2 quarts) mussels
150 ml (¼ pint) water
150 ml (¼ pint) dry white wine
1 small onion
2 tablespoons finely chopped parsley
Pinch of thyme
6 peppercorns

Wash, scrape and remove beards from the mussels. Place them in a large wide pan. Combine the water and wine in another pan and bring to the boil. Peel and finely chop the onion. Scatter the onion, parsley and thyme over the mussels, add the peppercorns and pour over the boiling liquid.

Cover and boil for about three minutes until the mussels have opened; discard any mussels that have *not* opened.

Brochettes de Moules

Serves 4

2 litres (1½–2 quarts) mussels, cooked as above
6 rashers streaky bacon
50 g (2 oz) cooked ham
1 egg, beaten
Dried breadcrumbs
Salt and pepper
Butter
Juice of 1 lemon

Drain the mussels and remove from their shells. Remove rinds from bacon and cut the bacon and ham into 2·5 cm (1 in) squares. Skewer the mussels, ham and bacon on four metal skewers, dip in beaten egg and roll in breadcrumbs. Season with salt and pepper and cook in butter until golden brown on all sides. Sprinkle with lemon juice before serving.

Mussels au Gratin

Serves 4

2 litres (1½–2 quarts) mussels, cooked as above
40 g (1½ oz) butter
2 tablespoons flour
2 egg yolks
Salt and pepper
1 tablespoon dry sherry
4 tablespoons fresh white breadcrumbs
50 g (2 oz) grated Emmenthal cheese
2 tablespoons melted butter
Pinch cayenne pepper

Drain the mussels, remove empty shells and place the mussels in their half shells in a fire-proof baking dish. Reserve the liquid and juices.

Melt the butter, add the flour and mix well. Gradually stir in the strained mussel liquid, beating continuously until the sauce is smooth and comes to the boil. Lower the heat and beat in egg yolks one by one. Season with salt and pepper and stir in the sherry.

Pour the sauce over the mussels. Combine the breadcrumbs and cheese, sprinkle this mixture on the sauce, pour over the melted butter, sprinkle with a little cayenne and brown quickly under a hot grill.

Stuffed Sea Trout

Serves 4

1 sea or salmon trout, about 1·5 kilos (3 lb)
100 g (4 oz) smoked salmon
6 anchovy fillets
1 sprig fresh dill
½ lemon cut into thin slices
3 tablespoons olive oil
2 tablespoons melted butter
Freshly ground black pepper

Ask your fishmonger to clean and gut the sea trout; leaving the head and tail on.

Cut 6 mm (¼ in) deep scores diagonally across both sides of the fish at 2·5 cm (1 in) intervals. Stuff the incisions with smoked salmon cut into thin strips and the anchovies cut in half lengthwise. Fill the centre of the fish with fresh dill and slices of lemon.

Place the fish on a well-oiled sheet of foil, pour over the remaining oil and melted butter and season generously with pepper. Close up the foil to make a neat parcel and bake in a moderate oven (180°C, 350°F, Reg. 4) for 35–40 minutes until the fish just comes away from the bone. The only way to judge this exactly is to unwrap the fish and test it after 25 minutes.

Scallops Mornay

Serves 4

6 medium scallops
150 ml (¼ pint) water
150 ml (¼ pint) white wine
2 slices lemon
1 slice onion
3 peppercorns
1 bay leaf
25 g (1 oz) butter
1 tablespoon flour
200 ml (7½ fl oz) milk
40 g (1½ oz) Parmesan cheese, grated
25 g (1 oz) Gruyère cheese, grated
Pinch of cayenne pepper
2 tablespoons single cream

Like all shellfish scallops respond well to being cooked with a classic Mornay sauce, delicately flavoured with a mixture of Gruyère and Parmesan cheese. If possible buy fresh Parmesan and grate it yourself, as its flavour is infinitely better than that of ready-grated.

Prepare the scallops by removing the coral and discarding the black vein that circles them. Wash gently in cold water and pat dry with kitchen paper.

Combine the water, wine, lemon, onion, peppercorns and bay leaf in a saucepan. Bring to the boil and simmer gently for five minutes. Strain and return the liquid to a clean pan, add the white part of the scallops and poach gently in the hot liquid for four minutes; add corals halfway through. Drain off and reserve the liquid. Cut the scallops into 6 mm (¼ in) thick slices and halve the corals. Divide them between four lightly greased scallop shells or individual dishes.

Melt the butter in a saucepan, add the flour and mix well. Gradually add the milk, stirring continuously over a medium high heat until the sauce is thick and smooth. Blend in enough of the reserved liquid to make a sauce of rich pouring consistency. Add two thirds of the Parmesan, the Gruyère and the cayenne pepper, mix well and stir over a low heat until the cheese has melted.

Blend in the cream and pour the sauce over the scallops. Top with the remaining Parmesan and brown under a hot grill before serving.

To make a more substantial dish the scallops can be placed in a ring of mashed potatoes or boiled rice.

Cold Scallops with a Light Curry Sauce

6 medium scallops
150 ml (¼ pint) white wine
150 ml (¼ pint) water
1 slice onion
3 peppercorns
1 bay leaf
¼ teaspoon curry powder
1 teaspoon tomato purée
150 ml (¼ pint) mayonnaise
150 ml (5 fl oz) double cream
1 lettuce
Quarters of lemon

Serves 4

Just a hint of curry flavouring is required for this sauce; the taste should be subtle and not overpoweringly spicy.

Prepare the scallops as above.

Combine the wine, water, onion, peppercorns and bay leaf in a saucepan, bring to the boil and simmer gently for five minutes. Strain and return the liquid to a clean pan.

Add the scallops to the pan and poach gently for four minutes; leave to cool in the liquid. Strain, reserving the liquid, cut the scallops into 6 mm (¼ in) slices and halve the corals.

Dissolve the curry powder in 1 tablespoon of the cooking liquid, blend in the tomato purée, add to the mayonnaise and mix well. Lightly beat the cream, mix in the curried mayonnaise and fold in the scallops.

Arrange on bed of crisp lettuce, garnish with quarters of lemon and chill before serving. Accompany with thin slices of buttered brown bread.

Meat

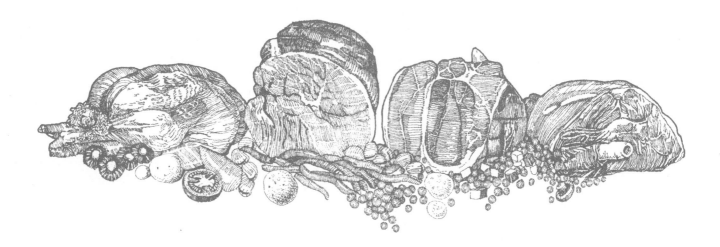

As meat will always be the most expensive item on your shopping list it makes sense to shop carefully and well for this commodity, especially as it is in meat that you will find the greatest discrepancy of both price and quality. Bargains in the meat field are not always worth having; you may well find cuts of meat on sale that seem exceptionally good value, especially if they are frozen, but you get the meat home only to find it is tough, tasteless and needs exceptionally long cooking. This applies particularly to beef which must be well hung and well matured in order to have a good taste and texture. On the other hand there certainly are bargains to be found in the meat line and it pays to shop around and compare prices before making a large purchase.

My attitude towards meat has changed considerably over the last ten years or so. When I first married and went to live in the West Country meat was eaten by the majority of people as often as once every day and taken as a matter of course. Gradually the price of that, as of so many things, has soared and soared and, in our family at least, a roast joint is a luxury which appears seldom. Instead of the more conservative methods of cooking large joints of meat by roasting or boiling, and instead of those almost criminally expensive grilling cuts like steaks and top-quality chops, I have turned towards methods and ways of cooking meat more economically, retaining the flavour and stretching the ingredients to sometimes surprising lengths.

Stewing and casseroling are, of course, well-tried methods of stretching meat and there is a lot to be said for these forms of cooking since the vegetables that are cooked with the meat not only help to tenderise the ingredients and add flavour but, in many cases, also take on the flavour of the meat itself. But there are more ways than these to stretch this expensive protein. I have learnt a lot from the Far East, where the price of meat is even higher than it is in this country; there they rely a lot on cutting meat and poultry into wafer-thin slices, using a razor-sharp knife. By chilling the meat in a deep-freeze for 20 minutes or so before it is to be sliced, in order to make it easier to cut, you can make it stretch to amazing lengths, and also enable even quite inferior cuts to be cooked in a surprisingly short time. Cut the meat against the grain and then, if you like, cut it again into thin matchstick strips; meat cut like this can be quickly fried, with vegetables, in a Chinese *wok* or a heavy frying pan, to make attractive dishes.

Beef

Good beef has a rich dark colour and the fat should be a rich yellow in colour. If beef is not to dry out during the cooking time there should be a fair ratio of fat to meat and the cut should always look moist when you buy it. Look out for rib joints for roasting and for chuck steak or skirt for stewing as these tend to provide the best value for money. If you are planning on a recipe based on minced beef it is always much better to buy suitable meat for mincing and then ask the butcher to mince it for you rather than buying ready minced beef which can often contain a high proportion of tough meat, fat or gristle. These days it is difficult for butchers to hang meat for any length of time and I find it helps to buy a joint a few days before it is required and let it stand in the bottom of the refrigerator. Cheaper cuts of meat can be infinitely improved by being marinated in a mixture of olive or vegetable oil, lemon juice or wine, herbs and seasoning. I have also had great success by buying a cheaper cut of stewing beef, marinating it and then freezing it for a month or so before using.

Roasting Chart for Beef

There are two basic methods of roasting meat: quick and slow. In my experience the better the quality of the joint you choose the more quickly it can be roasted; meat inclined to be dry or tough should be cooked by the slow method.

Quick Roasting
(220°C, 425°F, Reg. 7)
On the bone
15 minutes per ½ kilo (1 lb) and 15 minutes extra (allow a little extra if you do not like the centre too rare).
Off the bone
25 minutes per ½ kilo (1 lb) and 25 minutes extra.
Slow Roasting
(180°C, 350°F, Reg. 4)
On the bone
27 minutes per ½ kilo (1 lb) and 27 minutes extra.
Off the bone
35 minutes per ½ kilo (1 lb) and 35 minutes extra.
Allow an extra 5–10 minutes per ½ kilo (1 lb) for stuffed joints.

Veal

You will find that there are no recipes for veal included in this book. One has to have a few principles and since I dislike the methods used for rearing calves for veal I no longer eat this form of meat. Now I have found that very satisfactory escalopes (I used to be very fond of veal escalopes in all their many forms) can be made by beating breasts of chicken or fillets of pork out very thinly, dipping the slices in egg and breadcrumbs and then frying them in the usual way.

Lamb

One of the sad things that has happened to our society with regard to our eating patterns is, I believe, a sort of spoiling process which has led us to believe seasons no longer exist. We expect to eat lamb at Christmas, pork all year round and have beef whenever we want it and we feel thwarted when we are not able to do so.

But seasonal buying of fresh produce is as important as it ever was. If you want English lamb (and I maintain it is always a much better buy than imported lamb provided it is bought in season) you must buy it at the right time of the year when farmers are selling a quantity of lambs. If you insist on having home-grown lamb for an early Easter meal you are bound to have to pay a lot for the joint, whereas if you wait until later in the year you will be able to buy fresh lamb for a reasonable price.

Frozen lamb does lose some of its flavour and I would not

recommend using this meat for anything but made-up dishes where extra flavour and seasoning are added during the cooking time.

When you are buying lamb look for a good pink colour, moist flesh and clear white fat. The size of a joint you will buy will depend on the size of your family, but remember the larger the joint, the more flavour it will have. A more mature lamb may not be as mouthwateringly tender as a young one, but in many ways it will have a lot more going for it.

Roasting Chart for Lamb

Lamb joints need to be regularly basted during cooking and as the flesh is tender it responds best to being quick roasted. Quick roasting helps to seal in the juice keeping the joint moist and succulent.

Quick Roasting
(220°C, 425°F, Reg. 7)
On the bone
20 minutes per ½ kilo (1 lb) and 20 minutes extra.
Off the bone
25 minutes per pound and 25 minutes extra. Allow an extra 10–15 minutes per pound for stuffed joints.

Pork

Pork fluctuates considerably in price during the year so buy it when it is at its cheapest. I learn a lot by listening to those radio programmes which give an indication of food prices week by week. Look for meat that has a clear colour and looks fresh, because this will be the best indication of a good buy.

As well as pork do consider bacon joints on your shopping list; these can often be bought remarkably cheaply and make excellent eating for both hot and cold dishes.

Roasting Chart for Pork

Quick Roasting
(220°C, 425°F, Reg. 7)
On the bone
25 minutes per ½ kilo (1 lb) and 25 minutes extra.
Slow roasting
(180°C, 350°F, Reg. 4)
Off the bone
35 minutes per pound and 25 minutes extra.
Boiling Bacon and Gammon
Soak overnight to remove salt. Bring to the boil in fresh water and simmer for 25 minutes per ½ kilo (1 lb) and 25 minutes extra.

Offal

Many items of offal make delicious and inexpensive meals. Liver, kidneys and small hearts from lambs are excellent eating, and you can also produce delicious meals from sweetbreads, brains and even pig's tail or trotters. Offal is far cheaper here than it tends to be on the Continent for the simple reason that it is not yet as popular.

Beef Recipes

Basic Marinades for Meat

Lemon-based marinade :
3 tablespoons olive oil
Juice of 1 lemon
Freshly ground black pepper

Use for beef or lamb.

Red-wine-based marinade :
150 ml (¼ pint) olive or vegetable oil
½ teaspoon crushed black peppercorns
300 ml (½ pint) red wine
1 teaspoon crushed juniper berries
2 cloves
2 bay leaves
1 small onion or shallot, thinly sliced

Use for beef, pork or lamb.

Vinegar-based marinade :
300 ml (½ pint) olive or vegetable oil
5 tablespoons red or white wine vinegar
1 clove garlic, thinly sliced
1 teaspoon crushed black peppercorns
¼ teaspoon ground allspice
Thinly pared rind of one lemon

Use for beef or lamb.

Marinating meat makes sense especially if one is dealing with the cheaper cuts. Not only do the ingredients of a marinade help to break down the fibres of tough meat but they also help to add flavour to a cooked dish. Marinades, once used, can be skimmed off and refrigerated to use again provided they are stored for no longer than two weeks in a screw-topped jar. All these marinades are sufficient for 900 g (2 lb) of meat.

Slices of blade bone steak about 2·5 cm (1 in) thick marinated in the lemon marinade can be fried like rump steak. The red-wine version makes a good marinade for meat that is to be pot-roasted or braised.

Any of the cheaper cuts of meat that are to be stewed, casseroled or braised will benefit by being steeped in one of the marinades. Stews or casseroles can also be cooked on top of rather than in the stove, provided the cooking is done slowly.

Mix the marinade ingredients together and pour over the meat. Leave to marinate for 3–4 hours depending on thickness of meat, turning the cut every now and then.

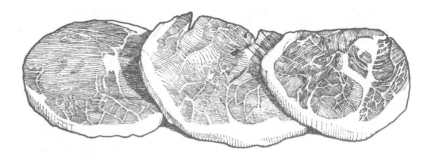

Herb-flavoured marinade:
450 ml ($\frac{3}{4}$ pint) tomato juice
4 tablespoons red wine vinegar
1 teaspoon thyme
1 teaspoon rosemary
$\frac{1}{2}$ teaspoon crushed white peppercorns
1 small onion or shallot, thinly sliced

Use for pork, beef or lamb.

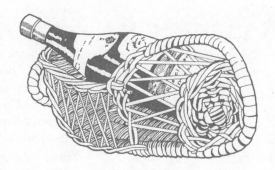

Fondue Bourguignonne

675 g (1$\frac{1}{2}$ lb) rump or fillet steak
Vegetable oil for cooking

Serves 4

Fondues are always fun to eat and can be made entirely over a fondue burner. Everyone cooks their own portions of meat by spearing them on skewers and cooking in hot oil for the desired length of time. The accompanying sauces need no cooking and make the meal colourful. If you feel rump or fillet is an extravagance, remember the money you are saving on cooking costs.

Half fill a fondue pot or copper saucepan with vegetable oil and heat until hot enough to brown a cube of bread in less than a minute. Regulate the flame to keep an even temperature.

Cut the meat into 2·5 cm (1 in) cubes, removing all fat and sinews. Divide into four portions and serve with a green and a tomato salad or with a mixed salad, and a selection of the following accompaniments:

Garlic or parsley butter, cut into thin slices
Horseradish sauce
Curried mayonnaise
Mayonnaise flavoured with garlic, chopped peppers and chopped raw onions
Tomato ketchup mixed with green pepper and finely chopped pickle
Vinaigrette dressing flavoured with finely chopped celery, chopped green pepper and chopped raw mushrooms

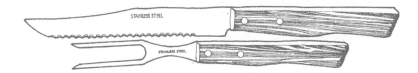

Daube de Boeuf

Serves 6

900 g (2 lb) top round of beef
75 g (3 oz) bacon
4 onions
2 carrots
2 sticks celery
2 cloves garlic
25 g (1 oz) lard
1 tablespoon olive oil
1 pig's trotter
300 ml (½ pint) red wine
225 g (8 oz) can tomatoes
Grated rind of ½ orange
Salt and freshly ground black pepper
Pinch of cinnamon and ginger
2 cloves
Bouquet garni

Cut the beef into 4 cm (1½ in) cubes. Chop the bacon. Peel and roughly chop the onions. Peel and thinly slice the carrots. Thickly slice the celery and peel and chop the garlic.

Heat the lard and olive oil in a heavy flame-proof casserole. Add the bacon and cook over a fast heat for two minutes. Add the onions, carrots, celery, garlic, meat and pig's trotter and continue to cook over a fast heat until the meat is browned on all sides. Pour over the wine, mix in the tomatoes, orange rind, seasoning, spices and bouquet garni, bring to the boil and cover tightly. Cook in a very slow oven (140°C, 275°F, Reg. 1) for about five hours until the beef is really tender.

Remove the bouquet garni, take out the pig's trotter, cut the meat off the bone and return it to the casserole. Skim any fat from the surface. Leave to cool completely if you are freezing, and check the seasoning after thawing and re-heating the casserole.

'I'm-only-here-for-the-beer' Casserole

Serves 4–5

900 g (2 lb) lean stewing steak
2 tablespoons dripping or vegetable oil
2 large onions, peeled and thinly sliced
1 large clove garlic, crushed
1 green pepper, finely chopped
1 tablespoon flour
300 ml (½ pint) strong stock
450 ml (¾ pint) brown ale
1 tablespoon tomato purée
Bouquet garni
Salt and freshly ground black pepper
¼ teaspoon ground nutmeg
Pinch of brown sugar
1 teaspoon white wine vinegar
4 thick slices white bread
French Dijon mustard

Cut the steak into bite-sized cubes. Heat the dripping or oil in a heavy flame-proof casserole, add the meat and brown quickly on all sides over high heat. Remove the meat with a slotted spoon and add the onion, garlic and pepper to the juices in the pan; cook until the onion is golden brown. Stir in the flour, mix well, add the meat and pour over the stock, ale and tomato purée. Add the bouquet garni, seasoning, nutmeg, sugar and vinegar, mix well and bring to the boil. Cover tightly and transfer to a pre-heated moderate oven (190°C, 375°F, Reg. 5); cook for about 1½ hours until the meat is fork tender.

Remove crusts from the bread and cut each slice into 4 cm (1½ in) wide fingers. Spread the slices thinly with mustard. Arrange them over the top of the casserole and return to the oven, uncovered, for a further 15 minutes until the bread rises to the surface and is crisply browned.

Note: if the casserole is to be re-heated the bread should not be added until then.

Curried Meat Balls in Vegetable Sauce

450 g (1 lb) British beef, minced
40 g (1½ oz) breadcrumbs
1 tablespoon very finely chopped onion
1 teaspoon salt
Generous pinch of freshly ground black pepper
2 tablespoons curry powder
1 small egg, lightly beaten
50 g (2 oz) butter
2 tablespoons vegetable oil
2 tablespoons water

The sauce:
100 g (4 oz) cabbage, finely shredded
2 onions, finely chopped
2 peppers, deseeded and chopped
1 large potato (peeled and diced)
300 ml (½ pint) boiling water
⅛ teaspoon freshly ground black pepper
½ teaspoon salt
2 tablespoons yoghurt

Serves 4

Mix the beef, breadcrumbs, onion, salt, pepper, curry powder and egg very thoroughly. Shape into small balls, about 2·5 cm (1 in) across. Heat the butter and oil and fry the meat balls until brown. Add the water, cover closely and simmer gently for 30 minutes.

To make the sauce put the cabbage, onion, peppers and potato into boiling water; add seasoning. Cover and simmer for 20 minutes, stirring occasionally, until they form a thick sauce. Add further seasoning to taste and stir in the yoghurt.

Drain the meat balls, pile in a heated serving dish and pour the sauce over.

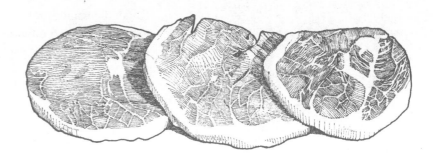

Beef Hot-pot

575 g (1¼ lb) shin beef
4 carrots
100 g (4 oz) mushrooms
12 shallots or small onions
450 g (1 lb) potatoes
40 g (1½ oz) dripping
15 g (½ oz) flour
150 ml (¼ pint) stock
Pinch of mace
1 teaspoon French Dijon mustard
Salt and freshly ground black pepper
1 tablespoon finely chopped parsley
1 tablespoon brandy
15 g (½ oz) butter

Serves 4

Trim off any gristle and cut the meat into 5 cm (2 in) strips. Peel and slice the carrots. Roughly chop the mushrooms. Peel the shallots, peel and thinly slice the potatoes.

Heat the dripping in a heavy fire-proof casserole. Add the meat and brown quickly over a high heat. Remove the meat with a slotted spoon and add the shallots to the fat. Cook over a medium heat until golden, then remove with a slotted spoon and mix the flour into the juices. Add the stock, mace and mustard to the juices and flour, mix well and season with salt and pepper. Add the meat, carrots, mushrooms, onions, parsley and brandy, stir well, top with a thick layer of the sliced potatoes and cover tightly.

Cook in a moderate oven (180°C, 350°F, Reg. 4) for 1¾ hours. Uncover the casserole, dot the potatoes with the butter and sprinkle with a little salt and pepper. Return to the oven for further 15 minutes or until the potatoes are golden brown.

The Genuine All-American Hamburger

450 g (1 lb) fresh beef steak
Salt and freshly ground black pepper
Butter for frying
4 soft rolls or baps

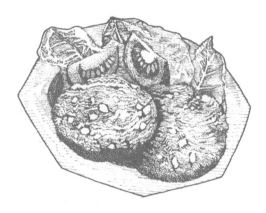

4 medium servings

Mince the meat twice through the coarse blades of a mincing machine, season with a *little* salt and pepper and shape into four thick flat cakes.

To fry

Heat enough butter to cover the bottom of a frying pan. Add the hamburgers and cook over a medium high heat for 3–5 minutes on each side. Add more seasoning half way through the cooking time. Place the cooked hamburgers in the centre of split rolls or baps and serve at once.

To grill

Brush the hamburgers with melted butter and cook under a medium high grill for 3–5 minutes on each side, adding more seasoning and more melted butter if necessary half-way through.

Variations

Add a little Tabasco and Worcestershire sauce to the basic recipe; or two tablespoons finely chopped parsley and chives.

   Serve the hamburgers with a layer of salad and home-made mayonnaise on top; or with fried onion rings and a sauce made from adding some bottled barbecue or tomato sauce to the pan juices.

Cheeseburgers

Basic hamburger recipe
4 slices of Gruyère cheese
4 slices tomato

Grill the hamburgers until they are half cooked through, turn over, cover with a slice of cheese and a slice of tomato and continue grilling until the cheese has melted.

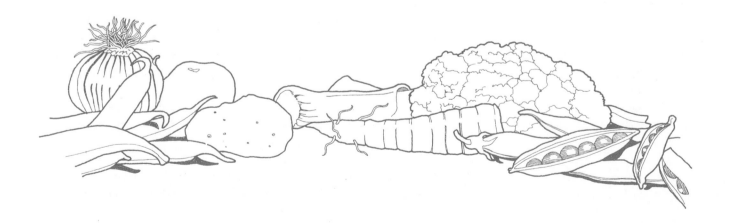

Individual Beef Pies

450 g (1 lb) cooked beef or lamb
1 medium onion
2 sticks celery
2 cloves garlic
4 anchovy fillets
1½ tablespoons dripping
Freshly ground black pepper
1½ tablespoons flour
150 ml (¼ pint) stock
425 g (15 oz) can tomatoes
About 400 g (14 oz) frozen puff pastry,
    thawed
1 small egg

Serves 4

Until the turn of this century anchovies were often used instead of salt to give taste and flavour to meat dishes. I find this form of 'seasoning' can make a leftover dish more interesting.

Small individual earthenware pots can be bought for a reasonable price from most kitchen stores and make attractive receptacles for serving leftover dishes.

Mince or finely chop the meat. Peel and finely chop the onion. Very finely chop the celery and crush the garlic. Drain off oil from the anchovies and finely chop the fillets.

Heat the dripping, add the onion, celery and garlic and cook over a low heat until the onion is soft and transparent. Add the meat, season with pepper and cook over a high heat, stirring continuously, for five minutes. Blend in the flour, mix well and gradually add the stock, stirring all the time so that no lumps form. Mix in the tomatoes and anchovy fillets, cover and simmer for 15 minutes. Divide the mixture between four earthenware dishes.

Roll out the pastry to about 3 mm (⅛ in) thickness and cut into four circles to fit the tops of the dishes. Damp the edges of the dishes and cover with pastry. Brush with beaten egg and cut a vent in the centre of each one. Bake in a hot oven (220°C, 425°F, Reg. 7) for about 15 minutes until the pastry is well risen and golden brown.

Beef Scallops with Tomatoes

350 g (12 oz) cold roast beef
3 large onions
425 g (15 oz) can tomatoes
¼ teaspoon oregano
Salt and freshly ground black pepper
1½ tablespoons dripping

Serves 4

Cut the meat into wafer-thin slices (or, if that is difficult, into very thin julienne strips) and arrange in the bottom of a shallow, lightly greased fire-proof dish. Peel and thinly slice the onions. Strain off juice from the tomatoes and chop the flesh.

Combine tomatoes, tomato juice and oregano in a saucepan and season with salt and pepper. Bring to the boil, cover and simmer for five minutes.

Heat the dripping in a frying pan. Add the onion and cook over a low heat until soft and transparent but not brown. Cover the meat with the onions and pour over the tomatoes. Cover the dish tightly with foil and bake in a moderate oven (180°C, 350°F, Reg. 4) for 25 minutes.

Boeuf Tartare

Serves 2

350 g (12 oz) minced fillet or rump steak, or
    the equivalent of scraped lean beef from a
    cheaper steak cut
1 teaspoon brandy
2 egg yolks
1 small onion, finely chopped
1 tablespoon drained, finely chopped pickled
    beetroot
1 tablespoon finely chopped capers
1 tablespoon finely chopped green pepper
1 tablespoon finely chopped parsley
Salt and freshly ground black pepper
French Dijon mustard
Worcestershire and Tabasco sauce

In restaurants the steak and the etceteras that go with it are usually mixed together by the *maître d'hôtel* before being served, but when I'm producing it at home I prefer to arrange the ingredients on individual plates in a decorative pattern and allow each person to add and mix in as much or as little 'hot' spices as they like. Following a Swedish tradition I often add some pickled beetroot to the ingredients.

One trick I did learn was to add a little brandy to the meat–not enough to taste the flavour of the spirit but just enough to enhance the taste of the meat. Fillet steak, rump or even a less expensive cut of steak can be used for the dish. The ideal is rump, which has a less bland texture and a richer taste than fillet. Fillet should be minced once through the coarse blades of a mincing machine. Rump should be minced twice to tenderise the meat.

Add brandy to the minced meat, form into 5cm (2 in) thick cakes and place one on each plate. Make a hollow in the centre of each cake large enough to take an egg yolk. Slide the yolk into the middle and surround the meat with a pattern of finely chopped onion, beetroot, capers and pepper. Sprinkle parsley over the surface and serve salt, pepper, mustard, Worcestershire and Tabasco sauce separately.

To eat, break up the egg yolk with a fork, draw the other ingredients into the meat and mix well, seasoning as required.

Serve with a green salad and a tomato salad made with peeled, thinly sliced tomatoes and very thin slices of young leeks tossed in a French dressing.

Savoury Minced Beef

Serves 4

1 large onion
100 g (4 oz) mushrooms
15 g (½ oz) butter
450 g (1 lb) minced beef
1 tablespoon flour
225 g (8 oz) can tomatoes
300 ml (½ pint) well-flavoured stock
1 tablespoon finely chopped parsley
Salt and freshly ground black pepper
Worcestershire and Tabasco sauce

This is always a popular dish with children, and can be made more or less savoury by altering the amounts of seasoning. Slow cooking ensures that the meat will be tender.

Peel and finely chop the onion; finely chop the mushrooms. Melt the butter in a saucepan, add the onions and cook until soft. Mix in the meat and cook over a high flame, stirring to prevent burning, until it is brown. Sprinkle with flour, cook for a further minute, then stir in mushrooms, tomatoes and stock. Add chopped parsley. Season with salt, pepper and a dash of Worcestershire and Tabasco sauce.

Cover and simmer over a low heat for 20–30 minutes until the meat is done. Serve in the centre of a ring of mashed potato.

Boiled Beef with Beer

1·8 kilos (4 lb) lean stewing beef, boned
    and rolled
1 teaspoon salt
12 black peppercorns, crushed
Generous pinch of ground mace, turmeric and
    cloves
4 large onions
1 bay leaf
Sprig of rosemary
Small sprig of thyme and sage
150 ml (¼ pint) red wine vinegar
100 g (4 oz) black treacle
1·2 litres (2 pints) light ale

Serves 8

This old country recipe gives meat a rich and satisfying taste. It is worth cooking a large piece so that you can enjoy it cold as well.

Ask your butcher to tie up the meat tightly. Combine the salt, peppercorns, mace, turmeric and cloves and mix well. Rub the meat all over with the spices and place in a deep dish. Top with the onions, peeled and sliced, and the herbs. Combine the vinegar with the black treacle and heat over a low flame until the treacle has melted. Cool and pour over the meat. Marinate for 12 hours, spooning the liquid in the bottom of the dish over the meat from time to time.

    Place both meat and marinade in a large heavy saucepan, pour over the ale and bring slowly to the boil. Cover tightly and simmer gently for about three hours until the meat is really tender. Remove the herbs and serve the meat surrounded by onions and cooking liquid.

Buster's Beef Stew

1 medium onion
200 ml (⅓ pint) red wine
Grated rind of 1 lemon
Bouquet garni
Pinch of salt and 5 peppercorns
1 tablespoon olive oil
900 g (2 lb) lean stewing beef
40 g (1½ oz) butter
1½ tablespoons flour
Juice of ½ orange
Small pinch of mace
12 small onions
4 rashers bacon
100 g (4 oz) button mushrooms
4–5 tablespoons brandy

Serves 4–6

Peel and roughly chop the medium onion. Combine onion, red wine, lemon rind, bouquet garni, salt, peppercorns and olive oil in a saucepan, bring to the boil, simmer for five minutes and cool. Cut the meat into neat 2·5 cm (1 in) cubes, cover with this marinade and leave overnight or for at least four hours in a cool place. Strain the marinade into a bowl, discard the onion and peppercorns and dry the meat with a clean cloth or kitchen paper.

    Melt the butter in a fire-proof casserole, add the meat and brown quickly on all sides over a high flame. Sprinkle over the flour and mix well. Pour over the strained marinade, orange juice and enough water to cover the meat. Mix in the mace and add the bouquet garni from the marinade. Cover tightly and cook in a slow oven (140°C, 275°F, Reg. 1) for one hour.

    Peel the small onions and mix them into the meat, cover with bacon rashers and replace the lid. Continue to cook for a further hour or until the meat is tender.

    Sauté the mushrooms in a little extra butter for about four minutes and mix them lightly into the stew. Check seasoning.

    Just before serving heat the brandy to just below boiling point, set it alight, pour the liquid over the stew and bring the dish flaming to the table.

Tomato Bredie

900 g (2 lb) good stewing steak
1·5 kilos (3 lb) ripe tomatoes (or substitute
   drained canned tomatoes)
2 large onions
2 tablespoons olive oil
1 tablespoon tomato purée
½ teaspoon curry powder
¼ teaspoon cinnamon
1 bay leaf
Salt and freshly ground black pepper
1 tablespoon brown sugar
2 hard-boiled eggs
1 tablespoon olive oil

Serves 4–6

An economical dish with South African origins that is easy to make and very well flavoured. I make and freeze it in bulk when our tomato season is at its height.

Cut the steak into 2·5 cm (1 in) cubes. Skin and quarter the tomatoes. Peel and thinly slice the onions.

Heat the olive oil in a frying pan, add the meat and cook quickly over a high heat until browned on all sides. Remove the meat with slotted spoon to a heavy fire-proof casserole. Add the onions to the pan and cook over a medium heat until light golden. Combine the onions, tomatoes, tomato purée, curry powder, cinnamon and bay leaf with the meat, season with salt and pepper and mix in the sugar. Cover tightly and simmer very slowly for 1–1½ hours until the meat is tender and the tomatoes have melted into a thick, aromatic purée.

Quarter the hard-boiled eggs and fry them in 1 tablespoon olive oil for two minutes. Drain off excess oil and add the eggs to the dish just before serving. Accompany with rice and a green salad.

Beef Stew

900 g (2 lb) lean stewing beef
2 onions
25 g (1 oz) butter
1 tablespoon olive oil
1½ tablespoons flour
Salt and freshly ground black pepper
1 bay leaf
300 ml (½ pint) red wine
Fresh parsley to garnish

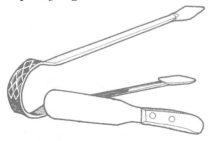

Serves 4–6

Cut the beef into neat 2·5 cm (1 in) cubes. Peel and thinly slice the onions. Melt the butter and oil in a heavy pan or frying pan. Add the onions and cook over a medium heat until soft and light yellow. Remove the onions with a slotted spoon, raise the heat and add the meat to the fat. Brown quickly on all sides. Sprinkle the meat with flour and transfer it to a casserole dish. Season with salt and pepper, cover with the onions and add the bay leaf.

Pour over the red wine and add enough water to cover the meat. Cover tightly and cook in a pre-heated slow oven (150°C, 300°F, Reg. 2) for 1½ hours or until the meat is tender.

Transfer to a clean dish and garnish with chopped parsley. Serve with mashed potatoes and a green vegetable or salad.

Variations

Blend one tablespoon tomato purée and ½ teaspoon paprika into the wine before pouring it over the meat.

Add 100 g (4 oz) sliced mushrooms, cooked in 25 g (1 oz) butter for three minutes, for the last ten minutes of cooking time.

Roast Entrecôte Steak–Farmhouse Style

2 fat rashers bacon
1 clove garlic
2 anchovy fillets
50 g (2 oz) butter
1½–2 kilos (3–5 lb) entrecôte steak
Freshly ground black pepper
1 tablespoon brandy

Serves 4

Rare red roast beef is the most delicious and succulent of all cold meat. Beef, unfortunately, is undeniably expensive but at least if you are planning to serve it cold your cut will be far more economical than a hot roast and you can afford to make up your saving by buying a really good cut which can, and should, be carved in wafer-thin slices. Serve the cold meat with a creamy horseradish sauce, a selection of mustards and a choice of pickles.

Entrecôte steak, cut from the top of the sirloin, is almost as tender as fillet and has a lot more flavour. Since it is difficult for butchers to hang meat properly in this country I would recommend buying the beef a few days before you plan to cook it and keeping it, lightly covered, in the bottom of the refrigerator.

Cut the bacon into very thin strips. Peel the garlic and cut into thin slivers. Chop the anchovy fillets and pound with the butter until smooth. Using a very thin, razor-sharp knife, cut small slashes on the outside of the meat and push the garlic and bacon into these narrow pockets. Rub the anchovy butter over the sides of the meat not covered with fat. Season with pepper. Pour over the brandy and roast in a pre-heated hot oven (220°C, 425°F, Reg. 7) for 15 minutes to the ½ kilo (1 lb) and 10 minutes extra, basting frequently.

Remove the meat on to a serving dish and leave to cool. When quite cold cover lightly with foil or greaseproof paper and keep in the refrigerator until required.

Strain the juices into a shallow pan and leave in a cold place for the fat to set. Carefully remove the fat and cut the rich jelly underneath into small cubes to use as a garnish for the meat.

Beef and Bacon Pie

1 onion
225 g (8 oz) bacon
225 g (8 oz) raw beef, minced
1 tablespoon plain flour
150 ml (¼ pint) water
Pinch of fresh mixed herbs
Salt and pepper
225 g (8 oz) shortcrust pastry

Serves 4

Chop the onion and bacon in small pieces, put in a heavy pan and cook gently until fat runs from the bacon and the onion is soft and golden. Add the mince and cook until it browns. Stir in the flour mixed with a little water, the rest of the water, herbs and seasoning and cook until the mixture is thick and well blended.

Roll the pastry into two rounds and line a 20 cm (8 in) pie plate with one. Put in the filling and cover with the second round of pastry.

Bake at 200°C, (400°F, Reg. 6) for 30 minutes.

Savoury Beef Puffs

Four 1 cm ($\frac{1}{2}$ in) fillet steaks
Salt and freshly ground black pepper
50 g (2 oz) butter
1 onion
100 g (4 oz) mushrooms
1 tablespoon finely chopped parsley
1 teaspoon lemon juice
Pinch of ground nutmeg
225 g (8 oz) puff pastry
1 egg, beaten

Serves 4

I find that by far the most exotic and exciting way of serving a dish which requires the imprisonment of every particle of flavour and delicious juice is by wrapping the ingredients in a well-sealed case of puff pastry. The light, inflated, golden brown exterior gives a special touch to any meal. I would suggest using frozen pastry.

Season the steaks with salt and pepper and fry in 15 g ($\frac{1}{2}$ oz) of the butter over a fierce heat for $\frac{1}{2}$ minute each side or until brown. Peel and finely chop the onion and finely chop the mushrooms. Cook together in the remaining butter, over a medium heat, until the onion is soft. Season with salt and pepper. Mix in the parsley, lemon juice and nutmeg and leave to cool.

Roll the puff pastry out thinly on a floured board and cut into eight circles about 1 cm ($\frac{3}{8}$ in) larger than the steaks; place a steak in the centre of each of four circles. Cover each steak with a quarter of the onion mixture and top with a second pastry circle. Damp the edges with water, seal together firmly and crimp the edges with a fork. Cut a nick in the centre of each puff, brush with beaten egg and chill in refrigerator for 30 minutes before baking.

Bake the puffs in a hot oven (220°C, 425°F, Reg. 7) for about 20 minutes until the pastry is well risen and golden brown. Serve at once.

Beef and Tomato Pie

2 large onions
675 g (1$\frac{1}{2}$ lb) tomatoes
25 g (1 oz) bacon fat
675 g (1$\frac{1}{2}$ lb) minced beef
1 tablespoon finely chopped parsley
Pinch of marjoram
Salt and freshly ground black pepper
2 tablespoons strong stock or meat glaze
50 g (2 oz) grated cheese
2 tablespoons dried breadcrumbs
15 g ($\frac{1}{2}$ oz) butter

Serves 4–5

Finely chop the onions and finely slice the tomatoes. Heat the bacon fat in a frying pan, add the onions and cook until soft. Mix in the meat and cook over a high heat, stirring continuously until the meat is brown. Remove from the heat, stir in the parsley and marjoram and season with salt and pepper.

Arrange half the tomatoes in the bottom of a casserole, cover with the meat mixture and top with the remaining tomatoes. Pour over the stock or meat glaze. Sprinkle over the cheese and breadcrumbs, dot with butter and bake in a moderate oven (190°C, 375°F, Reg. 5) for about one hour or until the meat is tender.

Leftover Meat and Cabbage Casserole

1 cabbage
1 clove garlic
225–275 g (8–10 oz) cooked beef or lamb
1 tablespoon dripping
½ tablespoon flour
150 ml (¼ pint) stock
3 tablespoons tomato purée
Salt and freshly ground black pepper
3 tablespoons fresh white breadcrumbs
15 g (½ oz) butter, melted

Serves 4

Clean and shred the cabbage and cook in a little boiling salted water until just tender. Drain well.

Crush the garlic and mince the meat through the coarse blades of a mincing machine. Heat the dripping in a frying pan, add garlic and meat and cook over a medium high heat for two minutes. Sprinkle over the flour and mix well. Gradually blend in the stock and tomato purée, season with salt and pepper, add the cabbage and cook over a low heat for five minutes.

Transfer the mixture to a shallow baking dish, sprinkle over the breadcrumbs, pour over the melted butter and bake in a hot oven (220°C, 425°F, Reg. 7) for about 15 minutes or until the breadcrumbs are crisp and golden brown.

Spiced Brisket of Beef

Salt and freshly ground black pepper
¼ teaspoon ground allspice
Small pinch of cayenne
900 g (2 lb) salt or cured beef joint
8 medium onions
3 large carrots
4 sticks celery
4 cloves garlic
6 bay leaves
600 ml (1 pint) dry cider, optional

Serves 4

The joy of this dish is that you literally leave it to cook itself and at the end not only have a succulent, tender and well-flavoured piece of meat, but also a rich and aromatic stock to use later.

Rub a mixture of salt (unless the meat is already salted), pepper, allspice and cayenne all over the meat. Peel the onions and leave them whole; peel and halve the carrots. Cut off the celery leaves and roughly chop the sticks. Peel and roughly chop the garlic.

Put the meat into a large saucepan and surround it with vegetables and garlic. Top with bay leaves and pour over the cider if using. Add enough cold water to cover the meat and bring slowly to the boil over a medium heat. Skim off any scum that rises to the surface, reduce the heat, cover very tightly and simmer slowly for 1¾ hours (the water should only just be moving–cooking too fast will toughen the meat) by which time the meat should be tender but not falling apart.

Discard the bay leaves, remove the meat and cut it into 6 mm (¼ in) thick slices. Arrange these on a heated serving dish, surround with strained vegetables and moisten with a little stock from the pan. Serve some of the remaining stock separately and have mustard and horseradish sauce on the table.

The beef can also be served cold in which case the cooking time should be reduced by 15 minutes and the meat left to cool in the stock with a weight on top to keep the flesh compact.

Marinated Beef with Carrots and Onions

3 tablespoons olive oil
2 cloves garlic
¼ teaspoon freshly ground black pepper
900 g (2 lb) stewing steak in one piece
450 g (1 lb) small onions or shallots
3 old carrots
75 g (3 oz) thinly sliced bacon rashers
150 ml (¼ pint) red wine
600 ml (1 pint) stock
1 bay leaf
2 tablespoons finely chopped parsley

Serves 4

Combine the oil, garlic and pepper. Pour this marinade over the meat and marinate for six hours, turning the meat every now and then.

Peel the onions; clean and thickly slice the carrots. Remove bacon rinds and wipe the meat with a clean cloth. Line a heavy pan or fire-proof casserole with half the bacon rashers. Put in the meat, cover with remaining rashers and pour over the wine. Cover and simmer gently for 1 hour. Add the stock and bay leaf and simmer for a further 30 minutes. Add the onion and carrot and continue to simmer until both meat and vegetables are tender. Taste for seasoning and remove the bay leaf before serving, sprinkled with parsley.

Yet another way to tenderise and flavour meat is to cook it slowly with beer, which has the same effect as marinating. Any lean stewing meat will respond well to this treatment; the cooking time will depend on the quality of the meat.

Mini Meat Balls

7 tablespoons white breadcrumbs or 2 boiled
    potatoes
300 ml (10 fl oz) cream
1½ tablespoons finely chopped raw onion
8 g (¼ oz) butter
450 g (1 lb) minced beef
100 g (4 oz) pork sausage meat
Salt, pepper and a pinch of allspice
1 egg
50 g (2 oz) margarine
2 tablespoons flour
300 ml (½ pint) stock
150 ml (5 fl oz) carton soured cream
Fresh parsley to garnish

8 small portions

Soak the breadcrumbs in the cream, or mash the potatoes with cream. Fry the onion in butter until soft. Combine the beef and sausage meat in a basin, season with salt, pepper and a pinch of allspice and mix with your hands until smooth. Stir in the egg and onion and mix well. Add the soaked breadcrumbs or potatoes and cream and work until smooth. Chill the mixture in the refrigerator and then form in small balls about 2 cm (¾ in) across.

Melt the margarine in a heavy frying pan. Add some of the meat balls (do not overcrowd) and fry over a high flame until brown on all sides. Lower the heat and continue to cook for a further 3–4 minutes. Remove with a slotted spoon and fry the remainder.

Add the flour to the juices in the pan and mix well until brown. Gradually add the stock, stirring continuously until the sauce is thick and smooth. Simmer for five minutes, taste for seasoning and blend in the soured cream. Pour this sauce over the meat balls, sprinkle with a little chopped parsley and serve piping hot.

Beef Casserole

900 g (2 lb) stewing beef
2 large onions
100 g (4 oz) firm button mushrooms
3 rashers streaky bacon
2 red peppers
40 g (1½ oz) butter
175 g (6 oz) frozen redcurrants or
    blackcurrants
2½ tablespoons flour
Salt and freshly ground black pepper
2 tablespoons soft brown sugar
Pinch of mace and allspice
300 ml (½ pint) Guinness
2 bay leaves
3 tablespoons finely chopped parsley

Serves 6

This is an invaluable dish to serve at the simplest of suppers or the most lavish of dinner parties. Accompany it with rice or mashed potatoes; garnish it with triangles of fried bread; or top it with pastry or rounds of your favourite scone mixture.

Cut the beef into 2·5 cm (1 in) cubes. Peel and chop the onions. Thickly slice the mushrooms. Remove rinds and chop the bacon. Remove core and seeds from the peppers and chop the flesh.

Melt the butter in a large heavy frying pan. Add the meat and cook over a high heat, stirring, until well browned. Remove to a casserole with a slotted spoon, add the bacon and cook until crisp. Add the onions and cook over low heat until soft and transparent. Add the mushrooms and cook for two minutes.

Transfer the bacon, onions and mushrooms to the casserole, add the peppers and currants and sprinkle with flour. Season with salt and pepper, add sugar, mace and allspice, mix well and pour over the Guinness. Add enough water to cover the ingredients, put in the bay leaves, cover tightly and cook in a slow oven (150°C, 300°F, Reg. 2) for three hours or until the meat is really tender. Remove the bay leaves, add the parsley and check seasoning.

Macaroni and Beef Pie

1 large onion
1 clove garlic
1 large green pepper
225 g (8 oz) can tomatoes
Stock
40 g (1½ oz) butter
2 tablespoons flour
Pinch of mixed herbs
Salt and freshly ground black pepper
225 g (8 oz) macaroni
225–275 g (8–10 oz) cooked beef, minced
50 g (2 oz) grated Cheddar cheese
4 tablespoons fresh white breadcrumbs
15 g (½ oz) butter, melted

Serves 4

Peel and finely chop the onion. Peel and crush the garlic. Remove core and seeds from the pepper and finely chop the flesh. Drain off tomato juice and add it to enough stock to make 300 ml (½ pint) of liquid. Chop the tomatoes.

Melt the butter in a saucepan. Add onion, garlic and pepper and cook over a low heat until the onion is soft and transparent. Mix in the flour and gradually blend in the stock, stirring continuously until the sauce comes to the boil and is thick and smooth. Add the mixed herbs, season with salt and pepper and simmer for three minutes.

Cook the macaroni in boiling salted water until just tender. Drain well and mix macaroni, tomatoes and meat into the sauce. Transfer to a fire-proof serving dish, sprinkle with cheese mixed with breadcrumbs and dribble over the melted butter. Bake in a moderate oven (190°C, 375°F, Reg. 5) for 20–25 minutes until the top of the pie is golden brown.

Old English Beef Casserole

Serves 6

900 g (2 lb) shin beef
4 large carrots
24 small shallots
2 tablespoons dripping or vegetable oil
3 teaspoons dry English mustard
Nearly 600 ml (1 pint) good stock, or water
    and one beef stock cube
1 teaspoon marjoram
Salt and freshly ground black pepper
1 tablespoon grated fresh or dried horseradish
2 tablespoons brandy

Cut the beef into 2 cm (¾ in) cubes. Peel the carrots and cut into same-sized cubes. Peel the shallots and leave whole. Melt the dripping in a heavy frying pan, add the meat and cook over a high heat until well browned on all sides. Remove with a slotted spoon. Add carrots and shallots to the juices in the pan and cook over a low heat, stirring to prevent sticking, until the shallots are nicely golden coloured on all sides. Remove with a slotted spoon. Stir the mustard into the juices in the pan and blend in 450 ml (¾ pint) of the stock.

Add the marjoram and season with salt and pepper. Return meat and vegetables to the pan, heat through and put into an earthenware casserole. Add remaining stock if necessary to cover the ingredients, cover tightly and cook in a low oven (160°C, 325°F, Reg. 3) for 2–3 hours or until the meat is tender. Just before serving stir in the horseradish and brandy.

Bosington Hash

Serves 4

2 rashers streaky bacon
275–350 g (10–12 oz) cooked beef
1 large onion
175 g (6 oz) cooked beetroot
350 g (12 oz) cooked potatoes
25 g (1 oz) dripping
2 tablespoons finely chopped parsley
Salt and freshly ground black pepper
4 eggs
3 tablespoons sour cream
A little paprika pepper

Remove rinds and finely chop the bacon. Cut the meat into very small cubes. Peel and finely chop the onion; dice the beetroot and potatoes.

Melt the dripping in a frying pan. Add the bacon and cook over a low heat for three minutes. Add the onion and continue to cook over a low heat until it is soft and transparent. Add potatoes, raise the heat a little and cook, stirring to prevent sticking, until they are golden brown.

Mix in the beetroot, meat and parsley, season with salt and pepper and toss over the heat until all ingredients are heated through. Turn on to a heated serving dish and keep warm. Fry the eggs and gently heat the sour cream.

Serve the hash with the eggs on top, a little sour cream poured over each one and a light sprinkling of paprika pepper over the cream.

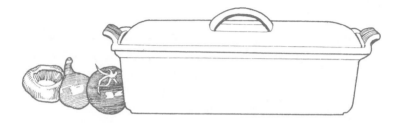

Lamb Recipes

North Country Ragoût

675 g (1½ lb) middle neck of lamb
225 g (8 oz) pig's kidney
12 shallots or very small onions
4 large carrots
Flour
Salt and freshly ground black pepper
25 g (1 oz) butter
1 tablespoon vegetable oil
2 tablespoons tomato purée
900 ml (1½ pints) light stock
Bouquet garni

Serves 4–5

Ragoûts, whether light or dark, are well-flavoured stews which used to be very popular; deservedly so as they are based on inexpensive cuts of meat, cooked with plenty of vegetables to stretch the meat further.

Cut the lamb into pieces but leave it on the bone. Cut the kidney into cubes about 2·5 cm (1 in) square, discarding any tough core. Peel the shallots; peel and slice the carrots.

Coat the meat in well-seasoned flour. Heat the butter and oil, add the meat and cook over a high heat until it is browned on all sides. Transfer to a casserole and add the shallots and carrots. Blend the tomato purée into the juices in the pan and gradually add the stock, stirring over a moderately high heat until the gravy is thick and smooth.

Season with salt and pepper, add the bouquet garni and pour gravy over the meat so that all the ingredients are covered. Cook in a slow oven (160°C, 325°F, Reg. 3) for about two hours or until the lamb is cooked through and tender.

Lamb and Rice Casserole

675 g (1½ lb) lamb, cut from a leg or
    shoulder
4 tablespoons olive oil
2 medium onions, peeled and chopped
2 leeks, thinly sliced
225 g (8 oz) can of tomatoes
Salt and freshly ground black pepper
Pinch of dried basil or oregano
75 g (3 oz) rice
600 ml (1 pint) boiling water
25 g (1 oz) finely grated Parmesan cheese
50 g (2 oz) grated Cheddar cheese

Serves 3–4

Cut the lamb into bite-sized cubes. Rub a casserole with some of the olive oil and put in the meat, onions, leeks, tomatoes and remaining oil. Season with salt and pepper, add the basil and mix well. Cover very tightly and cook in a moderately hot oven at 190°C (375°F, Reg. 5) for one hour.

Add the rice to the boiling water and mix into the casserole. Cover again and return to the oven for a further 30 minutes, adding more water if the casserole dries out too much (this will depend on the quality of the rice).

Remove the cover, sprinkle the surface with a mixture of the Parmesan and Cheddar cheese and return to the oven for about 10–15 minutes until the top is bubbling and golden brown.

Costa Brava Lamb Stew

2·5 litres (4 pints) hot water
900 g (2 lb) breast of lamb
2 stock cubes
2 onions
1 green pepper
50 g (2 oz) rice
Salt and freshly ground black pepper
225 g (8 oz) can tomatoes
1 small packet frozen peas
8 stuffed olives and a few raisins (optional)
1 egg
2 teaspoons olive oil
1 teaspoon vinegar

Serves 5–6

Rich meaty stews, meals in themselves with vegetables included, are the ideal food to produce over a small single burner. Meals like this take time to cook but their value has been proved by explorers throughout the ages.

To cook these stews, or hot-pots, a good heavy saucepan with a well-fitting lid is a necessity (cover the pan with a double layer of foil to ensure a complete seal before adding the lid) and a long-handled spoon is a help for stirring.

Heat the water while preparing the meat; trim off fat, cut bones and meat into small pieces. Melt this fat in a large saucepan over a high flame until the juice is extracted, add the meat and brown on both sides. Strain off any excess fat, pour over the water, add the stock cubes, mix well, cover and simmer for 1½ hours.

Roughly chop the onions and finely chop the green pepper; add these to the meat with the rice and season with salt and pepper. Re-cover and simmer for a further 30 minutes. Add the tomatoes, peas, olives and raisins. Give a good stir and cook for a further ten minutes.

Before serving beat the egg with the olive oil and vinegar and mix into the stew to give additional flavouring and a thicker consistency.

Lancashire Hot-pot

675 g (1½ lb) neck of lamb
1 lamb's kidney
450 g (1 lb) onions
900 g (2 lb) potatoes
Salt and freshly ground black pepper
300 ml (½ pint) stock

Serves 4

Traditionally this dish was made in an earthenware jar–hence the 'pot'.

Cut the lamb into pieces. Peel and thinly slice the onions; peel and slice the potatoes. Lightly grease a heavy casserole, arrange a layer of sliced potatoes on the bottom, cover with a layer of onions and some of the meat, and continue with the layers finishing with one of potatoes. Sprinkle the top layer with a generous pinch of salt and a screw of pepper and pour over the stock. Cover tightly–the casserole must be completely sealed, so if the lid is loose, place a layer of foil over the top before putting it on.

Bake the hot-pot in a hot oven (230°C, 450°F, Reg. 8) for 30 minutes, then reduce the heat to slow (150°C, 300°F, Reg. 2) and cook for a further 1½–2 hours until the meat is tender. Remove the cover for the last 30 minutes of cooking time to brown the top layer of potatoes.

Irish Stew

675 g (1½ lb) scrag or middle neck lamb
225 g (8 oz) lean green boiling bacon
225 g (8 oz) onions
675 g (1½ lb) potatoes
Dried marjoram
450 ml (¾ pint) stock or water
2 teaspoons mushroom ketchup or
    Worcestershire sauce
Salt and white pepper

Serves 4–6

Cut up the lamb. Remove rind and chop the bacon into small cubes. Peel and thinly slice the onions. Peel the potatoes and cut into pieces roughly the size of walnuts. Grease a heavy casserole and arrange the potatoes, meat, bacon and onions in layers, sprinkling each layer of meat with a little marjoram and finishing with a layer of potatoes.

Pour over the stock mixed with the mushroom ketchup or Worcestershire sauce and sprinkle over one teaspoon of salt and one of pepper. Cover tightly and bake in a hot oven (230°C, 450°F, Reg. 8) for 30 minutes, then reduce the heat to slow (150°C, 300°F, Reg. 2) and cook for a further 1½–2 hours until the meat is tender.

Lamb Squab Pie

75 g (3 oz) butter
6 lamb chops
2 onions
4 cooking apples
900 g (2 lb) potatoes
Pinch of rosemary
1 tablespoon finely chopped mint leaves
Salt and freshly ground black pepper
1 tablespoon soft brown sugar
300 ml (½ pint) chicken stock

Serves 6

Originally a squab pie would have been made with small pigeons. Today it is made with lamb in place of birds, but the combination of meat and apples remains the same. New potatoes make a perfect topping for this dish, that is pleasantly satisfying but not too heavy for a hot evening.

Melt two thirds of the butter in a frying pan. Add the chops and cook over a high heat for one minute on each side. Remove with a slotted spoon.

Peel and thinly slice the onions. Peel, core and slice the apples. Add the onion to the juices in the pan and cook over a low heat until soft and transparent. Remove with a slotted spoon, add the apple slices and cook gently for five minutes.

Peel and thinly slice the potatoes. Grease a baking dish well with butter. Arrange half the potato slices in the bottom of the dish, cover with chops and sprinkle over the rosemary and mint. Season with salt and plenty of pepper and top with apples, sugar and onions. Place the remaining potatoes in an overlapping layer on top of the dish and pour over the stock. Dot with the remaining butter and bake in a moderate oven (180°C, 350°F, Reg. 4) for one hour, by which time the meat should be tender and the potatoes an attractive golden brown.

Noisettes Diane

900 g (2 lb) best end neck of lamb, cut into
  noisettes
Oil and butter for frying
Salt and pepper

The sauce:
50 g (2 oz) lean bacon
50 g (2 oz) mushrooms
100 g (4 oz) courgettes
1 small onion
25 g (1 oz) butter
150 ml (¼ pint) stock
4 tablespoons sherry
Salt, pepper and mace
1 sprig mint, finely chopped
3 tablespoons cream, yoghurt or sour cream

Serves 4

To prepare noisettes leave a best end neck of lamb joint whole and begin cutting off the meat from the 'chine' or thinnest end of the bone. Keep your knife flat on the bones and cut downwards with short, even strokes. Try to keep the meat in as neat a shape as possible. Starting with the chined end, roll up the meat and tie securely with string at 2·5 cm (1 in) intervals. Cut through the meat between the string to make the plump, circular mini-steaks. The noisettes should have a thin layer of outside fat.

Heat enough equal quantities of oil and butter in a frying pan to come half-way up the sides of the noisettes. Season the meat with salt and pepper and cook in the hot fat until well browned on each side but still slightly pink in the centre; keep warm while making the sauce. Drain off the fat but reserve the meat juices.

Very finely chop the bacon, mushrooms, courgettes and onion. Melt the butter with the pan juices, add the bacon and onion and cook until the onion is soft and golden brown. Add the mushrooms and courgettes and continue cooking until the courgettes are just soft. Blend in the stock and sherry, season with salt, pepper and a pinch of mace, add the mint and simmer for five minutes.

Arrange the cooked noisettes in the centre of a ring of spaghetti, tagliatelli verdi or mashed potatoes, blend the cream into the sauce and pour over the meat.

Lamb Chops with Chestnuts

450 g (1 lb) chestnuts
10–12 small lamb chops
2 onions
Salt and freshly ground black pepper
½ teaspoon dried thyme
450 ml (¾ pint) stock
75 g (3 oz) butter
2 tablespoons finely chopped parsley

Serves 5–6

Peel the chestnuts by slitting them on their flat side, roasting in a moderate oven (200°C, 400°F, Reg. 6) for 12–15 minutes until the skins are brittle, then stripping off both outer and inner skins.

Trim off excess fat from the chops. Peel and thinly slice the onions and divide into rings. Arrange half the chops in the bottom of a greased baking dish. Season with salt and pepper, sprinkle with a little thyme and cover with a layer of half the onions and half the chestnuts. Repeat the layers, finishing off with chestnuts, pour over the stock, dot with butter, cover with foil and bake at 180°C (350°F, Reg. 4) for about one hour until the chops are tender.

Sprinkle over the chopped parsley and serve with mashed potatoes and crisp Brussels sprouts.

Cutlets en Chemise

8 small lamb cutlets, cut from best end of neck
Salt and freshly ground black pepper
50 g (2 oz) butter
1 small onion
50 g (2 oz) lean bacon
50 g (2 oz) mushrooms
2 ripe tomatoes
1 teaspoon tomato purée
2 teaspoons finely chopped parsley
225 g (8 oz) puff pastry
1 egg, beaten

Serves 4

Trim the cutlets, leaving about 1 cm ($\frac{1}{2}$ in) bare bone at the ends. Season with salt and pepper and cook in half the butter until tender. Leave to cool.

Peel and finely chop the onion. Finely chop the bacon and mushrooms; peel and finely chop the tomatoes. Melt the remaining butter, add the onion, bacon and mushrooms and cook for about three minutes over a medium heat. Add the tomatoes, tomato purée and parsley. Season with salt and pepper, cook for a further three minutes and then cool.

Roll the pastry out thinly on a floured board. Cut into eight oval shapes about 20 × 10 cm (8 × 4 in). Place a cutlet in the centre of each oval and cover with the savoury filling. Fold over the pastry, leaving a bit of bone exposed at one end, damp the edges and pinch together firmly to make a neat parcel. Brush with beaten egg and chill for 30 minutes before baking.

Bake the cutlets in a hot oven (220°C, 425°F, Reg. 7) for about 20 minutes until the pastry is well risen and golden brown. Before serving wrap protruding bones in foil.

Noisettes Roumanille

Olive oil
6 noisettes of lamb
Salt and freshly ground black pepper
Six 8 cm (3 in) rounds of bread
6 anchovy fillets
6 stuffed olives

Mornay Sauce:
50 g (2 oz) butter
1 tablespoon finely chopped onion
4 tablespoons flour
300 ml ($\frac{1}{2}$ pint) clear stock, or water and
   chicken stock cube
300 ml ($\frac{1}{2}$ pint) hot milk
75 g (3 oz) Gruyère cheese
1 tablespoon finely grated Parmesan cheese
Salt and white pepper
Pinch of nutmeg and cayenne

Serves 6

To prepare the noisettes see p. 84.

First make the Mornay sauce. Melt the butter, add the onion and cook until transparent. Blend in flour and gradually add stock and milk, stirring continuously over a high heat until the sauce is thick and smooth. Mix in Gruyère and Parmesan cheese and season with salt, white pepper and pinch of cayenne and nutmeg. Keep the sauce warm.

Heat three tablespoons of olive oil in heavy pan until smoking. Add the noisettes and cook over a high heat for four minutes on each side. Season with salt and pepper and keep warm while frying the bread in oil in a clean pan until crisp.

Place noisettes on the bread in a fire-proof baking dish, mask them generously with Mornay sauce and brown under the grill until nicely glazed. Top each with an anchovy wrapped around an olive.

Surround the noisettes with leaf spinach tossed in butter, chopped spring cabbage or grilled tomatoes.

Greek Moussaka

About 1·5 kilos (3 lb) lean lamb from a
    shoulder or leg
2 large onions
3 medium aubergines
4 tablespoons olive oil
150 ml (¼ pint) red wine
3 tablespoons tomato purée
4 tablespoons finely chopped parsley
Pinch of cinnamon
Salt and freshly ground black pepper
50 g (2 oz) dry white breadcrumbs
50 g (2 oz) grated Parmesan cheese
100 g (4 oz) butter
6 tablespoons flour
1·2 litres (2 pints) milk
4 eggs
100 g (4 oz) ricotta or cream cheese
Pinch of nutmeg

Moussaka makes a good main course for a dinner party at the time of year when aubergines are plentiful in the shops. This recipe is more than enough for eight servings, and it is possible to cut down on the meat and increase the aubergines.

The dish should be made the day before it is required in order to let the flavours develop; it actually improves by being re-heated.

Mince the meat through the coarse blades of a mincing machine. Finely chop the onions. Cut the aubergines into 6 mm (¼ in) thick slices, lengthwise.

Heat the oil in a large frying pan, add the aubergine slices and cook over a medium high heat until lightly browned. Remove with a slotted spoon, add the onion to the pan (with a little extra oil if necessary) and cook over medium heat until soft and transparent.

Mix in the meat and continue to cook for ten minutes, stirring to prevent sticking. Combine the wine and tomato purée, add the parsley and cinnamon and pour over the meat. Mix well, season with salt and pepper and cook for a further 15 minutes, stirring frequently.

Arrange aubergine slices and meat in layers sprinkled with breadcrumbs and Parmesan cheese in a lightly greased shallow oven-proof dish.

Melt the butter in a saucepan. Add the flour and mix well. Gradually blend in the milk, stirring continually over a medium high heat until the sauce comes to the boil and is thick and smooth.

Remove from the heat and beat in eggs and ricotta or cream cheese. Season with salt, pepper and a little nutmeg. Pour over the aubergine and meat and bake in moderate oven (160°C, 325°F, Reg. 3) for one hour and 15 minutes until the top is light golden brown. Remove from the oven and leave to settle for 15 minutes before cutting into large squares.

Paprika Lamb with Celery

Serves 4

450 g (1 lb) lean lamb from a leg or shoulder
1 large onion
4 sticks celery
4 tablespoons flour
1 teaspoon salt
1 teaspoon paprika
Pinch of ground nutmeg
3 tablespoons vegetable oil
300 ml ($\frac{1}{2}$ pint) water
150 ml ($\frac{1}{4}$ pint) dry white wine
2 bay leaves
3 tablespoons finely chopped celery leaves

Trim off excess fat from the lamb and cut the meat into 2·5 cm (1 in) cubes. Peel and chop the onion. Trim off top of sticks and leaves from celery and thickly slice the sticks. Combine the flour with the salt, paprika and nutmeg, add the meat and mix well to coat the meat on all sides with seasoned flour.

Heat the oil in a heavy saucepan, add the meat and cook over a high heat until it is lightly browned on all sides. Drain off excess oil and add the vegetables, water, wine and bay leaves. Mix well, bring to the boil and simmer, stirring every now and then to prevent sticking, for about one hour until the meat is tender.

Serve sprinkled with the chopped celery leaves.

Spanish Stuffed Lamb

Serves 6

$\frac{1}{4}$ teaspoon rosemary
1·2–1·5 kilo (2$\frac{1}{2}$–3 lb) boned shoulder of lamb
Salt and freshly ground black pepper
75 g (3 oz) bacon
1 small onion
1 clove garlic
12 pimento-stuffed olives
75 g (3 oz) cooked rice
Pinch of allspice
1 tablespoon finely chopped parsley
1 egg, beaten
2 drops Tabasco sauce
3 tablespoons dripping
1 heaped tablespoon flour
300 ml ($\frac{1}{2}$ pint) chicken stock
3 tablespoons red wine
1 teaspoon tomato purée

Any of this dish left over is excellent served cold.

Crush the rosemary with the back of a spoon. Spread the lamb, cut side up, on a board and rub it with salt, pepper and rosemary. Very finely chop the bacon and cook it, without extra fat, over a low heat for 4 minutes.

Peel and finely chop the onion. Crush the garlic and finely chop the stuffed olives. Combine the rice with the bacon, bacon fat, olives, onion, garlic, allspice, parsley, beaten egg and Tabasco, season with pepper and mix well.

Spread this stuffing on the lamb and roll up neatly. Tie with string at 5 cm (2 in) intervals, spread with the dripping and roast for 25 minutes to the $\frac{1}{2}$ kilo (1 lb) in a moderately hot oven (200°C, 400°F, Reg. 6).

Transfer the cooked joint to a heated serving dish, remove the string and keep warm. Add the flour to juices in the pan and mix over a high heat until it is brown. Gradually blend in the stock, stirring continuously, until the gravy is thick and smooth. Add the red wine and tomato purée and season with salt and pepper.

Cut the lamb into 6 mm ($\frac{1}{4}$ in) thick slices and serve the gravy separately.

China Chilo

900 g (2 lb) lamb cutlets
2 cabbage lettuces
4 spring onions
450 g (1 lb) peas
300 ml (½ pint) stock
1 teaspoon sugar
50 g (2 oz) butter
Tarragon (if liked)
1 cucumber, peeled and diced
225 g (8 oz) button mushrooms

Serves 4

Cut the meat into pieces, discarding the bones. Shred the lettuces, chop the onions and place them in a pan with the meat and peas. Add the stock, sugar, butter and tarragon. Cover the pan and gently stew for 1½–2 hours. Add the diced cucumber and whole mushrooms about 20 minutes before serving.

Devilled Lamb Chops

8 small lamb chops
1 clove garlic
½ teaspoon rosemary
1 teaspoon dry mustard
1 tablespoon brown sugar
2 tablespoons tomato ketchup
1 teaspoon white wine vinegar
3 tablespoons olive oil
Salt and freshly ground black pepper

Serves 4

Trim off excess fat from the chops. Crush the garlic in a garlic press or with a knife blade, combine it with the remaining ingredients and mix well. Pour the marinade over the chops and leave for at least four hours.

Grill the chops for 10–15 minutes, turning once and basting with a little marinade.

Rolled Stuffed Shoulder of Lamb

1 shoulder of lamb
4 tablespoons finely chopped parsley
Pinch rosemary and thyme
1 onion, finely chopped
1 clove garlic, crushed
Pinch of powdered ginger
175 g (6 oz) pork sausage-meat
Salt and pepper
2 tablespoons olive oil

Serves 6

Ask your butcher to bone the shoulder of lamb for you (but insist on keeping the bone–to make stock with).

Combine the herbs, onion, garlic, ginger and sausage-meat and mix well. Season with salt and pepper.

Spread out the meat, skin side down, and cover with stuffing. Roll the meat up neatly and tie at 5 cm (2 in) intervals with strong thin string.

Place the meat in a roasting tin, season with salt and pepper and brush with olive oil. Roast in a moderately hot oven (200°C, 400°F, Reg. 6) for 35 minutes to the ½ kilo (1 lb), basting frequently.

Make a gravy from the juices by mixing in a little wholemeal flour and some stock.

Noisettes Espagnole

350 g (12 oz) broad egg noodles
Salt and freshly ground black pepper
3 tablespoons olive oil
6 noisettes of lamb
20 g (¾ oz) butter

The sauce:
1 carrot
1 onion
20 g (¾ oz) butter
25 g (1 oz) flour
450 ml (¾ pint) tomato juice
Pinch of oregano and basil
2 tablespoons tomato purée
100 g (4 oz) lean ham, finely chopped

Serves 4–6

To prepare the noisettes see p. 84.

Make the sauce first. Peel and finely chop carrot and onion and cook in the butter until lightly browned. Add the flour and stir over a medium high heat until that, too, is golden. Gradually blend in the tomato juice, stirring continuously until the sauce comes to the boil. Add the herbs and tomato purée, season with salt and pepper and simmer for 30 minutes, stirring every now and then. Add the ham.

Cook the noodles in boiling salted water until tender (about 12 minutes), drain well and keep warm.

Heat the oil in a heavy frying pan until smoking. Add the noisettes and cook over a high heat for 4–6 minutes on each side. Season with salt and pepper and keep warm. Reserve the juices in the pan.

Heat the butter with the pan juices until melted. Scrape the pan with a wooden spoon to mix in all the residue, pour the liquid over the noodles and toss with two forks.

Put the noodles on heated serving dish, top with the noisettes and spoon over the sauce.

Pork and Ham Recipes

Cornish Farmhouse Cassoulet

450 g (1 lb) dried haricot beans
900 g (2 lb) belly pork
675 g (1½ lb) gammon
Salt, pepper and a bouquet garni
6 cabanos sausages
6 cloves garlic
3 tablespoons dripping
3 tablespoons finely chopped parsley

Serves 10–12

Cover the beans with water and soak overnight.

Cut the skin from the belly pork and discard most of the fat. Cut the skin and meat into 2·5 cm (1 in) strips. Cut the gammon into 2·5 cm (1 in) cubes. Line a large earthenware casserole with pork skin and fill with the beans (drained and rinsed), pork and gammon. Cover with cold water and add plenty of pepper, a small pinch of salt and the bouquet garni. Bring to the boil, cover tightly and cook in a slow oven (150°C, 300°F, Reg. 2) for 2½ hours. Add the cabanos, cut into 2·5 cm (1 in) pieces and continue cooking for a further 30 minutes.

Blanch the peeled garlic cloves in boiling water for ten minutes, pound them until smooth in a pestle and mortar and mix in the dripping and parsley.

Drain off half the liquid from the cassoulet, remove the bouquet garni, blend in the garlic mixture and return to the oven for a further ten minutes. Check for seasoning before serving.

Belly of Pork with Spiced Cabbage

Serves 4

675 g (1½ lb) belly pork
Salt and freshly ground black pepper
Pinch of cayenne
Ground ginger
1 onion
1 small cabbage
1 teaspoon caraway seeds
1 wineglass dry cider

Trim off the skin and some fat from the meat and cut into 2·5 cm (1 in) wide strips. Rub well with salt, pepper, cayenne and ginger and place on a wire rack over a roasting tin. Bake for 20 minutes in a hot oven (220°C, 425°F, Reg. 7). Remove the meat from the rack and drain off excess fat on kitchen paper.

Peel and finely chop the onion. Finely shred the cabbage. Place the vegetables in a lightly greased baking dish, mix in the caraway seeds, season with salt and pepper and moisten with cider. Arrange the meat on top of the vegetables, cover with a layer of foil and bake in a moderate oven (180°C, 350°F, Reg. 4) for about 40 minutes until the meat is tender. Serve with mashed potatoes.

Pork Teluchini

Serves 4

450 g (1 lb) pork tenderloin
1–2 eggs
Dried breadcrumbs
Salt, pepper and a pinch of paprika
100 g (4 oz) butter

Cut the tenderloin into 2·5 cm (1 in) slices, lay them between two sheets of greaseproof paper and pound gently with a rolling-pin or wooden mallet until they are evenly flattened to about 3 mm (⅛ in) thickness. Beat the egg until smooth; season the breadcrumbs with salt, pepper and paprika. Dip the slices of meat in the egg and coat with a generous layer of breadcrumbs.

Fry the meat slices in melted butter over a medium high heat until they are crisp and golden brown on each side. Drain well on crumpled kitchen paper and keep hot. Serve with tomato sauce, preferably home-made.

Prudency Pork

Serves 4

675–900 g (1½–2 lb) lean pork
Salt, pepper and a pinch of nutmeg
50 g (2 oz) butter
350 g (12 oz) cooked runner beans
1 tablespoon flour
300 ml (½ pint) milk
50 g (2 oz) grated cheese

Cut the meat into eight slices, season with salt and pepper and cook in half the butter until golden brown on both sides. Cover the bottom of a greased baking dish with cooked runner beans and arrange the pork slices on top.

Melt the rest of the butter in a saucepan. Add the flour and mix well. Gradually blend in the milk, stirring continuously until the sauce comes to the boil and is thick and smooth. Season with salt, pepper and a pinch of nutmeg. Pour the sauce over the meat and top with grated cheese.

Bake in a moderate oven (190°C, 375°F, Reg. 5) for 30 minutes.

Pinchpenny Pork with Fripperty Sauce

2 carrots
2 onions
1·2 kilos (2½ lb) belly pork
½ teaspoon sage
½ teaspoon thyme
2 bay leaves
1 tablespoon white wine vinegar
Salt
8 black peppercorns
1 egg, beaten
Dried breadcrumbs
Vegetable oil for frying

Fripperty Sauce:

1 onion
1 large cooking apple
15 g (½ oz) butter
225 g (8 oz) can tomatoes
Pinch of sage and thyme
1 teaspoon sugar
1 teaspoon lemon juice
Salt and pepper

Serves 4

Peel the carrots and cut them into quarters. Peel off the outer skins of the onions and cut each in half. Place the pork in a large saucepan, add the vegetables, herbs and vinegar, season with salt and whole peppercorns and pour over enough water to cover. Bring to the boil and simmer gently for about 1½ hours until the pork is tender. Drain off the liquid and keep it for soup stock.

Leave to cool for half an hour and pull out any bones. Press the meat flat with a plate covered with a heavy weight and refrigerate for at least two hours. Trim off the skin and excess fat and cut the meat into fingers about 2·5 cm (1 in) wide.

Dip the pork fingers into beaten egg seasoned with a little salt and pepper and coat in dried breadcrumbs. Fry in hot oil until crisp and golden brown. Drain on kitchen paper and serve hot with the following sauce.

Peel and finely chop the onion. Peel, core and chop the apple. Melt the butter in a saucepan, add the onion and apple and simmer over a medium low heat until the onion is transparent. Add tomatoes, herbs, sugar and lemon juice, season with salt and pepper, bring to the boil, cover and simmer for 20 minutes. Beat smooth with a wooden fork or wire whisk and check seasoning before serving.

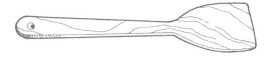

Herbaceous Pork Chop Casserole

3 large potatoes
2 cooking apples
1 onion
6 plump chops
Salt and freshly ground black pepper
Pinch of sage, thyme, and mace
1 tablespoon brown sugar
1 wineglass dry cider

Serves 6

Peel and thinly slice the potatoes. Peel, core and thinly slice the apples. Peel and finely chop the onion.

Trim skin from the chops and fry them briefly, with the skin, over a high heat until golden brown on both sides. Discard skin, drain off fat.

Arrange half the potatoes, apples and onion in a lightly greased baking dish; sprinkle with salt, pepper and half the herbs. Cover with the pork chops and top with the remaining potatoes, apples, onion and herbs. Season, sprinkle with sugar and pour over the cider and 1½ tablespoons of pork fat.

Cover with foil and bake in a moderate oven (180°C, 350°F, Reg. 4) for 50 minutes, removing the foil cover for the last ten minutes.

Kangaroo Pork

Serves 4–5

12 prunes
1 wineglass of port
1 onion
1 large cooking apple
900 g (2 lb) piece of boned shoulder of pork
Pinch of sage
Salt and freshly ground black pepper
1 tablespoon flour
300 ml (½ pint) stock

Soak the prunes until soft in the port, mixed with enough water to cover. Remove the stones. Peel and finely chop the onion and apple. Scrape the pork skin with a sharp knife and score through to make a lattice pattern. Cut a slit along the wide edge of the joint under the fat to form a deep cavity.

Combine the onion, apple, prunes and prune juices with a pinch of sage and season with salt and pepper. Stuff this mixture into the pocket. Place the pork on a rack in a roasting tin and cook without basting in a moderate oven (180°C, 350°F, Reg. 4) for 1½ hours or until the meat is cooked through.

Remove the pork and add the flour to the juices in the pan; blend in the stock to make gravy.

Stir-Fried Pork with Vegetables

Serves 4

450 g (1 lb) lean pork
1 tablespoon cornflour
½ teaspoon salt
½ teaspoon sugar
1½ tablespoons soya sauce
1 teaspoon sherry
2 carrots
6 spring onions
75 g (3 oz) young French beans or stringed
    runner beans
1 small white turnip
1 lettuce
50 g (2 oz) firm button mushrooms
4 tablespoons vegetable oil, preferably
    groundnut
1 teaspoon fresh ginger root,
    minced (obtainable at good delicatessen
    shops)
3 tablespoons chicken stock

Stir-frying is probably one of the oldest methods of cooking in the world. Yet it remains one of the most sophisticated ways of quick cooking. Stir-fried ingredients must be served as soon as they have been cooked.

Cut the pork diagonally into wafer-thin slices about 5 × 2·5 cm (2 × 1 in) wide. Dredge them with cornflour, sprinkle with salt, sugar, soya sauce and sherry and toss lightly to coat.

Peel and thinly slice the carrots on the diagonal and then cut into matchstick strips. Trim the spring onions, leaving on 5 cm (2 in) of green, and cut lengthwise into thin strips. Cut the beans diagonally into 6 mm (¼ in) thick slices. Peel the turnip and cut into very small dice. Shred the lettuce and very finely slice the mushrooms.

Turn heat under a wok or heavy frying pan to high and when it is hot through add half the oil, which should sizzle as it hits the pan. Add the pork slices, one by one, and stir lightly and continuously for three minutes. Remove with a slotted spoon. Add the remaining oil, heat and add ginger, carrots and turnips. Stir-fry for 1 minute. Add the remaining vegetables and continue to stir-fry over high heat for a further two minutes.

Add the pork and stock and continue to stir for two minutes longer, by which time the pork should be cooked and vegetables just tender. Serve at once with rice or noodles.

Salt Pork and Peas

225 g (8 oz) dried yellow peas
2 litres (3 pints) water
450 g (1 lb) salt pork
2 onions
¼ teaspoon ground ginger
1 teaspoon marjoram
Salt and white pepper

Serves 4–6

A traditional half meat/half soup dish from Sweden, this makes an inexpensive, hearty and nourishing family meal needing no additional vegetables.

Rinse the peas well in cold running water and put them in a large saucepan with the water. Cover and leave in a cold place overnight. The next day bring quickly to the boil, remove from the heat and skim off any outer skins floating on top. Simmer, covered, for two hours.

   Cut the pork into 5 cm (2 in) squares. Peel and roughly chop the onions.

   Add the pork, onions, ginger, marjoram and seasoning to the peas, bring to the boil, cover and continue to simmer for a further hour or until the pork is really tender. Serve in wide soup plates with mustard on the side.

Note: The soup should be fairly thick, and this will depend to some extent on the quality of the peas. If it becomes too thick add more water.

Rognons de Porc

4 pig's kidneys
100 g (4 oz) streaky bacon
175 g (6 oz) firm button mushrooms
Small bunch parsley
25 g (1 oz) butter
150 ml (¼ pint) red wine
1 teaspoon French Dijon mustard
Bouquet garni
Salt and freshly ground black pepper

Serves 4

Pig's kidneys are stronger than lamb's, so this is a rich dish that for a dinner party should be served after a light first course. Serve it with rice and broccoli or calabrese, or with triangles of crisply fried bread for a delicious supper dish.

If you want to remove some of the rather strong flavour soak the kidneys in milk or cold water for 3–4 hours before using. Cut in half, remove cores and cut the flesh into 1 cm (½ in) thick slices. Remove rinds and finely chop the bacon. Chop the mushrooms and finely chop the parsley.

   Heat the butter in a heavy frying pan, add the bacon and cook over a low heat, without browning, for three minutes. Add the kidneys and mushrooms and cook for a further two minutes, stirring to prevent sticking. Pour over the wine, raise the heat and allow it to bubble for one minute. Stir in the mustard, add the bouquet garni, season with salt and pepper, lower heat and simmer gently for 15 minutes. Remove the bouquet garni and sprinkle with parsley before serving.

Baked Sweet and Sour Ribs

Serves 4

1 rack pork ribs
3 tablespoons brown sugar
2 cloves garlic, crushed
2 tablespoons dry sherry
1 tablespoon vinegar
1 teaspoon ground ginger
2 tablespoons tomato juice
Salt and pepper
225 g (8 oz) rice
40 g (1½ oz) butter
1 onion
1 green pepper (finely chopped)

Use a sharp knife to remove the skin from the ribs and to cut three quarters of the way through the meat between the bones.

Keep aside the rice, onion, butter and green pepper. Combine all the other ingredients and mix well, seasoning with salt and pepper. Place the ribs in a baking dish and cover with the sauce, rubbing it into the meat with the back of a spoon.

Bake in a moderately hot oven (200°C, 400°F, Reg. 6) for about 1½ hours until the meat is really tender and almost black brown.

Meanwhile prepare the rice; boil until tender, drain, rinse in cold water and drain again to remove all excess water. Melt the butter in a saucepan, add the onion and green pepper and cook until soft. Stir in the rice and season with salt and pepper. Turn on to a serving dish and keep warm.

Separate the cooked ribs and arrange on the bed of rice. Leave the sauce to stand for five minutes, spoon off excess fat from the surface and pour the sauce over the ribs and rice.

Noisettes de Porc aux Pruneaux

Serves 4–5

25 prunes
200 ml (7½ fl oz) dry white wine
450 g (1 lb) pork fillet
Flour
Salt and freshly ground black pepper
50 g (2 oz) butter
2 tablespoons redcurrant jelly
150 ml (5 fl oz) single cream

Soak the prunes overnight in wine and remove stones. Very thinly slice the pork fillet, place the slices between two sheets of greaseproof paper and flatten with a mallet or the flat side of a meat chopper. Dredge the slices in seasoned flour.

Cook the prunes in wine for 30 minutes. Heat the butter until foaming in heavy saucepan. Add the pork slices and cook over a high heat until golden brown; arrange on a heated serving dish. Drain the cooked prunes, reserving the liquid, arrange around the pork and keep warm while making the sauce.

Put the liquid from the prunes into a small heavy pan and boil until reduced by about a third. Add the redcurrant jelly and stir until it has melted. Reduce the heat, mix in the cream, season with salt and pepper and heat through without boiling.

Pour sauce over the pork slices and serve at once.

Piquant Spare Ribs of Pork

1–1·5 kilos (2–3 lb) American cut pork
   spare ribs
3 tablespoons honey
2 tablespoons water
1 tablespoon tomato ketchup
1 teaspoon Worcestershire sauce
Squeeze of lemon juice
1½ tablespoons soya sauce
2 tablespoons brown sugar
Salt, pepper and a pinch of ground ginger

Serves 4–5

Spare ribs can only be satisfactorily eaten in the fingers, so it is a kindness to have a good supply of napkins and a clean damp cloth handy.

Separate the ribs and trim off the skin and some fat. Combine the remaining ingredients. Marinate the ribs in this liquid for at least four hours, turning them frequently to make sure the meat is well soaked.

Place ribs and sauce in a baking dish, cover with foil and bake for 1½–2 hours in a slow oven (150°C, 300°F, Reg. 2) until the meat is tender; baste about once every 30 minutes.

Drain off sauce from the ribs, leave to settle for a few minutes and spoon off any excess fat which rises to the surface. Serve the ribs in the centre of a ring of boiled rice or mashed poatoes with the sauce poured over them.

Pork Goulash

675 g (1½ lb) boned shoulder of pork
3 large onions
40 g (1½ oz) butter
½ tablespoon paprika
1 tablespoon flour
450 ml (¾ pint) dry cider
About 500 ml (¾ pint) stock
1 tablespoon tomato purée
Pinch of sage and thyme
3 bay leaves
Salt and freshly ground black pepper
675 g (1½ lb) potatoes

Serves 4

This aromatic stew makes a reasonably priced but very satisfying main dish. The flavour of paprika, which is not hot like cayenne, should be quite in evidence.

Cut the meat into 2·5 cm (1 in) squares. Peel and thinly slice the onions. Melt the butter in a heavy saucepan, add the meat and cook until lightly browned on all sides. Add the onions and cook for a further three minutes until soft and golden. Sprinkle over the paprika and flour and mix well. Cook, stirring continuously, over a medium high heat for a further three minutes and then stir in the cider and enough stock to ensure the meat is well covered. Add tomato purée, herbs and bay leaves, season with salt and pepper, cover and simmer gently for one hour.

Peel the potatoes and cut into 2·5 cm (1 in) cubes. Remove bay leaves from the goulash, add the potato and enough additional stock to cover them and continue to simmer for a further 30–40 minutes until the potatoes are cooked through and the meat is tender.

Wine-Braised Ham

Serves 4

8 slices ham
200 ml (7½ fl oz) sherry or Madeira
8 thin slices cheese (preferably Gruyère but
　Cheddar will do)
200 ml (7½ fl oz) double cream
1 tablespoon tomato purée
Salt, pepper and a pinch of paprika

Place the ham in a shallow baking dish and pour over the sherry or Madeira; leave to soak for 1–2 hours (this isn't essential but it does improve the flavour). Cover the ham with slices of cheese and pour over a sauce made by combining the cream with tomato purée, salt, pepper and a pinch of paprika.

Bake in a moderately hot oven (200°C, 400°F, Reg. 6) for 25–30 minutes and serve with boiled potatoes and a salad.

Ham and Celery Rolls in Cheese Sauce

Serves 4

1 can celery hearts, approx 450 g (1 lb)
8 thin slices ham
50 g (2 oz) button mushrooms
40 g (1½ oz) butter
25 g (1 oz) flour
300 ml (½ pint) milk
50 g (2 oz) grated cheese
Salt, pepper and a pinch of mace
1 tablespoon breadcrumbs

Drain off liquid from the celery (keep it to use when making stock), place half each heart in a slice of ham and roll up neatly.

Arrange the rolls in a lightly greased shallow baking dish. Thinly slice the mushrooms and cook for one minute in the butter; blend in the flour and gradually add the milk, stirring continuously over a medium heat until the mixture comes to the boil and the sauce is smooth. Lower the heat and cook for two minutes. Stir in half the cheese, season with salt, pepper and a small pinch of mace and pour over the ham.

Top with a mixture of remaining cheese and the breadcrumbs and heat under a hot grill until the sauce bubbles and the top is a crisp golden brown. Serve with a salad and mashed potatoes.

Ham Rolls Augustine

Serves 4

8 thin slices ham
Made English mustard
1 small can celery hearts, approx 225 g (8 oz)
1 small can sweetcorn, approx 225 g (8 oz)
1 small onion
5 tablespoons double cream
1 tablespoon finely chopped sweet pickle
150 ml (¼ pint) mayonnaise
Salt and pepper

Spread the ham slices with a little made English mustard on one side only. Drain the celery hearts and chop finely; drain the sweetcorn. Peel and very finely chop the onion. Beat the cream until stiff. Mix the sweet pickle into the mayonnaise and season well with salt and pepper. Fold in the whipped cream, celery and sweetcorn. Spread the mixture evenly on the mustard side of the ham and roll slices up neatly.

Arrange on a serving dish and garnish with salad.

Cabilla-Stuffed Ham with Chicory

8 small heads chicory
1·2 litres (2 pints) water
Juice of $\frac{1}{2}$ lemon
2 teaspoons sugar
4 hard-boiled eggs
4 tomatoes
8 thin slices ham
Salt and freshly ground black pepper
25 g (1 oz) butter
1 tablespoon flour
300 ml ($\frac{1}{2}$ pint) milk
100 g (4 oz) grated Cheddar cheese
$\frac{1}{4}$ teaspoon nutmeg

Serves 4

This is my own variation on a traditional theme, and a recipe I find extremely popular.

Trim off any discoloured leaves from the chicory and cut off 6 mm ($\frac{1}{4}$ in) of the stem. Bring the water to the boil with the lemon juice and sugar, add the chicory and blanch for ten minutes. Drain well, standing heads-down in a colander so that all water runs off.

Finely chop the hard-boiled eggs. Peel, remove core and seeds of the tomatoes and finely chop the flesh. Combine the egg and tomato and season with salt and pepper.

Lay a head of chicory on each slice of ham and make a slit half-way through the length of the chicory. Stuff with the egg and tomato mixture and roll the ham around them. Place the rolls in a lightly greased baking dish. Melt the butter in a saucepan, add the flour and mix well. Gradually blend in the milk, stirring continuously over a medium heat until the sauce comes to the boil and is thick and smooth. Add half the cheese and the nutmeg, season with salt and pepper and simmer for two minutes until the cheese is melted. Pour the sauce over the ham rolls. Sprinkle over the remaining cheese and bake in a moderate oven (180°C, 350°F, Reg. 4) for 30 minutes.

Miscellaneous Meat Recipes

Liver and Bacon Hot-pot

675 g (1$\frac{1}{2}$ lb) lamb's liver
Flour seasoned with salt and pepper
2 onions
4 carrots
6 rashers streaky bacon
900 g (2 lb) potatoes
2 tablespoons olive oil or 25 g (1 oz) butter
2 stock cubes
2 tablespoons tomato ketchup

Serves 5–6

Cut the liver into thin slices and coat well with seasoned flour. Peel and roughly chop the onions and carrots. Remove rinds and cut the bacon into 5 cm (2 in) pieces. Peel and slice the potatoes.

Heat the oil or butter, add the bacon and fry for three minutes over a medium heat. Add the liver and cook over a high heat until it is browned on all sides. Add the vegetables and pour over enough water to cover; bring to the boil, add stock cubes and tomato ketchup. Stir well, cover and simmer gently for about one hour until meat and vegetables are tender.

West Country Black Pudding or Hog's Pudding

450 g (1 lb) cooking apples
50 g (2 oz) sugar
2 tablespoons water
15 g (½ oz) butter
Salt, pepper and a pinch of sage
2 large onions
Fat for frying
1 black pudding or hog's pudding (approx
    450 g (1 lb))

Serves 4

Peel, core and slice the apples, combine them in a saucepan with the sugar and water, bring to the boil and simmer until tender. Mash into a purée, beat in the butter and season with salt, pepper and sage. Turn on to a heated dish and keep warm.

Peel and thinly slice the onions into rings and fry them over medium high heat until golden brown. Place the rings on top of the apple sauce. Cut the black pudding into 1 cm (½ in) thick slices and fry in hot fat until brown and crisp on both sides. Drain on kitchen paper and arrange on the onion slices. Serve at once with mashed potatoes and a green vegetable.

Ox Tongue with Madeira Sauce

1 pickled ox tongue
2 carrots
2 onions
6 peppercorns
1 bay leaf
Bouquet garni
50 g (2 oz) ham
25 g (1 oz) butter
25 g (1 oz) flour
450 ml (¾ pint) stock from cooking tongue
4 tablespoons Madeira or medium dry sherry
50 g (2 oz) sultanas
Salt and freshly ground black pepper

Serve this hot for one meal and then press the remainder to make a series of cold meals.

Soak the tongue in cold water for 12 hours. Peel and chop the carrots. Remove outer skin from the onions and cut them into quarters.

Place the tongue in a saucepan with the carrots, onions, peppercorns, bay leaf and bouquet garni. Cover with cold water, bring to the boil and skim off scum from surface. Cover and simmer for about 3½ hours until the tongue is tender and bones from the top can be easily removed. Strain off and reserve the stock. Remove any bones, gristle and excess fat from the tongue and peel off the skin. Place the tongue on a serving dish and keep warm.

Very finely chop the ham. Melt the butter in a saucepan, add the flour, mix well, and gradually blend in the stock, stirring over medium high heat until the sauce is thick and smooth. Add the Madeira, ham and sultanas, bring to the boil and simmer for ten minutes until the sauce is thick and rich looking. Season with salt and pepper and serve separately. Cut the tongue from the narrow end into thin slanting slices.

To press the remains of the tongue curl it round and fit it into a cake tin. Pour over enough stock to moisten, top with a plate and a heavy weight and leave in the refrigerator for 12 hours. To turn out run a knife around the side of the tongue and dip the tin into very hot water for about 30 seconds. Turn out and cut into thin slices across the top.

Rice Ring with Kidneys in Marsala Sauce

1 small onion
1 clove garlic
75 g (3 oz) butter
450 g (1 lb) long-grain rice
900 ml (1½ pints) stock, heated
4 lambs' kidneys
2 tablespoons flour
Salt and freshly ground black pepper
Vegetable oil for frying
1 wineglass Marsala or medium dry sherry
Finely grated Parmesan cheese
2 tablespoons finely chopped parsley

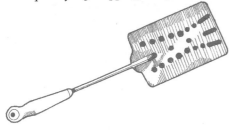

Serves 4

Peel and finely chop the onion and garlic. Melt two thirds of the butter in a heavy saucepan, add the onion and cook over a low heat until soft but not brown. Add the rice and mix well until it is transparent and the butter absorbed. Pour over the stock and cook over a low heat, stirring frequently, until the liquid is absorbed and the rice is tender (if the rice becomes too dry add a little extra stock).

Remove skin from the kidneys and cut out the hard core. Cut the kidneys into thin slices and toss them in the flour, seasoned with a little salt and pepper. Heat a little oil in a frying pan, add the kidneys and cook over a high heat until nicely browned on all sides. Pour in the Marsala, lower the heat and simmer gently for about ten minutes or until the kidneys are just cooked. Check seasoning and keep warm.

Beat the remaining butter and Parmesan into the cooked rice. Turn into a lightly greased ring mould and pat down lightly without compressing the rice too much. Place the ring in a moderately hot oven (200°C, 400°F, Reg. 6) for five minutes and then turn out on to a heated serving dish.

Spoon the kidneys into the centre of the mould and serve at once (this is important, because the rice ring will lose its shape if it is left to stand for any length of time) with a garnish of finely chopped parsley.

Devilled Creamed Kidneys

12 lambs' kidneys
1 tablespoon made English mustard
1 teaspoon Worcestershire sauce
Flour
Salt and pepper
100 g (4 oz) mushrooms
50 g (2 oz) butter
1 tablespoon brandy
150 ml (5 fl oz) canned consommé
Pinch of tarragon
3 tablespoons double cream
225 g (8 oz) rice
6 thin rashers streaky bacon

Serves 6

Soak the kidneys in iced water for 20 minutes, drain and dry well. Remove skins, cut in half and cut out the hard inner core. Spread the kidneys with mustard, sprinkle with Worcestershire sauce and lightly roll in seasoned flour. Thinly slice the mushrooms.

Heat the butter in a large frying pan, add the kidneys and cook for four minutes. Pour over the brandy, ignite with a lighted match and shake the pan until the flames subside. Add the mushrooms, mix well and cook over a medium heat for two minutes. Pour over the consommé, add the tarragon, cook for a few minutes and then stir in the cream. Heat through but do not allow the cream to boil.

Boil the rice until just tender and fry bacon rashers until crisp. Arrange the rice round a shallow serving dish, put the kidneys and mushrooms in the centre and arrange the bacon rashers on the rice.

Devilled Kidneys

8 lambs' kidneys
2 teaspoons made English mustard
1 teaspoon lemon juice
Few drops Worcestershire sauce
1 tablespoon olive or vegetable oil
Salt and cayenne pepper
2 onions
4 thin rashers lean bacon

Serves 4

For a change this can be served with a purée of cauliflower instead of potatoes, and with steamed broccoli or calabrese.

Remove the skin and any fat from the kidneys and cut them in half; remove fatty cores. Combine the mustard, lemon juice and Worcestershire sauce with the oil, salt and cayenne and brush the kidneys with the mixture. Leave them to stand in a cool place for an hour.

Peel and finely chop the onions. Remove rinds and cut the bacon into small pieces. Cook over a medium high heat, with the rinds but without extra fat, until crisp. Remove from the pan with a slotted spoon, discard rinds and drain bacon on kitchen paper.

Add the onions to the bacon fat in the pan and cook over a low heat until soft and pale golden. Lift out with a slotted spoon and drain on kitchen paper.

Grill the kidneys under a high heat for about six minutes, turning them half way through the cooking time (they should be nicely browned on the outside but still pleasantly pink in the centre). Arrange on a serving dish and top with the combined onions and bacon.

Stuffed Ox Heart

1 ox heart
1 onion
50 g (2 oz) mushrooms
50 g (2 oz) dried apricots
25 g (1 oz) butter
1 packet parsley and thyme stuffing
Salt and freshly ground black pepper
4 tablespoons dripping
4 large rashers streaky bacon

Serves 6

Trim the heart of any tough membrane, wash well and soak in cold water for two hours. Drain and dry well.

Peel and finely chop the onion. Chop the mushrooms and apricots. Melt the butter, add the onion and cook over low heat until soft and transparent. Add the mushrooms and cook for a further three minutes. Add the onion and mushroom, with apricot and the juices in the pan, to the packet stuffing and mix in enough boiling water to make a good stuffing consistency. Season with salt and pepper.

Leave the stuffing to cool, then pack it into the heart openings. Sew up the end with tough cotton and wrap the heart in lightly buttered foil; place in a saucepan, cover with cold water, bring to the boil and simmer for two hours. Drain off the water, unwrap the heart, place it in roasting dish, spread with dripping and cover with bacon rashers. Bake in a moderately hot oven (190°C, 375°F, Reg. 5) for one hour, basting frequently.

Make gravy from the juices in the pan and serve with mashed potatoes and a green vegetable.

Breaded Pork Trotters

4 pig's trotters
1 large stick celery
1 medium carrot
Salt and pepper
1 clove
2 bay leaves
1 onion
100 g (4 oz) white breadcrumbs
Fat or vegetable oil for deep-drying
1 tablespoon finely chopped parsley

Serves 4

White breadcrumbs play an important part in this delicious and cheap savoury dish.

Wash the trotters and singe off any hairs with a lighted match. Roughly chop the celery including the leaves. Peel and roughly chop the carrot. Place the trotters in a saucepan, cover them with cold water, season with salt and pepper and add the clove, bay leaves, carrot and celery. Bring slowly to the boil, cover and simmer slowly for about two hours or until the trotters are very tender when pierced with a fork. Don't try to cook them too fast or they will shrink and lose shape.

Peel the onion and pass it through a mincing machine or chop it very finely in a liquidiser, making sure you collect all the juice. Mix the breadcrumbs with the onion and season the mixture with salt and pepper.

Remove the trotters from the cooking liquid (this can be used as stock) and as soon as they are cool enough to handle cut in half, lengthwise, and ease out the bones. Coat the halved trotters in the onions and breadcrumb mixture and cook them in hot deep fat until crisp. Drain on kitchen paper and sprinkle with parsley.

Serve the trotters with horseradish sauce, or a mustard or sweet-and-sour sauce.

Calves' Liver with Avocado

4 avocado pears
Flour
Salt and pepper to taste
1 kilo (2½ lb) calves' liver, thinly sliced
6 tablespoons clarified butter for cooking
3 tablespoons butter for gravy
Lemon juice
Fresh parsley or chervil
120 ml (4 fl oz) Amontillado (or similar)
    sherry

Serves 6

After peeling the avocados remove stones and slice the flesh into lengthwise segments. Mix flour with salt and pepper. Dip the liver into the flour and shake off excess. Similarly dip the avocado slices. Heat the clarified butter in a frying pan and sauté liver for a couple of minutes on each side. Do the same with the avocados, but only for about a minute on each side.

Place the liver on a serving platter and put the avocado slices on top. Pour off the cooking butter from the pan. Add fresh butter and melt quickly. Add the lemon juice, chopped parsley or chervil and the sherry, mix together and pour over the platter while it sizzles.
Note: To clarify butter heat it in a saucepan until foaming and strain through muslin.

Stewed Oxtail with Olives

Serves 4–6

1 oxtail
4 rashers fat bacon
1 carrot
1 medium onion
1 stick celery
2 cloves garlic
8 stuffed olives
425 g (15 oz) can tomatoes
3 tablespoons olive oil
150 ml ($\frac{1}{4}$ pint) dry white wine or chicken stock
Freshly ground black pepper
Pinch of nutmeg
1 tablespoon sultanas

Cut the oxtail into joints (or ask your butcher to do this for you). Soak for 30 minutes in cold water, pat dry with kitchen paper and place in a heavy pan; cover with cold water, bring to the boil and simmer for 2 hours. A pressure cooker is ideal to cut down on cooking time for this kind of dish.

Remove rind and chop the bacon rashers. Peel and chop the carrot and onion. Thinly slice the celery and crush the garlic. Chop the stuffed olives. Roughly chop the tomatoes, reserving all the juice.

Strain the partially cooked oxtail (the stock can be used for soup). Heat the olive oil in a heavy saucepan, add the bacon and cook over a low heat for four minutes. Add the vegetables and cook over a high heat until the onions are golden brown. Add the oxtail pieces and brown quickly on all sides.

Pour over the wine, cook for three minutes, season with pepper and add tomatoes, garlic and nutmeg. Cover tightly and simmer for one hour or until the oxtail meat is falling off the bones. Mix in the sultanas and chopped olives and cook for a further two minutes before serving.

Ragoût of Tripe and Onions

Serves 4

570 g (1$\frac{1}{4}$ lb) dressed tripe
3 onions
225 g (8 oz) carrots
Bouquet garni with 1 bay leaf
Salt and white pepper
1 chicken stock cube
25 g (1 oz) butter
25 g (1 oz) flour
300 ml ($\frac{1}{2}$ pint) milk
Generous pinch of nutmeg
3 tablespoons finely chopped parsley

Tripe should not be overlooked as a nutritious and not-too-expensive food. Cooked with vegetables in this way it makes a first-class winter dish.

Cut the tripe into strips about 5 × 1 cm (2 × $\frac{1}{2}$ in). Peel and slice the onions and divide them into rings. Clean the carrots and cut into thin slices.

Place the tripe in a saucepan, cover with cold water, bring to the boil and then drain. Replace the drained tripe in clean saucepan with the onions, carrots, bouquet garni and seasoning. Cover with fresh cold water, add the crumbled chicken stock cube, bring to the boil, cover and simmer gently for 1$\frac{1}{2}$–2 hours until tripe is tender. Strain off and reserve the liquid and discard the bouquet garni.

Melt the butter in large heavy pan, add the flour and mix well. Gradually blend in the milk and 300 ml ($\frac{1}{2}$ pint) of the reserved cooking liquid, stirring continuously until the mixture comes to the boil and is thick and smooth. Mix in the nutmeg. Mix tripe and vegetables into the sauce, check seasoning and add the parsley. Simmer for ten minutes and serve at once.

Poultry and Game

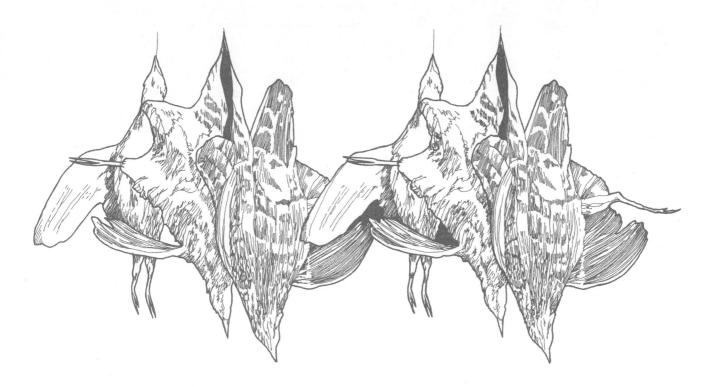

Chicken

Once the idea of almost every family in the country being able to eat chicken every Sunday for lunch was a dream. Now the dream has almost become a reality and chicken has replaced the roast beef of old England to a great extent as the most popular Sunday lunch (certainly on holidays and birthdays that is the roast my children always ask for). Chickens are a relatively reasonable price and new farming and freezing methods have made them readily available all the year round. Satisfactory as this situation might be, however, it does have some drawbacks. Roast chicken is no longer the excitement it once was, to

be greeted with cries of joy, and on the whole the flavour of poultry has suffered through intensive rearing procedures and freezing. Whatever the poultry suppliers say, those chickens that used to peck this and that from a farmyard had a lot more taste than the birds fed from automatic hoppers on a highly balanced diet, de-sexed at birth and brought up in dreary sterile batteries.

Whenever possible, and especially if you are looking for a bird to roast, shop around for a 'fresh not frozen' chicken, as these undoubtedly have more flavour than frozen birds. For those who have small families or live by themselves it is always possible to buy chicken joints (again look for the 'fresh not frozen' label). Add flavour to a roast bird with the addition of lemon, herbs, spices and seasonings. Best of all ensure a moist, well-flavoured Sunday roast chicken by combining herbs, spices, salt and freshly ground black pepper with softened butter and a little lemon juice; ease the skin from the breast of the bird using a small knife, making small snicking movements to separate it from the flesh and taking care not to pierce it; spread the softened butter under the skin and roast in the usual way. In order to get a crisp and rich golden brown skin on your bird, brush the skin with soya sauce before roasting–the effect is almost miraculous. Extra flavouring and tenderness can also be achieved by basting the bird with about three tablespoons of good stock half way through the cooking time.

Chickens are one of the most universally cooked meat meals in the world and there are thousands of exciting ways to cook them. They are not as cheap as they used to be but they can still be good value for money providing you make the best possible use of them. Leave roast chicken to stand for a good five minutes after roasting to allow the flesh to consolidate and thereby achieve more economical carving. Use raw or cooked carcasses to make the basis of a rich and nourishing chicken stock. Collect and freeze the livers from fresh birds to make chicken liver pâté, and use the necks, gizzards and hearts as a flavouring ingredient for gravy or stock.

By jointing a chicken you can not only produce some delicious and often economical dishes but you also have the basic carcass (left after taking off the breasts, legs and wings) for making a good stock for soups and sauces. Use a really sharp, fine-pointed knife and cut away the wishbone first. Slide the knife along the bones of the breast down to the top of the thighs and wings. The two breast portions of the chicken can be divided into fillets (this is a flattish slice of the breast which lies next to the breast bone and which can be pulled easily away from the rest of the breast) and a good 'steak' of tender chicken meat. Fillets and breast meat can be placed between two sheets of

greaseproof paper and beaten with a wooden mallet until almost double their size; the thin delicate slices of chicken can be poached in stock until tender or dipped in beaten egg and then breadcrumbs and fried like escalopes of veal.

In the Far East cooks perform miracles, stretching small amounts of raw chicken to almost incredible lengths. The meat is cut from the bone in thin slices and then cut into very thin strips. It is then quickly fried with very thinly sliced raw vegetables, spices and seasoning and moistened with a good stock made from chicken bones.

French cooks rely on more elaborate and extravagant methods to transform their poultry into spectacular dishes. From them we can learn a lot about the use of fresh herbs, especially tarragon, as a flavouring ingredient for the birds.

We in Britain also have our traditional, well-tried, chicken dishes, tasting so good it is not surprising they have stood up well to the test of time: succulent chicken pies, sometimes flavoured very liberally with parsley or leeks; nourishing chicken broths; and delicious mixtures of chicken poached with vegetables and herbs.

But perhaps it is the Americans above all who have made what almost amounts to a cult of chicken dishes. Certainly it was the Americans who realised the dream of having chicken at least once a week on their tables long before we did. Their cookery books positively burst with recipes for frying, grilling, roasting, barbecuing and stewing chicken, and their repertoire of chicken salads is amazing. One American cookery book I have in my library contains no less than one thousand recipes–all for chicken.

Almost as important as cooking your bird is the treatment you give it before it even gets to the pot. With a fresh bird, always remove the giblets as soon as you get it home, and wipe the inside with a clean damp cloth. If you plan to keep the bird for a day or two before cooking it place half a lemon and some celery in the cavity to keep the flesh sweet and provide extra flavour (the Romans used to feed their poultry celery for just this purpose). If the bird is frozen, defrost it slowly overnight in the bottom of the refrigerator and remove the giblets as soon as it has thawed.

Turkey

A revolution has occurred in the turkey market. Turkey breeders had a problem producing birds only wanted on just one, or maybe two, days a year. Then they decided to breed smaller birds, so making it possible for people to buy turkeys on more days a year than just at Christmas and Easter. They also introduced 'turkey products', pieces of turkey taken off the bone or sold in portions in all manner of cuts and guises. Turkey portions can be cooked in the same way as chicken; they have a slightly more defined flavour and may need a little extra cooking time but they make excellent eating.

Buying Your Christmas Turkey

Undoubtedly the best bird to buy is one that is 'farm fresh' and not frozen. Frozen birds may be less expensive, but they will not have as much flavour as a bird that has been bred to serve fresh because they are reared in a different way. Those turkeys which are brought up to be frozen live a more confined and shorter life than the birds which are to be sold fresh and this does affect the flavour. For the best bargains look for a 'farm fresh' bird in about the middle of November and put it in your own freezer. The price rises dramatically before Christmas so whatever bird you choose do (providing you own a deep-freeze) buy early so as not to be caught out by the appalling blackmail that tends to occur as Christmas approaches.

Roasting Turkey

One of the major problems when roasting a turkey is to keep the flesh moist and to prevent the breast becoming overcooked while the thicker and tougher joints of meat are still being tenderised. The best way I have discovered to do this (a method also used by Robert Carrier) is to drape the bird in muslin, first wrung out in cold water and then liberally soaked in melted butter. The bird is wrapped in the muslin, cooked in a hot oven (220°C, 425°F, Reg. 7) for 15 minutes to get it going and then finished in a moderate oven (180°C, 350°F, Reg. 4). During the cooking the juices in the pan should be poured from time to time over the muslin to keep it constantly moist.

With a very large turkey I reverse this method of cooking by wrapping it in the buttered muslin and putting it in the bottom of a very low oven (about 110°C, 225°F, Reg. $\frac{1}{4}$) overnight without basting, and then transferring it to a hot oven for the last hour, having removed the muslin to allow the skin to brown.

Cooking times for Turkey Roasted as Above

3 kilos (6 lb)	3–3½ hours
3–3.5 kilos (6–8 lb)	3½–4 hours
3.5–5 kilos (8–12 lb)	4–5½ hours
5–7 kilos (12–16 lb)	5½–6 hours
7–9 kilos (16–20 lb)	6½–8 hours

To test whether the turkey is cooked pierce the thickest part of the leg joint with a skewer. The juices that flow should be clear and not clouded with pink. Also the leg, if wiggled, should just move in its joint socket.

Game

Unfortunately for most people game has become an expensive commodity, but when the season is at its height, see below, there is no doubt that it is possible to buy some items of game for a fairly reasonable price and produce some really delicious and well flavoured dishes from it. Pigeons, for instance, if they are not the youngest and most tender, can be very good buys indeed, and although they may not be as grand as partridge or grouse they have a marvellous gamey flavour. The older pigeons require slow and careful cooking but the rewards are well worth reaping.

Hare also can be a good buy at the height of the season; it is extremely rich and quite a small amount goes a long way. Having experimented with various ways of cooking a hare I have come to the conclusion that the traditional British method of 'jugging' (originally the hare was literally cooked in a jug) is as good as, if not better than, any other way.

Older partridges, pheasants and grouse can also sometimes be found for a reasonable price, but don't attempt to roast them; only the young tender birds are fit for this, and anything else should be casseroled or used in raised pies or pâtés.

Seasons for Game

Grouse
The season begins on 12 August and continues until 10 December and while grouse are now extremely expensive at the beginning of the season and young birds will never be cheap, older grouse for casseroling, stewing or making into pies can usually be found for a reasonable price around the middle of the season.

Hare
Hares are in season from the beginning of August to the end of February and their price tends to drop towards the end of the season.

Partridge
1 September is the first day of the partridge season which lasts until 1 February and best buys are usually older birds bought at the end of the season.

Pheasant
Pheasant shooting lasts from 1 October to 10 December in Scotland and to 31 January in England and once the first few weeks of the season are over prices usually level off; old birds for casseroling or stewing often become very reasonable buys.

Wild Duck
These to my mind are amongst the best eating of all game birds but they are not all that easy to find. The duck season is from 1 August to the end of February and birds are usually more plentiful around October and November.

Chicken Recipes

Chicken with Lemon and Herb Sauce

1 roasting chicken, about 1·5 kilos (3 lb)
40 g (1½ oz) butter
1 tablespoon flour
300 ml (½ pint) strong chicken stock
Salt and freshly ground black pepper
¼ teaspoon grated nutmeg
Juice of ½ lemon
¼ tablespoon finely chopped fresh tarragon
½ tablespoon finely chopped fresh chervil
1 tablespoon finely chopped fresh parsley
2 tablespoons double cream

Serves 6

Boil or roast the chicken until tender (approx. 1–1½ hours in moderate oven). I prefer boiling it with a stock cube, half a lemon, an onion and a couple of carrots; if you roast it make sure it is well basted to keep the flesh moist.

Make a strong stock from the chicken giblets. Melt two thirds of the butter in a saucepan, add the flour and mix well. Gradually blend in the stock, stirring continously over a medium heat until the sauce is thick and smooth. Season with salt, pepper and nutmeg and simmer gently for five minutes. Blend in the remaining butter, add the lemon juice and herbs and stir in the cream. Check seasoning before serving. *Note:* If dried herbs are used, halve the quantities and soften them in the lemon juice for at least ten minutes before adding to the sauce.

Braised Chicken with Ham and Cheese

15 g (½ oz) butter and 1 tablespoon olive oil
1 chicken, about 1·5 kilos (3 lb)
900 ml (1½ pints) water
1 onion, peeled and chopped
¼ teaspoon tarragon
1 chicken stock cube
Salt and pepper
50 g (2 oz) butter
50 g (2 oz) flour
1 egg yolk
1 tablespoon cream
2 tomatoes
50 g (2 oz) cooked ham
50 g (2 oz) grated Cheddar cheese

Serves 4–6

Heat the butter and olive oil together in a large saucepan until very hot. Add the chicken and brown quickly on all sides. Add the water, onion, tarragon and stock cube. Season with salt and pepper, bring to the boil, cover and simmer for about 40 minutes until tender. Strain off the stock and leave the chicken to cool. Cut the chicken into eight pieces and arrange them on a serving dish.

Heat the butter in a saucepan and mix in the flour. Gradually blend in the stock–there should be 600 ml (1 pint)–stirring continuously over a medium heat until the sauce is thick and smooth. Beat the egg yolk with the cream and blend in a little of the sauce. Add the mixture to the sauce and heat through over a low heat without boiling. Check the seasoning and pour the sauce over the chicken pieces.

Peel and thinly slice the tomatoes and chop the ham. Arrange over the chicken and top with grated cheese. Heat through in a hot oven (220°C, 425°F, Reg. 7) until the top is golden brown.

Serve with boiled rice and a green salad.

Chicken Piri Piri

200 ml (7½ fl oz) olive or vegetable oil
Juice of 1 lemon
1 teaspoon chilli powder
Generous pinch of rosemary, oregano and
  tarragon
3 teaspoons tomato ketchup
Salt and freshly ground black pepper
4 chicken joints
Oil or fat for frying

Serves 4

The marinade in this recipe can be kept in a screw-topped jar and makes a delicious sauce for brushing over lamb chops, pork chops or tomatoes before grilling.

Combine the olive oil, lemon juice, chilli powder, herbs and tomato ketchup; season with salt and pepper. Wipe the chicken joints and score the flesh with a sharp knife. Leave them to marinate in the Piri Piri mixture for at least four hours, turning frequently to make sure they are well soaked.

Drain off the excess liquid and fry the joints in a shallow pan over a very high heat until well browned; lower the heat and continue cooking until the chicken is tender.

Note : To get the outside of the chicken joints really well browned the pan should be heated over the flame for a few minutes before they are added.

Jubilee Chicken

1 medium chicken
2 stock cubes
Bouquet garni
2 onions
450 g (1 lb) carrots
2 tablespoons olive oil
1 stick celery, finely chopped
575 g (20 oz) canned tomatoes
¼ teaspoon dried oregano
¼ teaspoon dried basil (or 1½ teaspoons fresh,
  finely chopped basil)
2 wineglasses dry white wine
2 bay leaves
Rind of 2 oranges, grated
Salt and freshly ground black pepper
Fresh parsley, chives or basil to garnish

Serves 6–8

This rather unusual way of serving cold chicken makes a good alternative to traditional mayonnaise-smothered cold chicken dishes.

Place the chicken in a large saucepan, cover with cold water and add the stock cubes, bouquet garni and one onion cut into quarters. Bring to the boil, cover and simmer gently for about 50 minutes or until the chicken is almost cooked. Remove from the heat and leave to cool in the liquid. Take out when cold, remove skin and cut the flesh into thin slices. Peel and finely chop the carrots and remaining onion.

Heat olive oil in saucepan, add carrots, celery and onion and cook over a low heat until the onion is transparent. Add the tomatoes, oregano, basil, wine, bay leaves and orange rind, season with salt and pepper, bring to the boil, cover and simmer for 30 minutes, stirring occasionally to break up the tomatoes. Remove the bay leaves and leave to cool. Add the chicken slices to the cold sauce and chill well before serving.

Serve the chicken sprinkled with finely chopped parsley, chives or fresh basil with a surround of watercress, rice salad, or, best of all, cold pasta mixed with peas and small snippets of ham tossed in mayonnaise.

Chicken à la Crème

Serves 6

1 chicken
450 ml (¾ pint) water
1 chicken stock cube
Bouquet garni
1 onion
1 stick celery
Salt, pepper and a pinch of celery salt
25 g (1 oz) butter
25 g (1 oz) flour
5 tablespoons dry vermouth
Juice of 1 lemon
150 ml (5 fl oz) single cream
Fresh parsley to garnish

Joint the chicken into eight pieces and place in a saucepan with the water, stock cube and bouquet garni. Add the onion, peeled and roughly chopped, and the celery cut into 2·5 cm (1 in) pieces. Season with salt, pepper and celery salt, bring to the boil, cover and simmer for about 20 minutes until tender. Strain off the stock and add a little water if necessary to make it up to 300 ml (½ pint). Arrange the chicken pieces on a serving dish.

Heat the butter in a saucepan until melted and stir in the flour. Gradually blend in the stock, stirring continuously over a medium heat until the sauce is thick and smooth. Add the vermouth, bring to the boil and simmer for three minutes. Check the seasoning, remove from the heat and blend in the lemon juice and cream. Pour the sauce over the chicken and heat through in a moderate oven (180°C, 350°F, Reg. 4) for about 20 minutes.

Garnish with finely chopped parsley and serve with boiled rice and green vegetables.

Simmered Chicken with Lemon Tarragon Sauce

Serves 6

1 chicken, about 1·5 kilos (3 lb)
1 large onion
1 clove garlic
2 carrots
1 stick celery
1 chicken stock cube
Bouquet garni
8 black peppercorns
½ lemon
150 ml (¼ pint) white wine
Lemon tarragon sauce (p. 158)
Fresh parsley or tarragon to garnish

Boiled chicken may sound dull, but this dish has a tenderness and subtlety hard to beat, with the added advantage of producing enough juices to make the base of a nourishing stock. The sauce is smooth and memorable.

Place the chicken in a saucepan with the gizzard, heart and neck (reserve the liver for garnishing a soup). Add the onion, garlic and carrots, peeled and roughly chopped, the celery stick cut into three, the stock cube, bouquet garni, peppercorns, lemon and white wine. Pour over enough water to cover the chicken, bring slowly to the boil, stir to dissolve the stock cube and simmer very slowly for one hour or until the bird is tender. Remove the chicken and strain off 300 ml (½ pint) stock (reserve the remaining stock and vegetables to re-boil with the chicken carcass to make a stronger stock for soup). Leave the chicken to cool, then carve, cutting the breast into thin slices and dividing up the joints. Arrange on a shallow serving dish.

Make the sauce as directed on p. 158, and pour over the chicken.

Heat through in a moderate oven (180°C, 350°F, Reg. 4) for about 15 minutes. Garnish with finely chopped fresh parsley or tarragon.

Malay Chicken Satay

675 g (1½ lb) chicken breasts
2·5 cm (1 in) piece fresh ginger root, peeled
1 onion
2 cloves garlic
1 teaspoon coriander seeds
3 tablespoons peanuts
Salt and freshly ground black pepper
Pinch of cayenne pepper
1 tablespoon honey
3 tablespoons lemon juice
1 tablespoon brown sugar
2 tablespoons soya sauce

Satay Sauce:
2 onions
100 g (4 oz) roasted peanuts
Pinch of chilli powder
2 tablespoons vegetable oil
150 ml (¼ pint) water
1 teaspoon brown sugar
1 tablespoon soya sauce
Juice of ½ lemon
Salt

Serves 4

Very thinly slice the chicken breasts and then cut into strips about 1 × 5 cm (½ × 2 in). Mince the ginger root, peel and very finely chop the onion. Crush the garlic and coriander seeds. Finely chop or mince peanuts. Combine all ingredients, add the chicken and marinate for at least three hours.

Thread the chicken strips on long skewers, putting about two or three on each one and leaving at least 10 cm (4 in) clear at one end. Grill over a hot fire, turning once or twice until the chicken is cooked, brown and slightly crisp around the edges. Dip into Satay sauce to eat.

Peel and chop one onion. Peel and chop the second onion and combine with peanuts and chilli powder in a liquidiser. Process until the mixture is reduced to a paste.

Heat the oil. Add chopped onion and cook over a medium heat until soft and golden. Add the paste and stir for three minutes. Gradually blend in the water, stirring all the time. Add the sugar and cook for five minutes. Mix in soya sauce and lemon juice and season if necessary with a little salt. Serve the sauce hot or warm. It can be made in advance and reheated over the fire.

Chicken with Grapefruit Sauce

1 medium chicken
Flour
Salt and pepper
70 g (2½ oz) butter
1 small can grapefruit segments
1 tablespoon grapefruit juice
150 ml (¼ pint) chicken stock
4 tablespoons sherry
Fresh parsley and fried bread to garnish

Serves 6

Cut the chicken flesh from the bones, dice it and roll in seasoned flour. Melt the butter in a frying pan, add the chicken and cook over a high heat to brown; lower the heat and cook gently until tender. Add the grapefruit segments, juice, chicken stock and sherry and mix well. Remove the chicken and grapefruit on to a warm serving dish with a slotted spoon and keep warm.

Boil up the sauce in the pan, stirring continuously, until the liquid is thick and reduced to about half the original quantity. Pour over the chicken and garnish with chopped parsley and triangles of crisply fried bread.

Chicken Blinis

900 ml (1½ pints) milk
25 g (1 oz) fresh yeast, or 15 g (½ oz) dried
1 tablespoon sugar
225 g (8 oz) plain flour
4 eggs, separated
10 g (½ oz) butter, melted
½ teaspoon salt
¾ teaspoon white pepper

The filling:

1 chicken, about 1·5 kilos (3 lb)
2 leeks
225 g (8 oz) firm button mushrooms
50 g (2 oz) butter
2 tablespoons flour
200 ml (7½ fl oz) chicken stock
150 ml (¼ pint) milk
2 tablespoons finely chopped canned pimento
2 egg yolks
5 tablespoons double cream
Salt and freshly ground black pepper
100 g (4 oz) grated Cheddar cheese

Serves 8

True Russian blinis are made with buckwheat flour, but this variation has the same light texture.

Warm half the milk to blood temperature (lukewarm). Crumble the yeast in a warm basin, add the sugar and gradually pour in the milk, stirring until the yeast is dissolved (or follow instructions given for dried yeast). Add the flour and mix well. Cover with a cloth and leave to rise in a warm place for two hours.

Beat the egg yolks with the remaining milk, add the butter and season with the salt and pepper. Add this to the risen yeast and mix well. Beat the egg whites until stiff and fold them into the batter. Cover again and leave to stand in a warm place for 30 minutes.

Lightly oil an omelette pan, heat until smoking and spoon a little batter into the centre; spread out thinly with a spatula and cook over a high heat until golden brown underneath; turn over and brown on the other side. Stack the pancakes as they are cooked.

Roast or boil the chicken until tender, leave to cool, remove all the flesh and cut into small dice. Thinly slice the leeks, boil until just tender and drain well. Thinly slice the mushrooms. Melt the butter in a large saucepan, add the sliced mushrooms and cook over a very low heat for three minutes. Add the flour and mix well; add the stock and milk, stirring continuously over a medium high heat until the sauce is thick and smooth. Add the chicken, leeks and pimento.

Beat the egg yolks with the cream and add to the chicken mixture. Cook, stirring continuously, over a medium heat without boiling for a further three minutes. Season with salt and pepper, spread the filling over the pancakes, roll each one up neatly, sprinkle with cheese and arrange in a lightly greased baking dish. Heat through in a moderate oven (180°C, 350°F, Reg. 4) until the filled pancakes are hot through and the cheese has melted.

Serve with a green vegetable or a salad.

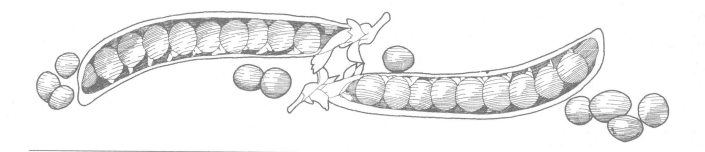

Chicken Curry

1 small chicken
2 onions
1 green pepper
1 stick celery
Bouquet garni
2 tablespoons oil
600 ml (1 pint) chicken stock
2 bananas
2 heaped tablespoons Madras curry powder
1 tablespoon plain flour
Grated rind and juice of 1 lemon
Salt and pepper
50 g (2 oz) blanched almonds

Serves 4

Remove the legs and wings from the chicken and cut off the breast. Cut the breast in half and separate the thigh from the leg bone. Peel and chop one onion. Remove core and seeds from the pepper and chop the flesh. Boil the carcass and giblets with one onion, the celery and a bouquet garni to make a strong stock.

Heat the oil in a fire-proof casserole dish. Add the chicken pieces, onion and pepper and cook over a medium high heat until the chicken is lightly browned on all sides. Add the chicken stock. Mash the bananas and blend in the curry powder, flour, lemon rind and juice, mixing well until a smooth paste is formed. Thin the paste with some of the chicken stock, then add it to the casserole and mix well. Bring to the boil, stirring to prevent any lumps forming in the sauce, season with salt and pepper, cover and simmer for 45 minutes. Add the almonds and serve with fluffy boiled rice.

Stuffed Pot-roasted Chicken

100 g (4 oz) long-grain rice
1 large chicken, about 2 kilos (4½ lb)
50 g (2 oz) butter
1 small green pepper
Salt and freshly ground black pepper
50 g (2 oz) raisins
450 g (1 lb) young carrots
450 g (1 lb) onions
450 g (1 lb) small tomatoes
¼ teaspoon rosemary
150 ml (¼ pint) dry cider

Serves 6

Lighter than a stew, cooked with spring vegetables, this dish is ideal for early summer days.

Cook the rice in boiling salted water for about 20 minutes until just tender. Drain well. Cook the chicken liver in a quarter of the butter for three minutes; reserve the juices and chop the liver. Remove seeds and core from the green pepper and finely chop the flesh. Combine the rice with 25 g (1 oz) of the remaining butter, liver and juices. Season with salt, mix in the raisins and chopped pepper. Stuff the chicken with this mixture.

Scrape the carrots and leave whole. Peel the onions and cut into quarters. Lightly grease a deep casserole dish and place the carrots, onions and tomatoes in the bottom.

Pound the rosemary in a mortar with a pestle. Add a little seasoning of salt and pepper and mix in the rest of the butter, softened. Rub the chicken with this mixture and place it in the casserole. Pour over the cider. Cover the casserole tightly and bake in a moderate oven (180°C, 350°F, Reg. 4) for 2½ hours or until the chicken is tender. Remove the lid for the last 10–15 minutes to brown the skin. Lift out the chicken with a slotted spoon, place it on a serving dish, surround with the strained vegetables and serve the gravy separately.

Roast Chicken Candide

Serves 4–5

½ lemon
15 g (½ oz) butter
1 small bunch parsley
1 medium roasting chicken
2 tablespoons olive oil
1 tablespoon lemon juice
1 teaspoon thyme
1 tablespoon tomato purée
Salt and pepper

Place the lemon, butter and parsley in the cavity of the chicken. Combine the olive oil, lemon juice, thyme and tomato purée and season with salt and pepper.

Place the chicken in a roasting dish and brush with the olive oil mixture. Roast in a hot oven (220°C, 425°F, Reg. 7) for 30 minutes and then lower the heat to very moderate (160°C, 325°F, Reg. 3) for a further 30–45 minutes or until tender. Baste frequently.

Place the chicken on a serving dish and serve with a gravy made from the juices in the pan and giblet stock.

Golden Chicken Hot-pot

Serves 4, with some left over

1 fresh chicken, about 1·5 kilos (3 lb)
4 sticks celery
675 g (1½ lb) potatoes
2 onions
2 cloves garlic (optional)
4 rashers lean bacon
1½ cans consommé
4 tablespoons vegetable oil
Salt and freshly ground black pepper
Grated rind of 1 lemon
15 g (½ oz) butter, melted

Remove giblets from the chicken. Chop the celery into 1 cm (½ in) thick slices. Peel the potatoes and cut into wedges the size of large walnuts. Peel and roughly chop the onions; peel and finely chop the garlic. Remove rinds and finely chop the bacon rashers. Open the consommé and leave in warm place for 20 minutes to melt.

Heat the oil in large fire-proof casserole. Add the bacon and vegetables and cook over a low heat, stirring every now and then, for about five minutes or until the onion is transparent. Remove the vegetables and bacon with a slotted spoon on to a spare plate, raise the heat and add the chicken to the juices in the casserole. Brown on all sides, turning it over with the spoon.

Remove the casserole from the heat, take out the chicken and arrange a thick layer of bacon and vegetables in the bottom. Place the chicken, breast side up, on top and pack the remaining vegetables around it. Season well with salt and pepper, sprinkle with the lemon rind and pour over the consommé. Cover with foil and the lid (to make sure the dish is well sealed) and cook in very moderate oven (160°C, 325°F, Reg. 3) for 1½ hours. Remove lid and foil for last ten minutes, smear the breast of the bird with butter and return it uncovered to the oven to brown.

Leave to settle for at least ten minutes before serving as this makes carving easier and more economical. With careful carving it should be possible to get four good servings from just over half the bird leaving enough for a chicken salad and chicken risotto for two meals.

Chicken Tandoori

Serves 4

*½ teaspoon each of cinnamon, cloves and
    cardamom*
4 cloves garlic
¼ teaspoon ground ginger
2 teaspoons paprika
150 g (5 oz) carton yoghurt
4 tablespoons olive or vegetable oil
1 small chicken, jointed

Combine the cinnamon with the cloves and cardamom seeds in a pestle and mortar and grind to a fine powder. Peel and very finely chop the garlic. Combine all the ingredients, mix well, pour over the chicken joint and leave to marinate for at least four hours.

Grill the joints, basting with marinade from time to time and turning half way through, for 20–25 minutes.

Sunday Special Chicken

Serves 4–5

2 tablespoons finely chopped parsley
½ teaspoon each of sage, thyme and chervil
75 g (3 oz) butter, softened
1 roasting chicken, about 1·5 kilos (3 lb)
½ lemon
Salt and pepper
Chicken giblets
150 ml (¼ pint) stock
2 tablespoons sherry
2 tablespoons flour
200 ml (7½ fl oz) single cream

Combine the herbs with half the butter and place inside the chicken. Rub it all over with lemon, salt and pepper. Heat the remaining butter in a frying pan and fry the chicken quickly until brown on all sides.

Place the chicken in a casserole with the neck, gizzard and heart. Add the stock and sherry to the pan juices, heat through and pour over the chicken. Cook, uncovered, in a moderate oven (190°C, 375°F, Reg. 5) for 1–1¼ hours until tender, basting to keep moist.

Remove the giblets, place the chicken on a heated serving dish and keep warm. Mix the flour with a little of the cooking liquid to make a smooth paste, blend in the rest of the liquid, bring to the boil and simmer for three minutes. Fry the chicken liver in a little butter or bacon fat for 3–4 minutes, rub through a fine sieve and add to the sauce. Mix in the cream, adjust the seasoning and heat through without boiling. Serve the sauce separately.

Quantock Chicken

Serves 4–5

1 green pepper
1 onion
100 g (4 oz) mushrooms
1 small chicken, jointed
Just under 300 ml (½ pint) medium dry cider
Salt and pepper
150 g (5 oz) carton yoghurt
1 tablespoon finely chopped parsley

Remove core and seeds from the green pepper and chop the flesh. Peel and chop the onion; halve the mushrooms. Put the chicken joints, vegetables and cider in an oven-proof casserole. Season with salt and pepper.

Cover tightly and cook in a moderate oven (180°C, 350°F, Reg. 4) for 1½ hours. Remove the lid, pour over the yoghurt and sprinkle with parsley just before serving.

Chicken Croquettes

Serves 4

225 g (8 oz) cooked chicken
1 small onion
25 g (1 oz) butter
2 tablespoons flour
300 ml ($\frac{1}{2}$ pint) chicken stock
2 egg yolks
Salt and freshly ground black pepper
Pinch of allspice and nutmeg
1$\frac{1}{4}$ tablespoons finely chopped parsley
Fine dried breadcrumbs
1 large egg, beaten
Lard or vegetable oil for frying
Fresh parsley to garnish

In one form or another this economical way of using up leftover chicken can be found throughout the British Isles, the Continent and the Near and Far East. The secret of crisp, succulent croquettes lies in keeping the mixture moist, chilling it well before attempting to shape it into croquettes, and rolling them in breadcrumbs before dipping them into beaten egg and breadcrumbs again. Seasonings should be fairly sharp and fully flavoured. Ham can be substituted for half the chicken quantity.

Mince the chicken. Peel and finely chop the onion. Melt the butter in a saucepan, add the onion and cook over a low heat for about five minutes until soft and transparent. Blend in the flour, mix well and gradually beat in the stock, stirring continuously until the mixture is thick. Beat in the egg yolks and then stir in the minced chicken. Season with salt, pepper, nutmeg and a hint of allspice and mix in the parsley. Spread the mixture out flat on a plate and refrigerate for two hours until firm.

Divide the mixture into eight portions and roll each one in breadcrumbs, moulding them into neat sausage shapes. Dip the croquettes in beaten egg and then into breadcrumbs again. Fry in about 2·5 cm (1 in) of hot lard or vegetable oil for 6–8 minutes. Turn halfway through cooking time, until crisp and golden brown. Drain well on kitchen paper and serve piled on a plate with a garnish of fresh parsley.

Mousse de Volaille

350 g (12 oz) streaky bacon
350 g (12 oz) onions
225 g (8 oz) cooked chicken breast
40 g (1½ oz) fresh white breadcrumbs
300 ml (½ pint) milk
25 g (1 oz) butter
1 egg
2 egg whites
1 teaspoon salt
⅛ teaspoon each of ground nutmeg, allspice and
    white pepper
150 ml (5 fl oz) double cream

Serves 6

Although this is a fairly spectacular dish it uses leftover chicken and is relatively inexpensive to produce. You can serve the mousse hot with lemon and tarragon, tomato or mushroom sauce, or leave it to cool and serve masked with a flavoured mayonnaise and garnished with salad.

Remove rinds from the bacon rashers. Peel and slice the onions. Mince the bacon and chicken twice through the fine blades of a mincing machine.

Combine the breadcrumbs and milk in a saucepan, bring to the boil and simmer, stirring, until the milk has been absorbed and the mixture is smooth. Leave to cool.

Melt the butter in a frying pan. Add the onions and cook over a low heat, stirring to prevent sticking, until very soft. Remove from the heat and leave to cool, then purée through a sieve or a food mill. Beat the whole egg with the egg whites until smooth. Combine all the ingredients and mix really well.

Butter a terrine or Pyrex dish, pack in the mixture and place in a baking tin. Pour in enough hot water to come half way up the sides of container and bake in a moderate oven (180°C, 350°F, Reg. 4) for 1½ hours or until the sides of the mousse come away from the container and a metal knitting needle plunged into the middle comes out clean.

To serve at once turn out, garnish with a little chopped parsley and serve with sauce on the side.

To serve cold leave to cool in the container and then chill well. Dip the container into boiling water, turn the mousse out on to a serving dish and mask with mayonnaise flavoured with a little tomato purée, curry powder or French Dijon mustard.

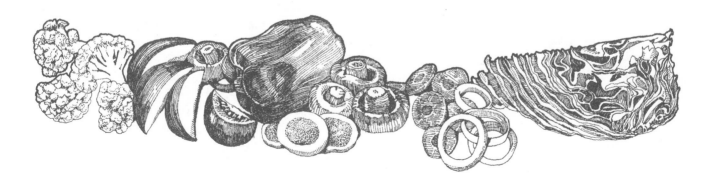

Game Recipes

Grouse Pie

2 *casseroling grouse*
450 g (1 lb) lean stewing steak
2 *onions*
Salt, freshly ground black pepper and cayenne
300 ml ($\frac{1}{2}$ pint) good stock
5 *tablespoons sherry*
225 g (8 oz) puff pastry
1 *egg yolk*

Serves 4

Cut each grouse in half from the front to the back. Cut the steak into thin strips about 6 mm × 4 cm ($\frac{1}{4}$ × 1$\frac{1}{2}$ in). Peel and very thinly slice the onions.

Arrange the steak in the bottom of a pie dish, cover with the onions and lay the grouse, cut side down, on top. Season with salt, pepper and a little cayenne, pour over the stock and seal tightly with foil. Cook in a moderate oven (180°C, 350°F, Reg. 5) for one hour. Remove from the heat, add the sherry and leave to cool for 15 minutes.

Roll out the pastry to about 6 mm ($\frac{1}{4}$ in) thickness and cover the pie dish with it. Brush over with beaten egg yolk and cut two air vents in the top. Return to a hot oven (220°C, 425°F, Reg. 7) and continue to cook for 20–30 minutes until the pastry is well risen and golden brown.

Jugged Hare

2 *onions*
2 *large carrots*
2 *sticks celery*
1 *hare, jointed (ask the butcher to reserve the blood)*
Flour
1$\frac{1}{2}$ *tablespoons dripping or bacon fat*
Bouquet garni
Thinly pared rind of $\frac{1}{2}$ lemon
Salt, freshly ground black pepper and cayenne
900 ml (1$\frac{1}{2}$ pints) good strong stock
2 *tablespoons redcurrant jelly*
120 ml (4 fl oz) port

Serves 6

Peel and thinly slice the onions. Peel and dice the carrots; thinly slice the celery. Dredge the hare joints in flour and fry them in the dripping until golden brown on all sides.

Place the joints in a thick earthenware jug with the vegetables, bouquet garni and lemon rind. Season with salt, pepper and cayenne and pour over the stock. Seal the jug tightly with foil and place it in a large saucepan. Add enough water to come to within 10 cm (4 in) of the top of the jug, bring to the boil and then simmer gently for about 2$\frac{1}{2}$–4 hours until the hare is tender.

Using a slotted spoon, remove hare and vegetables from the jug to a heated serving dish. Remove the bouquet garni and lemon rind and pour the juices into a saucepan. Add the hare's blood, redcurrant jelly and port and heat through, stirring continuously until the jelly has melted. Check seasoning and strain the sauce over the hare and vegetables.

Serve with extra redcurrant jelly on the side and small balls of sausage-meat fried until a crisp golden brown.

Pigeons en Casserole

2 large or 4 small pigeons
12 shallots
100 g (4 oz) salt pork or gammon
50 g (2 oz) butter
2 tablespoons flour
450 ml ($\frac{3}{4}$ pint) strong stock
150 ml ($\frac{1}{4}$ pint) red wine
Salt and freshly ground black pepper
Bouquet garni
100 g (4 oz) small firm button mushrooms
12 pimento-stuffed green olives
5 tablespoons sour cream
Fried bread to garnish

Serves 4

Split the pigeons in half along the breastbone and back, using kitchen scissors. Peel the shallots; dice the salt pork or gammon. Melt the butter in a heavy flame-proof casserole until foaming, add the pigeons and brown quickly on all sides. Remove the pigeons, add the pork or gammon and cook over a high heat for three minutes; remove with a slotted spoon. Add flour to the juices in the pan, stir well until it is brown and then gradually blend in the stock and wine, stirring constantly until the sauce comes to boil and is thick and smooth. Season with salt and pepper. Return the pigeons and pork to the casserole, add the shallots and bouquet garni, cover tightly and cook in a moderate oven (190°C, 375°F, Reg. 5) for 45 minutes. Add the mushrooms and olives and return to the oven for 15 minutes.

Transfer the pigeons, vegetables and olives to a heated serving dish. Remove the bouquet garni and blend the sour cream into the sauce. Check seasoning and pour the sauce over the pigeons before serving.

Garnish with triangles of fried bread and serve with boiled rice or mashed potatoes and a green vegetable.

Stuffings

Chestnut Stuffing

1·2 kilos (2$\frac{1}{2}$ lb) chestnuts
100 g (4 oz) lean bacon
Turkey heart and liver
100 g (4 oz) white breadcrumbs
Milk
2 eggs
1 onion, finely chopped
2 tablespoons finely chopped parsley
50 g (2 oz) butter, melted
Salt and freshly ground black pepper

Enough for a 4·5-kilo (10-lb) turkey

Using a sharp knife cut an incision through the skin of each chestnut from the base to the top and down the other side. Cover the chestnuts with cold water, bring to the boil and cook for eight minutes. Drain off the water and, as soon as the chestnuts are cool enough to handle, peel off outer and inner skins. Cover with more water and cook for a further 20–30 minutes until soft. Drain and mash slightly.

Remove the rinds and mince the rashers coarsely. Very finely chop the turkey heart and liver. Soak the breadcrumbs in milk and squeeze out excess liquid. Lightly beat the eggs.

Combine the breadcrumbs, bacon, heart, liver, onion, parsley and beaten eggs and mix in the melted butter. Add the chestnuts and season with salt and plenty of pepper.

Spicy Chestnut Stuffing

900 g (2 lb) fresh chestnuts
2 chicken livers
225 g (8 oz) streaky bacon
1 small onion
1 small green pepper
75 g (3 oz) butter
450 g (1 lb) pork sausage-meat
Salt and freshly ground black pepper
Pinch of allspice, nutmeg and ginger
½ wineglass brandy

Enough for a 6·5–8 kilo (15–18 lb) bird

A triumph of a stuffing with a subtle, almost Eastern taste to it. If you have a freezer you can prepare it well in advance.

Make a cross slit down the flat sides of chestnuts. Place them on a baking sheet and roast in a moderately hot oven (200°C, 400°F, Reg. 6) for 12–15 minutes until the skins crack and become brittle. Peel off outer and inner skins while the chestnuts are still warm.

Place the skinned chestnuts in a saucepan, cover with cold water, bring to the boil and simmer for about ten minutes until just tender. Drain and put through the coarse blades of a mincing machine.

Very finely chop or mince the chicken livers. Remove rinds and finely mince the bacon rashers. Peel and finely chop the onion. Remove core and seeds from the pepper and finely chop the flesh.

Melt the butter in a frying pan, add the onion, pepper and bacon and cook over a low heat until the onion is soft and transparent. Combine all the ingredients in a bowl and mix well. Leave to cool and then place in polythene bag, seal, label and freeze. Thaw for about five hours in the refrigerator before using.

Savoury Stuffing

175 g (6 oz) long-grain rice
225 g (8 oz) firm button mushrooms
1 onion
1 green pepper
50 g (2 oz) butter
450 g (1 lb) sausage-meat
¼ teaspoon each of sage and thyme
Salt and freshly ground black pepper
2 eggs, beaten

Enough for a 4·5 kilo (10 lb) turkey

Cook the rice in boiling salted water for about 20 minutes until the grains are just tender. Rinse in cold water and drain well. Finely chop the mushrooms; peel and finely chop the onion; remove core and seeds from the green pepper and finely chop the flesh.

Melt the butter, add the onion and pepper and cook over a low heat for three minutes until soft. Add mushrooms and sausage-meat, mix in the herbs, season with salt and pepper and cook gently for five minutes. Leave to cool and mix in the eggs.

Apple Stuffing

1 onion
3 cooking apples
15 g ($\frac{1}{2}$ oz) butter
450 g (1 lb) pork sausage-meat
Turkey or goose heart and liver
1 tablespoon olive oil
150 ml ($\frac{1}{4}$ pint) orange juice
Grated rind of 1 lemon
2 tablespoons finely chopped parsley
100 g (4 oz) fresh white breadcrumbs
Salt and freshly ground black pepper

For goose or turkey

Peel and finely chop the onion; peel, core and chop the apples. Melt the butter, add the onion and cook over a low heat for three minutes. Add the apples and sausage-meat and cook over a medium heat until lightly browned. Remove from the heat.

Finely chop the heart and liver and cook in the olive oil for two minutes. Add to the apples and sausage-meat and mix in the orange juice, lemon rind, parsley and breadcrumbs. Season with salt and pepper.

Vegetables

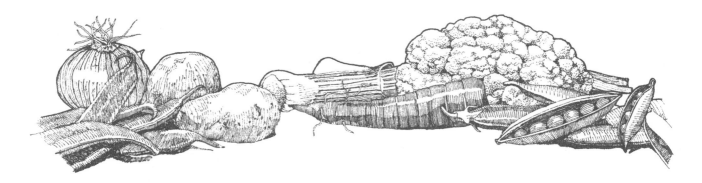

There is no doubt that all of us in today's world are going to have to cut down on our consumption of meat, poultry and fish if we have not in fact already done so. The price of these ingredients is bound to go on rising and although I am in no way an advocate of vegetarianism I am convinced that the best way to compromise in this direction is to supplement your main protein ingredients by partnering them with one or more interesting vegetable dishes. People in Britain, especially, have always been very conservative about vegetable cookery. It has tended to be plain and also, let us face it, somewhat dreary and often overcooked–everyone must have memories of school or boarding-house cabbage, soggy and swimming in soupy water. With this kind of vegetable you *need* hearty portions of a high protein ingredient to provide a satisfactory meal but if your vegetables are carefully and imaginatively cooked they become a positive asset, and a relatively inexpensive one, which enables you to halve the amount of meat, poultry or fish you serve with them. Forget about serving 'meat with two veg' and think more in terms of providing 'two veg with meat'.

Fresh vegetables help to provide a healthy and balanced diet and if you buy them when they are in season (rather than buying glasshouse or imported produce) they can be astonishingly good value for money. The most important thing is that they should be fresh and eaten as soon as possible after purchase; it is this point that the great chefs of the world, like Paul Bocuse and Michel Guérard, put such great emphasis on. Buy your vegetables as frequently as possible, rather than just once a week, and pick them carefully for firmness and colour and pay no attention to the greengrocer who tells you 'not to touch the goods'; sometimes the only way to tell whether or not a cauliflower is in its prime, whether courgettes are moist and firm or whether a tomato is really ripe, is to feel or smell it and, as a customer, I believe you have every right to do this.

Once bought, vegetables should be stored in a cool, dry and dark place and they should be prepared with care. When I specify in my recipes that a vegetable should be 'finely' chopped, I really do mean 'finely' and not hacked into chunks. The correct slicing, grating or chopping of vegetables can make all the difference to the consistency and success of a finished dish. When travelling in the Far East I learnt how much contrast of texture and even flavour can be derived from just one vegetable by the way in which it is prepared. *Al dente* is the phrase the Italians use for cooking vegetables just long enough to tenderise them without allowing them to become overcooked or 'mushy'. When in doubt undercook rather than overcook produce, remembering that it will continue to cook for a short time after you have removed it from the stove. Some people like to cook their fresh produce in plenty of fast-boiling salted water but I use a small amount of water (to which a little butter and salt has been added) covering most vegetables tightly so that they basically steam rather than boil. Drain all vegetables well and serve them as soon as possible.

Most of the flavour and goodness of vegetables lies nearest to the skin so peel them as thinly as possible and do not throw the peelings away—they can provide valuable goodness, flavouring and colour to a stock pot.

In this chapter the recipes are all for vegetable dishes, many of which can be served as a light supper or lunch main course but in the rest of the book you will find recipes where vegetables are combined with meat, fish and poultry to stretch the main ingredient and to give it extra flavour.

Cabbage with Onion Flakes

Serves 4

1 medium onion
1 small cabbage
40 g (1½ oz) butter
Salt, pepper and a pinch of nutmeg
2 tablespoons sour cream

Baked onion flakes can be used as here, to add flavour to another vegetable, or as a topping for minced meat or chicken dishes.

Peel and finely chop the onion. Spread it on a lightly greased baking sheet and bake in a moderate oven (180°C, 350°F, Reg. 4) for 20 minutes or until the onion is crisp and golden brown but not scorched. Spread on kitchen paper and leave to cool.

Shred the cabbage and cook it in 6 mm (¼ in) of boiling water for 8–10 minutes until just tender but still crisp. Drain off excess water and return the cabbage to a clean pan. Add the butter, season with salt, pepper and a pinch of nutmeg and mix lightly until the butter has melted. Mix in the sour cream and heat through without boiling. Arrange the cabbage in a serving dish and top with the onion flakes.

French Beans à la Grecque

Serves 4

450 g (1 lb) young French beans
Sauce as for mushrooms à la Grecque (p. 136)

Top and tail the beans and cook in boiling salted water for ten minutes only. Drain well.

Make the sauce, bring to the boil and simmer for five minutes. Add the beans and simmer for a further 5–8 minutes until they are tender but still firm. Remove the beans with a slotted spoon, bring the sauce back to the boil and cook over a high heat until it is reduced by about half.

Pour the sauce over the beans, cool and then refrigerate for at least four hours before serving.

Beetroot with Butter, Lemon Juice and Parsley

Serves 4

2 medium beetroots, cooked
40 g (1½ oz) butter
1 tablespoon granulated sugar
Juice of 1 lemon
2 tablespoons finely chopped parsley
Salt and paprika pepper

Cut the beetroot into thin matchstick strips. Melt the butter in a saucepan, add the sugar and cook over a low heat until the sugar has melted. Add the lemon juice and beetroot and cook for five minutes over a low heat, shaking the pan to prevent browning. Lightly mix in the parsley and season with a little salt and paprika.

Fèves à la Poulette

900 g (2 lb) broad beans
300 ml (½ pint) chicken stock
1 teaspoon sugar
Salt and white pepper
Bouquet garni (thyme, sage, savory,
*   marjoram, parsley)*
1 egg yolk
150 ml (5 fl oz) cream
1 tablespoon chopped parsley

Serves 4

The perfect accompaniment to a piece of boiled bacon or gammon.

Shell the beans and cook them in the boiling stock to which sugar, a pinch of salt and the bouquet garni have been added, until tender. Drain off and reserve the stock. Beat the egg yolk with the cream until smooth. Add a little of the reserved stock, beating all the time, then blend in the remainder. Heat the sauce over a low heat, stirring continuously until it thickens and reaches simmering point; do not allow to boil.

Add the beans and season with salt and white pepper. Top with parsley and serve at once.

Greens with Bacon

900 g (2 lb) greens
4 thin rashers streaky bacon
Salt
½ teaspoon lemon juice
Freshly ground black pepper

Serves 4

Fresh green vegetables are highly nutritious and also contain calcium, iron and vitamins A, B and C. But much of their goodness is lost through overcooking in too much water, so make sure that your greens are cooked in the minimum of water only long enough to tenderise them.

Trim off any tough stalks from the greens and wash if necessary. Fry the bacon without extra fat until crisp. Remove the rinds and return the rashers to the pan with the bacon fat and continue cooking over a low heat until all the fat has been extracted. Strain off the bacon fat and keep it warm. Crumble the rashers. Cover the bottom of a large saucepan with about 6 mm (¼ in) of water. Season with salt, bring to the boil and add the greens. Cook over a medium high heat for about 10–15 minutes until the greens are just tender.

Drain well and return to a clean pan. Add the lemon juice and season with pepper. Pour over the bacon fat, toss lightly to heat through and turn on to a heated serving dish. Sprinkle the top with crumbled bacon and serve at once.

Artichoke au Gratin

Serves 4

900 g (2 lb) Jerusalem artichokes
1 tablespoon lemon juice
450 ml (¾ pint) cheese sauce
50 g (2 oz) grated Gruyère and Parmesan
    cheese

Peel the artichokes and cover with cold water to which the lemon juice has been added. Bring to the boil and cook until just tender. Drain, cool and slice the artichokes and fold them in the cheese sauce.

    Transfer to a lightly greased baking dish, top with the grated cheese and bake in a moderately hot oven (200°C, 400°F, Reg. 6) for 20 minutes or until the dish is bubbling and the top golden brown.

Swedish Cabbage

Serves 4

900 g (2 lb) red cabbage
1 onion
2 cooking apples
25 g (1 oz) butter or dripping
1 teaspoon caraway seeds
2 tablespoons sugar
3 tablespoons white wine vinegar
150 ml (¼ pint) stock
Salt and pepper

This is superb with roast pork.

Shred the cabbage finely, removing all the core. Peel and finely chop the onion. Peel the apples, remove cores and cut the flesh into small dice. Heat the fat in a heavy saucepan, add the cabbage and cook gently for a few minutes. Mix in the onion and apples and cook until the onion is transparent.

    Stir in the remaining ingredients and season with salt and pepper. Simmer very gently for about 45 minutes until the cabbage is really tender and all the liquid has been absorbed. Check seasoning before serving.

Red Cabbage with Caraway Seeds

Serves 4

900 g (2 lb) red cabbage
1 onion
2 crisp eating apples
25 g (1 oz) butter or margarine, or 2
    tablespoons dripping
1½ teaspoons caraway seeds
2 tablespoons castor sugar
Salt
2½ tablespoons white wine vinegar
2½ tablespoons water

The perfect accompaniment to serve with sausages, with scalloped or mashed potatoes. Cook the cabbage slowly so as not to lose any of its rich red colour.

Remove hard core from the cabbage and finely shred the leaves. Peel and finely chop the onion. Peel, core and chop the apples. Melt the fat in a large heavy saucepan, add the cabbage and cook over a low heat until the fat is absorbed. Add the onion, apples, caraway seeds, sugar, salt, vinegar and water; mix well, cover tightly and cook over a low heat for about 15 minutes until the cabbage is soft. Remove the cover for the last ten minutes so that all the liquid is absorbed into the cabbage and it ends up moist but still slightly crunchy.

Mr Trumpington's Carrots

450 g (1 lb) young carrots
2 ripe tomatoes
50 g (2 oz) butter
1 teaspoon sugar
Salt and freshly ground black pepper
2 tablespoons chopped parsley
1 tablespoon flour
300 ml ($\frac{1}{2}$ pint) chicken stock

Serves 4

Scrape the carrots and cut into even 6 mm ($\frac{1}{4}$ in) thick slices. Cover the tomatoes with boiling water for two minutes, drain and slide off skins. Discard core and seeds and chop the flesh.

Melt the butter in a saucepan, add the carrots, tomatoes and sugar and season with salt and pepper. Mix in the parsley and stir over a low heat until the carrots are soft.

Remove the carrots and tomatoes with a slotted spoon and blend the flour into juices in the pan. Gradually mix in the stock, stirring continuously over a medium high heat until the sauce comes to the boil and is thick and smooth. Simmer for five minutes. Check seasoning, lightly mix in the carrots and tomatoes, heat through and serve at once.

Oriental Carrots

900 g (2 lb) carrots
1 small onion
100 g (4 oz) seedless raisins
1 tablespoon vegetable oil
2 teaspoons curry powder
100 g (4 oz) butter
Salt and freshly ground black pepper
3 teaspoons sugar
Finely chopped parsley

Serves 5–6

Carrots and potatoes are two of the few vegetables which, either young or old, are with us all the year round. Although full of nutrition they can become boring but they do respond well to such interesting flavouring as there is in the following dish.

Peel the carrots and slice them very thinly. Peel and finely chop the onion. Cover the raisins with cold water and leave to soak. Heat the oil in a heavy saucepan, add the onion and cook over a low heat until it is soft and transparent. Add the curry powder and stir over a low heat for one minute. Add the butter and heat until melted. Mix in the carrots tossing them well. Press a piece of lightly buttered greaseproof paper over the carrots, cover the saucepan with a tight-fitting lid and cook the carrots over as low a heat as possible for half an hour.

Drain and add the raisins and continue to cook the carrots for a further 30 minutes or until they are tender. Season with salt, pepper and sugar, tossing the carrots lightly, and serve topped with a sprinkling of finely chopped parsley.

Cauliflower Cheese

Serves 6

1 large cauliflower
100 g (4 oz) ham or 175 g (6 oz) cooked
   smoked haddock
2 large tomatoes
1 onion
40 g (1½ oz) butter
2 tablespoons flour
300 ml (½ pint) milk
2 eggs, separated
175 g (6 oz) grated Cheddar cheese
½ teaspoon made English mustard
Salt, pepper and a pinch of cayenne

Simple old favourites like this should not be overlooked. Well-made cauliflower cheese can be delicious enough to rival the most sophisticated and expensive of dishes. I add a small quantity of ham or flaked smoked haddock to give an additional flavour.

Simmer the cauliflower until tender, cool and divide into florets. Chop the ham or flake the haddock. Peel and chop the tomatoes; peel and finely chop onion.

Heat the butter in a large saucepan. Add the onion and cook over a low heat until soft and transparent. Add the flour, mix well and gradually blend in the milk. Stir continuously over a medium high heat until the sauce comes to the boil and is thick and smooth. Lower the heat and beat in the egg yolks, half the cheese, mustard and seasoning. Add the cauliflower, ham or haddock and tomatoes. Lightly fold in the egg whites, beaten until stiff.

Transfer to a fire-proof serving dish, top with the remaining cheese and bake in a moderate oven (180°C, 350°F, Reg. 4) for 30 minutes until risen and golden brown.

Braised Celery Hotch-potch

Serves 4–6

1 large or 2 smaller heads celery
2 carrots
1 medium onion
Salt and pepper
25 g (1 oz) butter
200 ml (7½ fl oz) water
1 chicken stock cube
1 teaspoon lemon juice

Because this vegetable dish is made of a mixture of vegetables it makes an admirable partner to any rather plain or mundane main course and provides the main interest point of a meal. A touch of lemon juice brings out the flavour of all the vegetables.

Separate the sticks of celery, trim off leaves and any tough fibres and cut them into 2·5 cm (1 in) pieces. Peel and thinly slice the carrots; peel and finely chop the onion. Blanch the celery in boiling salted water for about three minutes and drain well.

Arrange the vegetables in a buttered fire-proof dish, season with salt and pepper and dot with the butter. Heat the water, add the chicken stock cube and lemon juice and stir until the stock cube is dissolved. Pour the liquid over the vegetables, cover with foil and bake in a moderately hot oven (400°C, 600°F, Reg. 6) for 25–35 minutes until the vegetables are tender and have absorbed most of the liquid.

Celery in Cheese Sauce

1 large head celery
50 g (2 oz) butter
2 tablespoons flour
300 ml (½ pint) milk
75 g (3 oz) grated Cheddar cheese
4 tablespoons double cream
Celery salt and freshly ground black pepper
Pinch of nutmeg

Serves 4

To make this an inexpensive main course add some chopped ham to the sauce with the celery.

Wash the celery if necessary, divide up the sticks and trim off the leaves. Chop the sticks into 2·5 cm (1 in) pieces. Place in cold water with a little salt, bring to the boil and simmer until tender. Drain well.

Melt the butter, add the flour and mix well. Gradually blend in the milk, stirring continuously over a medium high heat until the sauce is thick and smooth. Mix in three-quarters of the cheese and all the cream; season with celery salt, pepper and nutmeg. Mix in the celery and turn into a heated serving dish. Sprinkle over the remaining cheese and brown quickly in a hot oven (220°C, 425°F, Reg. 7).

Purée of Florentine Fennel

2 large fennel roots
Juice of ½ lemon
25 g (1 oz) butter
4 tablespoons cream
Salt and freshly ground black pepper

Serves 4

This goes well with fish and chicken dishes.

Remove any tough outer layers and green leaves from the roots, then cut into thin slices. Combine the lemon juice with boiling salted water, add the fennel and cook for about 25 minutes until tender. Drain well and purée in a liquidiser or through a food mill. Melt the butter, add the fennel purée and heat through, mixing well. Blend in the cream and season well with salt and pepper.

Braised Cucumber

2 onions
1 cucumber
2 rashers bacon
450 ml (¾ pint) stock
Pinch of chervil
Salt and freshly ground black pepper

Serves 4

Peel and chop the onions. Peel the cucumber and cut the flesh into four lengthwise, and then into 5 cm (2 in) lengths. Remove rinds from the bacon, and most of the fat, cut the flesh into 6 mm (¼ in) strips and blanch in boiling water for three minutes; drain well.

Arrange onions, cucumber and bacon in a fire-proof baking dish, pour over the stock, add the chervil and season with a little salt and pepper. Cover tightly with foil and braise in a moderate oven (180°C, 350°F, Reg. 4) for 45 minutes until the cucumber is transparent but not mushy.

Old-fashioned Dandelion Greens

Serves 4

4 thin rashers streaky bacon
1-litre (2-pint) bowl loosely filled with
     dandelion leaves
1 hard-boiled egg
4 spring onions
4 egg yolks
5 tablespoons white wine vinegar
5 tablespoons water
2 tablespoons castor sugar
½ teaspoon salt
2 teaspoons dry English mustard
150 ml (5 fl oz) carton soured cream
Freshly ground pepper

Remove rind from the rashers and finely chop the bacon. Fry until crisp, without any additional fat, and drain well on kitchen paper.

Pick over the dandelion leaves, wash, shake to remove excess water, pat dry on kitchen paper and break into small pieces with your hands. Chop the hard-boiled egg. Finely chop the spring onions.

Beat the egg yolks and combine them, in the top of a double saucepan, with the vinegar, water, sugar, salt and mustard. Cook over simmering water, stirring continuously, until the sauce thickens enough to coat the back of a wooden spoon. Remove from the heat, stir in the soured cream and season with pepper. Add the chopped onions and fried bacon, pour over the leaves while still hot, toss lightly and top with the chopped hard-boiled egg. Serve at once.

Fried Marinated Courgettes

Serves 4

6 courgettes
Olive oil for frying
2 tomatoes
200 ml (8 fl oz) white wine vinegar
100 ml (4 fl oz) olive oil
Small clove garlic (optional)
5 chopped fresh leaves basil or 1 tablespoon
     dried
Salt and freshly ground black pepper
1 tablespoon chopped dill
1 tablespoon chopped parsley

This is one of those useful vegetable dishes that can, and should, be made well in advance, as it improves by being kept in the refrigerator for at least 24 hours before serving. Serve with any roast meat, hot or cold.

Cut the courgettes into finger-thick slices and fry gently in olive oil until golden but not mushy. Drain well on absorbent paper and arrange in a serving dish.

Peel the tomatoes (cover with boiling water for two minutes and slide off the skins). Remove the core and seeds and finely chop the flesh. Combine the olive oil and vinegar, add the crushed garlic and the basil. Mix well, add the chopped tomato, season with salt and pepper and pour this dressing over the courgettes. Sprinkle over the parsley and dill.

Leeks with Shredded Cabbage in a Supreme Sauce

8 medium leeks
1 small savoy cabbage
40 g (1½ oz) butter
1 tablespoon flour
300 ml (½ pint) chicken stock
Salt and pepper
Pinch of nutmeg
1 teaspoon lemon juice
150 ml (5 fl oz) double cream
1 tablespoon finely chopped parsley

Serves 4

A marvellous way of producing 'two veg' in one to serve with almost any main course, meat, poultry or fish–a good autumn dish.

Wash and trim the leeks, removing the outside leaves and leaving the leeks whole. Remove the outer leaves from the cabbage and finely shred the heart. Cook the leeks until just tender in boiling salted water. Remove the leeks from the water, drain well and keep them warm on a serving dish. Bring the water back to the boil, throw in the cabbage and cook, without a cover, for about three minutes until just tender. Drain well.

Melt the butter in a saucepan, add the flour and mix well. Gradually add the stock, stirring continuously over a medium high heat until the sauce is thick and smooth. Season with salt and pepper and a pinch of nutmeg and simmer over a low heat for three minutes. Add lemon juice and cream and heat through without boiling. Mix in cabbage and as soon as the sauce is hot pour it over the leeks. Garnish with the parsley.

Leek Pie

450 g (1 lb) leeks
40 g (1½ oz) butter
1½ tablespoons flour
300 ml (½ pint) milk
Salt and freshly ground black pepper
Pinch of nutmeg
25 g (1 oz) grated Cheddar cheese
2 large ripe tomatoes
450 g (1 lb) cooked, mashed potato

Serves 4

Clean the leeks, cut them into 5 cm (2 in) lengths and cook in boiling water until just tender. Drain well.

Melt two thirds of the butter in a saucepan, add the flour and mix well. Gradually blend in the milk, stirring continuously over a medium high heat until the sauce comes to the boil and is thick and smooth. Season with salt, pepper and nutmeg, mix in the grated cheese and cook for two minutes. Add leeks to the sauce and mix lightly.

Thinly slice the tomatoes. Arrange half of them in a lightly greased pie dish, cover with the leek mixture and top with remaining tomatoes. Spread over the mashed potato, brush with the remaining butter, melted, and bake in a moderately hot oven (190°C, 375°F, Reg. 5) for about 20 minutes until the pie is piping hot and the top nicely golden brown.

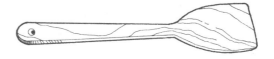

Devonshire Leek Pie

Serves 4

225 g (8 oz) shortcrust pastry
6 large leeks
300 ml (½ pint) milk
Salt and pepper
5 tablespoons single cream

Roll out the pastry to make a 'lid' for a large pie dish. Wash and trim the leeks and cut the white part (and a little of the green) into 2·5 cm (1 in) pieces.

Put into the milk with salt and pepper and simmer gently until the leeks are just tender. Pour into the pie dish and add the cream.

Cover with the pastry and bake at 200°C (400°F, Reg. 6) for 30 minutes. Serve hot with cold meat.

Ragoût of Cucumbers

Serves 6

2 large onions
2 cucumbers
25 g (1 oz) butter
4 tablespoons gravy or strong stock
2 tablespoons white wine
⅛ teaspoon mace
Salt and white pepper
1 tablespoon flour
15 g (½ oz) butter, softened
2 tablespoons finely chopped parsley

A cool, delicate vegetable to serve with chicken or fish dishes.

Peel and finely chop the onions. Peel the cucumbers and cut the flesh into 1 cm (½ in) dice. Melt the butter in a saucepan, add the onion and cucumber and cook over a low heat for 15 minutes, stirring occasionally to prevent browning. Add the gravy, white wine and mace, season with salt and pepper and cook for a further two minutes to incorporate the flavourings.

Blend the flour with the softened butter until smooth, mix into the ragoût and stir gently over a medium heat until the sauce has thickened and is smooth and shining. Sprinkle with parsley and serve.

To cook ahead: cook as above but leave the parsley to the last minute. Cover with foil and reheat in a moderate oven (180°C, 350°F, Reg. 4) for about 15 minutes until hot through. Sprinkle with parsley just before serving.

Onion Goulash

Serves 4

2 medium onions
1 medium cabbage
350 g (12 oz) tomatoes or 400 g (14 oz) can tomatoes
2 tablespoons olive oil or good dripping
Salt and pepper
¾ tablespoon paprika

Peel and thinly slice the onions. Very thinly shred the cabbage. Peel the tomatoes by dipping them in boiling water for two minutes and cut them into fairly small cubes.

Heat the oil or dripping in a heavy pan, add the onions and cabbage and cook over a medium heat, stirring every now and then to prevent burning, until the onions are soft and golden brown. Add the tomatoes: season with salt, pepper and paprika. Cover and simmer for 20 minutes.

Onion Ring Fritters

100 g (4 oz) flour
½ teaspoon salt
150 ml (¼ pint) light ale
1 egg
1 large onion
Oil for deep-frying

Serves 4

Combine the flour, salt, ale and egg and beat with a whisk until smooth. Peel the onion, cut into thin slices and divide carefully into rings. Coat the rings, one by one, in batter, drop them into very hot deep cooking oil and cook until crisp and brown. Fry only a few rings at a time without overcrowding in the pan. Drain on kitchen paper to remove excess fat and keep them warm.

Onions à la Grecque

675 g (1½ lb) small onions or shallots
6 juniper berries
300 ml (½ pint) dry white wine
150 ml (¼ pint) water
2 tablespoon castor sugar
5 tablespoons olive oil
1 tablespoon lemon juice
1 teaspoon finely grated lemon rind
2 tablespoons tomato ketchup
2 bay leaves
2 teaspoons finely chopped basil (or one teaspoon dried)
1 teaspoon dried oregano
Salt and freshly ground black pepper
2 tablespoons finely chopped parsley

Serves 5–6

Peel the onions or shallots. Crush the juniper berries. Combine the white wine, water, sugar, olive oil, lemon juice, lemon rind and tomato ketchup in a saucepan and mix well. Add the bay leaves, juniper berries, basil and oregano and season with pepper. Bring to the boil and add the onions.

Simmer the onions in the sauce over a low heat for about 20 minutes until they are just tender. Remove from the sauce with a slotted spoon and bring the sauce back to the boil again. Boil over high heat until reduced by about half and then strain through a fine sieve. Add the parsley, check for seasoning and pour the sauce over the onions. Refrigerate for at least four hours before serving.

Oven-fried Parsnips with Shallots

450 g (1 lb) parsnips
1 tablespoon lemon juice
Salt and freshly ground black pepper
Olive or vegetable oil
12 shallots or pickling onions
Fresh parsley to garnish

Serves 4–6

Peel the parsnips and cut them lengthwise into thin slices. Marinate the slices in lemon juice, salt and pepper for 30 minutes, drain well and pat dry on kitchen paper. Peel the shallots.

Heat about 1 cm (½ in) of oil in a shallow baking dish, put the vegetables into it and cook in a hot oven for 30 minutes until golden brown.

Drain off the oil and arrange the vegetables on a serving dish; sprinkle over a little finely chopped parsley and serve at once.

New Potatoes in their Skins

Serves 6

1·8 kilos (4 lb) new potatoes
50 g (2 oz) butter
1 tablespoon finely chopped mint
2 teaspoons coarse salt
Freshly ground black pepper

Wash the potatoes carefully, removing the dirt but not damaging the skins. Cover them with cold water, bring to the boil and cook over a medium high heat for about 20–30 minutes until just tender when pricked with a fork. Drain well.

Melt the butter in a saucepan. Add the potatoes and shake the pan over the heat until they are coated with butter. Add the mint, toss lightly and transfer to a heated serving dish. Sprinkle over the coarse salt and some pepper before serving.

Parsnips au Gratin

Serves 6

900 g (2 lb) parsnips
Juice of ½ lemon
½ teaspoon dry English mustard
50 g (2 oz) butter
2 tablespoons single cream or top of the milk
Salt, pepper and a pinch of nutmeg
2 tablespoons fresh white breadcrumbs
50 g (2 oz) grated Cheddar cheese

This goes really well with any ham, bacon or sausage dish, and can take the place of potatoes.

Peel the parsnips, chop them roughly and boil in salted water to which the lemon juice has been added for about 30 minutes until tender. Drain well and mash until smooth with a potato masher. Mix in the mustard. Add half the butter and the cream and beat well until the mixture is really smooth. Season with salt, pepper and nutmeg.

Spread in a lightly greased baking dish, top with breadcrumbs mixed with the cheese and dot with the remaining butter. Bake for about 20 minutes in a moderately hot oven (200°C, 400°F, Reg. 6) until hot through and golden brown.

Purée of Parsnip and Celery

Serves 4

1 head celery
1 large parsnip
Salt
2 eggs
150 ml (¼ pint) milk
100 g (4 oz) grated Cheddar cheese
Freshly ground black pepper
Ground nutmeg
Breadcrumbs

An unusual and extremely delicious winter vegetable dish. The sharpness of the celery counteracts the slight sweetness of the parsnip to make this a good partner to almost any main course.

Clean the celery, trim off tops of sticks and leaves and roughly chop the sticks. Peel and roughly chop the parsnip. Place both vegetables in a saucepan, cover with water, add a little salt, bring to the boil and simmer for about 30 minutes until tender. Drain well and purée through a food mill or in a liquidiser.

Beat the eggs until smooth. Beat the milk, eggs and cheese into the vegetable purée and season with pepper and pinch of nutmeg. Pile the purée into a baking dish, sprinkle with breadcrumbs and bake in a moderate oven (180°C, 350°F, Reg. 4) for 15 minutes until brown.

Parsnip Cakes

1 large parsnip
15 g (½ oz) butter
2 tablespoons flour
Salt and pepper
Dripping for frying

Serves 4

In the old days these used to be served for breakfast in farmhouse kitchens. They go well with any bacon or ham dishes.

Peel and roughly shop the parsnip and cook in boiling salted water until tender. Drain and mash with a potato masher until smooth and beat in the butter and flour until the mixture is well blended. Season with salt and pepper.

Melt just a little dripping in a really heavy frying pan, drop the parsnip mixture in spoonfuls into the pan and fry the cakes until golden brown on both sides.

Pot of Peas

1 rasher fat bacon
1 small onion
225 g (8 oz) can tomatoes
1 teaspoon honey
Salt and freshly ground black pepper
450 g (1 lb) peas, shelled
1 tablespoon finely chopped fresh mint

Serves 4–6

Remove rind and finely chop the bacon rasher; peel and finely chop the onion; roughly chop the tomatoes (I do this with a pair of scissors in the tin).

Cook the bacon, without additional fat, over a low heat until the fat runs and the bacon is beginning to shrivel. Add the onion and continue to cook over a low heat until soft and transparent. Add the tomatoes and honey, season with salt and pepper, bring to the boil and simmer for ten minutes. Add the peas and simmer until they are just cooked. Mix in the mint, check seasoning and serve at once.

Green Pea Soufflé

450 g (1 lb) frozen peas
2 leaves mint
40 g (1½ oz) butter
25 g (1 oz) flour
150 ml (¼ pint) milk
4 eggs, separated
Salt, pepper and paprika

Serves 4–6

Cook the peas until tender, with the mint, in boiling salted water. Drain well and purée through a sieve, a food mill or in a liquidiser.

Melt the butter in a saucepan. Add the flour and mix well. Gradually add the milk, beating vigorously until the mixture is thick and smooth. Leave to cool for 2–3 minutes and then beat in the egg yolks one by one. Mix in the pea purée and season with salt, pepper and a little paprika.

Beat the egg whites until stiff, fold them into the soufflé base and pour the mixture into a greased soufflé dish (it should be only just over half full to allow for rising).

Bake in a moderately hot oven (200°C, 400°F, Reg. 6) until well risen, slightly browned and a little cracked on the surface–about 30–35 minutes.

Mushrooms à la Grecque

Serves 4

450 g (1 lb) small firm button mushrooms
2 cloves garlic
2 ripe tomatoes
4 tablespoons olive oil
150 ml (¼ pint) dry white wine
150 ml (¼ pint) water
8 coriander seeds
2 bay leaves
1 sprig thyme
2 tablespoons tomato ketchup
2 teaspoons sugar
Salt and freshly ground black pepper

Cut the mushroom stalks off level with the caps. Crush the garlic through a garlic press or with a fork. Cover the tomatoes with boiling water for two minutes, then drain and peel. Cut out any tough core and finely chop the flesh. Combine the tomatoes, olive oil, wine, water, coriander seeds, herbs and garlic in a saucepan. Add the tomato ketchup and sugar and season with salt and pepper.

Bring to the boil, mix well and simmer for five minutes. Add the mushrooms and cook over a low heat for 4–5 minutes until they are just tender but not soggy. Remove the mushrooms with a slotted spoon. Bring the sauce back to the boil and boil hard until it is reduced by half. Remove thyme and bay leaves and pour the sauce over the mushrooms. This can be served hot or cold and makes a good first course. Florets of cauliflower, young French beans, courgettes and other young vegetables can be cooked in the same way.

Basic Potato Cakes

Serves 4

450 g (1 lb) mashed poatoes
15 g (½ oz) butter, melted
1 tablespoon grated raw onion
2 tablespoons flour
Salt and pepper
Bacon fat or dripping

Mix the mashed potatoes with the melted butter, grated onion and flour. Season with salt and pepper. Shape the potato mixture into a roll on a well-floured board and cut into 2·5 cm (1 in) thick slices. Press out to form flat cakes about half as thick.

Fry in hot fat until crisp and golden brown on both sides. The cakes will retain their shape better if they are chilled in a refrigerator for an hour or more before frying.

Herby Potato Cakes
Add 1 tablespoon finely chopped parsley and a pinch of dried sage to the basic recipe.

Cheese Potato Cakes
Add 50 g (2 oz) finely grated Cheddar cheese to the basic recipe.

Bacon Potato Cakes
Add two bacon rashers, crisply fried, drained on kitchen paper and crumbled, to the basic recipe.

Sausage and Potato Cakes
Replace 100 g (¼ lb) mashed potatoes with the same amount of sausage-meat and follow the basic recipe.

Potato, Onion and Tomato Pie

Serves 2–3

450 g (1 lb) potatoes
2 medium onions
1 small leek
3–4 tomatoes
70 g (2½ oz) butter
1½ tablespoons flour
300 ml (½ pint) milk
100 g (4 oz) grated Cheddar cheese
1 tablespoon made English mustard
Pinch of nutmeg and basil
Salt and freshly ground black pepper

Peel the potatoes and parboil them for 15 minutes, leave to cool and then cut into 6 mm (¼ in) thick slices. Peel and very finely slice the onions. Finely chop the leek. Peel and slice the tomatoes. Melt half the butter in a saucepan, add the flour and mix well. Gradually blend in the milk, stirring continuously over a medium heat until the sauce is thick and smooth. Add half the cheese, the mustard, nutmeg and basil, season with salt and pepper and stir over a low heat until the cheese has melted.

Arrange a layer of potato slices in a lightly greased shallow baking dish, cover with some of the onion, leek and tomato and pour over some of the sauce. Arrange the remaining vegetables in the same way, reserving a layer of potatoes for the topping. Sprinkle over the remaining cheese, dot with the remaining butter and bake in a moderate oven (180°C, 350°F, Reg. 4) for about 30 minutes until the top is golden brown.

Stuffed Baked Potatoes

Serves 6

6 large potatoes
Salt and pepper
75 g (3 oz) butter
225 g (8 oz) cream cheese
1 teaspoon mixed herbs
1 tablespoon finely chopped chives

Scrub potatoes, prick skins with a fork, dry well and rub with coarse salt. Bake in a moderate oven (190°C, 375°F, Reg. 5) for 1½ hours.

Cut a slice from the top of each potato, scoop out the inside into a bowl and mash until smooth with the butter, cheese and herbs. Season with salt and pepper and pile the mixture back into the potato cases. Bake for a further 20 minutes before serving.

Potato and Green Pepper Casserole

Serves 4–6

15 g (½ oz) butter
675 g (1½ lb) potatoes
1 large green pepper
2 rashers bacon
Salt and pepper
300 ml (½ pint) milk

Rub the sides of a casserole dish with a little of the butter. Peel the potatoes and cut into thin slices. Remove core and seeds from the pepper and finely chop the flesh. Remove rinds and cut the bacon rashers into thin strips.

Layer the potatoes and pepper in the casserole. Season with a little salt and pepper, pour over the milk and top with bacon strips. Dot with the remaining butter.

Bake the casserole in a moderate oven (180°C, 350°F, Reg. 4) for 30–40 minutes until the potatoes are tender.

Potato and Apple Casserole

Serves 4

450 g (1 lb) potatoes
3 cooking apples
1 medium onion
25 g (1 oz) butter
Salt and pepper
150 ml ($\frac{1}{4}$ pint) milk
5 tablespoons single cream

Peel and thinly slice the potatoes. Peel, core and thinly slice the apples. Peel and finely chop the onion. Arrange layers of potato, apple and onion in a buttered baking dish. Dot each layer with a little butter, season with salt and pepper and finish with a layer of potatoes.

Pour over the milk and cream and bake in a moderate oven (180°C, 350°F, Reg. 4) for about 40 minutes until the potatoes are soft through and the top is a good golden brown.

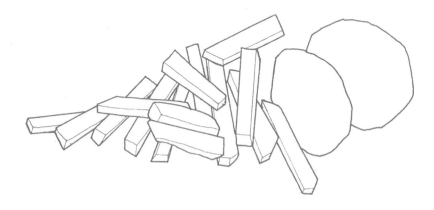

Pisto

Serves 6

2 large onions
2 cloves garlic
2 red or green peppers
3 large ripe tomatoes
4 courgettes
225–350 g (8–12 oz) cooked potatoes
4 tablespoons olive oil
Salt and freshly ground black pepper
1 tablespoon very finely chopped parsley
Pinch of oregano

When new potatoes are past their first flush of deliciousness this Spanish dish makes a good alternative to plain boiled or mashed potatoes.

Peel and thinly slice the onions and divide into rings. Crush the garlic. Remove the core and seeds of the peppers and cut the flesh into thin strips. Cover the tomatoes with boiling water, leave to stand for two minutes and then slide off the skins. Roughly chop the flesh. Cut the courgettes and potatoes into small cubes.

Heat the olive oil in a deep frying pan. Add the onion rings and garlic and cook over very low heat until the onion is transparent and pale yellow. Add the peppers and cook for further ten minutes until soft. Add the courgettes and tomatoes, season with salt and pepper, cover and simmer for 20 minutes. Add the potatoes, parsley and oregano, stir gently and cook for a further ten minutes.

Hot Potato Salad with Anchovies

Serves 4

900 g (2 lb) potatoes
3 spring onions
4 anchovy fillets
1 tablespoon finely chopped parsley
Freshly ground black pepper
300 ml (½ pint) mayonnaise

Peel the potatoes and cut them into small, even dice. Finely chop the spring onions. Drain and finely chop the anchovies. Cook the potatoes in boiling salted water until just tender and drain well.

Turn into a saucepan, mix in the spring onions, half the parsley and the anchovies, add a generous grinding of pepper and fold in the mayonnaise. Heat through, turn on to a serving dish and sprinkle with the remaining parsley.

Potato Pie

Serves 4

675 g (1½ lb) potatoes
1 clove garlic
1 large onion
3 tablespoons milk
2 tablespoons flour
Salt, pepper and a pinch of marjoram
25 g (1 oz) butter

A savoury potato pie makes a good accompaniment to roast meat, grills or cold dishes.

Peel the potatoes, grate through a coarse grater, rinse in cold water and drain well. Crush the garlic; peel and finely chop the onion.

Combine the milk and flour, mix well, season with salt and pepper and add a pinch of marjoram. Mix all the ingredients together, turn into a well-greased pie dish or casserole and dot with the butter.

Bake in a hot oven (220°C, 425°F, Reg. 7) for 30–35 minutes.

Crisp-Top Vegetable Pie

Serves 2–3

4 onions
1 clove garlic
1 green pepper
2 anchovy fillets
450 g (1 lb) boiled potatoes
425 g (15 oz) can tomatoes
2 tablespoons olive oil
Pinch of oregano
Freshly ground black pepper
1 tablespoon finely chopped parsley
50 g (2 oz) grated Cheddar cheese
15 g (½ oz) grated Parmesan cheese
1 packet potato crisps

Peel and very thinly slice the onions and crush the garlic clove. Remove core and seeds from green pepper and thinly slice the flesh. Very finely chop the anchovy fillets. Slice the potatoes. Drain off and reserve the tomato juice and slice the tomatoes.

Heat the oil in a heavy frying pan. Add the onion and garlic and cook for two minutes. Add the green pepper and cook over a medium low heat, without browning, until the onions are soft and pale yellow. Add the tomatoes, tomato juice, anchovies and oregano, season with pepper, cover and cook over a low heat for 15 minutes. Add the potatoes and parsley, stir lightly and heat through. Transfer to a shallow baking dish, top with the Cheddar and Parmesan cheese mixed with the crushed potato crisps and finish under a grill until the cheese melts and the topping is crisp.

Fried Potato and Apple Pancake

675 g (1½ lb) potatoes
1 cooking apple
1 tablespoon olive oil
15 g (½ oz) butter
Salt and freshly ground black pepper
¼ teaspoon ground nutmeg
Pinch of rosemary
1 tablespoon finely chopped parsley

Serves 6

A good combination which goes well with almost any main course, but especially with pork.

Peel the potatoes and cut into paper-thin slices, rinse in cold water and drain well. Peel, core and thinly slice the apple.

Heat the olive oil and butter together in a large frying pan until very hot. Add the potatoes and apple in one layer, season with salt and pepper and sprinkle with nutmeg and rosemary.

Cook over a high heat for eight minutes, then cover the pan, lower heat to medium and continue to cook for 20 minutes or until the potatoes are tender. Invert the pancake on to a heated serving dish and sprinkle with chopped parsley before serving.

Potato Kephtides

225 g (8 oz) tomatoes
4 spring onions
450 g (1 lb) cold mashed potatoes
40 g (1½ oz) flour
Salt and pepper
Dripping or olive oil

Serves 4

The most usual form of *kephtides* are made from meat–a sort of highly spiced hamburger grilled over charcoal. Travelling through Romania a few years ago we used to stop by roadside stalls and buy these and other highly seasoned meat or sausage combinations whenever we felt peckish. This recipe, however, is based on cold mashed potatoes and makes a marvellous way to use up any of those valuable leftovers. Serve the cakes with crisply fried bacon, sausages, or topped by a fried egg.

Peel and finely chop the tomatoes; very finely chop the spring onions. Mix the potatoes with tomatoes, flour and spring onions and season generously with salt and pepper. (If the mashed potatoes were not made with butter add 15 g (½ oz) melted butter as well.)

Refrigerate for about 30 minutes and then shape, with well-floured hands, into eight flat cakes about 6 mm (¼ in) thick.

Place the cakes on a baking sheet that has been well greased with dripping or oil and brush over the tops with more oil or melted dripping. Bake in a moderately hot oven (200°C, 400°F, Reg. 6) for about 15–20 minutes until they are crisp and light golden on top. Slide them off the baking sheet with a broad spatula so that they do not break up.

Spinach and Bacon Tart

450 g (1 lb) frozen spinach
25 g (1 oz) butter
2 eggs, beaten
3 tablespoons double cream
4 rashers streaky bacon
Salt and freshly ground black pepper
Finely grated nutmeg and ground saffron
25 cm (10 in) baked pastry case
50 g (2 oz) grated Gruyère or Cheddar cheese
Paprika pepper

Serves 6–8

The tart can be served hot as a first course, with a home-made tomato sauce as a main course, or left to cool and served cold with salad for a lunch or picnic dish.

Cook the spinach in a little boiling salted water until tender. Drain really well, pressing out excess liquid with the back of a wooden spoon. Chop with kitchen scissors, mix with the butter and leave to cool.

Beat the eggs with the cream until light and smooth. Remove rinds and chop the rashers. Fry the bacon without extra fat until crisp and drain on kitchen paper.

Add bacon and beaten eggs to the spinach, season with salt, pepper, a pinch of ground saffron and a little nutmeg and mix well. Fill the pastry case with spinach mixture, top with grated cheese and bake in a moderately hot oven (200°C, 400°F, Reg. 6) for about ten minutes until puffed and golden brown. Sprinkle with a little paprika pepper before serving.

Spinaci alla Borghese

900 g (2 lb) spinach
4 anchovy fillets
1 clove garlic
40 g (1½ oz) butter
¼ teaspoon freshly ground black pepper
Pinch of ground nutmeg

Serves 4

This way of cooking spinach is a winner, providing the spinach is cooked *al dente* and not allowed to subside into the soggy mush one so often gets.

Wash the spinach and shake well to remove excess water. Put in a large pan without extra water and cook over medium heat, stirring once or twice, for no longer than five minutes or until the spinach has just softened. Drain off any water in the pan.

Drain the anchovy fillets and chop finely. Peel the garlic clove and crush through a garlic press or with the back of a fork.

Melt the butter in a saucepan, add the anchovy fillets and garlic and cook over a low heat, stirring continuously, until the anchovies disappear into the butter and the garlic is quite transparent.

Add the spinach, season with pepper and nutmeg and toss over a low flame until hot through.

Spinach Lorenzo

Serves 4

450 g (1 lb) frozen spinach
1 small onion
1 large clove garlic
15 g (½ oz) butter
1 tablespoon lemon juice
Good pinch of cinnamon and paprika
Salt and pepper
Fried bread

Cook the frozen spinach in a little boiling salted water until hot through; drain well and chop.

Very finely chop the onion and garlic and cook in the butter on a low heat until transparent. Add the lemon juice and spinach; flavour with cinnamon and paprika and season with salt and pepper. Cover and simmer for five minutes.

Put the cooked spinach in a serving dish and surround with triangles of fried bread.

Glazed Turnip

Serves 4

1 large turnip
Salt and freshly ground black pepper
25 g (1 oz) butter
1 tablespoon soft brown sugar
2 tablespoons finely chopped parsley

Peel the turnip, cut it into 6 mm (¼ in) thick slices and then into thin sticks. Cook in plenty of fast-boiling salted water until cooked but still firm—about 20 minutes. Drain well.

Melt the butter in a saucepan, add the sugar and mix well, stirring over a medium heat until the sugar has melted and the mixture is syrupy. Add the turnip sticks and cook gently, shaking the pan to prevent sticking, for 10–15 minutes until the syrup is absorbed and the sticks are glazed. Lightly mix in the parsley and season generously with pepper.

Vegetable Casserole

Serves 4

675 g (1½ lb) potatoes
2 green peppers
1 medium onion
225 g (½ lb) tomatoes
175 g (6 oz) grated Cheddar cheese
1 tablespoon finely chopped parsley
Salt and pepper
300 ml (½ pint) stock
150 ml (5 fl oz) single cream

Peel and thinly slice the potatoes. Remove core and seeds from the peppers and cut the flesh into thin strips. Peel and thinly slice the onion. Skin the tomatoes and cut them into thin slices.

Arrange a third of the potatoes, peppers, onion and tomatoes in the bottom of a greased casserole dish; cover with a third of the grated cheese and finely chopped parsley. Sprinkle with a little salt and pepper and cover with two more similar layers of vegetables topped with cheese and parsley.

Combine the stock and cream and pour them over the ingredients. Cover tightly and cook in a moderate oven (180°C, 350°F, Reg. 4) for 45 minutes. Remove the cover and cook for a further 15 minutes to brown the top.

Stuffed Mediterranean Tomatoes

4 large ripe tomatoes
2 rashers bacon
1 small onion
2 cloves garlic (or large pinch dried oregano)
4 anchovy fillets, drained
2 tablespoons olive or vegetable oil
10 tablespoons coarsely grated fresh white breadcrumbs
2½ tablespoons finely chopped parsley
Salt and freshly ground black pepper
A little extra oil

Serves 4

If you like the strong sunshine flavouring of garlic you can add plenty of it to this dish. Otherwise use oregano which goes well with any cooked tomato dish. It makes a good first course, or can be served as an accompaniment to a main dish, providing that is a fairly plain one with ingredients that will not be swamped by the rich taste and aroma of the tomatoes.

Cut the tomatoes in half and carefully scoop out core, seeds and some of the pulp, leaving a firm case. Arrange the cases in a small oiled fire-proof dish.

Remove rinds and finely mince the bacon rashers. Peel and finely chop the onion; peel and crush the garlic; finely chop the anchovy fillets. Pass the tomato pulp through a coarse sieve or food mill.

Heat the oil in a frying pan. Add the bacon, onion and garlic and cook over a low heat until the onion is soft and transparent. Add the anchovies and continue to cook over low heat, stirring every now and then, for 3 minutes. Add 8 tablespoons of the breadcrumbs and cook for a further 2–3 minutes, stirring lightly until the crumbs are golden.

Add the tomato pulp, parsley and, for those who have chosen it, oregano. Season generously with salt and pepper. Fill the tomato cases with this mixture, top with the remaining breadcrumbs and a little more pepper and brush the tops and sides with oil.

Bake in a moderate oven (180°C, 350°F, Reg. 4) for 15–20 minutes.

Tomato Hanny

75 g (3 oz) brown breadcrumbs
100 g (4 oz) grated cheese
450 g (1 lb) tomatoes, thinly sliced
Salt and freshly ground black pepper
50 g (2 oz) butter
150 ml (¼ pint) milk
2 tablespoons cream
Paprika

Serves 4

An old-fashioned but useful dish to serve with a main course– delicious with fried sausages and bacon.

Grease a baking dish and cover the bottom with half the breadcrumbs and half the grated cheese. Cover with the sliced tomatoes, season with salt and pepper and dot with the butter. Pour over the milk mixed with cream and top with the remaining breadcrumbs and cheese.

Sprinkle with a little paprika and bake in a moderately hot oven (200°C, 400°F, Reg. 6) for about 20 minutes. Brown quickly under the grill before serving.

Provençal Tomatoes

Serves 4–6

8 ripe tomatoes
2 cloves garlic
4 anchovy fillets
3 tablespoons olive oil
½ tablespoon finely chopped parsley
1 teaspoon lemon juice
Salt and freshly ground black pepper

Halve the tomatoes and arrange them, cut side up, in a greased baking dish. Crush the garlic; drain and very finely chop the anchovy fillets.

Mix together the olive oil, garlic, anchovies, parsley and lemon juice and season with a little salt and plenty of pepper.

Spread this mixture over the surface of the tomatoes and grill under a high heat until slightly browned and sizzling.

Ratatouille

Serves 4–6

2 medium-large aubergines
3 small courgettes
2 red or green peppers
6 tomatoes
2 large onions
2 cloves garlic
6 tablespoons olive oil
1 tablespoon finely chopped parsley or chervil
Pinch of oregano
Salt and freshly ground black pepper

This Provençal dish loses nothing by being cooked in advance and kept in the refrigerator overnight to be re-heated the next day.

Cut the aubergines into small cubes, place them in a colander and lightly sprinkle with salt. Leave to 'sweat' for an hour, then wipe off excess moisture.

Cut the courgettes into small cubes. Remove the core and seeds of the peppers and cut the flesh into thin strips.

Pour boiling water over the tomatoes and leave to stand for two minutes, slide off the skins and roughly chop the flesh.

Peel and very thinly slice the onions and divide into rings. Crush the garlic through a garlic press or with a fork.

Heat the olive oil in a deep frying pan, add the onions and garlic and cook over a very low heat until the onions are pale yellow and transparent. Add the aubergines and peppers, cover tightly and simmer over a low heat for 30 minutes. Add the tomatoes, courgettes, parsley and oregano, season with plenty of freshly ground black pepper and continue to simmer with the lid on for a further 15 minutes. Remove the lid and cook for another ten minutes until the vegetables are all soft but not too mushy.

If you intend to serve the ratatouille as an hors d'oeuvre blend in a tablespoon of tomato purée when you add the tomatoes, chill after cooking and garnish with some fillets of anchovy and a few black olives.

Marinated Vegetables

1 green pepper
1 red pepper
3 tomatoes
½ small cauliflower
12 radishes
1 small onion
300 ml (½ pint) water
6 tablespoons olive oil
6 tablespoons dry white wine
Juice of 2 lemons
½ teaspoon dill
¼ teaspoon chervil
6 coriander seeds
1 bay leaf
Salt and freshly ground black pepper
100 g (4 oz.) firm button mushrooms
Small bunch watercress

Serves 6

If arranged with a little care this mixed vegetable platter looks very attractive.

Remove core and seeds from the peppers and cut the flesh into thin rings. Peel and thinly slice the tomatoes. Divide the cauliflower head into florets and thinly slice the radishes. Peel and slice the onion.

Combine water, olive oil, white wine, lemon juice, onion, herbs and seasoning in a saucepan, bring to the boil and simmer for ten minutes. Strain to remove the onion and herbs.

Place the peppers, cauliflower and mushrooms in a saucepan, pour over the hot marinade, bring to the boil and simmer gently until the cauliflower is just tender–it should have a bit of a crunch to it. Strain off the liquid and leave the vegetables to cool.

Arrange all the ingredients in rows on a flat serving dish and pour over enough of the cool liquid to moisten them. Chill before serving garnished with watercress.

Purée of Swede

1 swede
Salt and freshly ground black pepper
25 g (1 oz.) butter
3 tablespoons double cream
1 tablespoon finely chopped parsley or chives

Serves 4

Peel and roughly chop the swede and cook it until really tender in plenty of boiling salted water. Drain well and mash to a smooth purée with a potato masher or by passing through a food mill. The purée must be absolutely smooth or the dish will be a disappointment.

Return to a clean pan, season with salt and pepper, add the butter and cream and beat with a wire whisk until the mixture is light and fluffy. Pile on to a heated serving dish and scatter with chopped parsley or chives before serving.

Boiled Rice with Green Peppers

Serves 4

225 g (8 oz) long-grain rice
1 large onion
2 green peppers
2 tablespoons olive oil
25 g (1 oz) butter
Salt and freshly ground black pepper

In this recipe the rice is boiled first until tender and then reheated with onions and green peppers. The peppers should be tender but still slightly crisp.

Rinse the rice in cold water and drain it well. Boil in boiling salted water for about 15 minutes until the grains are tender but still separate. Drain, rinse in cold water and drain again.

Peel and finely chop the onion. Remove core and seeds from the green peppers and finely chop the flesh. Heat the olive oil in a frying pan, add the onion and cook over a medium heat until soft and transparent. Add the green peppers and cook for about five minutes until they are tender but not flabby. Add the rice, mix in the butter and season with salt and pepper. Stir over a medium low heat until the rice is hot through.

Orange and Almond Rice

Serves 4

1 onion
Rind of 1½ oranges
75 g (3 oz) butter
50 g (2 oz) blanched split almonds
½ teaspoon saffron
1 teaspoon hot water
350 g (12 oz) long-grain rice
200 ml (7½ fl oz) chicken stock, or water and stock cube
Salt and freshly ground black pepper

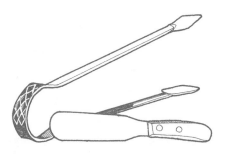

This Persian rice goes particularly well with roast duck or chicken and gives the whole meal a wonderfully aromatic taste.

Peel and very finely chop the onion. Thinly pare off the orange rind with a sharp potato peeler. Cut the rind into very thin julienne strips about 1 cm (½ in) long and blanch in boiling water for five minutes to remove the bitter taste.

Heat half the butter in a frying pan, add the onion and cook over a medium heat until soft and transparent–do not allow to brown. Add the orange rind and almonds and continue to cook over a low heat for five minutes. Pound the saffron to a powder in a mortar with a pestle and dissolve it in the hot water. Add to the onion, rind and almonds.

Wash the rice in cold water and drain well. Bring a saucepan half filled with water to the boil, add the rice and cook over a high heat for five minutes. Strain the rice and rinse again in cold water. Pour the stock into a heavy pan or casserole with a tight-fitting lid. Place half the onion mixture in the bottom, cover with the rice and top with the remaining onion mixture. Cover tightly and cook in a moderate oven (180°C, 350°F, Reg. 4) for about 40 minutes until the liquid has been absorbed and the rice is tender. Mix in the remaining butter and season with salt and pepper.

Spanish Rice

1 onion
1 clove garlic
75 g (3 oz) streaky bacon
225 g (8 oz) can tomatoes
1 tablespoon olive oil
350 g (12 oz) long-grain rice
2 teaspoons tomato purée
300 ml ($\frac{1}{2}$ pint) chicken stock, or water and
    stock cube
Freshly ground black pepper
175 g (6 oz) frozen peas
1 tablespoon finely chopped parsley

Serves 6

A colourful dish, this goes well with almost any main course.

Peel and finely chop the onion. Crush the garlic or squeeze through a garlic press. Remove rinds and finely chop the bacon rashers. Drain off and reserve the juice from the tomatoes and chop the flesh.

Heat the olive oil in a frying pan. Add the onion and garlic and cook over a medium heat until the onion is soft and transparent. Add the bacon and continue to cook for a further two minutes. Stir in the rice and cook over a low heat, without browning, until the rice is transparent. Add the tomatoes, tomato juice, purée and stock and mix well. Season with pepper, cover and cook very slowly for 30–40 minutes until all the moisture is absorbed and the rice is tender.

Cook the peas in boiling, salted water until tender, drain well and add them to the rice with the parsley just before serving.

Savoury Fried Rice

350 g (12 oz) long-grain rice
4 spring onions (or 1 small leek)
2 eggs
1 tablespoon water
Salt and freshly ground black pepper
2 tablespoons olive oil

Serves 4

This dish is based on the Eastern-type rice which accompanies so many dishes. It is extremely filling by itself and makes a good stretching side dish to serve with poultry or fish.

Wash the rice in cold water and drain well. Cook in boiling salted water for 20 minutes until tender and fluffy. Strain into a large sieve and hold under cold water for 30 seconds. Drain well, turn into a shallow dish and dry in a very low oven while cooking the onions and eggs.

Chop the spring onions or leek. Beat the eggs with the water and season with a little salt and pepper. Heat about half a tablespoon of the olive oil in an omelette pan. Add the beaten egg and cook over a medium high heat, stirring every now and then with a fork, until a thin pancake-like omelette has formed. Slide on to a plate and leave to cool; cut into thin strips with kitchen scissors when set firmly.

Heat the remaining oil in a large frying pan. Add the spring onion and cook over a low heat for two minutes. Add the rice, season with salt and pepper, mix well and heat through. Mix in the egg strips and serve as soon as possible.

Note: Instead of salt a spoonful of soya sauce can be added to the rice.

Italian Rice

2 onions
1 large green pepper
425 g (15 oz) can tomatoes
6 tablespoons olive oil
350 g (12 oz) long-grain rice
600 ml (1 pint) chicken stock (or water and
stock cubes)
Salt
Pinch of oregano
Pinch of chilli powder

Serves 5–6

Serve this with stews, pork, poultry or fish.

Peel and finely chop the onions. Remove core and seeds from the pepper and finely chop the flesh. Chop the tomatoes.

Heat the oil in a flame-proof casserole or heavy saucepan. Add the onions and pepper and cook over a medium high heat for three minutes, stirring to prevent browning. Add the rice and cook until it absorbs most of the oil and is transparent but not burnt. Add the tomatoes, stock, salt, oregano and chilli powder, mix well and bring to the boil. Cover tightly and simmer for about 30 minutes until the rice is tender and the liquid absorbed. Stir about once every ten minutes or so to prevent sticking, adding a little water if the mixture becomes too dry before the rice is cooked.

Some chopped parsley or grated cheese can be sprinkled over the surface of the rice before serving.

Sauces

This is a field in which the inventiveness and individuality of a cook can really run riot. No two sauces will ever be the same, however dedicatedly you follow a recipe, and this is part of their charm and excitement. Seasoning and flavouring play an important part here and I am sure that it is in tasting sauces that good cooks develop those sensitive taste buds that put them in a special class.

Good sauces can provide an almost endless variety of excitement and interest to the most plain and inexpensive of ingredients (though obviously you don't want to go mad by smothering a piece of inexpensive pollock with a wildly extravagant sauce made of caviar and truffles) and a good sauce can also complement a perfectly cooked main ingredient in a way that actually heightens its taste and flavour.

A few points should be born in mind when making the majority of classic sauces:

1. Sauces that contain eggs or cream should never be boiled.
2. If a sauce is to be made with stock it will benefit enormously by being made with a home-made stock that has been reduced so that it has a rich texture and flavour.
3. Seasoning increases in strength the more a sauce is cooked–it is easy to add more seasoning but it is very difficult to do anything about a sauce that has been over seasoned.

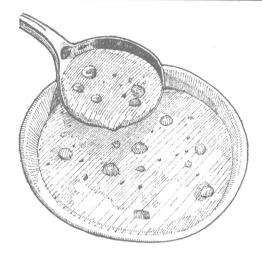

4. Herbs give a lift to a great many sauces. Whenever possible use fresh herbs but if you have to resort to the dried variety soak them in a little warm water or lemon juice before adding them to the sauce to help bring out their flavour and to lose that sometimes dusty taste.

5. One of the commonest faults that happen in sauce making is lumpiness. This is either caused by adding cold liquid to a hot sauce or by not beating the sauce enough as it cooks. I use a small wire whisk to beat most of my sauces with and make a point of stirring them as often as I can during the cooking time. A point that worries me about so many recipes for white sauces is that writers recommend the basic liaison of butter and flour should be removed from the stove while the milk or other liquid is being added. In my experience the best way to avoid any lumpiness in a sauce is to add the liquid, a little at a time, while the saucepan is over a moderately high heat, beating all the time until the sauce becomes smooth after each addition of liquid. This method usually works perfectly.

If you do find your sauce developing lumps you can eradicate them by putting the sauce into a liquidiser or passing it through a fine sieve.

6. Thicken sauces that are too thin by the addition of some double cream, one or two egg yolks beaten into the sauce or a mixture of softened butter and flour beaten together and then whisked into the sauce. Thin sauces that are too thick with milk or stock.

7. Add extra flavour to a sauce by mixing in a little lemon juice; white wine, red wine, sherry or vermouth; some finely chopped herbs; a stock cube; some Worcestershire or Tabasco sauce or mushroom ketchup; some anchovy essence for a sauce that is to accompany a fish dish; tomato purée or extra seasoning.

Above all be adventuresome with sauces. Follow the basic directions of a recipe but, if you feel like it, add a little chopped green or red pepper, some leftover ham (very finely chopped or shredded), the meat glaze from the drippings of a roast joint or any other ingredient you think might add pep to your sauce and make it an invention of your own kitchen.

White Sauce

25 g (1 oz) butter
2 tablespoons flour
300 ml (½ pint) milk
Salt and white pepper

A white sauce forms the basis of a good many other classic sauces and, providing the right procedure is followed, is quick and easy to make. Many cookery books recommend taking the saucepan from the stove once you have formed a 'roux' from butter and flour but I find this tends to make the sauce lumpy. I make my white sauces over a hot flame stirring vigorously to prevent the sauce colouring.

Melt the butter in a small saucepan. Add the flour and stir with a wooden spoon until the mixture forms a ball and comes cleanly away from the sides of the pan. Gradually beat in the milk, stirring continuously over a high heat until the sauce is thick and smooth. Lower the heat and simmer gently, stirring, for three minutes.

Variations

Use half stock or all white stock instead of the milk.

Enrich the sauce by beating one egg yolk and two tablespoons of double cream into the finished sauce and stirring over a low heat until thick and shining.

Give extra flavour by simmering the milk with an onion and a bouquet garni before straining it and adding it to the sauce.

Some white wine can be used to replace some of the milk.

Bread Sauce

1 medium onion
2 cloves
450 ml (¾ pint) milk
5 peppercorns
Salt
1 bay leaf
75 g (3 oz) white breadcrumbs
15 g (½ oz) butter
¼ teaspoon finely grated lemon rind
Pinch of nutmeg
Pinch of mixed herbs

To serve with poultry.

Remove onion skin and stick the cloves into the onion. Combine the onion, milk, peppercorns and a little salt in a saucepan with the bay leaf. Bring slowly to boiling point and then leave to stand in a warm place for 20 minutes to allow the flavours of the onion, cloves and bay leaf to infuse into the milk.

Strain into a clean pan. Return the onion to the milk and add the breadcrumbs, butter, lemon rind and a tiny pinch of ground nutmeg and mixed herbs. Cook slowly over a low heat for 15 minutes. Remove the onion, mix the sauce well with a wooden spoon and check to see if it needs more salt.

Ragu Sauce

Serves 6–8

1 onion
2 rashers bacon
1 carrot
1 stick celery
3 tablespoons olive or vegetable oil
75 g (3 oz) butter
175 g (6 oz) minced beef
1 pork sausage, skin removed
150 ml ($\frac{1}{4}$ pint) cheap dry white wine
1$\frac{1}{2}$ tablespoons tomato purée
300 ml ($\frac{1}{2}$ pint) stock
Salt and freshly ground black pepper
4 tablespoons single cream
50 g (2 oz) button mushrooms
1 clove garlic (optional)
2 tablespoons finely chopped parsley

A deliciously succulent blending of meats and vegetables cooked in wine and stock.

Peel and finely chop the onion. Remove rinds from the bacon rashers. Mince the carrot, celery and bacon through the coarse blades of a mincing machine.

Combine the oil and half the butter in a deep, heavy frying pan. Add the onion and minced ingredients and cook over a low heat, stirring to prevent browning, until the vegetables are soft and the onion is transparent. Add the meat and sausage, crumbled into pieces, and cook over a low heat, stirring with a fork, until the meat has browned. Add the wine and continue to stir until it has evaporated. Add the tomato purée, mix well and gradually blend in stock, stirring all the time. Season with salt and pepper and cook over a low heat for one hour. Mix in the cream and cook for a further three minutes. Do not let the cream boil.

Chop the mushrooms and garlic finely and cook gently for two minutes in 15 g ($\frac{1}{2}$ oz) of melted butter. Mix in the parsley. Add the mushroom mixture to the sauce with the remaining butter and cook, stirring, for a final three minutes.

Barbecue Sauce

2 small rashers fatty bacon
1 onion
4 celery leaves (or lovage leaves or $\frac{1}{2}$ teaspoon dried lovage)
225 g (8 oz) can tomatoes
2 tablespoons lemon juice
6 tablespoons tomato ketchup
1 tablespoon Worcestershire sauce
1$\frac{1}{2}$ tablespoons soft brown sugar
1 tablespoon French Dijon mustard
Salt and freshly ground black pepper

If this sauce is stored in a screw-topped jar it will keep well in the refrigerator for a week or two. It can be served hot or cold, as you like.

Very finely chop or mince the bacon. Peel and very finely chop the onion; finely chop the celery leaves. Break up the tomatoes with a fork.

Cook the bacon over a low heat until the fat melts. Add the onion and continue to cook over a low heat until it is soft and transparent. Add all the remaining ingredients, mix well, season with salt and pepper, bring to the boil and simmer for 15 minutes.

Mayonnaise

2 egg yolks
½ teaspoon dry English mustard
225 ml (8 fl oz) olive oil or sunflower oil
1½ tablespoons white wine vinegar
Salt and freshly ground black pepper

Those who are learning to cook find the making of mayonnaise one of the somewhat frightening mysteries of the kitchen, but like so many cookery procedures it gets faster and more simple the more you practise it. What happens is that oil beaten almost drop by drop into egg yolk forms a stiff emulsion producing a thick, glossy and satiny sauce; if the oil is added too quickly the mayonnaise will curdle and separate. Once one becomes proficient at making the sauce it is possible to feel the exact moment at which more oil can be added and to feel at exactly what speed it can be added to the yolks. It is probably the most satisfactory of all sauces to make.

Mayonnaise can be made in a blender or food processor but the sauce will be thicker and heavier than one that is made by hand.

Make sure all the ingredients are at the same temperature before you start. If your eggs are taken straight from the refrigerator and the oil is at room temperature the mayonnaise will almost always curdle.

Combine the egg yolks and mustard in a bowl and beat with a wooden spoon until smooth. Gradually add the oil from a small jug, a teaspoon at a time, beating continuously after each addition until the oil is absorbed by the yolks. When a smooth, thick emulsion has been formed the oil can be added a little more quickly. When all the oil has been used and the sauce is very thick and stiff add the vinegar, mix well and season with salt and pepper.

A lighter mayonnaise can be made by folding in a beaten white of egg just before serving.

Mayonnaise can be stored, in the refrigerator, in a screw-topped jar.

Sauce Espagnole

15 g (½ oz) meat dripping
2 tablespoons flour
450 ml (¾ pint) good dark stock
1 small onion
4 button mushrooms
50 g (2 oz) lean ham or bacon
2 tablespoons olive oil
200 ml (7½ fl oz) dry white wine
2 tablespoons tomato purée
½ teaspoon soya sauce
1 tablespoon finely chopped parsley
Freshly ground black pepper

Based on a brown sauce, this is one of the classic sauces that can be varied in any number of ways. Serve it with roast or braised meat, or re-heat leftover cold meat, chicken, ham or tongue in the sauce to make a delicious quick meal.

Make a brown sauce by melting the dripping, adding the flour and mixing well over a medium heat until the flour is well browned but not burnt. Gradually add the stock, stirring continuously until the sauce is thick and smooth. Bring to the boil, then remove from the heat and set aside.

Peel and finely chop the onion: finely chop the mushrooms and the ham or bacon. Heat the olive oil in a small saucepan, add the onion, mushrooms and ham and cook over a medium heat for three minutes. Add the wine, bring to the boil and boil vigorously for about five minutes or until the liquid is reduced by half. Blend in the brown sauce, tomato purée and soya sauce, add the parsley, season with a little pepper and simmer for a further five minutes before serving.

Chicken Liver Sauce

4 thin rashers streaky bacon
1 large onion
1 large carrot
1 tablespoon vegetable oil
450 g (1 lb) chicken livers, finely chopped
1 clove garlic
Pinch of oregano and sage
1 tablespoon tomato purée
150 ml (¼ pint) stock
150 ml (¼ pint) dry white wine
Salt and freshly ground black pepper

Serves 6

Chicken livers in bulk are easier to find than they used to be; now you can buy them in most supermarkets and from some butchers. The sauce can be served with pasta, with rice or with a wide variety of vegetable dishes to make a substantial supper dish. It goes well with courgettes, French or runner beans and can be used as a filling for aubergines, onions, tomatoes and cabbage leaves.

Remove rind and very finely chop the bacon rashers. Peel and very finely chop the onion and carrot. Heat the oil in a saucepan, add the bacon and cook over a low heat until it begins to crisp and the fat has melted. Add the onion and continue to cook over a low heat until it is soft and transparent. Add the carrot and cook for a further three minutes, stirring to prevent sticking. Add the chicken livers, stirring to prevent sticking, and cook over a high heat until they are browned. Peel and crush the garlic and add to the pan with the herbs.

Add the tomato purée, stock and wine, season with salt and pepper, mix well, cover and simmer for 20 minutes.

Mustard Sauce

300 ml (½ pint) milk
1 slice onion
1 slice carrot
1 bay leaf
Sprig of parsley
Small pinch of grated nutmeg
Salt and freshly ground black pepper
25 g (1 oz) butter
1½ tablespoons flour
2 teaspoons French Dijon mustard
5 tablespoons double cream

To serve with pork, bacon or ham dishes. The sauce also goes well with soft-boiled eggs.

Combine the milk in a pan with the onion, carrot, bay leaf, parsley, nutmeg and seasoning. Bring to just under boiling point, as slowly as possible to allow the flavouring ingredients to infuse into the milk. Remove from the heat and strain through a fine sieve.

In a clean pan, melt the butter, add the flour, mix well and gradually add the warm milk, stirring continuously over a medium heat until the sauce comes to the boil and is thick and smooth. Blend in the mustard and simmer very gently for three minutes. Whip the cream until thick and whisk it into the sauce to give a light, almost fluffy texture.

Sauce Infernale

1 chicken liver
2 teaspoons finely chopped parsley
2 teaspoons finely grated lemon rind
1 shallot, very finely chopped
6 tablespoons red wine
1 tablespoon French Dijon mustard
2 teaspoons lemon juice
Salt and freshly ground black pepper

Serves 4

A delicious, exciting accompaniment to roast game, roast chicken, steak or even hamburgers.

Finely chop the liver and mash it with a fork. Add all ingredients to the juices left in the pan from the roast game, chicken, steak or hamburgers. Mix really well and simmer for three minutes.

Cumberland Sauce

1 lemon
1 orange
100 g (4 oz) redcurrant jelly
1 tablespoon French Dijon mustard
150 ml (¼ pint) port
Salt and freshly ground black pepper

To serve with cold ham, tongue or game

Thinly remove the rind from the orange and lemon with a potato peeler and cut the peel into very thin julienne strips. Squeeze the juice of the orange and half the lemon. Blanch the peel in boiling water for five minutes and drain well.

Combine the redcurrant jelly, mustard, port, peels and fruit juice in a saucepan, season with salt and pepper and heat through, stirring until all the jelly has melted. Bring to the boil, then remove from the heat and leave to cool.

A Special Sauce for Fish

1 small onion
50 g (2 oz) peeled prawns
3 egg yolks
150 ml (5 fl oz) single cream
50 g (2 oz) butter
1 tablespoon flour
200 ml (7½ fl oz) fish stock, or water and 1
    chicken stock cube
1 tablespoon lemon juice
1 tablespoon finely chopped parsley
¼ teaspoon dried tarragon (or 2 teaspoons
    finely chopped fresh)
Salt and white pepper

A sauce on the extravagant side, but one that will enhance the flavour of any fish dish from steamed turbot to fried fish fingers. As egg yolks are added to the sauce it should be served when made and preferably not re-heated.

Peel and very finely chop the onion. Chop the prawns. Beat the egg yolks with the cream until the mixture is quite smooth.

Melt half the butter in a saucepan, add the flour and mix well without browning. Gradually blend in the stock, stirring continuously over a medium heat until the sauce is thick and smooth. Bring to the boil and simmer for three minutes. Whisk in cream and egg yolks with a wire whisk and continue to cook, whisking all the time, for a few minutes until the sauce is thick, shiny and foaming. Add the remaining butter, cut into small pieces, lemon juice, onion, prawns and herbs, season lightly and whisk until the butter has melted.

Olive and Almond Sauce

40 g (1½ oz) butter
3 tablespoons flour
300 ml (½ pint) chicken stock
8 olives
150 ml (5 fl oz) single cream
½ tablespoon lemon juice
50 g (2 oz) shredded almonds
Salt and white pepper

To serve with fish.

Melt the butter in a saucepan. Add the flour, mix well and gradually blend in the stock. Stir continuously over a medium heat until the sauce is thick and smooth. Simmer for three minutes.

Remove stones from the olives and cut the flesh into thin strips. Add cream to the sauce (do not boil) and mix in lemon juice, almonds and olives.

Season with salt and pepper and serve at once.

Apple, Sage and Redcurrant Sauce

3 cooking apples
1 tablespoon sugar
Juice of ½ lemon
3 tablespoons redcurrant jelly
25 g (1 oz) butter
½ teaspoon sage
Pinch of rosemary
Salt and freshly ground black pepper

Try this spicy mixture as a change from straight apple sauce to serve with pork or sausages.

Peel, core and roughly chop the apples. Combine the apples in a saucepan with the sugar, lemon juice, redcurrant jelly and butter. Add the herbs, season with a little salt and pepper and cook over a low heat until the apple becomes soft and mushy.

Beat well with a fork and serve either warm or cold.

Sauce Beurre Blanc

1 shallot or small onion
2 tablespoons white wine vinegar
Salt and white pepper
150 g (5 oz) butter

This classic French sauce is a winner for almost all poached fish.

Peel and finely chop the shallot. Combine the shallot and vinegar in a saucepan, season with salt and pepper and cook over a high heat until the liquid is reduced to about a quarter.

Add a quarter of the butter and mix well, keeping the pan over the heat. Bring to the boil, remove immediately and add the remaining butter, a little at a time, cut into small pieces, whisking with a wire whisk. The sauce should thicken and become the consistency of thin mayonnaise.

Creole Sauce

1 small onion
1 large green pepper
100 g (4 oz) firm button mushrooms
225 g (8 oz) can tomatoes
25 g (1 oz) butter
1 tablespoon flour
Pinch of oregano or basil
300 ml ($\frac{1}{2}$ pint) good stock
6 green olives
Salt, freshly ground black pepper and a pinch of chilli powder (or $\frac{1}{2}$ teaspoon finely chopped dried red chilli)
1 tablespoon sherry
1 tablespoon finely chopped parsley

Serve with pasta.

Peel and very finely chop the onion. Remove core and seeds from the pepper and finely chop the flesh. Finely chop the mushrooms. Roughly chop the tomatoes.

Melt the butter in a small heavy pan. Add the onion and pepper and cook over a low heat until the onion is soft and transparent. Add the mushrooms, sprinkle over the flour and mix well. Mix in the tomatoes, herbs and stock, add the olives and season well with salt, pepper and chilli powder. Bring to the boil, cover and simmer for 20 minutes. Add the sherry and parsley.

Gooseberry Mustard Sauce

225 g (8 oz) green gooseberries
50 g (2 oz) butter
1 tablespoon flour
300 ml ($\frac{1}{2}$ pint) water
1 tablespoon sugar
2 teaspoons made English mustard
1 teaspoon finely chopped fennel
Salt and pepper

To serve with grilled mackerel, kippers or other fish.

Top and tail the gooseberries and cook gently in boiling water until soft and yellow; strain and purée through a fine sieve. Melt a quarter of the butter in a saucepan, add the flour and mix well, then gradually blend in the water, stirring continuously until the sauce is smooth. Add the gooseberry purée, sugar, mustard and fennel, mix well and continue to simmer for a further three minutes.

Season with salt and pepper and blend in the remaining butter.

Lemon and Egg Sauce

6 eggs
½ chicken stock cube
Generous 150 ml (¼ pint) warm water
1½ tablespoons lemon juice
White pepper
2 tablespoons sour cream
2 tablespoons finely chopped parsley

Serves 2

Throughout the Balkans the lemon and egg combination appears time and time again in light, delicious soups, aromatic concoctions subtly flavoured and scattered with tender grains of rice.

To this typical sauce I add a little parsley and serve it over *ouefs mollets* as a first course or lunch dish. Although the texture is rich and satisfying the calorie content is surprisingly low, so it makes an ideal dish for the figure-conscious. Made in the same way as hollandaise sauce, it needs a little patience.

Boil four of the eggs in boiling water for five minutes. Plunge immediately into cold water, carefully peel off the shells and keep warm while making the sauce.

Beat the remaining eggs until smooth. Add the stock cube to the water and stir until dissolved. Place the beaten egg in a basin over hot (not boiling) water. Add the lemon juice, a drop at a time, stirring continuously with a wooden spoon. When all the lemon juice has been used, gradually pour in the stock and cook for about five minutes, stirring all the time, until the sauce is the consistency of mayonnaise. Season with pepper, mix in the sour cream and parsley and pour over the eggs.

Lemon Tarragon Sauce

40 g (1½ oz) butter
1 tablespoon flour
300 ml (½ pint) milk, or half milk and half chicken stock
2 teaspoons lemon juice
1 tablespoon finely chopped fresh tarragon
Salt and freshly ground black pepper
1 egg yolk
1–2 tablespoons double cream

Fresh herbs from the garden give almost any recipe a lift and a delicate flavouring that is unrivalled. They are easy to grow, and plants can be obtained from some of the better-class provision stores in London, top-quality market gardens, garden centres or large florists. Alternatively most can be successfully grown from seed.

This sauce goes well with egg, fish and chicken dishes and can be used to pep up some cold tongue or ham.

Melt the butter in a saucepan, add the flour and mix well. Gradually beat in the milk (or milk and stock), stirring continuously over a medium heat until the sauce comes to the boil and is thick and smooth.

Add the lemon juice and tarragon, salt and pepper, and simmer gently for four minutes. Beat the egg yolk with the cream, add the mixture to the sauce and mix well, stirring continuously over a low heat–do not allow to boil.

Egg Sauce

2 hard-boiled eggs
1 small onion
40 g (1½ oz) butter
1 tablespoon flour
300 ml (½ pint) milk
1 teaspoon made English mustard
Salt and pepper
2 tablespoons finely chopped parsley

Serves 4

An old-fashioned English sauce, this is delicious with any fried, poached or baked fish. The mustard gives a pleasant sharpness.

Chop the hard-boiled eggs. Peel and very finely chop the onion. Melt the butter in a saucepan. Add the onion and cook over a low heat until soft and transparent.

Add the flour and mix well. Gradually blend in the milk, stirring continually until the sauce is thick and smooth. Add the mustard, season with salt and pepper, bring to the boil and simmer for three minutes. Fold in the hard-boiled eggs and parsley and serve at once.

Hot Tomato Sauce

1 large onion
4 ripe tomatoes
2 tablespoons olive oil
1 teaspoon finely chopped parsley
1 teaspoon sugar
1 teaspoon white wine vinegar
Pinch of oregano
Salt and freshly ground black pepper

A delicious and quickly made sauce to serve with fish or grilled meat, this is like a sort of instant chutney. The flavour can be sharpened by adding a clove of crushed garlic, a pinch of chilli powder or a drop or two of Tabasco sauce.

Peel and finely chop the onion. Peel and chop the tomatoes. Heat the oil, add the onion and cook gently until transparent. Add remaining ingredients, season with salt and pepper, bring to the boil and simmer gently, stirring occasionally, for about 20 minutes until the onions and tomatoes have amalgamated to make a thick sauce.

Speedy Spaghetti Sauce

1 large onion
1–2 cloves garlic
2 tablespoons olive or vegetable oil
425 g (15 oz) can tomatoes
1 tablespoon tomato purée
425 g (15 oz) can minced meat
4 tablespoons red wine
4 anchovy fillets
¼ teaspoon dried mixed herbs
½ chicken or beef stock cube
Freshly ground black pepper

Serves 6

Peel and finely chop the onion. Squeeze the garlic through a garlic press or mash finely with a fork.

Heat the oil in a saucepan. Add the onion and garlic and cook over a low heat until soft and transparent. Drain the oil from the anchovies and very finely chop the fillets.

Add the tomatoes, tomato purée, minced meat and wine to the onions and mix well. Stir in the anchovy fillets, herbs and stock cube, bring to the boil and simmer for 20 minutes, stirring every now and then.

Season with pepper, pour over cooked spaghetti and sprinkle with some grated cheese.

Butter Sauces for Serving with Fish	Melted-butter sauces with some additional flavouring are quick to make and go well with most plain fish dishes. They can be poured over the fish or served separately. Allow about 15 g (½ oz) butter for each serving and be careful not to burn it while cooking.

Herb Butter

Add 1 tablespoon finely chopped fresh parsley and ½ teaspoon finely chopped dried herbs to every 50 g (2 oz) of melted butter. Cook gently for three minutes and season with salt and pepper.

Lemon and Dill Butter

Add 1 teaspoon fresh or dried, finely chopped dill and 1 teaspoon lemon juice to every 50 g (2 oz) melted butter and cook gently for three minutes. Season with salt, pepper and a pinch of paprika.

Anchovy and Egg Butter

Add 6 finely chopped anchovy fillets and 1 finely chopped hard-boiled egg to 50 g (2 oz) butter and simmer gently for five minutes. Season with pepper only.

Shrimp and Butter Sauce

1 small carton potted shrimps
50 g (2 oz) butter
Juice of ½ lemon
1 tablespoon very finely chopped parsley
Salt and freshly ground black pepper

Serves 4

To serve with plainly cooked fish.

Thaw the potted shrimps completely if they are frozen. Heat the butter until melted but do not allow to brown. Add the potted shrimps and stir continuously over a low heat until the butter from the shrimps has also melted.

Add the lemon juice and parsley, check the seasoning and serve at once.

Cucumber Mayonnaise

½ cucumber
Salt and pepper
1 teaspoon lemon juice
1 teaspoon French Dijon mustard
150 ml (¼ pint) home-made mayonnaise
1 teaspoon grated raw onion
1 tablespoon finely chopped sweet red pepper

Serves 4–6

To serve with chicken or fish.

Cut the rind off the cucumber. Coarsely grate the flesh, place in a sieve, sprinkle with salt and leave to sweat for 30 minutes. Press gently to remove excess liquid and pat dry on a clean cloth. Blend the lemon juice and mustard into the mayonnaise and mix well. Fold in the onion, pepper and cucumber and season with a little extra salt and pepper.

Use the sauce within an hour of making it.

Sauce Selina

2 egg yolks
¼ teaspoon dry mustard
Freshly ground black pepper
300 ml (½ pint) olive or vegetable oil
2 sprigs parsley
¼ teaspoon dried tarragon
1 teaspoon lemon juice
1 tablespoon finely chopped capers
1 tablespoon finely chopped green pepper
1 tablespoon chopped fresh or dried chives
1 finely chopped anchovy fillet
Pinch of cayenne pepper

Serve with chicken, steaks or grilled or fried fish.

Beat the egg yolks with the mustard until smooth. Add a good screw of pepper and gradually add the olive oil (drop by drop at first and then a teaspoon at a time) beating hard so the sauce thickens and emulsifies after each addition.

Blanch the parsley sprigs in boiling water for two minutes, drain well and chop very finely. Soak the tarragon in the lemon juice for five minutes. Beat the tarragon and lemon juice, a little at a time, into the egg yolk mixture. Mix in the capers, green pepper, chives and chopped anchovy fillet. Add a pinch of cayenne, check seasoning and leave to stand for at least 15 minutes to mature before serving.

Rhubarb Sauce

1·5 kilos (3 lb) rhubarb
225 g (8 oz) onions
450 ml (¾ pint) malt vinegar
Pinch of cayenne pepper
5 cloves
½ teaspoon salt
450 g (1 lb) sugar
3 teaspoons ground turmeric
2 teaspoons made English mustard

Serves 6–8

This sauce is excellent with fish, especially mackerel.

Wash the rhubarb and peel off any coarse strings. Cut into 2·5 cm (1 in) lengths. Peel and roughly chop the onions. Combine the rhubarb with 150 ml (¼ pint) of the vinegar, the onions, cayenne pepper, cloves and salt and simmer gently for one hour.

Rub the mixture through a fine sieve; or remove the cloves and pass through a food mill or purée in a liquidiser. Return the purée to a clean pan, add the remaining vinegar with the sugar and bring to the boil. Mix in the turmeric blended with the mustard and simmer the mixture over a medium heat until thick. Taste for seasoning, leave to cool for ten minutes and then pack in sterile jars, covering lightly.

Vera's Mayonnaise Sauce

300 ml (½ pint) home-made mayonnaise
2 tablespoons French Dijon mustard
1 tablespoon tomato ketchup
¼ teaspoon dried dill weed
2 drops Tabasco or chilli sauce
Salt and freshly ground black pepper
Juice of ½ lemon

Lobster, crab and all shellfish are so rich in flavour and texture that sometimes a plain home-made mayonnaise can be a little too bland. This is a sharper sauce with a bit of a bite to it to give the extra contrast which is needed.

Add the ingredients to the mayonnaise and mix well. Leave to stand in a cool place for about an hour before serving.

Avocado Mayonnaise

1 large egg yolk
Salt and pepper
½ teaspoon made English mustard
150 ml (¼ pint) olive oil
1 ripe avocado pear
Juice of 1 lemon
2 tablespoons single cream
1 teaspoon finely chopped fresh dill leaves

A rich, smooth sauce with an air of luxury about it and a subtle, cool colouring. Serve with cold fish, poultry or egg dishes.

Beat the egg yolk with salt, pepper and mustard until quite smooth. Gradually add the oil, drop by drop, beating continuously until each addition of oil has been absorbed and the sauce emulsifies. Continue to add the oil until it has all been absorbed and the mayonnaise is thick and shining.

Peel the avocado, remove stone and purée the flesh with lemon juice through a food mill or fine sieve (this can be done in a liquidiser but it is important that the avocado should be well mixed with lemon juice to prevent the flesh discolouring).

Add the avocado purée to the mayonnaise with the single cream (if the sauce is too thick add a little more cream) and taste for seasoning. Sprinkle over the chopped dill just before serving.

Sancreed Sauce for Smoked Mackerel

½ cucumber
150 ml (5 fl oz) double cream
3 tablespoons French Dijon mustard
2 tablespoons horseradish sauce
1 tablespoon finely chopped chives or spring
    onion tops
Salt and freshly ground black pepper

Serves 4–6

Allow half a large or one small smoked mackerel per serving.

Peel the cucumber. Grate the flesh through a coarse grater, sprinkle with a little salt and leave to sweat in a colander or sieve for 30 minutes. Squeeze off any excess liquid and pat dry on kitchen paper.

Lightly whip the cream until thick but not stiff. Mix in the mustard and horseradish sauce and fold in the cucumber and chives. Season with salt and pepper and chill until required.

Slimline Salad Dressing

150 ml (5 fl oz) carton yoghurt
1 teaspoon grated raw onion
1 teaspoon lemon juice
1 teaspoon made English mustard
2 teaspoons finely chopped mint
1 teaspoon finely chopped fresh tarragon
Salt, pepper and a pinch of cayenne

Combine all the ingredients, season, mix well and chill before serving.

Pinkerton Sauce

1 small clove garlic
2 tablespoons mango chutney, Branston pickle or piccalilli
1 teaspoon grated raw onion
1 tablespoon tomato ketchup
1 tablespoon finely chopped green or red pepper
200 ml (7½ fl oz) home-made mayonnaise, or a good bottled mayonnaise
Worcestershire sauce (optional)

Another version of mayonnaise, spiked with tomato chutney. It can be used as a dressing for a shellfish cocktail, as a barbecue sauce, or as an accompaniment to a bland dish such as salmon mousse.

Peel the garlic clove and squeeze through a garlic press or crush with a fork. Chop the chutney until fine. Add the onion, garlic, tomato ketchup, pepper and chutney to the mayonnaise and mix well. If a really piquant flavour is required mix in a few drops of Worcestershire sauce.

Cucumber and Soured Cream Sauce

½ cucumber
1 teaspoon lemon juice
150 ml (5 fl oz) carton soured cream
1 hard-boiled egg
½ tablespoon very finely chopped parsley
Salt and pepper
Pinch of cayenne
½ teaspoon finely chopped fresh dill, if available

Serves 4–6

Serve as a salad dressing with fish, chicken or cold meat.

Peel the cucumber. Coarsely grate the flesh, place in a sieve, sprinkle lightly with salt and leave it to sweat for 30 minutes. Drain off the excess liquid and pat dry with a clean cloth.

Blend the lemon juice into the soured cream. Finely chop the hard-boiled egg and add it to the sauce with the parsley and cucumber. Season with salt and pepper, spoon the sauce into a serving dish and top with a very light dusting of cayenne and some finely chopped fresh dill.

Basic Tomato Purée

1·3 kilos (3 lb) ripe tomatoes
1 large onion
1 tablespoon olive oil
150 ml (¼ pint) water
1 chicken stock cube
Juice of 1 lemon
1 teaspoon sugar
Pinch of sage, thyme and basil
1 tablespoon finely chopped parsley
Salt and pepper

Peel and roughly chop the tomatoes and onion. Heat the olive oil in a saucepan, add the onion and cook over a low heat until soft. Add all the other ingredients, season with salt and pepper, bring to the boil and simmer for 15–20 minutes.

Purée the mixture through a fine sieve, a food mill or in a liquidiser.

Home-made Tomato Purée

1 large onion
2 cloves garlic
1½ tablespoons olive oil
575 g (20 oz) canned tomatoes
1 teaspoon grated orange rind
½ teaspoon mixed dried oregano, thyme, savory
  and basil
1 bay leaf
2 teaspoons sugar
Salt and freshly ground black pepper
Few drops Tabasco sauce

Use this purée with a light hand as the flavour is concentrated. Add it to home-made mayonnaise to make a rich sauce for fish salad or prawn cocktail. Use a teaspoonful to colour sour cream to be used as a garnish. Add to a white sauce made with chicken stock to go with grilled chicken, or use it in my baked eggs dish (p. 178).

Peel and mince the onion; peel and crush the garlic cloves. Heat the oil in a heavy saucepan. Add the onion and garlic and cook over a low heat, stirring to prevent burning, until the onion is soft and transparent. Add the tomatoes, orange rind, herbs and sugar and season with salt and plenty of pepper. Bring to the boil and cook over a medium high heat, stirring occasionally, for 20 minutes.

Remove the bay leaf and purée through a fine sieve or food mill. Return the purée to a clean pan and boil over a high heat, stirring every now and then, until it is reduced to a rich, dark red paste (there should be about half the quantity you started with). Add a few drops of Tabasco sauce and mix well. Turn the purée into a screw-topped jar and store in the refrigerator.

Note: You can turn the purée into ice-cube containers and store it in the deep freeze, but I find it just as easy to make a new batch at the beginning of each week.

Spiky Sauce

4 sprigs parsley
8 pimento-stuffed olives
1 teaspoon capers
1 small garlic clove
1 teaspoon finely grated raw onion
1 teaspoon made English mustard
300 ml (½ pint) home-made mayonnaise
Salt and pepper

Based on a tartare sauce usually served with fish, this goes equally well with charcoal-grilled steak or hamburgers and makes a change from a more conventional barbecue sauce.

Remove stalks from the parsley and finely chop the leaves. Very finely chop olives and capers. Squeeze garlic through garlic press or crush with a fork. Combine all ingredients, mix well and taste for seasoning before serving.

Curried Mayonnaise

1 small onion or shallot
2 ripe tomatoes
1 tablespoon olive or vegetable oil
1 teaspoon curry powder
1 teaspoon lemon juice
300 ml (½ pint) home-made or bottled
    mayonnaise

People too often make the mistake of trying to flavour a mayonnaise with raw curry powder, which results in a rather gritty texture. If a little more time and trouble is taken the result will be a delicious, smoothly rich sauce that makes an ideal partner to cold chicken, fish, egg or rice dishes.

Peel and finely chop the onion; peel and finely chop the tomatoes. Heat the oil in a small saucepan. Add the onion and cook over a low heat until soft and transparent. Mix in the tomatoes, curry powder and lemon juice, bring to the boil and simmer gently for 20 minutes. Leave to cool, rub through a very fine sieve and blend into the mayonnaise.

Smetacress Dressing

½ bunch watercress
½ teaspoon lemon juice
About 5 tablespoons milk
150 ml (5 fl oz) carton soured cream
Salt and freshly ground black pepper
50 g (2 oz) chopped walnuts

This can be used on mixed salads but goes especially well with cold chicken or meat salads–try a combination of cold chicken, diced apple and cooked, diced new potatoes.

Remove the stalks from the watercress (add these to stock for flavouring) and finely chop the leaves. Blend the lemon juice and milk with the soured cream and season with salt and pepper. Fold in the watercress and walnuts and refrigerate for about 30 minutes before serving. If the dressing is too thick add a little extra milk.

Quickly-Made Meals

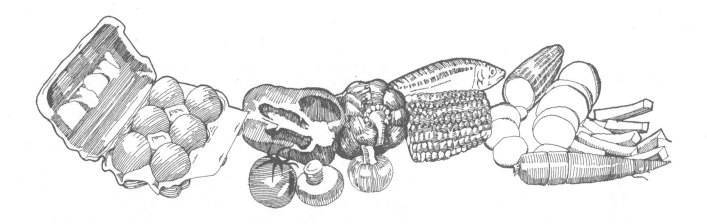

I have always maintained that the reason why cookery books continue to be published in such large quantities and why there is such a demand for cookery articles and features in newspapers and magazines (and long may it last!) is because basically we are all looking for a certain kind of magic; a miracle recipe that will result in our being able to produce the perfect meal in fifteen minutes, a meal which feeds six people for under 50 pence a head and stuns our family and friends. Fortunately for cookery writers such a recipe does not exist. Good cooking requires care, a certain skill and a modicum of patience; there are a few reliable short cuts but few ways of cheating with any great success.

But don't be depressed by that opening homily. There are many occasions when the food you serve, although it must be appetising and attractive, does not need to be of high culinary standard, and when time is infinitely more important than *haute cuisine*. This section will, I hope, help to fill this role. The dishes can be served for lunch, a high tea, supper, or to have after the cinema. Their common factor is that they are all simple, quick to make and inexpensive.

Tortilla with Spinach

450 g (1 lb) potatoes
2 large onions
6 eggs
Salt and freshly ground black pepper
50 g (2 oz) ham
4 tablespoons olive or vegetable oil
450 g (1 lb) frozen spinach

Serves 4

Peel the potatoes and cut them into small dice. Peel and finely chop the onions. Beat the eggs and season them with salt and pepper. Finely chop the ham and mix it into the eggs.

Heat the oil in a non-stick frying pan, add the potatoes and onions, cover with a saucepan lid and cook over a low heat, shaking now and then to prevent sticking, for about 15 minutes until the potatoes are tender. Cook the spinach in a little boiling, salted water until tender, drain well and chop roughly with kitchen scissors.

Add the spinach to the onions and potatoes and mix well. Pour over the beaten eggs and ham and cook over a low heat. Lift the bottom of the omelette with the prongs of a fork as it sets to allow more liquid to spread over the bottom of the pan.

As soon as the omelette is solid enough to turn out invert it on to a warmed serving dish. Serve at once with a green salad and a tomato salad sprinkled with a little basil or oregano.

Basic Omelette

8 eggs
Salt and white pepper
25 g (1 oz) butter

Serves 4

Beat the eggs with a fork until whites and yolks are amalgamated but not in any way fluffy (you should not beat air into the eggs). Season lightly with salt and pepper.

Heat the butter in a large omelette pan until it begins to foam, without letting it brown. Add the beaten egg and cook over a high heat, stirring lightly with a fork, until just beginning to set. Shake the pan over the heat every now and then. As soon as the eggs are just set through slide the omelette on to a warm serving dish, folding it in half as you do so. Brush a little butter from the pan over the top to give a glossy sheen and serve at once.

Fines herbes (finely chopped parsley, chives and a little thyme) can be mixed into the basic mixture or sprinkled on to the finished omelette, or mix in any of the following ingredients to produce alternative flavours: a little flaked tunny fish; some peeled and finely chopped tomatoes; chopped ham or cooked bacon; 2 tablespoons diced aubergines fried in butter and drained; thinly sliced button mushrooms fried in butter and drained; grated Cheddar or Gruyère cheese.

Omelettes can also be filled with sauces or cooked ingredients.

Spanish Omelette

Serves 4

1 small onion
50 g (2 oz) cooked ham
1 cooked potato
50 g (2 oz) firm button mushrooms
5 eggs
1 tablespoon water
2 teaspoons finely chopped parsley
Salt and white pepper
75 g (3 oz) butter
1 tablespoon cooked peas

A substantial Spanish omelette makes good use of eggs as well as all kinds of leftovers. Other cooked vegetables can be substituted for the peas and the mushrooms. You can add peeled and chopped tomatoes to the basic recipe, or use lightly-cooked bacon rashers instead of ham.

Peel and finely chop the onion. Cut the ham into small dice. Dice the potato and finely slice the mushrooms. Beat the eggs lightly with water, add the parsley and season with salt and pepper.

Melt the butter in an omelette pan. Add the onion and cook over a low heat until soft and transparent. Add the ham, mushrooms, potato and peas and cook for $1\frac{1}{2}$ minutes until hot through. Pour over the egg mixture and stir lightly with a fork. Cook over a moderate heat until the eggs are just lightly set (do not stir). Put the pan under a hot grill to brown. Slide on to a serving dish and serve at once.

Omelette Mousseline

Serves 4

6 eggs, separated
2 tablespoons single cream
40 g ($1\frac{1}{2}$ oz) finely grated Cheddar cheese
Salt and white pepper
25 g (1 oz) butter
300 ml ($\frac{1}{2}$ pint) home-made tomato sauce
 (p. 159)

This cheese-flavoured omelette, lighter and rather more dry than an ordinary one, contains hot tomato sauce.

Beat yolks with the cream until smooth, mix in the cheese and season with salt and pepper. Beat the whites until fluffy but not stiff and fold lightly into the yolks.

Melt the butter in an omelette pan until foaming but not brown. Pour in the omelette mixture and cook over a high heat, scoring through with a wooden spatula to encourage even cooking. As soon as the omelette has set, slide half of it from the pan on to a heated serving dish, pour over the hot tomato sauce and flip the remaining half over. Serve at once.

Omelette Arnold Bennett

225 g (8 oz) smoked haddock
50 g (2 oz) butter
4 large eggs, separated
150 ml (5 fl oz) single cream
50 g (2 oz) grated Cheddar cheese
Pepper

Serves 4

Poach the haddock until tender in a little water and 15 g (½ oz) of the butter. Drain well, remove any skin and bones and flake the fish.

Beat the egg yolks with half the cream, add the haddock and half the cheese and season with a little pepper. Whip the egg whites lightly and fold into the yolks.

Melt the remaining butter in an omelette pan, add the egg mixture and cook over a medium high heat until just set–the top should still be slightly loose and creamy. Slide, without folding, on to a heated serving dish, pour over remaining cream, top with the remaining grated cheese and brown quickly under a hot grill. Serve at once.

Shepherd's Omelette

100 g (4 oz) cooked meat, poultry or ham
1 onion
1 cooked potato
1 tomato
4 eggs
4 tablespoons single cream
Pinch of dried mixed herbs
Salt and pepper
40 g (1½ oz) butter
50 g (2 oz) cooked peas or beans

Serves 4

Finely chop the meat. Peel and finely chop the onion. Cut the potato into small dice. Peel and chop the tomato. Beat the eggs with the cream, mix in a pinch of mixed herbs and season with salt and pepper.

Melt the butter in a large omelette pan or non-stick frying pan. Add the onion and cook gently until transparent and a light gold in colour. Add the meat, potato, tomatoes and peas or beans; cook over a medium heat for five minutes. Pour over the egg mixture and cook quickly until the egg has set; ease the omelette away from the sides of the pan to allow raw egg mixture to cook.

Serve at once with French bread and a green salad.

Chinese Pancake Omelettes

1 onion
1 red or green pepper
2 sticks celery
6 eggs
Salt and pepper
Vegetable oil
Soya sauce

Serves 4

Peel and very finely chop the onion. Remove core and seeds from the pepper and very finely chop the flesh. Thinly slice the celery sticks. Beat the eggs lightly with a little salt and pepper. Add the prepared vegetables and mix well.

Cover the bottom of a non-stick omelette pan with a thin layer of oil. Heat through and add a large spoonful of the egg mixture, swirling it round until thinly and evenly distributed. Cook over a medium hot flame until brown underneath. Flip over and cook the other side until golden brown. Roll up like a pancake and repeat with remaining mixture.

Serve with rice and soya sauce.

Omelette Suzanne

Serves 4

4 thin rashers bacon
100 g (4 oz) cream cheese
5 eggs, separated
200 ml (7½ fl oz) single cream
Salt and pepper
25 g (1 oz) grated Cheddar cheese
50 g (2 oz) butter

Remove rinds and cut the bacon rashers into thin matchstick strips. Fry, without extra fat, until crisp and drain on kitchen paper. Combine with the cream cheese.

Beat the egg yolks with half the cream. Lightly whip the whites and fold them into the yolk mixture with a little salt and pepper. Add the grated cheese to the remaining cream.

Heat the butter in an omelette pan, add the egg mixture and cook over a medium high heat, cutting through the omelette with a knife as it cooks. When the eggs have just set cover with cream cheese and bacon, fold in half and slide on to a heated serving dish.

Pour over the cream and cheese mixture and brown quickly under a hot grill. Serve at once.

Egg Savouries

Serves 4

225 g (8 oz) ham
225 g (8 oz) mashed potatoes
1 tablespoon finely chopped parsley
Salt and pepper
4 rashers streaky bacon
4 eggs

Finely mince the ham and mix with the mashed potatoes and parsley. Season with salt and pepper and form into four flat rounds about 2·5 cm (1 in) thick. Remove rinds from the bacon and wrap the rashers round the sides of each cake. Fasten in place with a cocktail stick.

Bake the cakes in a moderately hot oven (200°C, 400°F, Reg. 6) for 20 minutes until the bacon is cooked and the cakes are golden brown. Arrange on a serving dish.

Poach four eggs and serve on top of the cakes.

Mediterranean Fried Eggs

Serves 4

1 onion
1 green pepper
4 rashers bacon
1½ tablespoons olive oil
Salt and pepper
4 eggs

Peel and finely slice the onion. Remove core and seeds from the green pepper and cut the flesh into very thin strips. Remove rinds and cut the bacon into small pieces.

Heat the oil in a non-stick frying pan. Add the onion, pepper and bacon, season and cook over a medium heat until the onions are transparent. Break over the eggs, cover with a lid or foil and continue to cook over a low heat for a further three minutes until the eggs are just firm.

Slide carefully on to a warm serving dish.

Curried Eggs

6 hard-boiled eggs
2 onions
1 cooking apple
15 g (½ oz) butter
1 tablespoon olive oil
1 tablespoon curry powder
2 teaspoons tomato purée
300 ml (½ pint) chicken stock, or water and
  stock cube
1 teaspoon lemon juice
1 tablespoon sultanas
1 tablespoon finely chopped parsley

Serves 3–6

Serve these hot as a light main course or cold as a substantial starter. The taste of curry is not over-strong; the end result has the subtle flavouring of an Eastern dish.

Shell and halve the hard-boiled eggs. Peel and thinly slice the onions and divide into rings. Peel the apple, core and cut into small dice. Melt the butter and oil in a frying pan, add the onion rings and cook over medium low heat until soft and transparent. Blend in the curry powder and tomato purée and mix well. Add the stock and cook over a medium heat, stirring continuously, for five minutes. Add the lemon juice, apple and sultanas and continue to cook for a further eight minutes until the apple is soft. Add the eggs, heat through and transfer to a serving dish.
Serve hot or cold garnished with parsley.

Paprika Eggs

4 eggs
1 large onion
50 g (2 oz) butter
1 tablespoon flour
Scant 300 ml (½ pint) milk
2 teaspoons paprika
1½ tablespoons tomato purée
2 tablespoons dry vermouth
Pinch of chervil and basil
Salt and freshly ground black pepper
1 tablespoon cream

Serves 2

Lightly hard-boil the eggs in boiling slightly salted water for five minutes. Immediately run them under cold water and carefully peel off the shells.
Peel and very thinly slice the onion and divide it into rings. Melt one quarter of the butter in a frying pan, add the onion rings and cook over a medium low heat until soft and pale yellow. Arrange in the bottom of a fire-proof serving dish and place the eggs on top.
Heat the remaining butter in a saucepan, add the flour and mix well. Gradually blend in the milk, stirring continuously over a medium heat until the sauce is thick and smooth. Add the paprika, tomato purée, dry vermouth, herbs and seasoning and mix well. Simmer over a very low heat for five minutes, stirring occasionally to allow the flavours to infuse into the sauce. Add the cream and pour the sauce over the eggs and onions. Heat through in a moderately hot oven (200°C, 400°F, Reg. 6) for about five minutes before serving.
Serve the eggs with rice or mashed potatoes. A salad of chicory, thin matchsticks of Gruyère cheese and chopped walnuts, tossed in a vinaigrette dressing, is a nice accompaniment.

Eggs and Bacon in Baked Bread Cases

1 small white loaf
70 g (2½ oz) melted butter
4 eggs
2 rashers bacon
2 tablespoons cream
Salt and pepper

Serves 4

Cut the bread into 7 cm (3 in) thick slices. Remove the crusts and, using a sharp knife, cut out the inside of each slice to within 6 mm (¼ in) of the sides and the bottom to make a neat case. Brush the cases with melted butter and bake in a medium oven until light golden brown. Leave to cool.

Break an egg into each case and bake in a moderate oven (180°C, 350°F, Reg. 4) for about ten minutes until the eggs are just set.

While the eggs are baking finely chop the bacon, after removing the rind, and fry without extra fat until crisp.

Pour a little seasoned cream over each cooked egg, sprinkle with bacon pieces and serve at once.

Scrambled Eggs with Bacon and Mushrooms

2 rashers bacon
50 g (2 oz) firm button mushrooms
6 eggs
1 tablespoon top of the milk
Salt and pepper
25 g (1 oz) butter

Serves 4

Heat a small saucepan of water until boiling. Remove the rind from the bacon, drop the rashers into the water and simmer for ten minutes. Remove, drain well and cut into small pieces.

Thinly slice the mushrooms. Beat the eggs with the milk and season with salt and pepper.

Melt the butter in a saucepan, add the bacon and mushrooms and cook over a low heat for three minutes. Mix in the eggs and cook over a low heat, stirring occasionally, until they begin to set.

Transfer to a heated serving dish and serve at once.

Travellers' Breakfast

4 rashers lean bacon
4 eggs
1 large can baked beans
Breadcrumbs
15 g (½ oz) butter

Serves 4

Remove rinds and cut the bacon into thin strips; cook over a medium heat without extra fat until tender. Place bacon and bacon fat in the bottom of a fire-proof baking dish.

Poach the eggs lightly in boiling salted water, drain well and trim off any untidy edges with a pair of kitchen scissors.

Arrange the eggs on the bacon and cover with the baked beans. Sprinkle a layer of breadcrumbs over the surface of the dish and dot with small pieces of butter.

Bake the dish in a hot oven (220°C, 425°F, Reg. 7) for about 15 minutes until the top is golden brown and the ingredients hot through. Serve with buttered toast cut into 'soldiers'.

Juan's Baked Eggs with Prawns and Pimento

200 g (7 oz) can pimentos
1 small onion
1 clove garlic
1 tablespoon olive oil
A few drops Tabasco sauce
Pinch of oregano and basil
50 g (2 oz) peeled prawns
Salt and freshly ground black pepper
4 eggs

Serves 2

Drain the pimentos and thinly slice the flesh. Peel and thinly slice the onion and divide into rings. Peel the garlic and squeeze through a garlic press or crush with a fork. Heat the olive oil in a saucepan, add the garlic and onion and cook over a low heat until the onion is very soft and transparent.

Add the pimento, Tabasco and herbs, cover and continue to cook over a low heat for ten minutes. Mix in the prawns, season with salt and pepper and turn into a serving dish. Push the mixture to the sides to make four hollows and break the eggs into these. Bake in a moderate oven (180°C, 350°F, Reg. 4) for about eight minutes until the whites are just set but the yolks still soft–the time varies a little from oven to oven.

Serve the eggs at once with rice cooked in chicken broth, or triangles of crisply fried bread; and with a salad of lettuce hearts, cut into quarters, tomatoes, peeled and quartered, slices of celery and stoned black olives, tossed in a dressing to which a pinch of sugar, a hint of mustard and just a little touch of aniseed and tarragon have been added.

Piperade

2 rashers fat bacon
3 large ripe tomatoes
2 green peppers
1 small onion
6 eggs
2 tablespoons cream
Salt and pepper

Serves 4

A delicious mixture of eggs, tomatoes, onion and green peppers which can be served hot or cold. Thin slices of prosciutto or ham and a green or mixed salad should accompany the dish.

Remove rinds, finely chop the bacon rashers and fry them gently until the fat has melted.

Peel and chop the tomatoes. Remove core and seeds from the green peppers and cut the flesh into thin strips. Peel and very thinly slice the onion and divide into rings. Add the vegetables to the bacon and cook slowly, stirring every now and then to prevent browning, for about 20 minutes or until the green peppers are quite soft.

Beat the eggs with the cream and pour over the vegetables. Season with salt and pepper and cook gently, stirring with a light hand, over a low heat until the eggs are just set.

Turn on to a serving dish and serve at once, or leave to get cold and cut into wedges like a cake.

Creamy Eggs and Bacon on Toast

Serves 4

4 hard-boiled eggs
50 g (2 oz) mushrooms
4 rashers lean bacon
25 g (1 oz) butter
25 g (1 oz) flour
300 ml ($\frac{1}{2}$ pint) milk
Salt and pepper

Roughly chop the eggs and thinly slice the mushrooms.

Remove rinds and fry bacon until crisp; drain well on kitchen paper and chop finely. Cook the mushrooms in a little extra butter, over a gentle heat, for three minutes.

Heat the butter in a saucepan, add the flour and mix well until the mixture forms a ball and come away from the sides of the pan. Gradually blend in the milk, stirring continuously over a medium high heat, until the sauce is thick and smooth. Fold in the eggs, bacon and mushrooms, season with salt and pepper and heat through.

Pile the hot, creamy eggs and bacon on to four pieces of generously buttered hot toast and serve at once.

Cauliflower with Scrambled Eggs

Serves 4

1 small cauliflower
1 onion
4 large eggs
40 g (1$\frac{1}{2}$ oz) butter
Pinch of caraway seeds
Salt and white pepper
Slices of buttered toast

An unusual Czechoslovakian supper dish that has a special taste all of its own.

Steam the cauliflower until just cooked but still quite crisp. Cool and divide into florets. Peel and very thinly slice the onion. Beat the eggs with a fork.

Melt the butter in a saucepan. Add the onion and cook over a low heat until soft and transparent. Add the cauliflower florets and caraway seeds and cook over a low heat for three minutes, stirring to prevent sticking. Add the eggs, season with salt and pepper and cook gently, stirring lightly until just set.

Serve on buttered toast.

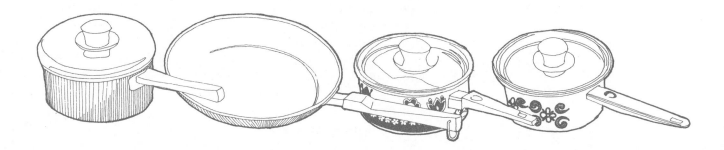

Egg and Anchovy Pie

6 hard-boiled eggs
1 can anchovies
Milk
2 boiled potatoes
25 g (1 oz) butter
2 tablespoons flour
450 ml (¾ pint) milk
Salt and freshly ground black pepper
2 tablespoons parsley
Browned breadcrumbs
A little melted butter

Serves 4

A dish that is as simple to make as it is good to eat.

Shell and roughly chop the hard-boiled eggs. Soak the anchovy fillets in milk for ten minutes to remove excess salt. Squeeze out milk and finely chop the fillets. Cut the potatoes into very small dice.

Melt the butter, add the flour and mix well. Gradually add the milk, stirring continuously over a medium high heat until the sauce comes to the boil and is thick and smooth. Season with salt and pepper and simmer for three minutes. Add the hard-boiled eggs, anchovies, potato and parsley and mix lightly.

Transfer the mixture to a lightly greased fire-proof serving dish, cover with a thin layer of breadcrumbs and dribble over a little melted butter. Bake in a moderate oven (180°C, 350°F, Reg. 4) for 20–30 minutes and serve with a salad or green vegetables.

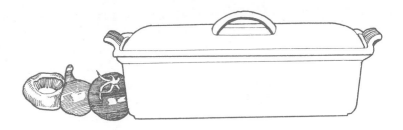

Smothered Eggs

2 onions
100 g (4 oz) mushrooms
2 tablespoons olive oil
Salt and pepper
1 tablespoon tomato purée
6–8 hard-boiled eggs
25 g (1 oz) butter
1 tablespoon flour
300 ml (½ pint) milk
75 g (3 oz) grated Cheddar cheese
2 tablespoons cream

Serves 4

Peel and thinly slice the onions and divide into rings. Thinly slice the mushrooms. Heat the oil in a frying pan, add the onions and cook over a medium heat until soft and pale golden. Add the mushrooms and cook for a further 2–3 minutes until just soft. Season with salt and pepper and stir in the tomato purée. Arrange the mixture in the bottom of a shallow baking dish and top with the hard-boiled eggs, halved and placed cut side down.

Melt the butter in a saucepan, add the flour and mix well. Gradually blend in the milk, stirring continuously until the sauce comes to the boil and is thick and smooth. Mix in two thirds of the cheese, add the cream and cook over a low heat until the cheese has melted. Check seasoning and pour the sauce evenly over the eggs.

Top with the remaining grated cheese and brown under a hot grill.

Panzerotti

The filling:

40 g (1½ oz) butter
4 tablespoons flour
300 ml (½ pint) milk
4 tablespoons cream cheese
5 tablespoons finely grated Parmesan cheese
1 egg, well beaten
Salt and freshly ground black pepper
100 g (4 oz) finely chopped ham

The pancakes:

6 tablespoons flour
Pinch of salt
200 ml (7 fl oz) milk
2 eggs, well beaten
Olive or vegetable oil for frying

The sauce:

1 onion
1 clove garlic
2 tablespoons olive oil
400 g (14 oz) canned tomatoes
Small pinch of oregano and basil
Salt and freshly ground black pepper
100 g (4 oz) mozzarella cheese, sliced
Parmesan cheese

Serves 4–6

Delicious pancakes, stuffed with cream cheese and ham and served with tomato sauce; my own version of a dish I once enjoyed in a small Tuscan restaurant.

Make the filling first. Melt the butter in a small heavy pan. Add the flour and mix well until the mixture forms a ball and comes away from the sides of the pan. Gradually add the milk, stirring continuously over a medium high heat until mixture is smooth and just comes to the boil. Remove from the heat. Allow to cool for ten minutes and then beat in the cream cheese, Parmesan and egg. Season with salt and pepper and mix in the chopped ham. Refrigerate for at least 30 minutes.

Then make the pancakes. Put flour into a bowl with a pinch of salt. Gradually beat in the milk with wooden spoon, and when it has all been incorporated, beat with a rotary whisk until smooth. Beat in the eggs. Heat a thin film of oil in a non-stick pan until it is smoking. Add about two tablespoons of the batter and swirl it around until it forms an even layer across the bottom. Cook for about 1½ minutes until the pancake is set and slightly browned on the bottom; turn over and cook for a further 1½ minutes until golden brown and firm but still pliable and not brittle. As the pancakes are cooked pile them on a plate with greaseproof paper between each one.

Now make the sauce. Peel and finely chop the onion and garlic. Heat the oil, add the onion and garlic and cook over a medium high heat until the onion is soft and transparent. Add the tomatoes and herbs, season with salt and pepper and mix well to break up the tomatoes. Bring to the boil and simmer for 20 minutes, stirring occasionally to prevent sticking.

Spread the chilled filling over the pancakes and roll up tightly. Cut the rolled pancakes into 2·5 cm (1 in) thick slices. Spread two thirds of the tomato sauce over the bottom of a fire-proof serving dish and place the pancakes, cut sides up, on top. Arrange the slices of mozzarella cheese on top, cover with the remaining tomato sauce and sprinkle with Parmesan.

Bake in a moderately hot oven (200°C, 400°F, Reg. 6) for 15 minutes until hot through and bubbling.

Portuguese Eggs

2 large onions
2 green peppers
6 hard-boiled eggs
3 tablespoons olive oil
425 g (15 oz) can tomatoes
1 tablespoon tomato purée
Pinch of basil and oregano
Salt and freshly ground black pepper
1 can anchovy fillets
Milk

Serves 4

An excellent main course supper with a southern flavour.

Peel and very thinly slice the onions. Remove core and seeds from the peppers and cut the flesh into thin strips. Halve the hard-boiled eggs.

Heat the olive oil in a frying pan. Add the onion and peppers and cook over low heat until the onions are soft and transparent. Add the tomatoes, tomato purée and herbs, season with salt and pepper and bring to the boil. Cover and simmer gently for 20 minutes, stirring every now and then to break up the tomatoes. Soak the anchovy fillets in milk for five minutes, drain well and pat dry on kitchen paper.

Arrange the eggs, cut side down, in a lightly greased shallow fire-proof serving dish and cover with the vegetables. Top with a criss-cross pattern of anchovy fillets and heat through in a moderate oven (180°C, 350°F, Reg. 4) before serving.

Accompany with garlic bread and a crisp green salad.

Oeufs Mollets in Bread Nests

4 large and 1 small egg
50 g (2 oz) fat bacon
Olive oil
1 small onion
3 tomatoes
Salt and pepper
Four 2 cm ($\frac{3}{4}$ in) thick slices of bread with
  crusts trimmed off; or four large bread rolls
2 teaspoons very finely chopped parsley

Serves 4 as a first course, 2 as a main course

Cook the four large eggs in boiling salted water for six minutes. Plunge them into cold water, carefully remove the shells and keep warm in hand-hot water. Cook the small egg in boiling salted water for ten minutes, then plunge into cold water. Remove shell and chop the hard-boiled egg.

Very finely chop the bacon, combine with 1 tablespoon of olive oil and cook over a medium high heat, stirring to prevent sticking, for three minutes. Add the onion, very finely chopped, and the tomatoes, peeled and chopped, and cook over a high heat, so that the sauce reduces, for 20 minutes. Rub through a sieve and season with salt and pepper.

Carefully cut out the centre of the bread slices, leaving a rim about 6 mm ($\frac{1}{4}$ in) thick; or cut a slice off the top of each roll and scoop out the soft bread inside. Brush the slices or rolls with olive oil and bake in a hot oven (230°C, 450°F, Reg. 8) for five minutes until crisp and golden brown. Arrange an egg in each nest, pour over the sauce and garnish with hard-boiled egg mixed with chopped parsley. Serve at once.

Baked Eggs with Tomato Purée and Cream

For each serving:
15 g (½ oz) butter
2 teaspoons tomato purée
2 eggs
Salt and freshly ground black pepper
2 teaspoons double cream
1 teaspoon very finely chopped fresh chervil or
    parsley

One of my favourite supper dishes when I am on my own.

Place the butter in the bottom of a ramekin dish large enough to take the two eggs and put into a moderate oven (180°C, 350°F, Reg. 4) just long enough for the butter to melt. Mix tomato purée into the melted butter and break in the eggs. Season with salt and pepper and return to the oven for 6–8 minutes until the eggs are lightly set. Pour over the cream, sprinkle over the chervil or parsley and serve at once with toast or hot French bread.

Alternatively place the ramekins in a covered frying pan half-filled with boiling water. Cook over a gentle heat for ten minutes or until set.

Oeufs Mollets with Herb Sauce

4 eggs
70 g (2½ oz) butter
2 teaspoons flour
150 ml (¼ pint) chicken stock or consommé
1 tablespoon finely chopped parsley
Pinch of dried tarragon
Salt and freshly ground black pepper
1 teaspoon lemon juice
4 slices of buttered toast

Serves 4 as a first course, 2 as a main course

Cook the eggs in boiling, salted water for exactly six minutes, keeping the water on the boil the whole time. Plunge them immediately into cold water to prevent further cooking (the eggs should still be slightly soft inside–*mollet*–and not hard-boiled). Carefully remove the shells and then keep the eggs warm in hand-hot water.

Heat half the butter, add the flour and mix well. Gradually blend in the stock, stirring continuously over a medium heat until the sauce is smooth, thick and shiny. Add the parsley and tarragon, season with salt and pepper and blend in a further 15 g (½ oz) of the butter. Simmer gently for 20 minutes. Remove from the heat and mix in the lemon juice and remaining butter. Beat well.

Place an egg on each slice of buttered toast, pour over the sauce and heat through quickly in a hot oven.

Oeufs Mollets with Prawns

8 eggs
175 g (6 oz) peeled prawns
50 g (2 oz) butter
1½ tablespoons flour
300 ml (½ pint) milk
75 g (3 oz) grated Gruyère cheese
Salt and white pepper
1 egg yolk
2 tablespoons double cream
Cayenne pepper
2 slices white bread
Fat for frying

Serves 4

Cook the eggs in boiling water for five minutes and immediately transfer to cold water. Peel them carefully and arrange with the prawns in a lightly greased baking dish.

Melt the butter in a saucepan. Add the flour and mix well. Gradually add the milk, stirring continuously over a moderately high heat until the sauce is thick and smooth. Add the cheese, season with salt and pepper and cook gently, stirring, until the cheese has melted. Beat the egg yolk with the cream and blend into the sauce.

Pour the sauce over the eggs and prawns, sprinkle with a little cayenne and cook under a hot grill until the sauce bubbles and has a golden brown crust. Serve with triangles of fried bread.

Cheese Soufflés Surprises

50 g (2 oz) butter
50 g (2 oz) flour
300 ml (½ pint) milk
3 eggs, separated
1 teaspoon made English mustard
100 g (4 oz) finely grated Cheddar cheese
Salt and pepper
4 whole eggs

Serves 4

Like all soufflés, these wait for no man, and must be brought straight to the table as soon as they are ready.

Heat the butter until melted; add the flour and mix well. Gradually blend in the milk, stirring continuously until the mixture is thick and smooth. Remove from the heat and beat in the three egg yolks, one at a time, and the mustard and grated cheese. Season with salt and pepper. Break the four whole eggs into separate cups; beat the three egg whites until stiff and fold them lightly into the cheese base.

Put half of the soufflé mixture into four well-buttered ramekin dishes. Carefully slide a whole raw egg into the centre of each dish and spoon over remaining soufflé mixture.

Bake in a hot oven (220°C, 425°F, Reg. 7) for 8–12 minutes until the soufflés are well risen and their tops are a crusty brown. Serve at once. The eggs in the centre should be set, with whites firm but yolks still soft.

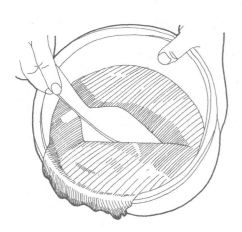

Cheese Pancakes

Serves 4

100 g (4 oz) plain flour
¼ teaspoon salt
1 egg
300 ml (½ pint) milk, or half milk half water
4 tablespoons grated cheese
A little lard or cooking oil

Sieve the flour and salt into a basin. Break the egg into a cup. Make a hollow in the flour with the back of a tablespoon, drop in the egg and add a little of the milk. Stir the egg and milk with a wooden spoon, gradually drawing in the flour. Add the remaining milk little by little. When the mixture is smooth, beat it with your wooden spoon until little air bubbles appear. Sieve it into a jug, add the cheese and stir.

Heat a teaspoonful of oil in a small frying pan. Pour a tablespoon of the batter into the centre of the pan, tilting the pan so the mixture runs all over the bottom. Cook for about two minutes or until the edges look brown and crispy. Turn the pancake over with a fish slice and cook the other side. Take it out of the pan and put it on a plate. Now repeat the performance.

You can wrap your pancakes round any of these fillings: a small tin of baked beans, heated up; leftover meat or vegetables, well heated up and sizzling hot; a fried egg; some fried bacon; a small tin of sweetcorn, heated up; well-fried sausages, or Frankfurter sausages.

Baked Onion, Bacon and Apples

Serves 4

4 large or 6 medium onions
2 cooking apples
8 thin rashers bacon
100 g (4 oz) fresh white breadcrumbs
200 ml (7½ fl oz) stock
Salt and freshly ground black pepper

This dish can be served as a main course for supper with a salad and hot French bread, or it can be used as a marvellous accompaniment to pork, lamb or duck dishes.

Peel and slice the onions. Peel, core and slice the apples. Fry the bacon rashers without any extra fat over a medium high heat until crisp. Reserve the bacon fat, remove the rinds and finely chop the rashers. Add the breadcrumbs to the bacon fat and cook over a high heat until golden brown.

Lightly grease a baking dish. Arrange alternate layers of onion, apple and bacon in the dish, pour over the stock, season lightly and top with the breadcrumbs.

Cover the dish with foil and bake in a moderate oven (190°C, 375°F, Reg. 5) for 30 minutes. Remove the foil and continue to cook for another 15 minutes to brown the top.

Athenian Baked Casserole

2 small aubergines
450 g (1 lb) courgettes
1–3 cloves garlic
1 small onion
Olive or sunflower oil
675 g (1½ lb) ripe tomatoes
Salt and freshly ground black pepper
½ teaspoon mixed herbs
2 tablespoons fresh white breadcrumbs
Anchovy fillets

Serves 4–6

Don't be concerned when aubergines discolour as they are cut; this does not affect their flavour and disappears as they cook. As they contain a fair amount of water they are often sliced, sprinkled with salt and left to sweat before being dried and cooked.

This dish can be served hot or cold, either as a first course or as a vegetarian main course. It is delicious spread on fresh rye bread or crisp slices of French bread.

Cut the aubergines into 6 mm (¼ in) slices. Slice the courgettes. Peel the garlic and crush the cloves with the back of a fork. Peel and thinly slice the onion and divide into rings.

Heat 2 tablespoons of oil in a large heavy frying pan, add the onion and garlic and cook over a low heat until the onion is soft and transparent. Remove onion and garlic with a slotted spoon. Fry the courgettes in the pan juices over a low heat, adding more oil if necessary, for three minutes, turning the slices once. Remove the courgettes and fry the aubergines for three minutes.

If the tomatoes are the Mediterranean variety they will not need to be peeled before slicing, but English ones should be (cover with boiling water, leave for one minute then drain and slide off skins).

Arrange half the courgette and aubergine in a greased casserole dish. Cover with the onion, half the tomato slices, the rest of the courgette and aubergine and finish with the remaining tomato slices. Season the layers with salt and pepper and sprinkle in the herbs. Sprinkle with the breadcrumbs and top with anchovy fillets cut into very thin strips. Dribble over one tablespoon of oil and bake in a moderate oven (180°C, 350°F, Reg. 4) for 45 minutes.

Savoury Aubergines

Serves 4

100 g (4 oz) long-grain rice
2 large or 4 small aubergines
Salt
Olive oil for frying
50 g (2 oz) bacon
1 large onion
1 clove garlic
225 g (8 oz) can tomatoes
150 g (5 oz) carton yoghurt
Freshly ground black pepper
50 g (2 oz) grated cheese

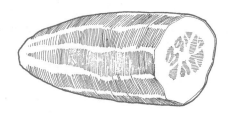

Cook the rice in boiling salted water, rinse in cold water and drain.

Cut the aubergines in half and, using a sharp knife, cut round the edge of the flesh without piercing skin. Score through centre of flesh, making a criss-cross pattern, and sprinkle with salt. Heat two tablespoons of olive oil in a large frying pan. Add aubergines, cut side down, cover with a lid and cook over a moderate heat for 20 minutes or until the flesh is soft. Leave to cool, scoop out flesh from the skins and chop finely. (Reserve the skins.)

Finely chop or mince the bacon. Peel and finely chop onion and garlic. Heat one tablespoon of olive oil, add the bacon, onion and garlic and cook over a medium heat until the onions are transparent. Add the tomatoes, season with salt and pepper and cook for a further three minutes. Remove from the heat and mix in the rice, yoghurt and aubergine flesh; season with pepper. Fill the aubergine skins with this mixture and arrange in a lightly greased baking dish.

Cover lightly with foil and bake for 15–20 minutes in a moderately hot oven (200°C, 400°F, Reg. 6). Sprinkle with cheese and brown quickly under a hot grill.

Toad in the Hole

Serves 4

450 g (1 lb) pork sausages
Dripping
175 g (6 oz) flour
Pinch of salt and a little white pepper
2 eggs
Pinch of sage and thyme
600 ml (1 pint) milk

If your sausages are those lovely herby ones you will not need to add herbs to the batter.

Divide each sausage into two by twisting gently in the centre two or three times and cutting through the links. Fry sausages in a little dripping over a low heat until well browned on all sides (cooking slowly will prevent their exploding).

Put the flour in a basin with salt and pepper. Make a well in the centre, break in the eggs and beat from the centre with a wooden spoon, gradually incorporating flour and eggs. When the mixture is thick add the herbs and milk and beat with a rotary whisk until smooth and free from lumps.

Put two tablespoons of dripping into a fire-proof baking dish, add the mini-sausages and heat through in the oven until the dripping is very hot. Gently pour in the batter and bake for about 25 minutes at 220°C (425°F, Reg. 7) until the batter is well puffed and brown. Serve at once with gravy or tomato sauce.

Jerusalem Artichokes with Bacon and Parsley Sauce

300 ml (½ pint) milk
1 small onion, peeled
1 stick celery
2 cloves
6 black peppercorns
4 large Jerusalem artichokes
Juice of ½ lemon
4 large rashers streaky bacon
25 g (1 oz) butter
1 tablespoon flour
Salt and white pepper
3 tablespoons finely chopped parsley

Serves 4

This is my interpretation of a dish which I believe originated in France, where Jerusalem artichokes are still given the respect they deserve. They are knobbly-looking tubers, quite unlike the more familiar globe artichokes.

Combine the milk, onion, celery, cloves and peppercorns in a saucepan and bring to the boil. Cover, simmer for 20 minutes and strain. Peel the artichokes, trimming off protuberances to give smooth egg-like shapes. Place in cold salted water to which the lemon juice has been added, bring to the boil and cook for 20–30 minutes until they are tender but not mushy. Drain well.

Remove rinds from the bacon and cook the rashers without extra fat over a low heat for five minutes; drain off excess fat.

Melt the butter in a saucepan, add the flour and mix well. Gradually add the strained milk, stirring continuously over a medium high heat until the sauce is thick and smooth. Season with salt and pepper and simmer for four minutes. Mix in the chopped parsley. Wrap the cooked bacon around the artichokes and put under the grill for a few minutes to crisp up the bacon and heat the artichokes. Then serve on four plates with the artichokes in the centre and parsley sauce around them.

Huntingdon Fidget Pie

450 g (1 lb) streaky bacon
225 g (8 oz) onions
450 g (1 lb) cooking apples
Salt and pepper
150 ml (¼ pint) cider
225 g (8 oz) plain flour
100 g (4 oz) butter
Beaten egg or milk

Serves 4–6

Remove rind from the bacon and dice the rashers. Peel and chop the onions; core and chop the apples. Mix all well together and season. Put into a 1-litre (2-pint) pie dish and pour over the cider.

Sieve the flour with a pinch of salt. Rub in the butter until mixture resembles breadcrumbs. Mix with just enough water to form a firm dough. Roll out and cover the pie. Make four cuts from the centre about 8 cm (3 in) long and fold back triangles of pastry to expose the filling. Decorate with pastry crescents around the edge.

Brush the pie with beaten egg or milk and bake for 20 minutes in a hot oven (230°C, 450°F, Reg. 8). Lower the heat to moderate (180°C, 350°F, Reg. 4) and bake for a further 30 minutes until crisp and golden.

Hungarian Goulash

Serves 6

1 green pepper
2 onions
675 g (1½ lb) potatoes
1 tablespoon olive oil or 15 g (½ oz) butter
Two 425 g (15 oz) cans braised steak
1 can tomato soup
1 tablespoon paprika pepper
Pinch of sugar
1 bay leaf
Salt and freshly ground black pepper

Finely chop the green pepper and onions. Peel and slice the potatoes. Heat the oil or butter, add the pepper and onion and cook until the onion is soft and golden. Mix in the meat, potatoes and tomato soup. Add the paprika pepper, sugar and bay leaf. Season well with salt and pepper and thin, if necessary, with a little water.

Bring the goulash to the boil, lower the heat and simmer until the potatoes are just soft; about 25 minutes. Check seasoning and remove bay leaf before serving.

Mediterranean Macaroni and Cauliflower Cheese

Serves 6

1 small cauliflower
225 g (8 oz) macaroni
400 g (14 oz) canned tomatoes
175 g (6 oz) ham
3 hard-boiled eggs
Pinch of saffron
50 g (2 oz) butter
50 g (2 oz) flour
450 ml (¾ pint) milk
100 g (4 oz) grated Cheddar cheese
Salt and freshly ground black pepper
50 g (2 oz) fresh white breadcrumbs
A little melted butter

This is a hotch-potch family dish that doesn't take long to prepare, is inexpensive and will satisfy everyone. It can be made in advance and the only accompaniment it needs is a green or mixed salad. Leftover chicken, cooked rashers of bacon or sliced cooked sausages can be used instead of ham.

Steam the cauliflower until just tender but still crisp. Cook the macaroni in boiling salted water until tender and drain well. Drain off the tomato juice (this can be used in soups or stews) and roughly chop the tomatoes. Chop the ham and quarter the hard-boiled eggs. Combine these ingredients in a fire-proof serving dish.

Infuse the saffron in 150 ml (¼ pint) of boiling water. Melt the butter in a heavy pan. Add the flour and mix well. Gradually blend in the milk, stirring continuously over a high heat until thick and smooth. Add half the cheese and continue to stir until it has melted.

Blend in the saffron water and season with salt and pepper. Pour the sauce over the other ingredients, mixing lightly with a fork. Scatter the breadcrumbs and remaining cheese over the top and dribble over a little melted butter.

Bake in a moderate oven (180°C, 350°F, Reg. 4) until hot through and golden brown on the surface; 20–30 minutes.

Spaghetti or Tagliatelle Carbonara

50 g (2 oz) ham
3 eggs
50 g (2 oz) finely grated cheese
Salt and pepper
450 g (1 lb) spaghetti or tagliatelle
50 g (2 oz) butter
2 tablespoons cream

Serves 6 as a first course, 4 as a main course

Ideally this should be made with thin ribbon tagliatelle flavoured with spinach, but thicker noodles or spaghetti make a good substitute. The sauce is light and subtle and so makes the dish ideal to serve as a first course.

Finely chop the ham, beat the eggs with a fork and combine ham, eggs and half the cheese; season with salt and pepper.

Cook the spaghetti or tagliatelle in boiling salted water until just tender, drain well and rinse in cool water. Return the spaghetti or tagliatelle to a saucepan with the butter and stir gently over a low flame until the butter melts. Pour over the egg mixture and continue to stir, without breaking the pasta, until the egg is on the point of setting (the sauce should be liquid, not scrambled).

Add the cream, check seasoning, turn on to a serving dish and sprinkle with the remaining cheese before serving.

Spaghetti al Formaggio

1 clove garlic
1 small onion
450 g (1 lb) ripe tomatoes (or use canned ones)
675 g (1½ lb) spaghetti
3 tablespoons olive oil
2 tablespoons finely chopped parsley
1 tablespoon dried basil (or 2 teaspoons finely chopped fresh basil)
Salt and pepper
100 g (4 oz) finely grated pecorino, Cheddar or Gruyère cheese

Serves 6

Pasta should be served as quickly as possible after it has been cooked. The cooking time will range from 10 to 20 minutes, according to thickness, and the finished pasta should be firm, not mushy.

Peel and crush the garlic clove. Peel and finely chop the onion. Peel and chop the tomatoes. Put the spaghetti into a large saucepan of fast-boiling salted water and stir with a wooden spoon during cooking to prevent it from sticking.

Heat the olive oil in a small saucepan. Add the garlic and onion and cook over a medium heat until the onion is soft and transparent. Add the tomatoes and herbs and season with salt and pepper. Bring to the boil and cook over a medium high heat for 15 minutes.

Drain the cooked spaghetti, rinse quickly in running cold water and turn at once into a well-heated heat-proof serving dish, preferably earthenware. Pour over the sauce, mix well and top with grated cheese.

Bake in a moderately hot oven (200°C, 400°F, Reg. 6) for 5–10 minutes until the cheese has melted.

Serve at once with a green salad of fennel roots, lettuce and thinly shredded green peppers.

Spaghetti alla Rustica

675 g (1½ lb) spaghetti
Salt and freshly ground black pepper
25 g (1 oz) butter
1 can anchovy fillets
Milk
2 cloves garlic
50 g (2 oz) firm button mushrooms
1 small onion
6 tablespoons olive oil
1 teaspoon oregano
1 tablespoon finely chopped parsley
50–100 g (2–4 oz) grated Parmesan cheese

Serves 6

Cook the spaghetti in boiling salted water. Drain well and stir in the butter.

Soak the anchovies in a little milk for five minutes to remove oil and salt; squeeze out milk and pat dry with kitchen paper. Finely chop the anchovies, very thinly slice the mushrooms, crush the garlic cloves, peel and finely chop the onion.

Heat the olive oil in a saucepan, add the garlic and onion and cook until transparent. Add anchovies and mushrooms, oregano and parsley, season with pepper and cook over a low heat, stirring gently, for ten minutes.

Turn the spaghetti into a heated earthenware dish, mix in the sauce and sprinkle with grated cheese. Serve at once.

Spaghetti al Burro

450 g (1 lb) spaghetti
70 g (2½ oz) butter
Salt and freshly ground black pepper
50 g (2 oz) grated Parmesan cheese

Serves 4

Robin, that non-gourmet husband of mine, maintains that the only way spaghetti should really be eaten is quite plain with just a dressing of butter, freshly ground black pepper and grated Parmesan cheese. Here is the recipe for other purists to follow.

Cook the spaghetti until just tender in boiling salted water over a fast heat, stirring it every now and then with a wooden spoon to prevent sticking.

Drain well and rinse quickly in cold running water. Melt the butter in a fire-proof serving dish. Add the spaghetti, season with salt and plenty of pepper and toss over a low heat so that all the butter is absorbed into the pasta.

Sprinkle over the cheese and serve at once with a salad of thinly sliced tomatoes, very thinly sliced raw onion, slivers of red pepper and some stoned black olives dressed with a vinaigrette flavoured with fresh herbs.

Spaghetti with Tomato and the Fat of Ham

900 g (2 lb) fresh tomatoes (don't use canned)
75 g (3 oz) butter
1 tablespoon chopped onion
75 g (3 oz) ham fat, chopped
Salt and freshly ground black pepper
675 g (1½ lb) spaghetti or vermicelli
1 tablespoon chopped fresh basil
100 g (4 oz) grated Parmesan cheese

Serves 6

Put the tomatoes in boiling water for one minute. Peel, take out seeds and liquid, shake dry and cut the flesh into strips.

Put a third of the butter in a frying pan with the chopped onion, ham fat and a good sprinkling of pepper. Cook over a moderate heat until the onion turns golden. Add the tomato strips, season with salt and cook for 15 minutes.

When the spaghetti or vermicelli has been cooked and drained, put in a serving dish. Add the remaining butter in small pats, with the basil, half the Parmesan and the tomato sauce. Mix well and serve accompanied by the rest of the cheese.

Bacon Rashers with Spaghetti

225 g (8 oz) spaghetti
8 thick rashers back bacon
1 small onion, chopped
225 g (8 oz) small tomatoes
50 g (2 oz) grated Samsoe or Gruyère cheese
50 g (2 oz) butter
Salt and freshly ground black pepper
1 tablespoon finely chopped parsley

Serves 4

Boil the spaghetti in plenty of salted water for ten minutes. Drain well and keep hot. Remove bacon rinds and fry the rashers, without extra fat, until tender; keep hot. Add the onion to the bacon fat and cook over a medium heat until soft; remove with a slotted spoon and mix with the cooked spaghetti. Add the whole tomatoes to the bacon fat and cook gently for three minutes.

Mix the spaghetti with the grated cheese and butter in a clean pan and heat through until piping hot. Season with plenty of salt and pepper and transfer to a hot serving dish. Arrange the bacon and tomatoes on top of the spaghetti and sprinkle over the parsley. Serve at once.

Ham and Mushroom Risotto

225 g (8 oz) long-grain rice
2 onions
50 g (2 oz) firm mushrooms
100 g (4 oz) ham
3 tablespoons olive oil
4 tablespoons stock
Pinch of mixed herbs
Salt and freshly ground black pepper
Grated Parmesan cheese

Serves 4

Cook the rice until just tender in boiling salted water. Peel and finely chop the onions. Thinly slice the mushrooms and chop the ham. Heat the olive oil in a large frying pan, add the onions and cook over a medium heat until transparent; add the mushrooms and cook for two minutes. Mix in the rice, ham, stock and herbs, season with salt and pepper and heat through for five minutes, stirring gently to avoid breaking up the mushrooms.

Serve sprinkled with Parmesan.

Spaghetti al Guanciale

675 g (1½ lb) spaghetti
Salt and freshly ground black pepper
25 g (1 oz) butter
225 g (8 oz) streaky bacon
1 medium onion
225 g (8 oz) can tomatoes
2 tablespoons olive oil
1 tablespoon finely chopped parsley
1 sprig marjoram (or ½ teaspoon dried
   marjoram)
50–100 g (2–4 oz) grated Parmesan cheese

Serves 6

A simple spaghetti dish from the region of Umbria in Italy with the classic rich tomato sauce flavoured with marjoram that, when I make it, transports me immediately to this lovely part of the country.

Cook the spaghetti in boiling salted water, drain and stir in the butter. Remove rinds and cut the bacon into small dice. Peel and finely chop the onion. Drain off excess liquid from the tomatoes.

Heat the olive oil in a saucepan, add the bacon and cook gently for five minutes. Add the onion and cook until soft. Stir in the tomatoes, parsley and marjoram, season with salt and pepper, bring to the boil and simmer for ten minutes.

Turn the spaghetti into a heated earthenware dish (rubbed with a clove of garlic if you like), mix in the sauce and sprinkle over the grated cheese. Serve at once.

Danish Pizza

The filling:
6 rashers streaky bacon
40 g (1½ oz) Danish mozzarella cheese
1 small onion
25 g (1 oz) butter
225 g (8 oz) can tomatoes
½ level teaspoon mixed herbs
Freshly ground black pepper

The dough:
100 g (4 oz) self-raising flour
½ level teaspoon salt
70 g (2½ oz) butter, melted
1 tablespoon olive oil

Serves 2–3

Remove the rind from the bacon and fry or grill the rashers lightly on one side.

Cut the mozzarella into 1 cm (½ in) strips. Chop the onion and fry in the butter until soft. Drain and add the tomatoes, herbs and pepper and cook gently for five minutes, breaking the tomatoes and stirring them with a fork. Increase the heat and boil the sauce for a few minutes to reduce the excess liquid.

Mix the flour and salt in a bowl, add one tablespoon of the melted butter and enough cold water to make a soft dough. Roll out on a floured board to an 18 cm (7 in) round.

Heat the remaining butter with the oil in a 20 cm (8 in) frying pan, put in the dough and cook over a medium heat for about four minutes until the underneath is golden brown. Carefully turn over and spread with the tomato mixture: arrange the bacon rashers on top and cover with strips of cheese. Cook for a further four minutes and brown under a pre-heated grill until the bacon is sizzling and the cheese has melted.

Nasi Goreng

2 eggs
Salt and freshly ground black pepper
Olive oil for frying
225 g (8 oz) long-grain rice
300 ml (½ pint) water
1 large onion
1 small clove garlic
225 g (8 oz) lean pork
2 shallots or small leeks
1 tablespoon soya sauce
1¼ tablespoons dried onion flakes

Serves 4

This is an Indonesian fried rice dish.

Beat the eggs and season with salt and pepper. Heat a little olive oil in an omelette pan, add half the egg and cook over a medium heat until just set. Slide on to a plate and repeat with the remainder. Slide the second omelette on top of the first and leave to cool. Keeping the cooked omelettes one on top of the other, roll up pancake-style and cut into very thin slices.

Place the rice in a colander, rinse through with plenty of cold running water and drain well. Bring the water to the boil, add the rice, season with a little salt and bring back to the boil, stirring continuously. Cover the saucepan tightly, turn the heat very low and cook until tender. The water should all be absorbed in 20 minutes.

Peel and very finely chop the onion. Peel and crush the garlic. Cut the pork into thin matchstick strips. Peel and very finely chop the shallots or thinly slice the white part of the leeks.

Heat two tablespoons of oil in a frying pan. Add the onion and garlic and cook over a medium low heat until the onion is soft and transparent. Add the pork and soya sauce and cook gently for 10–15 minutes until the pork is tender. Add the finely chopped shallots or leeks and the cooked rice and cook, mixing well, for five minutes.

Fry the onion flakes in one tablespoon of oil for a few minutes until golden brown and drain on kitchen paper.

Turn the nasi goreng on to a heated serving dish and sprinkle over the strips of omelette and the crisp onion flakes.

Mushroom Risotto

1 onion
225 g (8 oz) button mushrooms
100 g (4 oz) butter
150 ml (¼ pint) white wine
350 g (12 oz) long-grain rice
1·2 litres (2 pints) stock
50 g (2 oz) grated Parmesan cheese
Salt and freshly ground black pepper

Serves 4

Peel and finely chop the onion. Thinly slice the mushrooms. Melt half the butter in a heavy pan, add the onion and cook without browning until soft and transparent. Add the mushrooms, pour over the wine, stir well and cook for a further three minutes until the wine is absorbed. Add the rice, cook until it is lightly coloured and then stir in a cupful of the stock. Cook over a low heat until the liquid is absorbed, then gradually add the rest of the stock, cooking the risotto for about 20 minutes until the rice is cooked but not mushy. Stir in the remaining butter and the cheese and season with salt and pepper.

Leave to stand for 2–3 minutes before serving to enable the flavour of the cheese to penetrate the rice.

Supper Pot

450 g (1 lb) bacon joint or pieces
2 onions
2 large carrots
225 g (8 oz) lentils
3 tablespoons dripping
2 bay leaves
Pinch of thyme and sage
Freshly ground black pepper
2 tablespoons finely chopped parsley
1 clove garlic

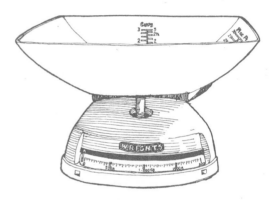

Serves 6

This dish has a base of richly flavoured lentils and is finished like a French cassoulet to give a touch of extra sophistication. Try to buy green lentils rather than the less well-flavoured orange variety, and shop for those untidy trimmings of bacon joints which can often be found at a very reasonable price.

This sort of cold-weather dish is extremely suitable for pressure cooking, but you have to be careful not to allow the ingredients to get too dry, so check with the handbook that goes with your cooker.

Remove rind from the bacon, cutting it off as thinly as possible. Cut the meat into 1 cm ($\frac{1}{2}$ in) square dice. Peel and roughly chop the onions. Peel and dice the carrots. Wash the lentils in cold water.

Cover the bacon with cold water, bring to the boil and drain to remove any excess salt. Melt 2 tablespoons of the dripping in a large heavy pan. Add the onion and carrots and cook over a low heat, stirring, until the onion is soft and transparent. Add the lentils, bacon, bay leaves, thyme and sage, mix well and season with pepper. Cover with 900 ml ($1\frac{1}{2}$ pints) cold water, bring to the boil and simmer gently for one hour. Uncover the pan and cook for a further 15 minutes until the liquid has been absorbed and the lentils are tender.

Mix together $1\frac{1}{2}$ tablespoons parsley, the garlic, crushed, and the remaining tablespoon of dripping. Mix into the pan, check seasoning and serve with the remaining parsley sprinkled over the top. Leeks, cabbage or Brussels sprouts can be served on the side.

Cheese, Bacon and Potato Pie

6 potatoes
2 large onions
6 rashers bacon
25 g (1 oz) butter
25 g (1 oz) flour
300 ml ($\frac{1}{2}$ pint) milk
225 g (8 oz) grated cheese
Salt and pepper

Serves 4

Peel and thinly slice the potatoes and onions. Remove rinds, chop the bacon and cook gently for five minutes without additional fat. Lightly grease a fire-proof dish and fill with alternating layers of potato, onion and bacon.

Melt the butter, add the flour and mix well. Gradually blend in the milk, stirring continuously until the sauce comes to the boil and is thick and smooth. Stir in 175 g (6 oz) of the grated cheese and season with salt and pepper. Pour the sauce into the dish and top with the remaining cheese.

Bake in a moderate oven (190°C, 375°F, Reg. 5) for 45 minutes and serve with a salad or green vegetable.

Quiche aux Crevettes

Quiche pastry (p. 258)
2 ripe tomatoes
4 spring onions
1 tablespoon tomato purée
150 ml (5 fl oz) double cream
2 eggs
100 g (4 oz) grated cheese
225 g (8 oz) peeled prawns
Salt, pepper and a pinch of cayenne
50 g (2 oz) cheese in one piece

Serves 6 as a first course, 4 as a main course

Line a 23 cm (9 in) flan case with the pastry. Peel and very thinly slice the tomatoes and arrange them in the bottom of the flan. Very finely chop the onions.

Whisk the tomato purée into the cream until well blended but not thick. Beat in the eggs and the grated cheese, fold in the prawns and onions and season with salt, pepper and cayenne. Pour the mixture into the flan and top with the whole cheese cut into very thin strips and arranged in a lattice pattern. Refrigerate for 30 minutes.

Bake the quiche in a moderately hot oven (200°C, 400°F, Reg. 6) for about 30 minutes until the pastry is crisp and the filling golden brown.

Note: If you like your pastry especially crisp you can bake the case 'blind' before adding the filling (see notes on p. 256).

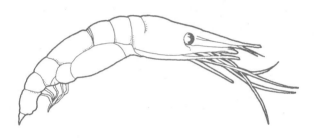

Quiche Astoria

Quiche pastry (p. 258)
1 large onion
25 g (1 oz) butter
175 g (6 oz) cooked ham
2 eggs
225 g (8 oz) soft cream cheese
150 ml (5 fl oz) double cream
Salt, pepper and a pinch of cayenne

Serves 6 as a first course, 4 as a main course

One of my favourite quiche recipes which can be served hot or cold.

Line a 23 cm (9 in) flan case with the pastry. Peel and very thinly slice the onion. Heat the butter and cook the onion until soft and transparent; leave to cool.

Finely chop the ham. Beat the eggs and blend in the cream cheese and cream. Season with salt, pepper and cayenne.

Arrange the onions in the bottom of the flan, cover with ham and spread over the cream cheese mixture. Refrigerate for 30 minutes and bake in a moderately hot oven (200°C, 400°F, Reg. 6) until the pastry is crisp and the filling light gold.

Note: To ensure the bottom as well as the sides of the pastry case are crisp the case can be baked 'blind' for a short time before filling (see notes on p. 256).

Quiche with Ham and Spinach

Quiche pastry (p. 258)
225 g (8 oz) frozen spinach
1 large onion
15 g (½ oz) butter
100 g (4 oz) cooked ham
2 eggs
150 ml (5 fl oz) double cream
Salt, pepper and a pinch of paprika
175 g (6 oz) grated Cheddar cheese

Serves 6 as a first course, 4 as a main course

Line a 23 cm (9 in) flan case with the pastry. Cook the spinach in boiling salted water until tender, drain very well and leave to cool. Peel and very finely chop the onion, cook until soft and transparent in the butter and leave to cool. Finely chop the ham.

Beat the eggs with the cream and fold in the spinach, onion and ham. Season with salt, pepper and paprika, add 100 g (4 oz) of the cheese and spread in the flan case. Sprinkle over the remaining cheese and refrigerate for 30 minutes.

Bake the quiche in a moderately hot oven (200°C, 400°F, Reg. 6) for 30 minutes until the pastry is crisp and the filling golden brown. *Note:* To ensure the bottom as well as the sides of the pastry are crisp the case can be baked 'blind' for a short time before filling (see notes on p. 256).

Tomandillas

4 slices thick-cut white bread
Lard, dripping or vegetable oil for frying
4 tablespoons soured cream
2 teaspoons made horseradish sauce
Salt and freshly ground black pepper
1 large ripe tomato
1 small can liver pâté
4 anchovy fillets

Serves 4

Serve these as a first course, or a light supper dish to make when time is short. Soured cream is cheaper than fresh cream, makes a good substitute for savoury dishes, keeps well and should be obtainable at supermarkets.

Cut large circles from the bread slices and fry the rounds to a crisp golden brown in hot fat or oil; drain on kitchen paper. Mix the soured cream with the horseradish sauce and season with salt and pepper. Thinly slice the tomato.

Spread the fried bread with the pâté and arrange a few slices of tomato on each. Top with the soured cream mixture and garnish each serving with an anchovy fillet, split lengthwise and arranged in a cross.

Flippit Cakes

50 g (2 oz) cooked mashed potato
100 g (4 oz) cooked mashed parsnip
50 g (2 oz) flour
100 g (4 oz) ham
1 tablespoon finely chopped parsley
Salt and freshly ground black pepper
Lard or dripping for frying

Serves 4

The mashed potato and parsnip combination is one I am very fond of. In this recipe these leftover vegetables go towards producing a delicious supper dish.

Combine the potato and parsnip, add the flour and beat until the mixture is smooth. Finely chop the ham and add to the mashed vegetables with the parsley. Season with salt and pepper and mix well.

Using well-floured hands shape the mixture into eight round flat cakes. Fry the cakes in hot lard or dripping for about three minutes on each side until crisp and golden brown.

Stuffed Roast Onions

4 large onions
100 g (4 oz) minced cooked meat (chicken, ham, or fried sausage-meat)
Small pinch of thyme, sage and finely chopped parsley
Salt and pepper
Flour
50 g (2 oz) butter

Serves 4

Peel the onions and parboil them for 15 minutes. Drain well and leave to cool. Using a small sharp pointed knife remove about a third of the onions from their centres. Mix the minced meat with the herbs, season with salt and pepper and stuff the filling carefully into the onion cavities.

Arrange the onions in a well-buttered baking dish, dredge them with flour and season with a little salt and pepper. Top each onion with a knob of butter and bake in moderate oven (180°C, 350°F, Reg. 4) for about 40 minutes, basting every now and then with juices from the pan.

Prawn Kedgeree

225 g (8 oz) long-grain rice
Salt and freshly ground black pepper
1 small onion
100 g (4 oz) butter
1 teaspoon curry powder
3 hard-boiled eggs
225 g (8 oz) peeled prawns
4 tablespoons double cream

Serves 4

Cook the rice in boiling salted water until tender. Drain, rinse in cold water and leave in a sieve to drain off all excess liquid.

Peel and very finely chop the onion. Heat the butter in a large heavy frying pan, add the onion and cook over a low heat until soft and transparent. Mix in the curry powder and continue to cook very slowly, stirring to prevent sticking, for five minutes.

Peel and quarter the hard-boiled eggs. Add the rice and prawns to the curry mixture and mix lightly. Add the hard-boiled eggs and heat through gently.

Taste for seasoning, lightly mix in the cream and serve at once.

Prawns in Cider Sauce

350 g (12 oz) best-quality frozen prawns
2 slices raw onion
Pinch of mixed or bouquet garni herbs
300 ml ($\frac{1}{2}$ pint) medium dry cider
70 g ($2\frac{1}{2}$ oz) butter
1$\frac{1}{2}$ tablespoons flour
Salt, freshly ground black pepper and a tiny
   pinch of mace
2 hard-boiled eggs

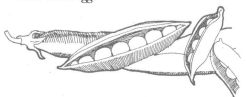

Serves 4

A delicious supper dish, first course, or part of a buffet meal.

Leave the prawns to thaw at room temperature for three hours. Combine the onion, herbs and cider in a heavy saucepan and boil until the cider is reduced by half (I found this takes about 15 minutes over a high flame). Pass through a fine sieve.

Melt the butter in a saucepan, add the prawns and heat through well until the mixture bubbles. Sprinkle over the flour and stir until it is well mixed with the prawns. Gradually pour over the reduced cider, stirring continuously over a high heat until the sauce is smooth; add seasoning, mace and hard-boiled eggs, chopped. Simmer for just three minutes to incorporate the flavourings.

Serve with slices of buttered brown bread, hot toast or French bread.

Savoury Bacon Rolls

100 g (4 oz) mushrooms
1 onion
25 g (1 oz) bacon fat
225 g (8 oz) minced meat
1 tablespoon tomato ketchup
$\frac{1}{4}$ teaspoon Worcestershire sauce
1 tablespoon finely chopped parsley
Freshly ground black pepper
12 very thin bacon rashers
50 g (2 oz) grated cheese
Mashed potato

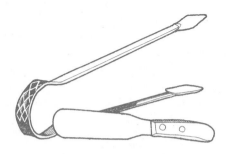

Serves 6

I have purposely left out salt in this recipe as most bacon tends to be a little on the salty side.

Finely chop the mushrooms and mince the onion. Heat the bacon fat in a frying pan, add the onion and cook over a medium heat until soft and transparent. Add the mushrooms and meat and cook for a further five minutes. Stir in the tomato ketchup, Worcestershire sauce and chopped parsley. Season the mixture with pepper and cook gently for 3–4 minutes. Leave the filling to cool while you cut off the bacon rinds with a pair of kitchen scissors, leaving all the fat on the rashers.

Spread the bacon rashers out flat and cover each one with the meat filling. Roll them up neatly and arrange in a lightly greased baking dish. Cover with a thin layer of grated cheese and bake in a moderately hot oven (200°C, 400°F, Reg 6) until the bacon is cooked; 15–20 minutes.

Place a ring of mashed potato round a serving dish and pile the bacon rolls in the centre.

Baked Cheese Blintzes

200 g (7 oz) plain flour
100 g (4 oz) mashed boiled potatoes
1 egg
450 ml (¾ pint) milk
25 g (1 oz) butter, melted
Salt and white pepper
Olive oil or lard for frying
100 g (4 oz) grated Cheddar cheese
4 tablespoons sour cream

Serves 4

Combine the flour, potato, egg, milk and melted butter and beat with a rotary whisk until the mixture is smooth. Season with salt and pepper.

Heat a thin film of oil or lard in an omelette pan and add a spoonful of batter, swirling it round the pan until the bottom is thinly coated. Cook over a medium high heat until the underside is a little browned, turn over and cook on the other side for a couple more minutes. Slide the pancake on to a round fire-proof serving dish that has been well greased with extra butter.

Sprinkle the pancake with a little cheese and continue to stack pancakes as you cook them, with grated cheese between each layer. Spread the sour cream over the top of the final pancake and sprinkle with the remaining cheese. Bake the stack in a moderately hot oven (200°C, 400°F, Reg. 6) for 20 minutes.

To serve cut the stack of pancakes into thick cake-shaped wedges.

Savoury Potato Cakes with Ham and Eggs

450 g (1 lb) potatoes
50 g (2 oz) butter
Salt and freshly ground black pepper
75 g (3 oz) self-raising flour
50 g (2 oz) ham
50 g (2 oz) chopped bacon
Bacon fat, lard or dripping for frying
4 eggs

Serves 4

A high-tea recipe that makes a mouth-watering supper dish.

Peel, roughly chop and boil the potatoes until tender. Drain well and mash until smooth with the butter, season with salt and pepper. Beat in the flour to make a stiffish dough and leave to cool. Chop the ham, remove rinds from the bacon and finely chop the rashers. Cook the bacon without extra fat over a low heat for about five minutes until tender. Drain on kitchen paper and mix into the dough.

Roll out the dough on a well-floured board to about 6 mm (¼ in) thickness and cut into twelve 8 cm (3 in) diameter cakes. Fry in the bacon fat, lard or dripping for 3–4 minutes a side until crisp and golden brown. Arrange on a warm serving dish, top with chopped ham and keep warm.

Fry the eggs and slide them neatly on to the potato cakes. Serve at once.

Soufflés with Almonds

Serves 4

30 g (1¼ oz) butter
½ teaspoon paprika pepper
350 g (12 oz) mixed crab meat (fresh or frozen)
15 g (½ oz) flour
150 ml (¼ pint) milk
Salt and freshly ground black pepper
Few drops Tabasco sauce
2 tablespoons cream
3 egg yolks
4 egg whites
15 g (½ oz) Parmesan cheese
50 g (2 oz) flaked almonds

Melt the butter in a saucepan, add the paprika and cook slowly for one minute. Mix in the crab meat, sprinkle with the flour and mix well. Gradually blend in the milk, stirring continuously over a moderate heat until the mixture comes to the boil and is thick and smooth. Season with salt, pepper and Tabasco. Remove the pan from the heat and beat in the cream and egg yolks one by one. Whip the whites until stiff and fold lightly into the crab mixture.

Turn into four well-greased individual soufflé dishes, sprinkle with cheese and almonds and bake in a moderate oven (180°C, 350°F, Reg. 4) for 15–20 minutes until well risen and firm to touch. Serve at once.

Courgette Soufflé with Cheese and Ham

Serves 4–6

450 g (1 lb) courgettes
1 small onion
40 g (1½ oz) butter
50 g (2 oz) ham
25 g (1 oz) flour
150 ml (¼ pint) milk
4 eggs, separated
50 g (2 oz) grated cheese

Thinly slice the courgettes. Peel and finely chop the onion. Cook them together in one-third of the butter until tender and purée through a coarse sieve or a food mill. Chop ham finely and mix in with purée.

Melt the remaining butter in a saucepan. Add the flour and mix well. Gradually blend in the milk, stirring vigorously, until the mixture is thick and smooth. Remove saucepan from heat, add egg yolks one at a time, beating the mixture between each addition. Leave to cool for a few minutes and mix in the courgette and ham mixture and grated cheese. Season with salt, pepper and cayenne.

Beat the egg whites until stiff, fold them into the soufflé and turn into a greased soufflé dish. Bake in a moderately hot oven (200°C, 400°F, Reg. 6) for about 30–40 minutes until well risen, light golden on the top and very slightly cracked across the surface.

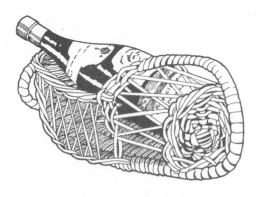

Souffléd Ham Welsh Rarebit

25 g (1 oz.) butter
25 g (1 oz.) flour
150 ml (¼ pint) milk
225 g (8 oz) grated cheese
1 tablespoon beer
Salt and pepper
2 eggs, separated
4 slices ham
4 slices buttered toast
1 teaspoon made English mustard

Serves 4

A quickly made supper dish with savoury overtones.

Heat the butter in a saucepan, add the flour and mix well. Gradually blend in the milk, stirring continuously until the sauce comes to the boil and is thick and smooth. Add 175 g (6 oz) of the cheese, the beer and enough salt and pepper to season. Remove from the heat and beat in the egg yolks one by one. Beat the egg whites until stiff.

Place a slice of ham on each piece of buttered toast and spread with a little mustard. Fold the egg whites into the cheese mixture, pile over the ham and top with the remaining grated cheese. Put under a hot grill until puffed out and golden brown.

Baked Croustades

1 large white unsliced loaf at least 2 days old
Melted butter

These cases can be kept for 2–3 days in an airtight container. Smaller *croustades* can be made to fill and serve with soup or as cocktail canapés.

Remove end crusts and cut the loaf into slices at least 2·5 cm (1 in) thick. Remove the crusts and with a sharp-pointed knife make a cut inside the slice 6 mm (¼ in) from the edge and to within the same distance of the bottom. Carefully remove the bread from the centre leaving a neat square case. Brush the *croustades* with melted butter and bake in a moderately hot oven (200°C, 400°F, Reg. 6) for 10–15 minutes until firm, crisp and a light gold in colour.

Prawn and chive filling for croustades
4 baked croustades *(see above)*
40 g (1½ oz) butter
2 tablespoons flour
300 ml (½ pint) milk
1 tablespoon sherry
1 tablespoon double cream
225 g (8 oz) frozen prawns
1 tablespoon chopped chives
Salt, freshly ground black pepper and a pinch of cayenne

Serves 4

Melt the butter in a saucepan. Add the flour, mix well and gradually blend in the milk, stirring continuously until the sauce is thick and smooth. Bring to the boil, lower the heat and simmer for two minutes. Stir in the sherry, cream, prawns and chives, season with salt, pepper and cayenne and cook gently for a further three minutes.

Pour the filling into the prepared cases and heat through in a moderate oven (180°C, 350°F, Reg. 4) before serving.

Ham Pancakes

Serves 4

100 g (4 oz) plain flour
150 ml (¼ pint) water
1 tablespoon olive oil
75 g (3 oz) ham
Salt and pepper
1 egg white
Oil for frying

These pancakes can be served for breakfast or as a light lunch or supper dish with vegetables or salad.

Sieve the flour into a bowl. Gradually mix in enough water to make a smooth paste. Add the remaining water and the oil and beat for three minutes.

Chop the ham into small pieces, add it to the batter and season with a little salt and pepper. Leave the batter to stand for at least 15 minutes. Whisk the egg white until stiff and fold it into the batter just before cooking.

Pour a thin film of oil into a non-stick frying pan and heat until smoking. Drop four separate tablespoons of batter into the pan and flatten them into a neat round shape with the back of a spatula as they begin to cook. Cook the pancakes over a medium high heat, turning once, until golden brown on each side. Place on a hot plate and keep warm while the remaining pancakes are being cooked.

Friday Night Special

Serves 4–6

1 tablespoon olive oil
1 clove garlic, finely chopped
1 small onion, finely chopped
425 g (15 oz) can tomatoes
1 level tablespoon tomato purée
½ level teaspoon castor sugar
¼ level teaspoon sage
Salt and freshly ground black pepper
Fat or oil for frying
12 fish cakes
12 thin slices Cheddar cheese

Heat the oil in a pan and cook the garlic and onion over a medium heat until the onion is transparent. Add the tomatoes with their juice, the tomato purée, sugar and sage; season with salt and pepper. Bring this sauce to the boil, then simmer for five minutes.

Heat the fat in a heavy-based pan and fry the fish cakes until crisp and golden on both sides. Top the drained fish cakes with cheese and grill until the cheese has melted. Arrange on a serving dish and pour over the sauce.

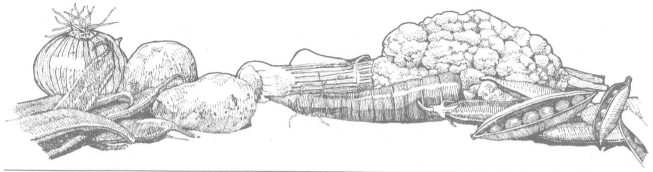

Baked Tomatoes

12 large firm tomatoes
1 finely chopped onion
40–50 g (1½–2 oz) butter
175 g (6 oz) cooked minced meat
100 g (4 oz) cooked rice
2–3 tablespoons stock
1 tablespoon single cream
2 teaspoons Worcestershire sauce
2 tablespoons chopped parsley
Freshly ground black pepper
50 g (2 oz) grated cheese
1 tablespoon breadcrumbs

Serves 6

A little leftover meat and rice can be made into a savoury filling for tomatoes. Serve them with green beans.

Cut a thin slice from the top of each tomato and scoop out the pulp. Cook the onion in the butter until soft. Add the meat, rice, stock, cream, Worcestershire sauce and parsley. Season with pepper and cook for three minutes.

Fill the tomato cases with the meat mixture and put in a lightly buttered oven-proof dish. Sprinkle with the grated cheese and breadcrumbs and bake in the centre of a pre-heated oven at 190°C (375°F, Reg. 5) for 15–20 minutes.

Serena's Macaroni Cheese

225 g (8 oz) macaroni
175 g (6 oz) grated Cheddar or Double
    Gloucester cheese
450 ml (¾ pint) white sauce
Salt and freshly ground black pepper
100 g (4 oz) cooked, diced ham
4 large skinned and chopped tomatoes
2 tablespoons fresh white breadcrumbs
25 g (1 oz) butter, melted

Serves 4–6

Ham and fresh tomatoes add colour and flavour to a plain macaroni cheese. For a richer, lighter macaroni cheese with a soufflé effect, beat two egg yolks into the white sauce and fold two stiffly beaten egg whites into the ingredients before spooning into the baking dish.

Cook the macaroni uncovered in plenty of boiling water for about 15 minutes. Stir 100 g (4 oz) of the cheese into the white sauce and season to taste. Fold the drained macaroni, ham and tomatoes into the sauce and spoon the mixture into a buttered oven-proof dish. Mix the remaining cheese with the breadcrumbs. Sprinkle over the macaroni and pour melted butter over.

Bake near the top of a preheated oven at 200°C (400°F, Reg. 6) for 20 minutes or until the top is crisp and golden.

Serve hot with a crisp winter salad or a green vegetable.

Anchovy Tom

Serves 4

8 anchovy fillets
Oil for frying
4 diagonal slices of French bread 1 cm ($\frac{1}{2}$ in)
thick
8 slices of ripe tomato 1 cm ($\frac{1}{2}$ in) thick
4 tablespoons soured cream

This is a dish I invented for a young friend of mine who was home from school for the holidays and at fifteen years of age had sophisticated tastes. Since the original success of Anchovy Tom I have served it frequently as both a first course and as a supper dish.

Drain the anchovy fillets and cut each fillet in half lengthwise. Heat the oil in a frying pan, add the slices of bread and fry on both sides until crisp and golden brown. Drain well on kitchen paper and leave to cool.

Arrange the slices of bread on each plate; cover with two slices of tomato, side by side. Whip the sour cream until thick and spoon on top of each tomato slice, garnish with criss-cross anchovy strips and serve chilled.

Chicken Liver and Water Chestnut Savoury

Serves 4

100 g (4 oz) chicken livers
1 small can water chestnuts
5 tablespoons port
8 thin rashers streaky bacon
2 teaspoons soya sauce
4 slices white bread
Butter

The soft well-flavoured texture of chicken livers, combined with crisp crunchy water chestnuts wrapped in bacon, make this Chinese titbit a perfect after-dinner savoury. Tinned water chestnuts and soya sauce can be bought from most delicatessen shops.

Cut the chicken livers into eight pieces. Cut the water chestnuts into slices 6 mm ($\frac{1}{4}$ in) thick and marinate them in port for at least 30 minutes. Trim off rinds from the bacon rashers. Dip the chicken livers into soya sauce and place with a slice of water chestnut on each rasher of bacon; roll up neatly.

Place the rolls in a lightly greased baking dish and cook in a moderately hot oven (200°C, 400°F, Reg. 6) for 10–15 minutes until the bacon is crisp. Serve on buttered toast.

Salads and Summer Food

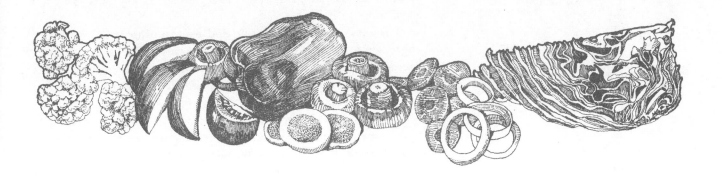

Much of the pleasure and excitement of summer is provided by lovely, icicle-fresh, ice-cream-coloured foods, or those that you cook out of doors on a barbecue, open fire or even a camping stove. Even if the weather is so hot that you don't feel like eating much, if the food is attractive and good to taste life and living will benefit.

Anything limp, insipidly coloured or drearily garnished will dull the appetite, and you would have been better off serving a plain meal of French bread, British cheese and home-made pickles. This is still, incidentally, one of the nicest forms of picnic food, providing the bread is fresh and crisp, the cheese is mature and well coloured and the pickles are full of flavour.

Salads, for instance, must be fresh and crisp (limp lettuce is worse than no lettuce at all). Tomatoes must be ripe and, as far as I am concerned, that large and ugly, but delicious, Mediterranean variety, peeled before they are presented as a salad dish or garnish. Dishes which include gelatine should be firm, but not the consistency of thick plastic. Those dishes which are to be served with mayonnaise or its variations should not be made up too long before they are required, so that the sauces do not have a chance to develop that unattractive film of discoloured skin over their surface. Food that is to be served cold must also be chilled, preferably in the refrigerator,

until the moment it is to be served, and not allowed to sit around in a warm or sunny place.

When you are preparing cold food, whether it is merely a matter of preparing ingredients, or of cooking them and leaving them to cool down, remember that they will need more seasoning than food that is to be served hot. Be generous with the salt and (that great favourite of all cookery writers) the freshly ground black pepper; be eager, but not too eager, with fresh herbs and remember that the hotter the weather the more liberally you can sprinkle in or on those hot chilli flavourings.

It is easy to be conservative and even boring with your salad ingredients, so always look for alternatives. Raw leeks, for instance, are delicious instead of spring onions. Miniature courgettes, thinly sliced, make a good salad ingredient and so do the young leaves of spinach. Raw mushrooms, providing they are small and firm, are another good salad ingredient and instead of just adding grated raw carrot to your winter salads try also grating raw beetroot, turnip and swede for pleasant and nutty flavouring.

If you want to keep salad ingredients, clean them well, dry thoroughly and store in a sealed polythene box in the bottom of the refrigerator. Crisp up vegetable salad ingredients in a bowl of cold water to which ice cubes have been added and never dress green salads until the last minute before they are to be served—the dressing quickly turns them limp.

Dandelion Salad Niçoise

1 litre (2 pint) bowl loosely filled with young
    dandelion leaves
1 small can tuna fish
2 hard-boiled eggs
1 small onion
12 black olives
½ green pepper
8 anchovy fillets
Vinaigrette dressing

Serves 4

A dish that makes a good first course or a luncheon salad.

Pick over, wash and dry the dandelion leaves. Drain the tuna and break into chunks with a fork. Quarter the hard-boiled eggs. Peel and thinly slice the onion and divide into rings. Halve and stone the olives. Remove seeds and core from the green pepper and cut the flesh into thin strips.

Arrange all the ingredients attractively in a salad bowl and pour over the dressing. Toss lightly before serving.

Rillettes de Porc

900 g (2 lb) belly of pork
¼ teaspoon dried thyme
2 cloves of garlic
Salt and freshly ground black pepper

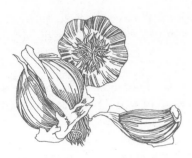

Serves 4–6

Remove all skin and bones from the pork and cut the flesh into small cubes about 1 cm (½ in) across. Place in an oven-proof dish with the thyme and garlic, peeled and crushed. Season generously with salt and pepper, cover tightly with foil and bake in a slow oven (150°C, 300°F, Reg. 2) for three hours until the meat is flaking and thoroughly tender.

Strain off the liquid fat and remove any large tough pieces of pork fat. Taking a little of the meat at a time, put it into a bowl and shred it apart with two forks until it is divided into fine strands. Pack firmly into an earthenware pot, pour over the strained cooking juices and fat and chill until solid. The *rillettes* can be kept for at least three weeks in a refrigerator.

Another delicious form of *rillettes* can be made by combining equal quantities of pork belly with rabbit to make a rather lighter dish.

Pork and Bacon Terrine

675 g (1½ lb) lean pork from the shoulder
100 g (4 oz) ham in one piece
450 g (1 lb) belly of pork, skin removed
2 cloves garlic
150 ml (¼ pint) rich stock or gravy juices
2 tablespoons brandy
4 juniper berries, crushed
Pinch of sage, thyme and oregano
1 tablespoon finely chopped parsley
Salt and pepper
225 g (8 oz) streaky bacon
2 onions
50 g (2 oz) butter
2 small eggs
1 tablespoon flour

Serves 6

Chop (preferably don't mince) the pork, ham and belly of pork very finely until the pieces are no larger than small peas. Add the garlic, crushed, mix in the stock, brandy, juniper berries, herbs and a generous seasoning of salt and pepper, stir well, cover and leave in a cool place for at least five hours.

Remove rinds, cut the bacon into thin strips and use all except four to line a well-greased 1-litre (2-pint) terrine. Peel and finely chop the onions and soften them in the butter until transparent. Beat the eggs well, mix in the flour to make a smooth paste and blend into the meat mixture with the onions and the butter they were softened in. Press the mixture firmly into the terrine and cover with the remaining strips of bacon and a double layer of foil.

Stand the terrine in a dish of hot water and bake in a moderate oven (180°C, 350°F, Reg. 4) for about two hours until the meat has shrunk from the sides of the dish and a thin knife blade comes out clean after being inserted into the centre. Return the foil cover to prevent drying, cool and leave to set firm overnight.

Cucumber with Soured Cream

1 large cucumber
Salt
150 ml (5 fl oz) soured cream
1 tablespoon finely chopped dill
1 tablespoon finely chopped chives or spring
  onion tops
1 tablespoon finely chopped mint
½ teaspoon castor sugar
1 small clove garlic
Freshly ground black pepper
Paprika pepper

Serves 4

This is an old summer favourite. Serve it as a sauce for fish or barbecued food; use it as a dip with sticks of crisp green pepper; serve it as part of a hot weather hors d'oeuvre or as a salad side dish. To make it into a delicious starter cocktail add prawns, a little tomato ketchup and a dash of Worcestershire sauce and Tabasco and serve on a bed of chopped lettuce.

The garlic is optional and if you don't have any fresh dill available (a herb well worth growing if you can) soften a little dried dill in lemon juice before adding.

Peel and coarsely grate the cucumber. Place in a sieve, sprinkle with salt and leave to stand for 30 minutes in a cool place. Press firmly to remove excess water and pat dry with kitchen paper.

Squeeze the garlic through a garlic press or crush with a fork. Combine all ingredients, mix lightly and season with pepper. Sprinkle the top with paprika and chill well before serving.

Savoury Tomato Tartlets

225 g (8 oz) shortcrust pastry
1 onion
1 clove garlic
425 g (15 oz) can tomatoes
2 canned pimentos
1½ tablespoons olive oil
Pinch of sugar
½ tablespoon finely chopped marjoram
Salt and freshly ground black pepper
6 basil leaves

Serves 6 as a first course

This can be served as a starter, as part of a picnic or as an accompaniment to a main course.

Roll out the pastry thinly and line six patty tins (I use flattish tins about 10 cm (4 in) across). Bake the cases blind in a hot oven (220°C, 425°F, Reg. 7) until crisp and golden brown. Leave to cool on a wire rack.

Peel and finely chop the onion; crush the garlic. Chop the tomatoes, reserving all the juice, and chop the pimentos. Heat the oil in a saucepan, add the onion and garlic and cook over a low heat until the onion is soft and transparent. Mix in the tomatoes, tomato juice, pimentos, sugar and marjoram and season with salt and pepper. Bring to the boil and cook over a medium low heat, without covering, for about 20 minutes until the mixture is the consistency of a thick sauce. Leave to cool.

Fill the pastry cases with the tomato mixture and garnish each with a basil leaf. Serve cold as first course or re-heat in a moderate oven (180°C, 350°F, Reg. 4) to serve with a main course, adding basil leaves after re-heating.

Deauville Salad

1 lettuce
50 g (2 oz) ham, or you can substitute Spam
    or luncheon meat
100 g (4 oz) frozen peas
2 tomatoes
2 crisp eating apples
2 sticks celery
1 teaspoon lemon juice
¼ teaspoon dried tarragon
150 ml (¼ pint) bought or home-made
    mayonnaise
2 tablespoons double or single cream
Few drops Tabasco sauce
2 tablespoons chopped canned pimento
2 hard-boiled eggs

Serves 4

Wash and dry the lettuce and arrange in a shallow serving dish. Chop the meat. Cook the frozen peas, drain and leave to cool. Cover the tomatoes with boiling water, leave for one minute and then slide off skins and remove core and seeds. Chop the tomato flesh. Peel, core and dice the apples; chop the celery. Soak the tarragon in the lemon juice for a few minutes to soften the leaves.

Combine the mayonnaise, cream and lemon juice and mix in a few drops of Tabasco sauce. Add the ham, tomatoes, pimento, apples, peas and celery and mix lightly.

Pile the salad on to the lettuce leaves and garnish with slices of hard-boiled egg.

Summer Spice Dip

150 ml (5 fl oz) carton soured cream
1 tablespoon mayonnaise
2 tablespoons tomato ketchup
1 teaspoon Worcestershire sauce
1 tablespoon finely chopped spring onions
1 tablespoon finely chopped green pepper

Yield: approx ⅓ pint

Add some peeled prawns or chopped hard-boiled egg to this dip and you have an exciting sandwich filling.

Combine the soured cream, mayonnaise, tomato ketchup and Worcestershire sauce and mix well. Fold in the onions and pepper. Chill before serving.

Cold Lemon and Herb Chicken

2 spring chickens (poussins)
100 g (4 oz) butter, softened
Juice of 1 lemon
1 teaspoon dried rosemary
1 teaspoon dried oregano
½ teaspoon rock salt
Freshly ground black pepper

Serves 4

Wipe inside and outside of the chickens with a damp cloth. Blend together the butter, lemon juice, herbs, salt and a generous sprinkling of pepper. Spread a little of the mixture inside the chicken and rub the rest over the outside.

Roast the chickens in a moderately hot oven (200°C, 400°F, Reg. 6), basting frequently in the juices, until they are golden brown and tender—about 30–40 minutes depending on size. Leave to cool and split in half.

Egg and Tomato Salad

Serves 4

8 tomatoes
8 hard-boiled eggs
1 can anchovy fillets
Milk
8 black olives
1 tablespoon finely chopped parsley
1 tablespoon finely chopped chives
150 ml ($\frac{1}{4}$ pint) vinaigrette dressing

A popular summer dish in rural France which varies from simplicity itself to a sophisticated and elegant platter of fanned-out tomatoes, interspersed with egg slices, anchovy fillets and chopped parsley. Serve a mayonnaise lightly flavoured with garlic on the side.

Cover the tomatoes with boiling water for two minutes, drain, peel and cut into thin slices. Peel and slice the eggs, reserving half an egg. Soak the anchovy fillets in milk for ten minutes to remove excess salt; drain the fillets, pat dry on kitchen paper and cut each one in half lengthwise. Remove stones and chop the flesh from the olives.

Arrange a layer of tomatoes and egg slices in a glass dish. Cover with some of the anchovies and some chopped olives. Sprinkle with a little parsley and chives and pour over a little dressing. Continue in layers until all the main ingredients are used up. Sprinkle the dish with remaining parsley and chives and the reserved half an egg, finely chopped, and pour over remaining vinaigrette.

Refrigerate for at least 30 minutes and serve with the mayonnaise, a green salad and hot crusty French bread.

Spinach, Mushroom and Bacon Salad

Serves 4

450 g (1 lb) young spinach
100 g (4 oz) firm button mushrooms
Juice of 1 lemon
4 rashers lean bacon
1 teaspoon made English mustard
Salt and freshly ground black pepper

This delicious summer salad, made with the small leaves of fresh spinach, can either be served as a main course or as a starter.

Strip the tender leaves off the spinach stalks (the coarser leaves and stalks can be used for soup) and wash them in ice-cold water to clean and freshen. Pat dry gently on kitchen paper or in a clean cloth.

Thinly slice the mushrooms and blanch them in boiling salted water, to which a little lemon juice has been added, for two minutes. Drain and cool.

Grill the bacon rashers until crisp, drain well on kitchen paper, leave to cool and then crumble into small pieces.

Arrange the spinach and mushrooms on a serving dish. Combine the lemon juice and mustard, mix well and season with salt and pepper. Mix in the bacon and pour the dressing over the spinach. Chill well before serving.

Midsummer Meat Salad

450 g (1 lb) cooked beef, lamb or pork
4 ripe tomatoes
1 large clove garlic
1 tablespoon finely chopped parsley
1 tablespoon finely chopped fresh chervil or
    basil (or ¼ teaspoon dried herbs soaked in a
    little warm water)
4 tablespoons olive oil
1 tablespoon white wine vinegar
Grated rind of ½ lemon
Salt and freshly ground black pepper
1 crisp green pepper

Serves 4

A salad of new potatoes in mayonnaise goes very well with this dish.

Cut the meat into very thin slices and then into neat julienne strips about 3 mm (⅛ in) wide. Cover the tomatoes with boiling water for two minutes, peel off skins, discard cores and seeds and finely chop the flesh. Peel and very finely chop the garlic.

Combine the tomatoes, garlic, parsley, chervil or basil, olive oil, vinegar and lemon rind and mix well. Season with salt and pepper. Add the meat and toss with a fork until all the ingredients are amalgamated. Chill for at least two hours.

Pile the meat salad on to a serving dish and garnish with thin rings of green pepper.

Carnival Meat Salad

225 g (8 oz) cooked beef or lamb
100 g (4 oz) cooked ham
100 g (4 oz) leftover cooked beans, peas or
    carrots.
50 g (2 oz) firm button mushrooms
Juice of ½ lemon
5 tablespoons double or soured cream
150 ml (¼ pint) home-made mayonnaise
Salt and freshly ground pepper
1 crisp eating apple (a Granny Smith is
    ideal)
Lettuce, finely shredded

Serves 4

Cut the meat and ham into thin slices and then into neat julienne strips about 3 mm (⅛ in) wide. Cut the beans or carrots into small dice. Very thinly slice the mushrooms and blanch in boiling salted water, to which the lemon juice has been added, for two minutes. Drain well and leave to cool.

Mix the cream with the mayonnaise and season with salt and pepper. Mix in the meat, ham, vegetables and the apple (peeled, cored and cut into small dice). Pile on to a serving dish, surround with lettuce and refrigerate for at least one hour before serving.

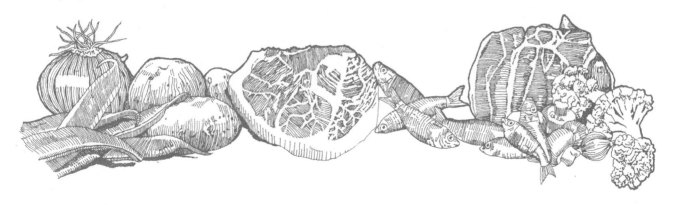

Jellied Chicken and Bacon

1 onion
1 young boiling fowl
Bouquet garni
1 tablespoon sherry
Salt and pepper
900 g (2 lb) bacon in a piece
2 cloves
1 tablespoon brown sugar
2 teaspoons white wine vinegar
4 tablespoons finely chopped parsley

Serves 6

Remove any coarse earthy skins from the onion but leave on the inner brown ones; cut into quarters. Place the chicken in a fairly large pan with the onion and bouquet garni. Add the sherry and just enough water to cover. Season with a little salt and pepper, bring to the boil and simmer slowly for about 1½ hours until the chicken is tender throughout.

Soak the bacon if it has been salted, cover it with water, add the cloves, brown sugar and vinegar and bring slowly to the boil. Skim off any scum from the surface, cover and simmer gently for 1½–2 hours until tender. Strain the chicken liquid through a very fine sieve. Cut the chicken and bacon into thin slices while still warm and pack tightly in a bowl in alternate layers.

Remove all possible fat from the chicken stock (first with a spoon and then with absorbent kitchen paper). Mix the parsley with the stock. Pour enough stock into the bowl to cover the meat and top with a plate and a heavy weight. Cool and then leave to set in the refrigerator for at least ten hours. Dip the mould into hot water, turn out and garnish with salad ingredients.

Tasmanian Chicken Salad

1 boiling fowl
1 chicken stock cube
1 lemon
1 onion, peeled and sliced
Bouquet garni
Salt and freshly ground black pepper
2 crisp eating apples
1 can water chestnuts
2 green peppers
2 spring onions
300 ml (½ pint) mayonnaise
1 teaspoon lemon juice
25 g (1 oz) split almonds, roasted
Lettuce leaves

Serves 4–6

Cook the chicken until tender in enough water to cover, with the stock cube, the lemon, cut into quarters, onion, bouquet garni and seasoning. Leave to cool in the stock and cut the meat into neat cubes when cold.

Peel, core and dice the apples. Drain and thinly slice the water chestnuts. Discard core and seeds from the green peppers; chop the flesh of one and cut the other into thin strips. Chop the spring onions.

Put the mayonnaise in a large bowl, add the lemon juice and check seasoning. Add the chicken, apple, water chestnuts and chopped pepper. Arrange on crisp lettuce leaves in a serving dish, sprinkle with the roasted almonds and decorate with the strips of green pepper. Chill well before serving.

Britannia Duck Terrine

70 g (2½ oz) butter, softened
Salt and freshly ground black pepper
Pinch of sage
1·5-kilo (3½-lb) duck with giblets
450 g (1 lb) lean pork, coarsely minced
225 g (8 oz) pork fat, coarsely minced
2 cloves garlic
6 juniper berries
Pinch of mace and thyme
1½ tablespoons brandy
½ tablespoon concentrated frozen orange juice
225 g (8 oz) thinly cut fat bacon rashers
2 bay leaves

For garnishing:
½ orange, peeled and thinly sliced
Juniper berries
Small bay leaves
1 teaspoon gelatine powder
1 can consommé
1 tablespoon sherry
½ tablespoon concentrated orange juice

Serves 6

A rich and extremely well-flavoured terrine that takes time to make, this is an excellent main course with a memorable taste. Ask your butcher to mince the pork and pork fat for you.

For a more gamey flavour two wild ducks can be used in this dish and remember that both bones and neck of the duck make an excellent stock for rich nourishing soups, especially borsch.

Season the butter with salt, pepper and sage. Rub the duck all over with the butter and roast it in a fairly hot oven (220°C, 425°F, Reg. 7) for 25 minutes, basting frequently. Remove and leave to cool. Cut off the skin, neatly trim off all the breast meat and cut into thin, 6 mm (¼ in) strips. Remove the rest of the flesh and mince it through the coarse blades of a mincing machine with the liver, heart and gizzard.

Mix the minced duck with the pork and pork fat and blend in the garlic and juniper berries (crushed with a fork), the mace, thyme, brandy and orange juice. Season with salt and pepper.

Remove rinds from the bacon and line a 1-litre (2-pint) earthenware terrine with three-quarters of the rashers. Pack in half of the minced mixture. Arrange strips of duck breast in the centre and pack in the remaining mince. Cover with the remaining rashers and top with the bay leaves. Press the mixture firmly into the terrine and place a piece of well-buttered greaseproof paper over the top before sealing with a well-fitting lid.

Place the terrine in a roasting pan with enough cold water to come 2·5 cm (1 in) up the side of the terrine. Cook in the centre of a pre-heated very slow oven (140°C, 275°F, Reg. 1) for three hours. Remove the lid and bay leaves. Place a plate on the meat with a heavy weight on top and leave to set for at least eight hours until firm.

Dip the terrine dish quickly into a bowl of very hot water and turn out. Clean the dish carefully and return the terrine.

To garnish, arrange slices of orange, juniper berries and small bay leaves in a pattern on the top. Dissolve the gelatine in 2 tablespoons of the consommé over a low heat. Combine with the rest of the consommé, the sherry and orange juice and mix well. Pour the consommé over the top of the terrine so that it forms a thin glaze and fills in cracks along the sides. Refrigerate until the jelly has set firm.

Serve the terrine cut into thin slices with baked potatoes in their jackets; or with hot French bread and two salads, one of chicory, grated carrots and thin rings of green pepper, another of finely shredded crisp lettuce. Add vinaigrette dressing to the salads at the last minute and toss lightly before serving.

Meat Salad

Serves 4

350–450 g (12–16 oz) cooked meat–beef,
    lamb, ham, tongue, etc. or a mixture
2 sticks celery
50 g (2 oz) mushrooms
Juice of ½ lemon
100–175 g (4–6 oz) cooked or tinned
    vegetables
2 teaspoons Dijon mustard
1 tablespoon made horseradish sauce
300 ml (½ pint) mayonnaise
Salt and pepper
1 tablespoon sultanas
1 tablespoon finely chopped green pepper
Lettuce and tomato to garnish

Finely shred the meat and thinly slice the celery sticks and mushrooms. Toss the mushrooms in the lemon juice to preserve their colour. Chop the cooked vegetables if necessary.

Add mustard and horseradish sauce to mayonnaise, season with salt and pepper and mix well. Fold in the remaining ingredients, pile on to a serving dish and garnish with lettuce leaves and slices of tomato.

Scandinavian Salad

Serves 4

5 tablespoons double cream
2 tablespoons horseradish sauce
1 teaspoon made mustard
1 teaspoon capers
Salt, pepper and a pinch of paprika
8 thin slices cooked roast beef
Lettuce, shredded
2 tomatoes
1 beetroot, cooked
1 green pepper
Vinaigrette dressing

Whip the cream until stiff and combine with the horseradish sauce and mustard. Finely chop the capers; fold them into the sauce and season it with a little salt, pepper and paprika. Spread some of this sauce on each slice of beef and roll it up neatly. Arrange the rolls on a bed of lettuce in the centre of a large serving dish.

Peel and thinly slice the tomatoes, thinly slice the beetroot, remove core and seeds from the green pepper and finely chop the flesh. Arrange the tomato and beetroot slices around the beef rolls, sprinkle over the green pepper and dribble some vinaigrette dressing over the vegetables.

Cover the dish with foil or a slightly damp cloth to prevent the beef drying and serve chilled.

Bean and Tuna Salad

250 g (9½ oz) canned white beans in brine
1 medium can tuna fish
1 generous bunch parsley
1 small clove garlic, crushed
3 tablespoons olive oil
1 tablespoon white wine or cider vinegar
1 teaspoon French Dijon mustard
Salt and freshly ground black pepper
1 tablespoon finely chopped chives
1 small onion
6 black olives, stoned

Serves 4 as a first course

Drain off brine from the beans. Pour off oil from the tuna, reserve oil and flake the fish. Mince the parsley through the fine blades of a mincing machine. Combine the parsley, garlic, tuna oil, olive oil, vinegar, mustard, salt, pepper and chives in a screw-topped jar and shake hard until well mixed.

Add the dressing to the beans and tuna fish and mix lightly. Turn on to a serving dish, top with thin rings of raw onion and slices of black olives and chill well before serving with hot toast or French bread.

Clarabelle

15 g (½ oz) gelatine powder
300 ml (½ pint) water
150 ml (¾ pint) white wine
Juice of 1 lemon
1 large cucumber
Salt and freshly ground black pepper
150 ml (5 fl oz) double cream
1 tablespoon finely chopped dill
1 tablespoon finely chopped chives
4 spring onions (white part only), finely
    chopped
Pinch of castor sugar

Serves 6

A summer dish that is so cool to look at that it really sharpens any appetite. The jellied mould can be filled in the centre with any number of delicious variations. A mixture of watercress and prawns, for instance, with a sharp French dressing; or try pasta shells mixed with mayonnaise and chopped tongue, or ham and tomatoes and black olives. A fish salad in a cocktail sauce would be good or cold chicken, diced, with a curried mayonnaise.

Mix the gelatine with a little of the water and heat gently, stirring, until it dissolves. Combine the gelatine, water, wine and lemon juice and refrigerate until just beginning to set. Peel and coarsely grate the cucumber, put into a sieve and sprinkle generously with salt. Leave to stand for 30 minutes, then drain well. Whip the cream until thick.

Add the cucumber, dill, chives and onions to the jellied mixture with the sugar and mix lightly. Season with pepper. Mix in the cream and pour into a ring mould. Refrigerate until set and turn on to a serving dish.

Cauliflower Vinaigrette with . Prawns

1 cauliflower
2 tomatoes
8 black olives, stoned
4 tablespoons olive oil
2 tablespoons white wine vinegar
1 teaspoon finely chopped onion
1 teaspoon finely chopped parsley
1 teaspoon finely chopped chives or spring onion
    tops
Salt and freshly ground black pepper
100 g (4 oz) peeled prawns

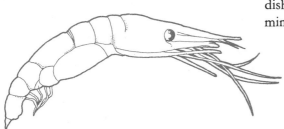

Serves 4

Cut off green leaves from the cauliflower (the ribs can be cut into matchstick strips and cooked as a vegetable in its own right) and divide the cauliflower head into florets. Cook them in boiling salted water, to which a little lemon juice has been added, for about 8–10 minutes–they must be crisp for this dish–remembering that they will go on cooking for a little while after they have been removed from the water. Drain well.

Immerse the tomatoes in boiling water for one minute. Drain, slide off skins, halve and scoop out seeds, cutting out central core. Cut the flesh into small dice. Cut the olives into thin strips.

Combine the olive oil, vinegar, onion, parsley and chives in a screw-top jar. Season with salt and pepper and shake well.

Combine the cauliflower, prawns, tomatoes and olives in a serving dish, pour over the dressing, toss lightly and refrigerate for 30 minutes before serving.

Sinclaire Salad

1 kipper
275–350 g (10–12 oz) cooked chicken
4 sticks celery
1 small green pepper
1 teaspoon made horseradish sauce
3 tablespoons mayonnaise
2 tablespoons sour cream
Salt, pepper and a pinch of cayenne
1 teaspoon grated raw onion
1 bunch watercress
8 black olives (optional)

Serves 4

A good buffet or quick lunch dish. Serve it with a hot potato baked in its jacket or with hot French bread and butter.

Place the kipper, tail end up, in a jug and pour over enough boiling water to reach the tail. Leave for five minutes, drain off the water, remove skin and bones and flake the flesh.

Chop the chicken meat. Remove leaves and any coarse fibres from the sides of celery sticks and chop the flesh. Remove core and seeds from the pepper and finely chop the flesh.

Combine the horseradish, mayonnaise and sour cream (or single cream mixed with lemon juice) and season with salt, pepper and cayenne. Add the chicken, kipper, onion, celery and pepper and mix lightly. Remove any coarse stalks from the watercress, arrange the leaves around a serving dish and pile the salad in the centre. Garnish with halved and stoned black olives.

Mediterranean Prawn Salad

350 g (12 oz) frozen French beans (or 1 can
   stringless French beans)
4 tablespoons olive oil
1 tablespoon lemon juice
½ teaspoon Dijon mustard
Salt and freshly ground black pepper
175 g (6 oz) frozen prawns, thawed
2 hard-boiled eggs

Serves 4

Cook the beans until just tender in a little boiling salted water. Drain well.

Combine the oil with lemon juice and mustard in screw-top jar and season well. Shake until well mixed. Pour half this dressing over the prawns and leave to stand for 30 minutes while beans are cooling.

Halve the eggs, take out the yolks and chop the whites. Toss the beans, prawns and white of eggs in the remaining dressing and turn on to a serving dish.

Garnish with egg yolks rubbed through a coarse sieve to give a 'mimosa' effect and serve chilled with slices of buttered brown bread.

Crabmeat and Rice Salad

4 large cooked crab claws
2 cloves garlic
300 ml (½ pint) home-made mayonnaise
Pinch of mace
4 small firm tomatoes
1 small onion
1 green pepper
225 g (8 oz) rice
Salt and freshly ground black pepper

Serves 4

Crack the claws (I do this by wrapping them in a clean cloth and tapping with a hammer), remove all the meat and chop it coarsely.

Squeeze the garlic through a garlic press or crush with a fork and mix with the mayonnaise with the mace. Peel and chop the tomatoes, finely chop the onion and green pepper.

Cook the rice in boiling salted water until just tender. Drain, rinse through with cold water and drain again. Mix the rice with the mayonnaise, fold in the crab, tomato, onion and pepper and season with salt and plenty of pepper.

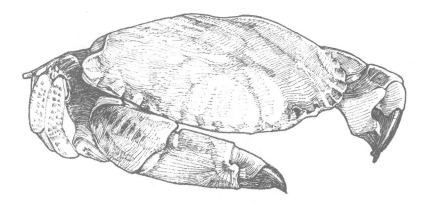

Salade Écossaise

Serves 4

1 clove garlic
1 head crisp lettuce (preferably Cos)
½ teaspoon French Dijon mustard
6 tablespoons olive oil
Juice of ½ lemon
Pinch of sugar
Salt and freshly ground black pepper
450 g (1 lb) young French beans
450 g (1 lb) fresh salmon
3 firm tomatoes
8 black olives
2 hard-boiled eggs
1 can anchovy fillets
2 tablespoons finely chopped chives

Rub a salad bowl with the garlic clove. Remove outer leaves from the lettuce, cut the heart into eight pieces and arrange in the bottom of the bowl. Combine the mustard, 4 tablespoons of the olive oil, lemon juice, sugar and seasoning and mix well.

Top and tail the beans, cook until just tender in boiling salted water, drain well and toss in the dressing while still warm.

Brush the salmon with the remaining olive oil, season with salt and pepper, wrap in foil and bake in a moderately hot oven (200°C, 400°F, Reg. 6) for about 20 minutes until just cooked. Leave to cool, remove skin and bones and break into eight pieces.

Skin and quarter the tomatoes. Stone the olives and quarter the hard-boiled eggs. Drain the anchovy fillets.

Arrange the beans in the centre of the lettuce, top with salmon and garnish with tomatoes, hard-boiled eggs and anchovies. Sprinkle with the chives and serve well chilled.

Fish Salad

Serves 4–6

225 g (8 oz) cooked white fish
1 cucumber
4 firm tomatoes
2 hard-boiled eggs
8 anchovy fillets
Milk
100 g (4 oz) black olives
3 tablespoons olive oil
1 clove garlic
1 tablespoon white wine vinegar
½ teaspoon mustard
Salt and freshly ground black pepper
1 tablespoon finely chopped parsley or chervil
1 tablespoon finely chopped chives or spring
   onion tops
2 crisp lettuce hearts
100 g (4 oz) peeled prawns
225 g (8 oz) cooked young French beans
175 g (6 oz) cooked peas

Any good-quality white fish (sole, haddock, turbot, halibut, etc.) is delicious combined with peeled prawns and served with salad ingredients and a vinaigrette dressing. This is really a salad *niçoise*, using alternative ingredients to the rather oily and heavy tinned tuna fish.

Divide the fish into large flakes with a fork. Remove the peel from the cucumber and cut the flesh into 5 cm (2 in) long finger-thick pieces. Peel the tomatoes by dropping them into boiling water for two minutes and then sliding off the skins; cut into quarters. Shell and quarter the hard-boiled eggs. Soak the anchovy fillets in milk for five minutes, squeeze out excess liquid and pat dry with kitchen paper. Stone the olives.

Combine the olive oil, garlic clove, vinegar and mustard in a screw-top jar. Season with salt and pepper and shake to mix well. Remove the garlic and add the parsley and chives.

Cut the lettuce hearts into quarters and arrange them around the outside of a serving bowl. Arrange the beans, peas, cucumber, tomatoes and hard-boiled eggs on the lettuce. Pile the fish and prawns in the centre and garnish with the anchovy fillets and olives. Pour over the dressing and refrigerate before serving.

Waldorf Salad

4 crisp eating apples (Cox's, Newtons or
    Granny Smiths are all good)
Juice of ½ lemon
1 head celery
6 walnuts, shelled
200 ml (7½ fl oz) home-made mayonnaise
2 tablespoons double cream
Salt and white pepper

Serves 4

If you have some leftover chicken, ham or tongue, some of this cut into small dice will turn this salad into a good lunch dish.

Peel and core the apples and cut the flesh into small dice. Sprinkle with lemon juice to prevent them going brown. Trim off the leaves and any tough fibres from the celery and chop the stalks. Peel the walnuts and chop. Combine the mayonnaise with the cream, season with salt and pepper, add the apples, celery and walnuts and toss lightly to mix. Pile on to a serving dish and serve chilled.

Mexican Bean Salad

225 g (8 oz) salami or garlic sausage
200 g (7 oz) canned luncheon meat
200 g (7 oz) canned kidney beans
200 g (7 oz) canned butter beans
100 g (4 oz) frozen peas
1 large onion
1 lettuce
5 tablespoons olive oil
3 tablespoons white wine vinegar
½ teaspoon dry mustard
1 clove garlic
Salt and freshly ground black pepper
Pinch of sugar
Pinch of chilli powder
1 tablespoon tomato ketchup
Few drops of Tabasco sauce

Serves 4

This is a filling salad exceptionally quick to make. As you may guess from its name, the dish is a hot-tasting one. If the idea scares you a bit go easy with the chilli powder and Tabasco sauce. Served as the main course of a meal this salad makes an exciting and unusual change.

Cut the salami and luncheon meat into small cubes. Drain off liquid from the tinned beans; cook, drain and cool the peas. Place meat and vegetables in a large bowl and chill well.

Peel and very thinly slice the onion and shred the lettuce leaves.

Place the olive oil, vinegar, mustard, garlic, salt, pepper, sugar, chilli powder, tomato ketchup and Tabasco in a screw-top jar and shake very well. Strain the dressing over the meat and vegetables and mix it in gently so as not to break up the beans. Arrange the salad on a bed of lettuce leaves and top with a layer of thinly sliced raw onion.

Serve well chilled with hot French bread.

Tomato Salad with Fresh Basil

4 large or 6 small firm ripe tomatoes
1 small onion
4 anchovy fillets
Milk
50 g (2 oz) mozzarella cheese
2 sprigs fresh basil
3 tablespoons olive oil
1 tablespoon white wine vinegar
½ teaspoon French Dijon mustard
Salt and freshly ground black pepper

Serves 4

A wonderful spring or summer salad which can be served as a light first course or as an accompaniment to a main course of fish or chicken. Mozzarella (a smooth Italian cheese) can now be bought from most delicatessen shops.

Peel the tomatoes by dropping them in boiling water for two minutes and then sliding off the skins. Cut the tomatoes into thin slices and arrange them in a shallow serving dish. Peel the onion, cut it into thin slices and divide into rings. Drain off the oil from the anchovies, soak them in milk for five minutes to remove excess salt and cut each one in half lengthwise. Cut the cheese into matchstick strips about 2·5 cm (1 in) long. Chop the basil as gently as possible to avoid bruising the leaves.

Arrange the onion rings, anchovy fillets and cheese over the tomatoes and sprinkle with basil. Combine the olive oil, vinegar and mustard in a screw-top jar, season with salt and pepper and shake to mix well. Pour the dressing over the salad and refrigerate before serving.

Midsummer Salad

675 g (1½ lb) young runner beans
1 bunch radishes
1 can anchovy fillets
2 hard-boiled eggs
4 tablespoons olive oil
1 tablespoon white wine vinegar
½ teaspoon French Dijon mustard
Salt, freshly ground black pepper and cayenne

Serves 4

Like all salads this is best served with fresh French bread crisped in a hot oven and buttered.

Top and tail the beans, remove any strings from the sides and cut into 2·5 cm (1 in) slices. Remove leaves from the radishes, wash well and cut into thin slices. Drop the slices into iced water to crisp and drain well.

Drain the anchovy fillets and split each one in half lengthwise. Remove the whites from the hard-boiled eggs (use for a sandwich filling, mixed into mayonnaise or sandwich spread).

Combine the olive oil, vinegar and mustard and mix well. Season with a little salt, pepper and small pinch of cayenne. Add the beans and radishes to the dressing, toss lightly and turn into a serving dish. Rub the egg yolks through a sieve and sprinkle over the salad. Garnish with anchovy fillets arranged in a lattice pattern and refrigerate before serving.

Jellied Cabbage and Red Pepper Salad

1 packet lemon jelly
2 tablespoons white wine
225 g (8 oz) white cabbage
1 red pepper
1 orange
Lettuce leaves to garnish

Serves 4–6

This salad can be served as a first course with a home-made mayonnaise flavoured with lemon juice and tarragon.

Make up the jelly according to the instructions on the packet but substituting two tablespoons of white wine for two tablespoons of water. Leave in a cool place until the jelly begins to thicken and set.

Finely shred the white cabbage. Remove core and seeds of the red pepper and cut the flesh into thin strips. Peel the orange, divide it into segments and remove the membrane.

Gently fold the cabbage, pepper and orange segments into the semi-set jelly and pour into a mould or basin. Leave to set firm, turn out and garnish with lettuce leaves.

Caesar Salad

1 Cos lettuce
2 hard-boiled eggs
½ cucumber
4 spring onions
2 tomatoes
100 g (4 oz) Cheddar cheese
2 thin slices bread
Vegetable oil for frying
¼ teaspoon mustard
3 tablespoons olive oil
1 tablespoon white wine vinegar
Salt and freshly ground black pepper

Serves 4

Remove tough outer leaves from the lettuce. Wash the heart in cold running water, shake well to remove excess water and dry by patting lightly with a clean tea-towel. Cut it into six segments, put into a serving bowl and crisp up by leaving in the refrigerator for about 20 minutes.

Chop the hard-boiled eggs, peel and dice the cucumber, clean and slice the onions, peel and thinly slice the tomatoes and coarsely grate the cheese.

Remove crusts from the bread and cut the slices into small dice. Fry until crisp and golden brown in a little oil; leave to cool. Combine the mustard, olive oil, vinegar, salt and pepper in a screw-top jar and shake well.

Arrange all the ingredients over the lettuce, pour over the dressing and chill before serving.

Potato and Courgette Salad

450 g (1 lb) new potatoes
225 g (8 oz) baby courgettes
2 spring onions
150 ml (¼ pint) home-made mayonnaise
2 tablespoons single cream
Salt and freshly ground black pepper
2 tablespoons freshly chopped parsley

Serves 4

Man (or, for that matter, woman or child) cannot live off barbecued meat alone. They need the trimmings of some hot, crusty French bread and a cool crunchy salad to complete their enjoyment. In summer there are crisp baby courgettes which cry out to be eaten raw and which make the perfect partner to a salad of sweet new potatoes.

Scrape the potatoes and boil in salted water until just tender, cool and cut into small dice. Wash the courgettes in cold running water, cut off the stalk and dice the flesh. Chop the spring onions.
  Combine the potatoes, courgettes and onions and pour over the mayonnaise mixed with cream. Season with a little salt and pepper and toss lightly. Refrigerate for at least 30 minutes and sprinkle with parsley just before serving.

Courgette Salad

6 courgettes
6 tablespoons dry white wine
4 tablespoons olive oil
1 tablespoon tarragon vinegar
1 tablespoon very finely chopped onion
1 small clove garlic (optional)
Salt and freshly ground black pepper
1 tablespoon finely chopped parsley

Serves 4

A cool, fresh-tasting salad that goes well with cold chicken.

Cook the courgettes in boiling salted water, for about five minutes until just tender but not mushy. Drain, cool and cut into 1 cm (½ in) thick slices. Place in a colander and leave to drain for a further 20 minutes.
  Combine the wine, olive oil, vinegar and chopped onion. Add the garlic, crushed, and season with salt and pepper.
  Arrange the courgette slices in a serving dish, pour over the dressing and sprinkle with chopped parsley. Chill well before serving.

Red Pepper Salad

1 large red pepper
1 small fennel root
1 shallot
3 tablespoons olive oil
1 tablespoon white wine vinegar
½ teaspoon French Dijon mustard
Salt and freshly ground black pepper

Serves 4

Remove core and seeds from the pepper and cut the flesh into thin strips. Remove any tough outer layers from the fennel and trim off any green leaves. Cut the fennel into small strips. Peel the shallot, cut into thin slices and divide into rings. Combine the pepper, fennel and shallot in a salad bowl.
  Put the olive oil, vinegar and mustard into a screw-top jar, season with salt and pepper and shake to mix well. Pour the dressing over the salad and chill for 30 minutes before serving.

Grape and Cucumber Salad with Mint

225 g (8 oz) white grapes
½ cucumber
½ teaspoon made English mustard
Salt and freshly ground black pepper
1 tablespoon white wine vinegar
3 tablespoons olive oil
4 leaves fresh mint

Serves 4

A cool, cool salad with sweet/sour overtones that makes a delicious summer accompaniment for hot or cold roast chicken.

Halve and pip the grapes. Peel the cucumber, cut the flesh into very thin matchstick pieces about 2·5 cm (1 in) long, place them in a colander, cover with a plate and leave for 30 minutes to get rid of excess liquid.

Combine the mustard with a small pinch of salt and a generous screw of pepper. Beat a little vinegar at a time into the mustard until the mixture is smooth. Add the olive oil and mix well. Finely chop the mint and add it to the dressing.

Put the grapes and cucumber into a glass serving dish, pour over the dressing and chill well.

Perfection Salad

1 small white cabbage
1 head celery
15 g (½ oz) gelatine
450 ml (¾ pint) water
100 g (4 oz) sugar
5 tablespoons white wine vinegar
1 tablespoon lemon juice
Salt and white pepper
2 tablespoons finely chopped canned pimento
150 ml (¼ pint) home-made mayonnaise
1 tablespoon tomato ketchup
2 tablespoons double cream
Worcestershire sauce
Lettuce leaves

Serves 4–6

Imported celery now makes it possible for us to have this crisp salad ingredient all the year round. This classic American recipe combines celery with shredded cabbage to make an extremely good hot-weather accompaniment to cold dishes.

Remove any hard core and very finely shred the cabbage leaves. Trim off leaves from the celery and very thinly slice the stalks.

Combine the gelatine with five tablespoons of the water and the sugar; heat slowly until the gelatine dissolves. Add the remaining water, vinegar and lemon juice and season with a little salt and white pepper. Mix well and refrigerate until just beginning to set. Fold in the cabbage, celery and pimento, turn into a ring mould that has been dipped in cold water and refrigerate until set firm.

Combine the mayonnaise with the tomato ketchup and cream, flavour with few drops of Worcestershire sauce and with salt and pepper if necessary.

Dip the mould in very hot water, turn out on to a bed of crisp lettuce leaves and spoon the mayonnaise into the centre of the ring.

Spring Potato Salad

900 g (2 lb) new potatoes
2 hard-boiled eggs
3 anchovy fillets
4 tablespoons olive oil
1 tablespoon white wine or cider vinegar
3 tablespoons finely chopped chives
1 tablespoon finely chopped parsley
Pinch of paprika and celery salt (or use salad seasoning)
Freshly ground black pepper
2 thin rashers streaky bacon

Serves 6

Scrub the potatoes and boil in their skins until just tender. Leave until just cool enough to handle. Chop the hard-boiled eggs; drain and finely chop the anchovy fillets. Combine the oil, wine or vinegar, herbs and seasonings and mix well. Fry the bacon rashers without extra fat until crisp, drain on kitchen paper and crumble.

Peel and cut the still-warm potatoes into small cubes. Combine with the egg and anchovy, pour over the dressing and toss lightly. Top with the crumbled bacon and chill for an hour before serving.

Jacqueline's Salad

1 crisp lettuce heart
1 bunch watercress
1 bunch radishes
1 clove garlic
3 tablespoons olive oil
1 teaspoon Dijon mustard
1 tablespoon white wine vinegar
Salt and freshly ground black pepper
50 g (2 oz) shelled walnuts

Serves 4

Roughly shred the lettuce and remove stalks from the watercress.

Trim and thickly slice the radishes. Rub a wooden bowl with the garlic and discard. Combine the olive oil, mustard and vinegar in the wooden bowl. Season with salt and pepper and mix well. Add the salad ingredients and toss lightly just before serving.

Dandelion Caesar Salad

1 large bunch young dandelion leaves
1 hard-boiled egg
2 rashers streaky bacon (rinds removed)
2 slices white bread (crusts removed)
2 tablespoons vegetable oil
Vinaigrette dressing
Pinch of sugar
½ teaspoon Dijon mustard

Serves 4

A perfect partner to cold roast chicken, cold ham or tongue.

Wash the dandelion leaves and dry well. Chop the hard-boiled egg. Chop the bacon, fry without extra fat until crisp and drain on kitchen paper. Cut the bread into small cubes, add oil to bacon fat in the pan and fry cubes until golden brown; drain on kitchen paper.

Place the leaves in a salad bowl, top with chopped egg, bread cubes and bacon, pour over a dressing made with vinaigrette mixed with the sugar and mustard and toss lightly. The salad should be served as soon as the dressing has been added.

Austrian Cucumber Salad

1 cucumber
Salt and freshly ground black pepper
The white part of 3 spring onions, very finely
     chopped
3 tablespoons olive oil
1 tablespoon white wine vinegar
½ tablespoon French Dijon mustard
3 tablespoons very finely chopped parsley

Serves 4

An accompanying cucumber salad is a must if you can afford salmon these days. The salad also goes well with more humble fish salads as well as with cold meat or poultry. In Austria they combine the cucumber with a generous quantity of very finely chopped parsley and French dressing.

Peel and very thinly slice the cucumber, spread out on a flat plate and sprinkle with salt. Leave to stand for one hour, then drain off excess liquid and pat dry on kitchen paper. Very finely chop the spring onions.

Combine the olive oil, vinegar and mustard in a screw-top jar, season with salt and pepper and shake to mix well. Add the parsley and onion to the dressing. Put the cucumber into a serving dish, pour over the dressing and chill well before serving.

Potato and Vegetable Salad

450 g (1 lb) cooked potatoes
100 g (4 oz) cooked beans or carrots
1 small onion
2 teaspoons tomato ketchup
1 teaspoon water
1 teaspoon lemon juice
1 teaspoon curry powder
1 tablespoon cream
300 ml (½ pint) mayonnaise
1 tablespoon Branston pickle
Salt and pepper
100 g (4 oz) cooked peas

Serves 4–6

Serve with cold meat, poultry or tinned salmon.

Cut the potatoes into small dice; chop the beans or dice the carrots (these can be tinned if necessary). Peel and finely chop the onion.

Combine the tomato ketchup, water, lemon juice, curry powder and cream, mix well and leave to stand for five minutes until curry powder has dissolved. Add this mixture to the mayonnaise with the pickle and mix well. Season with salt and pepper and fold in the prepared vegetables and the peas.

Coleslaw

Serves 4

1 small firm white cabbage
2 crisp red-skinned eating apples
1 tablespoon orange juice
1 tablespoon lemon juice
1 teaspoon English dry mustard
1 teaspoon Worcestershire sauce
200 ml (7½ fl oz) home-made mayonnaise or a
    good-quality bottled one
4 tablespoons single cream
Salt and freshly ground black pepper
175 g (6 oz) raisins
2 tablespoons finely chopped raw onion
1 tablespoon thinly sliced pimento-stuffed olives
1 tablespoon finely chopped parsley

This popular American salad is full of nutrition and goes well with anything from hamburgers to cold chicken. You can buy it ready-made in many supermarkets and delicatessen stores, but the one you make at home is always just that much fresher and more delicious.

Remove core from the cabbage and very finely shred the leaves. Remove apple cores and finely dice the flesh, leaving the skin on.

Combine the orange and lemon juice with mustard and Worcestershire sauce; mix well. Blend this mixture into the mayonnaise with the cream; mix well and season, if necessary, with salt and pepper. Add the cabbage, apple, raisins, onion, olives and parsley and toss lightly. Turn into a serving bowl and chill before serving.

Mixed Vegetable Salad

Serves 4–6

½ small white cabbage
1 small cooked beetroot
100 g (4 oz) French beans
225 g (8 oz) young carrots
½ red pepper
3 tablespoons olive oil
1 tablespoon white wine vinegar
1 teaspoon French Dijon mustard
1 clove garlic, crushed (optional)
Salt and freshly ground black pepper
1 tablespoon finely chopped capers

Remove outside leaves and core from the cabbage; finely shred the leaves. Cut the beetroot into very fine matchstick strips. Cook the beans and carrots until just tender. When cool cut the beans into 5 cm (2 in) lengths and the carrots into matchstick strips. Remove core and seeds from the pepper and cut the flesh into thin strips.

Combine olive oil, vinegar and mustard (with the garlic if used) in a screw-topped jar, season and shake to mix well.

Combine all the ingredients in a bowl, pour over the dressing and toss lightly so as not to break up the beetroot. Chill before serving.

Puddings

Should one call them puddings, sweets or desserts? The trouble is that fashions change and what is correct one year may not be the next. I have always disliked the word 'sweets', and I find 'desserts' rather grand for anything less than a creation of jelly, topped by ice-cream, topped by meringue, topped by hot chocolate sauce. So I prefer to stick to the old-fashioned but nevertheless workable term puddings, which to my mind covers anything from ice-cream to an extravagance of profiteroles.

You may find that this section, compared to the rest of the book, is a trifle (if you will forgive the pun) thin. The reason is quite simply that, being almost fanatically figure-conscious as my loyal readers will know well, but at the same time greedy, I find that by the time puddings come to the table I have no room left to enjoy them. There are, of course, many people who enjoy puddings more than first or main courses and I certainly always try to provide something delicious and sweet at the end of a supper, lunch or dinner party. But I must admit that when I am cooking seriously in the kitchen for much of the day I prefer to rely mainly on cheese and fresh fruit to end the meal.

I fear I do protest too much because, however much I mind about my figure I also really do secretly love puddings. So on the following

pages you will see those that I find relatively quick and easy to make, exceptionally delicious to taste and on the whole not too terribly fattening.

Remember that when you are dealing with cold puddings they must, above all things, *look* attractive. A few golden brown almonds scattered over the pudding are a far better form of garnish than the traditional glacé cherries or slivers of angelica and they also add a pleasant crunch to the dish. And do serve cold puddings well chilled.

Ice-cream, on the other hand, sometimes suffers from being too cold. It wants to be taken from the freezer about ten minutes before being served and allowed to 'breathe' before being scooped or cut into servings.

If you are fortunate enough to have your own garden, utilise it to make your summer puddings even more attractive. Moulded puddings which are to be turned out, for instance, look sensational if they are served on a bed of fresh vine leaves or the glossy leaves of camellias. And if you have blackcurrants you can infuse the leaves into a sugar syrup for a fruit salad to give a delicious muscat grape flavouring.

Basic Ice-Cream

4 egg yolks
175 g (6 oz) granulated sugar
4 tablespoons water
1 teaspoon vanilla essence
300 ml (10 fl oz) double cream
50 g (2 oz) castor sugar
300 ml (10 fl oz) single cream

Serves 4–5

Beat the egg yolks until pale and fluffy. Combine the granulated sugar with the water and boil for five minutes. Mix in the vanilla essence. Pour the hot syrup on to the egg yolks in a slow stream, beating constantly with a rotary whisk (this can be done with an electric beater or in a liquidiser with the motor running slow).

Whip the double cream with the castor sugar until thick but not stiff and gradually beat in the single cream (the whipped double cream will provide body and the end result should be very similar to using all double cream).

Fold the whipped cream into the egg mousse base, pour into freezer trays or tins and freeze in the freezing compartment of a refrigerator or in a deep-freeze (set at the lowest temperature).

Remove the mixture from the freezer when it has frozen to a depth of 1 cm ($\frac{1}{2}$ in) around the edges, turn into a bowl and beat well. Return to the freezer and repeat the beating process once more when it has partially solidified. Allow to freeze solid and pack carefully.

Rum and Raisin Ice-Cream
225 g (8 oz) sultanas
5 tablespoons white rum

Soak the sultanas in the rum for two hours. Mix the soaked sultanas into the egg mousse base.

Lemon and Honey Ice-Cream
3 tablespoons honey
Juice of 2 lemons

Melt the honey over a low heat and mix in the lemon juice. Leave to cool and mix into the egg mousse base.

Blackcurrant Ice-Cream

450 g (1 lb) blackcurrants
225 g (8 oz) sugar
150 ml (¼ pint) water
300 ml (10 fl oz) double cream
4 tablespoons Cassis (blackcurrant liqueur)

Serves 4

Combine the blackcurrants, sugar and water in a saucepan, bring to the boil, cover and simmer until the fruit is soft. Purée through a sieve or a food mill and leave to cool.

Beat the cream until stiff. Fold it into the blackcurrant purée and mix only enough to blend. Turn the mixture into a metal tray and freeze in the ice-making compartment of a refrigerator until the edges begin to freeze and crystallise. Remove from the refrigerator, turn into a bowl and beat until smooth. Return to the tray and freeze for a further hour, beat once more and freeze again until solid.

Remove from the refrigerator ten minutes before required and scoop into individual glasses. Pour one tablespoon of Cassis over each serving.

Lemon Ice-Cream with Raspberry Sauce

Grated rinds of 2 lemons
Juice of 3 lemons
175 g (6 oz) castor sugar
300 ml (½ pint) milk
300 ml (10 fl oz) double cream

The sauce:
225 g (8 oz) packet frozen raspberries
75 g (3 oz) castor sugar
1 tablespoon kirsch

Serves 4–6

Beat the lemon rind, lemon juice and sugar until smooth. Gradually add the milk and cream, beating continuously until the sugar has completely dissolved. Pour into a freezing tray and freeze until the mixture begins to crystallise around the edges. Turn into a bowl and beat with a rotary whisk or electric beater until thick and smooth. Return to the freezing tray and freeze until firm.

To make the sauce combine the raspberries and sugar in a saucepan and heat gently until the fruit is soft and the sugar has dissolved. Purée through a fine sieve and mix in the kirsch.

Remove the ice-cream from the freezer about ten minutes before serving. The sauce should be made just before serving.

Brown Bread Ice-Cream

Serves 4

300 ml (10 fl oz) double cream
300 ml (10 fl oz) single cream
150 g (5 oz) castor sugar
¼ teaspoon vanilla essence
4 tablespoons water
100 g (4 oz) granulated sugar
175 g (6 oz) brown breadcrumbs
1 tablespoon rum

This has a coolness and texture that goes like a dream with blackberries and hazel-nuts.

Beat the creams and castor sugar together until thick, add the vanilla essence and freeze in shallow trays until firm but not solid. Combine the water and half the granulated sugar in a saucepan, bring to the boil and cook over a high heat for four minutes. Leave to cool.

Sprinkle the remaining granulated sugar over the breadcrumbs and bake in a moderate oven (180°C, 350°F, Reg. 4) for about 15 minutes until well browned. Leave to cool.

Turn the frozen cream into a basin, beat until smooth and blend in the sugar syrup and rum. Fold in the breadcrumbs, return to the trays and freeze until firm.

Bombe Princess

Serves 6

3 egg whites
75 g (3 oz) castor sugar
450 ml (15 fl oz) double cream
4 pieces of ginger preserved in syrup
2 tablespoons castor sugar
Grated rind of 1 lemon
3 tablespoons kirsch

An attractive-looking ice-cream cake with an evocative flavour and texture–something really different. If you don't like making meringues, don't be put off by this recipe. Bought meringues can be substituted; or if you make them yourself and they discolour or break it doesn't matter in the least.

Whisk the egg whites until stiff. Add half the sugar and continue beating for one minute. Fold in the remaining sugar with a fork. Well oil a baking sheet with olive oil. Drop dollops of the meringue mixture on to the sheet from a tablespoon.

Bake the meringues in a cool oven (110°C, 225°F, Reg. ¼) for two hours until firm. Turn off the heat and leave to dry out for 15 minutes. Remove from the baking sheet and break into small pieces when cool.

Whisk the cream until it will form light peaks. Finely chop the ginger. Fold the ginger, castor sugar, lemon rind, kirsch and meringue into the cream.

Lightly oil a cake tin with a removable bottom. Spoon in the cream mixture and smooth it down firmly with the back of a wooden spoon. Cover tightly with foil and freeze in a deep-freeze or freezing compartment of a refrigerator for at least four hours.

Turn the ice-cream cake out ten minutes before serving and accompany it with a fresh fruit salad.

Liqueur Water Ice

750 ml (1¼ pints) water
350 g (12 oz) sugar
Juice of 1 lemon
150 ml (5 fl oz) liqueur

Serves 6

This is, frankly, prohibitively expensive–but next time you want to splash out and make an impression without breaking your back to do so, here is a sweet which is made in minutes and is blatantly luxurious. Use crème de menthe, crème de cassis or an orange-flavoured liqueur such as Grand Marnier. Serve the ice in fine glass goblets, topped with a little sweetened whipped cream. Pour over a little more liqueur just before serving and hand round a plate of almond biscuits.

Combine the water and sugar, bring slowly to the boil and then boil as fast as possible for five minutes. Leave to cool and mix in the lemon juice. Pour into a freezing tray and freeze, stirring every now and then as the sides become solidified.

When the mixture is all crystallised, mix in the liqueur and continue to freeze until almost solid.

Gooseberry and Blackcurrant Leaf Sorbet

675 g (1½ lb) sugar
300 ml (½ pint) water
900 g (2 lb) gooseberries, topped and tailed
2 handfuls blackcurrant leaves
Juice of 1 lemon
1 egg white

Serves 6

In this recipe an infusion of blackcurrant leaves gives the gooseberries an unusual musky flavouring.

Combine the sugar and water, bring slowly to the boil and boil as fast as possible for five minutes. Add the gooseberries and simmer for five minutes if the berries are soft and ripe, ten minutes if they are hard and green. Add the blackcurrant leaves and leave to infuse in the hot fruit for 20 minutes. Remove leaves and strain the juice through a fine nylon sieve. Press the fruit gently to extract all the flavour.

Add the lemon juice, pour the syrup into a shallow tray and freeze at the lowest possible temperature. When the mixture has frozen to a depth of 1 cm (½ in) around the sides of the tray give it a good stir to break up the ice crystals. Continue to stir every now and then until the ice is almost solid.

Whip the egg white until stiff. Turn the ice into a bowl and beat until it is mushy. Fold in the egg white, mix well and return to a freezing tray. Freeze until solid.

Orange and Lemon Sorbet

Serves 6

85 g (3½ oz) sugar
150 ml (¼ pint) water
2 teaspoons gelatine powder
Juice of 2 lemons
600 ml (1 pint) fresh or frozen orange juice
1 egg white

A little gelatine added to the sorbet stops it melting too quickly.

Combine the sugar and water and boil until the sugar has dissolved; leave to cool. Dissolve the gelatine in the lemon juice over a low heat. Combine the syrup, orange juice and lemon juice, mix well and pour into an ice-making tray. Freeze in the freezing compartment of a refrigerator until crystals have formed but the mixture is not quite solid.

Beat to a mush. Whip the egg white until stiff, fold it into the fruit juice and return to the freezer. Freeze until firm and serve in glasses or goblets which have been chilled in the refrigerator. Serve with chocolate mints.

Sweet Clementines

Serves 6

12 clementines
450 ml (¾ pint) water
225 g (8 oz) granulated sugar
Finely grated rind and juice of 1 lemon
Pinch of cinnamon

Wash and dry the clementines. Cut them, skin and all, into wafer-thin slices.

Combine the water, sugar, lemon juice, rind and cinnamon in a heavy saucepan. Bring to the boil and cook until the sugar has dissolved. Add the clementine slices and simmer gently for an hour until the skins are translucent and tender.

Leave until cold and chill well before serving.

Fresh Pear and Orange Jelly

Serves 4

15 g (½ oz) gelatine powder
450 ml (¾ pint) fresh orange juice
Scant 150 ml (¼ pint) dry white wine
4 ripe eating pears

Dissolve the gelatine in 150 ml (¼ pint) of the orange juice over a low heat. Mix in the remaining orange juice and the white wine and leave to cool. Chill the jelly until it is just beginning to thicken.

Peel the pears, cut each one in half and scoop out the core and pips with a small teaspoon. Put the pear halves together again and stand each one in a glass goblet. Pour the jelly mixture over the pears and leave in the refrigerator to set.

Serve well chilled and if you have any mint in your garden top each serving with a tiny sprig.

Caramel Oranges

8 oranges
225 g (8 oz) granulated sugar
150 ml (¼ pint) cold water
150 ml (¼ pint) warm water

Thinly cut the rind from one orange without removing any white pith or membrane. Cut it into thin strips, blanch in boiling water for one minute and drain well. Using a sharp knife, cut the skin and membrane from all the oranges until they are pared down to the flesh only. Cut into slices, removing any pips, and then reshape by sticking them together with toothpicks. Place in a glass bowl and sprinkle with strips of blanched peel.

Combine the sugar with the cold water in a heavy saucepan and heat over a low flame, without stirring, until the sugar has dissolved. Bring to the boil and cook over a high flame, still without stirring, until the sugar turns to a rich, golden brown caramel. Remove from the heat and, protecting your hand from spatters with a cloth, pour in the warm water, stirring to dissolve the caramel. Leave to cool.

Pour the cooled caramel mixture over the oranges and chill well before serving.

Blackcurrant Jelly

450 g (1 lb) blackcurrants
300 ml (½ pint) water
225 g (8 oz) sugar
Gelatine powder
2 tablespoons port
200 ml (7½ fl oz) double cream
1 tablespoon castor sugar
2 drops vanilla essence
40 g (1½ oz) slivered blanched almonds

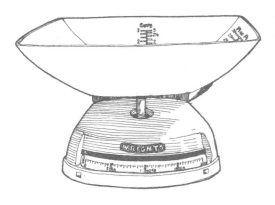

Serves 6

This can be made in a round mould, masked with whipped cream, sweetened and with just a suspicion of vanilla essence, and then sprinkled with toasted split almonds. You cut the pudding like a cake and the contrast of white cream and dark jelly is stunning.

Combine the blackcurrants, water, and sugar in a saucepan, bring to the boil, cover and simmer until the fruit is soft. Rub through a fine sieve or a food mill and measure the resulting purée. Soften 1 envelope of gelatine powder–15 g (½ oz)–for every 600 ml (1 pint) of purée in a little water over a low heat until dissolved. Mix the gelatine and port with the purée and pour into a bowl. Chill until set.

Whip the cream until stiff, sweeten it with the castor sugar and flavour with the vanilla essence. Mix well. Dip the bowl into very hot water, turn out the jelly on to a serving dish and mask with whipped cream. Toast the almonds under a hot grill until golden brown, cool and scatter them over the pudding.

If you have any redcurrants you can surround the pudding with the red fruit.

Chilled Oranges

Serves 4

4 oranges
5 tablespoons white rum
75 g (3 oz.) sugar
2 tablespoons hot water

Peel the oranges and remove all the white pith and membrane. Cut into very thin slices and remove the pips. Arrange neatly on four plates.

Combine the rum, sugar and water and stir until the sugar has dissolved; sprinkle the mixture over the oranges and chill the fruit for at least two hours before serving.

Melon and Wine Jelly

Serves 4–6

150 ml (¼ pint) water
175 g (6 oz) sugar
4 tablespoons finely chopped fresh mint
1 large Ogen melon
1½ tablespoons gelatine powder
Juice of 2 lemons
300 ml (½ pint) dry white wine
8–12 mint leaves
1 egg white
Castor sugar

Combine the water and sugar in a saucepan, simmer gently until the sugar has dissolved, bring to the boil and cook over a high heat for five minutes. Add the chopped mint and leave to cool. Strain the syrup and discard the mint.

Halve the melon, remove the seeds and scoop out the flesh with a ball scoop.

Dissolve the gelatine in the lemon juice over a very low heat. Add the gelatine to the sugar syrup and mix in the wine. Chill the jelly in the refrigerator until it begins to thicken. Mix in the melon, pour into a mould and chill until set firm.

Brush the mint leaves with lightly beaten egg white and dip them into castor sugar. Arrange on a wire rack and dry in a cool oven (100°C, 225°F, Reg. ¼) for about an hour until crisp.

Dip the mould into very hot water, turn it out on to a serving plate and decorate with the frosted mint leaves.

Red Wine Jelly

Serves 4–6

15 g (½ oz) gelatine powder
150 ml (¼ pint) hot water
175 g (6 oz) castor sugar
175 g (6 oz) redcurrant jelly
½ bottle red wine

This jelly is best eaten just as it is, without further adornment, in order to savour the delightful flavour to the full, although a little lightly whipped cream may be used to decorate it.

Melt the gelatine in the hot water and stir until completely dissolved.

Mix the sugar and redcurrant jelly thoroughly together in a saucepan and heat gently over a low flame. When melted add the gelatine and mix well. Lastly add the wine and remove from the heat. Pour into individual glasses and allow to set.

Red Winter Jelly

300 ml (½ pint) water
Rind and juice of 1 lemon and ½ orange
1 stick cinnamon
2 cloves
1½ tablespoons redcurrant jelly (or better still, home-made bramble jelly)
150 ml (5 fl oz) port (British will do)
Sugar to taste
15 g (½ oz) gelatine powder
150 ml (5 fl oz) double cream
1 drop vanilla essence
1 teaspoon castor sugar
40 g (1½ oz) nibbed almonds

Serves 4

A marvellously rich jelly of a grown-up variety. A good follower to a rich main course, and a sweet that looks attractive served in narrow wine glasses with long stems.

Combine the water, lemon and orange rind (grated) and juices, cinnamon and cloves in a saucepan. Add the jelly and cook over a medium heat, stirring continuously, until the jelly has melted. Simmer gently for ten minutes. Add the port and enough sugar to sweeten (this will depend on sweetness of the port, but the final mixture should not be too sickly). Return to the boil, remove from the heat, strain through a fine sieve and cool.

Soften the gelatine in about 3 tablespoons of water and melt over a low heat. Add to the port mixture and mix well. Pour into narrow glasses and leave in a cold place to set.

Whip the cream until stiff, add the vanilla essence and castor sugar and pile on top of the jelly. Toast the almonds under a hot grill until golden brown and scatter over the cream. Serve well chilled.

Tangerine Crème Brûlée

6 egg yolks
50 g (2 oz) castor sugar
Grated rind of 4 small tangerines, mandarins or clementines
900 ml (30 fl oz) double cream
Juice of 2 small tangerines, mandarins or clementines
Castor sugar for the topping

Serves 8

This is a classic *crème brûlée* with a rather subtle and sophisticated hint of tangerine to prevent it being too rich. Usually *crème brûlée* is made in a large flat dish, but it is easier to serve if done in individual small pots or ramekins.

Beat the egg yolks with the castor sugar until white and fluffy. Add the tangerine rind to the cream and heat over a low flame until almost boiling. Pour the hot cream over the egg yolk mixture, beating all the time. Strain the custard through a fine sieve into the top of a double boiler and cook over simmering water, stirring continuously, until the custard thickens and will coat the back of a wooden spoon. *Do not allow to boil.*

Cool the custard, mix in tangerine juice and pour into eight small heat-proof pots or ramekin dishes. Leave to set in the refrigerator for at least eight hours.

Dust the top of the custard with a 3 mm (⅛ in) thickness of castor sugar and brown quickly under a hot grill until the top is melted and golden brown. Chill again for at least an hour before serving.

French Raspberry and Redcurrant Tart

The pastry:
50 g (2 oz) butter
100 g (4 oz) flour
1 small egg white
75 g (3 oz) castor sugar
2 drops vanilla essence

The filling:
225 g (8 oz) cream cheese
175 g (6 oz) castor sugar
Grated rind of ½ lemon
1 tablespoon orange juice
1 tablespoon double cream
225 g (8 oz) raspberries
100 g (4 oz) redcurrants
4 tablespoons redcurrant jelly
1 tablespoon water

Serves 4–6

Rub the butter into the flour until the mixture resembles coarse breadcrumbs. Make a well in the centre, add the egg white, sugar and vanilla and knead, adding a little water if necessary, into a smooth dough. Wrap in a clean cloth and refrigerate for at least 30 minutes.

Roll out the pastry thinly and line a 23 cm (9 in) flan tin. Prick the bottom with a fork and refrigerate again until firm. Bake blind in a moderate oven (190°C, 375°F, Reg. 5) for 20 minutes until crisp and golden brown. Leave to cool in the tin.

Combine the cream cheese, sugar, lemon rind, orange juice and cream and mix well. Spread the mixture in the flan case and top with the raspberries and redcurrants, stalks removed.

Combine the redcurrant jelly and water in a saucepan and heat gently until the jelly has melted. Cool and pour the jelly over the fruit. Refrigerate and serve with plain or whipped cream.

Tarte Celeste

One 25 cm (10 in) pie case, baked blind (see p. 256)
50 g (2 oz) currants
2 tablespoons rum or Calvados
6 crisp, slightly sharp eating apples (Granny Smiths are ideal)
40 g (1½ oz) butter
175 g (6 oz) soft brown sugar
225 g (8 oz) apricot jam (or dried apricots, soaked, sweetened and puréed)
50 g (2 oz) nibbed or chopped blanched almonds

Serves 6–8

A rich dessert ideal for following a lightish first course.

Combine the currants with the rum or Calvados and leave fruit to soak for 2 hours.

Peel, core and slice the apples into rings, putting them into lightly salted cold water as they are prepared to prevent browning. Melt the butter in a large, heavy frying pan. Strain off the water and pat the apples dry. Place them in the frying pan, sprinkle with the brown sugar and cook over a low heat, shaking the pan every now and then to prevent sticking, until soft and transparent but not mushy. Leave to cool.

Melt the apricot jam over a low heat and mix in the soaked currants and the almonds.

Spread the apples over the cooked pastry case and top with the apricot mixture. Chill before serving. For an even more splendid effect the top of the tart can be spread with lightly whipped cream before serving.

Dark Berry Salad

350 g (12 oz) blackberries
225 g (8 oz) fresh or frozen raspberries
100 g (4 oz) frozen blackcurrants
100 g (4 oz) castor sugar
150 ml (¼ pint) water
Juice of ½ lemon
5 tablespoons black cherry jam

Serves 6

If frozen thaw the berries in the refrigerator overnight.

Combine the sugar, water and lemon juice and bring slowly to the boil, stirring every now and then to prevent sticking. Simmer for one minute, mix in the black cherry jam and leave to get cold.

Combine all the berries in a serving bowl, pour over the syrup, mix lightly and leave in refrigerator for at least one hour before serving.

Cherry Picker Flan

225 g (8 oz) shortcrust pastry
450 g (1 lb) cherries
Grated rind of 1 lemon
2 tablespoons sugar
3 tablespoons water
2 small eggs
100 g (4 oz) ground almonds
100 g (4 oz) castor sugar

Serves 4

Roll the pastry out thinly and line a 20 cm (8 in) flan case. Line the case with greaseproof paper, fill with dried peas or beans and bake blind in a hot oven (220°C, 425°F, Reg. 7) for 15 minutes until firm. Remove peas and paper and leave to cool.

Stone the cherries and put them in a saucepan with the lemon rind, sugar and water. Cook over a medium heat for five minutes and leave to cool.

Beat the eggs and mix with the ground almonds and castor sugar to make a thick paste. Arrange the cherries in the flan case, cover with almond paste and bake in a moderate oven (190°C, 375°F, Reg. 5) for 30 minutes until the pastry and topping are golden brown.

Serve hot or cold.

Highland Fling

4 fresh peaches
Juice of 2 lemons
2 tablespoons honey
2 tablespoons whisky
150 ml (5 fl oz) cream

Serves 4

Simplicity is so often the essence of good food and the following recipe for a quick fruit sweet combines simplicity with a fresh, unusual flavour.

Peel the peaches by covering with boiling water for 30 seconds, draining and sliding off the skins; remove stones and cut into thin slices. Arrange in four glasses or goblets.

Combine the lemon juice and honey in a saucepan and heat gently, stirring well, until the honey has melted. Add the whisky and pour over the peaches.

Leave until cold and top with whipped cream.

Cherries Jubilee

Serves 4

1 family-size carton vanilla or Cornish ice-
    cream
2 large cans pitted black cherries
3 tablespoons kirsch or brandy

Place the ice-cream on a serving dish in the deep-freeze or the ice-making compartment of the refrigerator. Drain the cherries (drink the juice instead of orange juice for breakfast).

At the last minute remove the ice-cream from the refrigerator and pile the cherries on top. Heat the kirsch or brandy in a small saucepan, set alight, pour over the cherries and bring the dish still flaming to the table.

Rancin

Serves 6

6 thin slices white bread
Butter
900 g (2 lb) ripe slightly tart cherries
75 g (3 oz) vanilla sugar

A delicious Alsatian pudding with a taste that belies its simplicity. Cherry stoners can be bought in most hardware shops.

Remove the crusts from the bread and butter the slices. Arrange half the slices in a well-greased baking dish.

Stone the cherries and arrange them on the bread. Cover with the remaining buttered slices and sprinkle over the vanilla sugar. Bake the pudding in a moderately hot oven (200°C, 400°F, Reg. 6) for 15 minutes until the top is a rich golden brown. Serve hot with whipped or double cream.

Note: To make vanilla sugar put 225 g (8 oz) castor sugar in a jar. Add one or two vanilla pods, shake the jar well, cover and leave for at least a week before using.

Tuscan Fruit Salad

Serves 4

2 oranges
Rind of 1 lemon
450 ml ($\frac{3}{4}$ pint) water
4 tablespoons thick honey
1 tablespoon lemon juice
2 tablespoons brandy
2 bananas
2 pears
2 eating apples
50 g (2 oz) unblanched almonds

Cut the orange and lemon rind off the fruit in very thin slivers so that you have skin only and no white membrane. Cut the slivers into the thinnest possible strips.

Combine the water, honey and lemon juice in a saucepan, bring to the boil, add orange and lemon slivers and simmer gently for 20 minutes. Leave the syrup to cool and add the brandy.

Remove white pith and membrane and cut the oranges into very thin slices. Peel and thinly slice bananas. Peel, core and slice the pears and apples. Combine all the fruit in a bowl and pour over the syrup.

Toast the almonds under a hot grill for three minutes. Cool, chop coarsely and scatter over the fruit salad before serving.

Croquembouche

Choux pastry (p. 260)
300 ml (10 fl oz) double cream
1 tablespoon castor sugar
¼ teaspoon vanilla essence
275 g (10 oz) granulated sugar

Serves 8

This is a spectacular dessert which tastes as good as it looks.

Follow the directions for making profiteroles on page 260 and bake. Whip the cream until stiff and blend in the castor sugar and vanilla essence. Fill the hollow puffs with the cream.

Heat the granulated sugar in a dry heavy pan over a medium heat until it melts and turns to a golden syrup. Lower the heat and keep the sugar melted while assembling the sweet.

Arrange a layer of cream-filled puffs on a serving dish, pour over a thin layer of melted sugar and quickly press a second layer of puffs on to the syrup. Continue with the layers, making a pyramid shape, and finish off by dribbling the remaining syrup over the puffs.

Serve the sweet well chilled and divide the profiteroles with two forks.

Brandied Cherries

1·5 kilos (3 lb) cherries
300–450 ml (½–¾ pint) cooking brandy
275 g (10 oz) castor sugar
4 tablespoons water
¼ teaspoon ground cinnamon
4 cloves

Serves 6–8

A recipe to stretch out the cherry season; make it when they are at their cheapest.

Wipe the fruit with a damp cloth and remove the stalks. Pack them tightly but without crushing into sterilised glass jars (I use large empty instant coffee jars) and pour over enough brandy to cover. Close the jars tightly and leave in a cool place for 4–6 weeks.

Strain off brandy from the cherries and put on one side.

Combine the sugar, water, cinnamon and cloves in a saucepan. Cook gently for 20 minutes until the sugar has dissolved and the flavour of the spices has been released. Strain the syrup and mix it with the brandy. Cool and pour back into the jars over the fruit. Seal the jars carefully and store for at least two weeks before serving.

If the jars are correctly sealed the fruit will keep almost indefinitely. It makes an exotic pudding to serve at any time with ice-cream or *crème Chantilly*.

Pineapple and Ginger Fruit Salad

Serves 4

1 small pineapple
4 pieces stem ginger in syrup
150 ml (¼ pint) fresh or frozen orange juice
2 tablespoons ginger syrup
25 g (1 oz) blanched flaked almonds

A cool, rather sharp and refreshing end to a meal.

Using a sharp knife slice off the pineapple skin. Quarter the pineapple, remove hard core and cut the flesh into finger-sized pieces. Finely chop the stem ginger.

Combine the pineapple and ginger in a serving bowl and pour over the orange juice mixed with ginger syrup (if the pineapple is very tart you may need to add a little castor sugar to the juice).

Refrigerate until required and sprinkle over the almonds, toasted under a hot grill until golden brown, just before serving.

Cleveland Terrace Summer Salad

Serves 6

675 g (1½ lb) strawberries
Castor sugar
150 ml (¼ pint) rosé wine
1 tablespoon brandy
White of 1 egg
325 g (11 oz) canned lychees

Remove hulls from the strawberries, cut each one in half and place in a bowl with some sugar (the amount depends on the sweetness of the fruit), the rosé and the brandy. Refrigerate for two hours.

Break up the egg white with a fork. Brush a rim of egg white around the top of a glass serving bowl and dip the rim in castor sugar to give a frosted effect. Combine the strawberries and lychees in the bowl, add enough syrup from the lychees to cover and stir gently. Chill before serving.

Mulled Fruit Cocktail

Serves 6

1 small melon or 450 g (1 lb) frozen melon
   balls
Grated rind and juice of 1½ oranges
150 ml (5 fl oz) port
1 tablespoon redcurrant jelly
40 g (1½ oz) sugar
Pinch of nutmeg and cinnamon
2 cloves
450 g (1 lb) frozen raspberries

Fruit that freezes well can be a boon in winter. Raspberries are best of all, providing they are thawed with the greatest possible care. Thaw them overnight in their wrappings in the refrigerator–this way there should be virtually no loss of juice.

Halve the melon, remove seeds and scoop out the flesh with a ball scoop. Combine the orange rind, juice, port and redcurrant jelly in a saucepan with the sugar, nutmeg, cinnamon and cloves. Bring gently to the boil and simmer, stirring continuously over a very low heat until the jelly and sugar have dissolved. Remove from the heat and leave to cool.

Combine the raspberries and melon in individual glass goblets or a glass bowl. Pour over the cool liquid and refrigerate for at least one hour before serving.

Winter Fruit Salad

100 g (4 oz) dried apricots
50 g (2 oz) sugar
Juice of 1 lemon
3 crisp eating apples
25 g (1 oz) unblanched almonds

Serves 6

Cover the apricots with cold water and leave to soak overnight. Drain, cut into thin strips and put in a saucepan. Measure the liquid in which they were soaked and make it up with water to 300 ml ($\frac{1}{2}$ pint). Add this liquid to the apricots with the sugar and lemon juice. Bring to the boil, simmer gently for 20 minutes and leave to cool. Check sweetness to taste.

Peel, core and dice the apples and add them to the cooled apricots. Roughly chop the almonds and toast them under a hot grill for 2–3 minutes until crisp. Add to the fruit, mix well and chill.

Ginger Group

4 small ripe melons
8 pieces of ginger preserved in syrup
200 ml (7$\frac{1}{2}$ fl oz) double cream
4 tablespoons ginger syrup
2 tablespoons Drambuie or brandy

Serves 4

Melon and ginger are old and well-tried companions.

Cut a thin slice off the top of the melons and scoop out the flesh with a small ball scoop. Chop the preserved ginger. Whip the double cream until thick and stiff and gradually beat in the ginger syrup and Drambuie or brandy. Fold in the melon balls and chopped ginger, spoon the mixture into the melon shells, piling it up high, and refrigerate for at least an hour.

Rhubarb Pudding

1 packet trifle sponge cakes
450 g (1 lb) rhubarb
5 tablespoons water
50 g (2 oz) sugar
200 ml (7$\frac{1}{2}$ fl oz) double cream
2 teaspoons castor sugar
1 drop vanilla essence

Serves 6

Made on the same principle as summer pudding, this has a wonderfully fresh and pleasant taste.

Cut the cakes into thin slices and use some of them to line a pudding basin. Wash the rhubarb, peel off any coarse strings and cut the stalks into 1 cm ($\frac{1}{2}$ in) pieces. Combine the rhubarb, water and 50 g (2 oz) sugar in a saucepan, bring to the boil and simmer gently for about 20 minutes or until the rhubarb is cooked through. Pour half the rhubarb into the basin and cover with a layer of sponge. Add the remaining rhubarb and cover with a final layer of sponge. Place a plate on top, weight it down with a heavy object and refrigerate the pudding overnight or for at least eight hours.

To turn the pudding out loosen the edges with a spatula dipped in hot water, invert on to a serving plate and tap the bottom of the basin with a wooden spoon. Mask the pudding with the cream, whipped until stiff and flavoured with the castor sugar and vanilla essence.

Rhubarb Pie

350 g (12 oz) flour
Pinch of salt
175 g (6 oz) butter or margarine
3–4 tablespoons cold water
675 g (1½ lb) rhubarb
100 g (4 oz) soft brown sugar
Grated rind of ½ lemon
3 tablespoons cream

Serves 4–6

Sieve the flour and salt into a basin. Add the butter and cut it into the flour with two sharp knives until the size of mature peas and well-coated with flour. Using fingertips, rub butter and flour together until the mixture resembles coarse breadcrumbs. Add just enough cold water to make a stiff paste and knead the pastry until smooth. Wrap in a clean cloth and refrigerate for 30 minutes.

Roll the pastry out thinly and divide into two. Use half to line a 20–22 cm (8–9 in) flan dish and fill with rhubarb cut into 2·5 cm (1 in) pieces. Sprinkle over the sugar and lemon rind and cover with a lid of the remaining pastry.

Cut two slits in pastry, brush with some of the cream and bake in a hot oven (220°C, 425°F, Reg. 7) for 45 minutes. Pour the remaining cream into the pie through one of the slits, using a small funnel, and bake for a further 10–15 minutes. Serve hot or cold.

Crème de Abacate

3 ripe avocado pears
1 tablespoon lemon juice
175 g (6 oz) castor sugar
Pinch of salt
300 ml (½ pint) milk
150 ml (5 fl oz) cream
4 tablespoons port
25 g (1 oz) blanched chopped almonds

Serves 6

A Brazilian delicacy to soothe the digestion at the end of a rich meal.

Peel the avocados, remove stones and sprinkle the flesh with the lemon juice and sugar. Leave to stand for ten minutes. Add the salt and mash the avocados with a fork; mix in the milk and purée through a fine sieve (this can also be done in a liquidiser).

Add the cream and port, spoon into six glass goblets or wine glasses and chill well. Toast the almonds for 1–2 minutes under a hot grill, cool and sprinkle over the surface before serving.

Yoghurt Mousse

15 g (½ oz) gelatine powder
150 ml (¼ pint) water
2 crisp eating apples
200 ml (7½ fl oz) double cream
450 g (1 lb) carton black cherry yoghurt
3 egg whites

Serves 5–6

Combine the gelatine and water and heat over a low flame until the gelatine has dissolved. Remove from the heat and leave to cool.

Peel the apples, remove cores and cut the flesh into small dice. Whip the cream until stiff. Blend the gelatine into the yoghurt, add apples and mix well. Beat egg whites until stiff. Lightly mix in whipped cream and fold in the egg white.

Spoon into a glass dish or individual glass goblets and chill for at least 30 minutes before serving.

Rhubarb Batter Pudding

350 g (12 oz) rhubarb
2 large eggs
1 egg white
½ teaspoon ground ginger
2 tablespoons flour
4 tablespoons castor sugar
5 tablespoons double cream
5 tablespoons milk

Serves 4

Rhubarb and ginger are well tried companions and the following recipe makes a good end-of-winter pudding.

Wash the rhubarb and peel off any coarse strings. Cut it into 1 cm (½ in) pieces and place in the bottom of a baking dish. Beat the eggs and egg white until well blended; add the ginger and flour. Add half the sugar, whisking well, and then beat in the cream and milk. Leave the batter to stand for 30 minutes. Sprinkle the rhubarb with the remaining sugar, pour over the batter and bake in a moderately hot oven (200°C, 400°F, Reg. 6) for about 25 minutes until golden brown.

Rich Fritter Batter

175 g (6 oz) flour
¼ teaspoon salt
Pinch of pepper
1 tablespoon olive oil
2 eggs, separated
200 ml (7½ fl oz) flat beer

Sieve the flour, salt and pepper into a bowl; add the olive oil, beaten egg yolks and the beer. Beat until smooth. Cover and leave to mature in the refrigerator for at least two hours before using. At the last minute fold in the egg whites, stiffly beaten.

Make sure your fritter ingredients are of an even size and free of moisture, dip them in the batter mixture and fry until golden brown in deep fat. Drain on kitchen paper and put immediately into a moderate oven while the remaining fritters are cooked.

Make the fritters from elderflower heads, slices of banana or slices of peeled and cored apple.

Italian Stuffed Peaches

4 large peaches
2 tablespoons castor sugar
15 g (½ oz) unsalted butter
1 egg yolk
75 g (3 oz) macaroons
1 teaspoon lemon juice
1 teaspoon brandy

Serves 4

Peel the peaches by covering with boiling water for 30 seconds, draining and sliding off the skins. Cut them in half, remove stones and scoop out a little of the peach flesh to make room for the filling.

Cream the sugar with the butter until the mixture is smooth. Add the egg yolk and beat well.

Crush the macaroons with a rolling pin. Combine the butter mixture with the macaroons, lemon juice and brandy and press into the peach cavities.

Place the peaches in a lightly buttered baking dish and bake in a moderate oven (180°C, 350°F, Reg. 4) for 20 minutes. Serve warm with cream.

Pêche Melba

1 egg
2 egg yolks
150 g (5 oz) castor sugar
300 ml (½ pint) milk
Few drops vanilla essence
300 ml (10 fl oz) double cream
3 large peaches
600 ml (1 pint) water
225 g (8 oz) sugar
50 g (2 oz) slivered almonds
350 g (12 oz) raspberries

Serves 6

First make the ice-cream. Beat the egg and egg yolks with 75 g (3 oz) of the castor sugar until light and pale yellow. Bring the milk to just below boiling point and pour it over the egg mixture, beating all the time.

Strain this custard through a fine sieve into a heavy-bottomed pan and cook over a very low heat, stirring continuously, until the mixture thickens enough to coat the back of the wooden spoon. Add the vanilla essence, pour the custard into a bowl and leave to cool. Whip the cream until thick and fold it as lightly as possible into the custard.

Pour the ice-cream into freezing trays and put in a deep-freeze or in the ice-making compartment of the refrigerator until the ice-cream is frozen to a depth of about 1 cm (½ in) around the sides of the trays. Turn the half-frozen ice-cream into a bowl and beat with a rotary whisk until smooth. Return to the freezing trays and freeze until firm.

Put the peaches in a bowl and cover with boiling water for 30 seconds; drain and slide off the skins. Halve the peaches, remove stones. Boil the water with 225 g (8 oz) sugar until the sugar has dissolved.

Poach the peaches in the sugar syrup for five minutes, remove with a slotted spoon and boil the syrup until reduced to about two-thirds of the original volume. Leave to cool.

Toast the almonds under a hot grill for a few minutes until golden brown. Rub the raspberries through a fine sieve to remove the pips and mix the purée with the remaining castor sugar.

Put two scoops of ice-cream into glass goblets, top with a peach half and a little of the peach syrup and spoon over the raspberry purée. Scatter the roasted almonds over the top and serve at once.

Fresh peaches or nectarines are delicious with the first of the season's blackberries, too. Peel fresh peaches, cut them into halves (remove stones) and pile blackberries over the top. Sprinkle with a little lemon juice and sugar and serve with double cream.

Old English Syllabub

2 eggs, separated
100 g (4 oz) castor sugar
150 ml (¼ pint) milk
300 ml (10 fl oz) single cream
150 ml (¼ pint) sherry
Finely grated rind of ½ lemon
Grated nutmeg

Serves 6

A true syllabub should be made with milk fresh from the cow, and mixed with the eggs and sugar while still warm and foaming. If you don't happen to have a cow ready for milking on your doorstep excellent results can be obtained by using bottled milk and single cream, providing the egg whites are only added at the very end.

Beat the egg yolks with the sugar until light and almost white. Gradually add the milk and cream, beating all the time until the mixture is smooth. Blend in the sherry, add the lemon rind and leave to stand for an hour.

Just before serving whip the egg whites until stiff, fold them into the syllabub and sprinkle with a little grated nutmeg.

Strawberry Cream Gâteau

450 g (1 lb) puff pastry
Castor sugar for dusting
300 ml (10 fl oz) double cream
50 g (2 oz) castor sugar
2 drops vanilla essence
450 g (1 lb) strawberries, hulled and sliced
Icing sugar

Serves 6

Puff pastry is such a time-consuming thing to make oneself that I have no compunction in buying a frozen variety, and I defy anyone to tell the difference.

Roll the pastry out very thinly and cut into three circles about 20 cm (8 in) across. Brush the surface of each with a little water and sprinkle over a very thin dusting of castor sugar. Place on a dampened baking sheet and bake in a hot oven (230°C, 450°F, Reg. 8) for 5–10 minutes until well risen and golden brown. Leave to cool on the baking sheet and then split each circle horizontally in two with a long sharp knife.

Whip the cream until stiff and mix in the sugar and vanilla essence. Spread all but one of the pastry circles with the cream and cover with the strawberries. Sandwich neatly together and top with the remaining circle.

Sieve a little icing sugar over the top and refrigerate until ready to serve.

Pineapple Alaska

Serves 6

1 medium pineapple
600 ml (1 pint) home-made or bought
  ice-cream
3 egg whites
75 g (3 oz) castor sugar

This is an absolutely spectacular pudding to serve for a special occasion when pineapples are not too expensive. But as it requires a certain sleight of hand it should, like a new hairstyle, be practised on the family first.

In advance: remove and reserve top of the pineapple. Remove skin from the rest, gouging out any pips left in the fruit with a potato peeler or small spoon. Cut the pineapple into six slices, removing the core from each one. Reshape the pineapple on a fire-proof serving dish, filling the core and masking the sides with ice-cream. Put into the freezer.

Beat the egg whites until stiff and lightly fold in the sugar. Smother the sides and top of pineapple with this meringue, crown with the reserved top and freeze until five minutes before serving time.

Put the frozen pineapple dish into a moderately hot oven (200°C, 400°F, Reg. 6) and bake for five minutes or until the meringue is crisped and a light golden colour. Serve at once, slicing sideways to give each person one of the cut slices.

Lemon Pineapple Soufflé

Serves 6

450 g (16 oz) can pineapple chunks
15 g (½ oz) gelatine powder
2 eggs, separated
100 g (4 oz) castor sugar
Juice of 1 lemon
300 ml (10 fl oz) double cream
Black grapes to decorate

Drain off the pineapple juice. Mix two tablespoons of this juice with the gelatine and heat slowly over a very low heat until the gelatine has melted.

Beat the egg yolks with the sugar until light, smooth and pale yellow. Add the lemon juice and 150 ml (¼ pint) of pineapple juice and mix well. Stir in the gelatine and leave until thickening but not yet set firm (about 10–15 minutes).

Beat the egg whites until stiff. Beat the cream until stiff (doing it this way round you don't need to wash the whisk in between beating whites and cream). Add the pineapple chunks to the egg yolk mixture and quickly fold in the cream and lastly the egg whites.

Transfer to a glass serving dish and leave to set firm in the refrigerator – about an hour. Decorate with black grapes, halved and with pips removed.

Traditional Lemon Soufflé with Praline

3 eggs, separated
150 g (5 oz.) castor sugar
Rind and juice of 2 lemons
15 g (½ oz) gelatine powder
4 tablespoons hot water
150 ml (5 fl oz) single cream
150 ml (5 fl oz) double cream
100 g (4 oz) blanched almonds
100 g (4 oz) granulated sugar

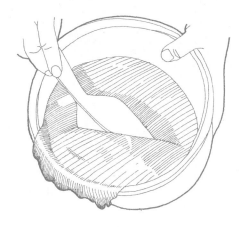

Serves 6

As a hot-weather pudding few sweets can beat this light, airy, lemony concoction. But it must be made properly with the egg yolks being whisked over hot water; taking short cuts will result in a heavier and sometimes even cloying end product. The crisp praline gives an attractive finish and a delicious contrast in texture.

Combine the egg yolks, castor sugar, grated lemon rind and juice in a bowl, place over a saucepan of hot water and cook, whisking all the time, over a medium heat for five minutes until the mixture is like thick custard. Remove from the saucepan and continue to whisk until the mixture has cooled and is light and pale yellow.

Dissolve the gelatine in the hot water and add it to the egg yolk mixture. Whip the double and single cream together until thick. Whip the egg whites until they form stiff peaks. Fold the cream and then the egg whites lightly into the egg yolk mixture.

Wrap a collar of greaseproof paper around a soufflé dish and pour in the soufflé mixture so that it rises inside the collar about 5 cm (2 in) above the top of the dish. Refrigerate until set firm and gently remove the collar.

Toast the almonds under a hot grill until golden brown. Combine the granulated sugar with two tablespoons of water in a saucepan and cook to a thick syrup over a medium heat. Add the almonds and continue to cook, without stirring, until the mixture is a rich toffee colour. Pour at once on to an oiled marble slab or Fomica top and leave to set into praline. Crush with a rolling pin and sprinkle over the top and sides of the soufflé before serving.

Light Prune Soufflé

225 g (8 oz) prunes
4 egg whites
8 tablespoons castor sugar
1 tablespoon nibbed almonds

Serves 4

Cover the prunes with water and leave to soak overnight. Cook in the juice for 10–15 minutes until tender. Drain, cool, remove stones and chop the flesh.

Whip the egg whites until foaming. Add a little of the sugar and a little of the fruit and nuts at a time, whisking vigorously until the ingredients are all incorporated and the egg whites are stiff.

Pour into a lightly oiled soufflé dish and bake in a moderate oven (180°C, 350°F, Reg. 4) for 30 minutes. Serve immediately with cream.

Lemon Soufflé

50 g (2 oz) butter
1 tablespoon flour
200 ml (7½ fl oz) milk
Grated rind and juice of 1 large lemon
2 teaspoons brandy
75 g (3 oz) castor sugar
2 large eggs, separated

Serves 4

Melt the butter, add the flour and mix well; remove from the heat. Gradually add the milk, stirring continuously, until the mixture is thick and smooth. Beat in the lemon rind and juice, brandy and sugar. Add the egg yolks one by one, beating until they are well blended into the basic soufflé mixture.

In a clean bowl, beat the egg whites until stiff but not dry and fold them into the soufflé base with a fork. Pour the mixture into a lightly greased soufflé dish about 18 cm (7 in) across. Place the dish in a roasting tin half filled with hot water and bake in a moderate oven (180°C, 350°F, Reg. 4) for 40 minutes.

Serve at once with a jug of fresh cream.

Sweet Soufflé Omelette

8 small eggs, separated
75 g (3 oz) castor sugar
2 drops vanilla essence
15 g (½ oz) butter
4 tablespoons of strawberry or raspberry jam
Icing sugar

Serves 4–5

Beat the egg yolks until light and fluffy with the sugar and vanilla essence. Beat the whites until stiff and fold lightly into the yolk mixture.

Melt the butter until foaming but not brown in a non-stick frying pan. Add the omelette mixture, cover the pan and cook over a medium low heat for about ten minutes until the bottom is golden brown (score through the omelette with a knife in a few places half-way through to ensure even cooking).

Spread the omelette with warm jam. Slide on to a plate, folding in half, and dust the top with a little icing sugar.

No-crust Lemon Cheese Pie

225 g (8 oz) cottage cheese
2 egg yolks
40 g (1½ oz) sugar
25 g (1 oz) plain flour
300 ml (½ pint) milk
Grated rind and juice of 1 lemon
¼ teaspoon vanilla essence
2 egg whites
50 g (2 oz) castor sugar

Serves 4

Press the cottage cheese through a fine sieve. Beat the egg yolks with the sugar, flour and a little of the milk until the mixture is smooth. Heat the remaining milk to boiling point and pour it slowly into the egg mixture, beating all the time. Pour this custard into a clean pan and bring slowly to the boil, stirring continuously.

Remove from the heat, leave to cool for about five minutes and add the lemon rind, juice, cottage cheese and vanilla essence. Pour into an oven-proof pie dish and top with a meringue made by whisking the egg whites until stiff and then folding in the castor sugar.

Bake in a moderate oven (180°C, 350°F, Reg. 4) for 20 minutes until lightly browned. The pie can be served hot or cold.

Apple-filled Pancakes

2 eggs, separated
600 ml (1 pint) milk
150 g (5 oz) plain flour
2 teaspoons sugar
2 drops vanilla essence
Olive oil or lard for frying

The filling:
900 g (2 lb) cooking apples
5 tablespoons water
50 g (2 oz) sugar
Juice of 1 lemon

The topping:
2 tablespoons apricot jam
2 teaspoons lemon juice
25 g (1 oz) split blanched almonds

Serves 4–6

Beat the egg yolks with some of the milk, add the flour and sugar and mix to a smooth batter. Mix in the remaining milk and the vanilla essence.

Heat a little olive oil or lard in a non-stick frying pan, add enough batter to form a thin film over the surface of the pan and cook until the pancake is golden brown on the bottom. Turn over and brown on the other side. Stack the cooked pancakes on a plate and keep warm.

Peel, core and roughly chop the apples. Stew them with the water, sugar and lemon juice until tender and purée through a sieve.

Place a generous dollop of this filling in each pancake, roll up neatly and arrange in a lightly greased shallow baking dish.

Combine the apricot jam, lemon juice and almonds and spread the mixture over the pancakes. Heat through in a hot oven or under a hot grill and serve at once.

Swiss Pancakes

100 g (4 oz) flour
Pinch of salt
1 egg
150 ml ($\frac{1}{4}$ pint) milk
150 ml ($\frac{1}{4}$ pint) water
Rind of $\frac{1}{2}$ orange
Olive oil for frying

The filling:
400 g (14 oz) canned stoned black cherries in
    syrup
1 tablespoon kirsch (optional)
2 tablespoons apricot jam
Juice of $\frac{1}{2}$ orange

Serves 4

Combine the flour and salt in a bowl, mix in the egg, add the milk and water and beat with a rotary whisk until the batter is smooth. Mix in the finely grated orange rind. Pour the batter into a jug and leave to stand in the refrigerator for 30 minutes before using. Beat again with the rotary whisk just before using.

Brush an omelette pan with a thin veil of olive oil and heat over a high flame. Pour in about one tablespoon of batter, swirling it around until it forms a wafer-thin even layer over the pan. Cook over a medium heat for about $1\frac{1}{2}$ minutes, then turn over and continue to cook until the underneath is golden brown. Stack the pancakes and keep warm until required.

Strain off the juice from the cherries and store. Add the kirsch to the cherries. Combine the apricot jam and orange juice in a saucepan and heat gently until the jam has melted. Place a spoonful of cherries in each pancake and roll up neatly. Arrange pancakes in a lightly buttered fire-proof serving dish and spread over the melted jam.

Heat the pancakes through in a moderate oven until the jam is bubbling and the pancakes are piping hot. Serve at once with cream.

Pancakes with Orange Butter

Serves 4–5

150 g (5 oz) plain flour
300 ml (½ pint) milk
2 eggs, separated
25 g (1 oz) sugar
25 g (1 oz) butter
Olive oil for frying

The filling:

50 g (2 oz) unsalted butter
50 g (2 oz) castor sugar
Grated rind and juice of 1 orange
Grated rind of ½ lemon

Mix the flour and milk together with a wire whisk until the mixture is smooth. Add the egg yolks and sugar and beat well. Melt the butter and blend it into the batter. Whip the egg whites until stiff and fold them into the batter.

Heat a very thin film of oil in a non-stick frying pan. Add a little batter and swirl it around until it just covers the bottom of the pan. Cook the pancake over a medium high heat until golden brown; turn over and cook the other side. Stack the cooked pancakes one on top of the other and continue until the batter is used up. Leave them to cool.

Beat the butter with the castor sugar until pale and creamy and blend in the orange juice and orange and lemon rind. Spread a little of the filling on the pancakes and fold each one into four. Arrange in a buttered baking dish, dot with a little extra butter and heat through in a moderately hot oven (200°C, 400°F, Reg. 6).

Somerset Apple Cake

Serves 4–6

4 apples
75 g (3 oz) butter
150 ml (¼ pint) milk
2 eggs
3 tablespoons sugar
50 g (2 oz) plain flour

Peel and slice the apples and fry in hot butter. Mix the milk, eggs, sugar and flour. Stir in the apples and butter. Put in a greased 18 cm (7 in) sponge sandwich tin and bake in a moderately hot oven (190°C, 375°F, Reg. 5) for 20 minutes.

Turn out, sprinkle with extra sugar and brown in the oven or under the grill.

Rum-baked Apples

Serves 4

4 large cooking apples
40 g (1½ oz) unsalted butter
75 g (3 oz) raisins
4 tablespoons rum
6 tablespoons apricot jam
¼ teaspoon ground nutmeg

Wash the apples and make a hole through the centres with an apple corer. Rub the skins with a little softened butter. Place each apple on a piece of well-buttered foil about 20 cm (8 in) square.

Combine the raisins, rum and apricot jam, mix well and pack into the apples. Dust the top of each apple with a little ground nutmeg, draw up the sides of the foil to make neat sealed parcels and place in a shallow baking dish.

Cook in a moderately hot oven (200°C, 400°F, Reg. 6) for about 20 minutes. Test to see if they are tender by lightly squeezing one of the parcels.

Serve the apples in their foil with cream on the side.

Bananas Flambé

3 bananas (ripe but on no account discoloured by brown spots)
40 g (1½ oz) butter
½ teaspoon lemon juice
3 tablespoons sugar
3 tablespoons rum

As the secret of most flambé dishes is quick cooking and instant serving, cooking at the table is ideal. The perfect cooking vessel is a copper frying pan, but if you haven't got one of those an attractive enamelled frying pan will do.

Peel the bananas and cut in half lengthwise. Melt the butter over a medium low heat without browning. Add the bananas, cut side up, sprinkle with the lemon juice, increase the heat slightly and cook for two minutes. Gently turn the bananas over without breaking them, sprinkle over the sugar and cook for a further two minutes or until the sugar has all melted. Pour over the rum, heat through until it bubbles, then set alight and serve immediately on warmed plates.

Serve with plenty of fresh cream.

Apple and Blackberry Pie

225 g (8 oz) blackberries
100 g (4 oz) castor sugar
Grated rind and juice of ½ lemon
450 g (1 lb) cooking apples
225 g (8 oz) shortcrust pastry
1 tablespoon finely chopped lemon balm (optional)
Pinch of cinnamon
Milk

Serves 4

I put lemon balm with my blackberries to add something just a little bit special to the pie. Lemon balm is a perennial herb, easy to grow and indeed, like mint, hard to stop once it gets going. Stewing the blackberries first and removing some of their juice prevents them being too liquid.

Combine the blackberries, sugar, lemon rind and juice, bring to the boil in a saucepan. Simmer gently for ten minutes, place the blackberries in a sieve and reserve their juice.

Peel, core and slice the apples. Divide the pastry into two, one half slightly larger than the other. Roll out the smaller to line a 20 cm (8 in) pie plate and the other to a circle about 1 cm (½ in) larger.

Spread the apple slices on the pastry, cover with the blackberries and pour over four tablespoons of blackberry liquid. Sprinkle over the lemon balm and cinnamon. Damp the edge of the pastry, cover with the second circle and press firmly together with the prongs of a fork. Cut an air vent in the top and brush with milk. Bake in a moderately hot oven (200°C, 400°F, Reg. 6) for 20 minutes, then lower the heat to very moderate (160°C, 325°F, Reg. 3) and cook for a further 20 minutes.

Sprinkle with sugar and serve warm or cold.

Apple and Blackberry Crisp

3 cooking apples
450 g (1 lb) blackberries
2 tablespoons sugar
Finely grated rind and juice of 1 orange
150 g (5 oz) flour
40 g (1½ oz) sugar
75 g (3 oz) butter
½ teaspoon ground cinnamon
15 g (½ oz) finely chopped blanched almonds

Serves 4

In this recipe the top layer of apples prevents the juice of the blackberries seeping into the crisp crunchy topping.

Peel, core and slice the apples. Wash and dry the blackberries if necessary.

Arrange half the apples in the bottom of a lightly buttered fireproof dish, add the blackberries mixed with the two tablespoons of sugar and cover with the remaining apples. Pour over the orange juice. Mix the flour and sugar together and rub in the butter with the fingertips until the mixture resembles breadcrumbs. Add the orange rind, cinnamon and almonds and sprinkle the mixture over the fruit.

Bake in a hot oven (220°C, 425°F, Reg. 7) for about 20 minutes until crisp and golden brown.

Stewed Apples and Blackberries with Cider

150 ml (¼ pint) cider
150 ml (¼ pint) water
175 g (6 oz) castor sugar
450 g (1 lb) eating apples
450 g (1 lb) blackberries
1 tablespoon cornflour

Serves 6

Serve the stewed fruit with cream, or use it as a filling for flans and pies.

Combine the cider, water and sugar in a saucepan and heat slowly, stirring occasionally, until the sugar has dissolved. Bring to the boil and simmer for two minutes.

Peel, core and slice the apples. Add them to the syrup, bring to the boil and simmer for one minute. Add the blackberries, bring back to the boil and remove immediately from the heat. Cover tightly and leave to stand for 15 minutes.

Strain off the juices and mix the cornflour with one tablespoon of juice until you have a smooth paste. Stir in the remaining juice and put the mixture into a clean saucepan. Bring to the boil, stirring all the time, until the sauce is thick, clear and shining. Pour over the fruit.

To serve by itself, refrigerate the fruit for at least two hours and accompany with raw or clotted cream.

Fruit Puffs

450 g (1 lb) apples
1 tablespoon water
25 g (1 oz) butter
100 g (4 oz) brown sugar
450 g (1 lb) blackberries
225 g (8 oz) flaky or puff pastry
1 egg, beaten; or a little milk

Serves 4

Peel, core and thinly slice the apples and simmer gently in a saucepan with the water, butter and sugar until soft but not mushy. Drain off excess liquid, mix in the blackberries and leave to cool.

Roll out the pastry to 3 mm ($\frac{1}{8}$ in) thickness and cut into saucer-size circles. Put a heaped tablespoon of fruit in the centre of each circle, damp round the edge and fold in half. Crimp firmly together with a fork, brush over with beaten egg or milk and cut an air vent in the top of each puff.

Bake in a hot oven (220°C, 425°F, Reg. 7) for 15–20 minutes until golden brown.

Bramble Conserve

675 g (1$\frac{1}{2}$ lb) cooking apples
675 g (1$\frac{1}{2}$ lb) blackberries
Grated rind and juice of $\frac{1}{2}$ lemon
Sugar

This is ideal to serve with ice-cream or a rice pudding.

Roughly chop the apples without removing peels or cores. Place with the blackberries, lemon rind and juice in a saucepan, just cover with water, bring slowly to the boil and simmer until the apples are soft. Rub the fruit through a fine sieve, weigh the pulp and add 450 g (1 lb) sugar to each 450 g (1 lb) of fruit pulp.

Boil the fruit in a clean saucepan for half an hour, stirring continuously to prevent burning or sticking. Pour into a mould and leave to set firm in a cool place. Turn out before serving and cut into wedges.

September Delight

675 g (1$\frac{1}{2}$ lb) blackberries, freshly picked
4–5 tablespoons Cassis
2 tablespoons brandy
Juice of $\frac{1}{2}$ a lemon
175 g (6 oz) sugar
200 ml (7$\frac{1}{2}$ fl oz) double cream
2 tablespoons red wine
2 tablespoons icing sugar

Serves 6

Cassis is a blackcurrant cordial (or liqueur), smooth as satin and delicious as nectar. Combined with blackberries it makes one of the most perfect desserts I know. Top it with a rose-coloured cream and you have what can only be called a dream.

Put the blackberries in a bowl and pour over the Cassis, brandy and lemon juice. Sprinkle with the 175 g (6 oz) sugar and leave to marinate in the refrigerator overnight. Spoon into individual glasses.

Whip the cream until thick. Blend in the wine and icing sugar and top each glass of fruit with a generous dollop of cream. Serve well chilled.

Blackberry Fool

450 g (1 lb) blackberries
100 g (4 oz) castor sugar
Juice of ½ lemon
1 tablespoon Cassis (blackcurrant liqueur)
300 ml (10 fl oz) double cream
1 egg white
50 g (2 oz) blanched flaked almonds

Serves 6

Fruit fools are very much a part of the traditional English scene, and they are quick to make and fresh to taste. They look particularly pretty if you serve them in individual glass goblets or wine glasses.

Place the blackberries in a heavy pan, add the sugar and cook over a low heat, stirring every now and then, for 15 minutes until soft. Sieve the fruit or pass it through a food mill to remove pips; leave the purée to cool. Add the lemon juice and Cassis and mix well.

Beat the cream until thick; whip the egg white until stiff. Blend the cream with the blackberry purée and lightly fold in the egg white. Spoon the mixture into glass goblets and chill before serving. Top with the almonds toasted to a crisp golden brown under a hot grill.

Queen of Puddings

150 ml (¼ pint) Jersey milk
25 g (1 oz) unsalted butter
Finely grated rind of 1 lemon
2 eggs, separated
50 g (2 oz) castor sugar
75 g (3 oz) white breadcrumbs
3 tablespoons black cherry jam

Serves 4

This old-fashioned nursery pudding can either be a dream or a dreary disaster. Add lemon to the filling to give it a zip, use black cherry jam instead of the traditional raspberry and you have a pudding that every man, whatever his age, will love. To lift the pudding into the gourmet class add a tablespoon of sherry to the custard base.

Heat the milk with the butter and lemon rind until it reaches boiling point. Beat the egg yolks with half the sugar until the mixture is pale and light in texture. Beat the hot milk into the egg yolks. Put the breadcrumbs into a lightly buttered 1 litre (2 pint) soufflé dish and strain over the custard mixture. Mix lightly and bake in a moderate oven (180°C, 350°F, Reg. 4) for 20–30 minutes until just set. Remove and leave to cool for ten minutes.

Meanwhile heat the jam in a saucepan until just melted and spread it over the pudding. Whip the egg whites until stiff and lightly fold in the remaining sugar. Pile this meringue on top of the pudding and bake for a further 15 minutes until the meringue is set and lightly coloured. Serve at once with fresh cream.

Steamed Chocolate Pudding

150 g (5 oz) stale sponge cake
75 g (3 oz) Bourneville slab chocolate
150 ml ($\frac{1}{4}$ pint) milk
50 g (2 oz) butter, softened
2$\frac{1}{2}$ tablespoons castor sugar
2 large eggs, separated
2 drops vanilla essence

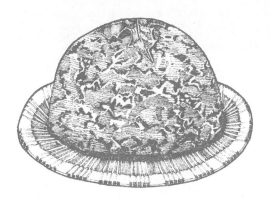

Serves 6

Break the sponge cake into smallish crumbs and put into a bowl. Break the chocolate into little pieces and combine with the milk in a small saucepan. Heat, stirring occasionally, until the chocolate has melted and pour over the sponge crumbs. Leave to stand for 20 minutes.

Beat the butter and sugar until light and fluffy. Beat in the egg yolks one by one, then mix in the soaked crumbs and vanilla essence.

Beat the egg whites until stiff and fold lightly into the chocolate base. Turn the mixture into a well-buttered pudding basin (the mixture should only half fill it) and cover tightly with lightly greased foil.

Place in a saucepan with enough boiling water to come half way up the basin and steam for 1$\frac{1}{2}$ hours or until set.

Turn out the pudding, dust with castor sugar and serve with chocolate sauce or cream.

Steamed Batter Pudding

175 g (6 oz) plain flour
Pinch of salt
1 tablespoon castor sugar
Grated rind of 1 small lemon
2 eggs, separated
175 ml (6 fl oz) milk

Serves 4

Sieve the flour and salt into a bowl. Add the sugar and lemon rind and mix well. Make a well in the centre, and place the egg yolks and milk in it. Using a wooden spoon gradually draw the flour into the egg yolks and milk, beating well until all the ingredients are well mixed. Finish by beating with a rotary whisk until the batter is smooth.

Beat the egg whites until stiff and fold them lightly into the batter. Half fill a well-greased pudding basin with the batter, cover tightly with a sheet of lightly buttered foil and place in a large saucepan with enough water to come half way up the basin. Cover the pan tightly and steam for 1$\frac{1}{2}$–2 hours until well risen and fairly firm.

Turn out and serve with a lemon sauce, hot jam or marmalade, or a sauce made by melting brown sugar with a little butter and flavouring it with lemon rind and a little lemon juice.

Monmouth Pudding

Serves 4

1 small white loaf
Hot milk
2 tablespoons castor sugar
50 g (2 oz) butter
Few drops vanilla essence
2 egg whites
Strawberry or raspberry jam

Perhaps one of the most economical puddings of all, as its basic ingredients are a small stale loaf and egg whites which may well be left over from a recipe like mayonnaise.

Remove crusts and crumble the loaf. Place the crumbs in a basin and pour over just enough hot milk to cover. Leave to stand for 15 minutes then beat in the sugar, butter and vanilla essence. Whip the egg whites until really stiff and fold into the crumb mixture. Spread the bottom of a lightly greased baking dish with a thin layer of jam, cover with a third of the pudding mixture, dot with more jam and then continue with alternate layers, finishing with a layer of mixture.

Bake in a slow oven (150°C, 300°F, Reg. 2) for about 45 minutes until set. Dust with castor sugar and serve with cream.

Biscuits Amandines

Serves 6

75 g (3 oz) blanched split almonds
100 g (4 oz) sugar
5 tablespoons water
2 egg whites
300 ml (10 fl oz) cream
4 tablespoons Marsala

Toast the almonds under a hot grill until dark golden brown. Leave to cool and crush into small crumbs with a rolling pin.

Combine the sugar and water in a saucepan, bring to the boil and continue boiling until the sugar reaches the crack stage–150°C or 300°F.

Whip the egg whites until stiff and gradually beat in the hot syrup. Leave to cool. Whip the cream until thick.

Reserve some of the crushed almonds for decoration and fold the rest, with the cream and Marsala, into the egg white mixture.

Turn into six small dishes and freeze until solid in the ice-making compartment of the refrigerator. Remove from the refrigerator a short time before serving as they should be iced but not rock-hard when eaten.

Brandy Butter

Serves 6

100 g (4 oz) unsalted butter
100 g (4 oz) icing sugar
2 tablespoons brandy
Grated rind of 1 orange

Soften the butter and cream it with a wooden spoon until fluffy. Very gradually add the sugar, teaspoon by teaspoon, beating well until the sauce is white.

Beat in the brandy drop by drop and add the grated orange rind.

Butterscotch and Almond Sauce

100 g (4 oz) unsalted butter
150 g (5 oz) soft brown sugar
1 tablespoon lemon juice
150 ml (5 fl oz) double cream
50 g (2 oz) blanched slivered almonds
2 drops vanilla essence (optional)

Serves 4–6

A rich glistening sauce which needs long slow cooking. Serve it hot or cold over vanilla, chocolate or coffee ice-cream.

Cut the butter into small pieces and combine it in the top of a double boiler with the sugar, lemon juice and cream. Stir over hot, not boiling, water until the butter has melted. Cook over a low heat for 30–45 minutes, stirring occasionally, until the sauce is thick and shining.

Toast the almonds under a hot grill until golden brown. Add to the sauce with vanilla essence if used.

Chocolate Fudge Sauce

50 g (2 oz) unsweetened block chocolate
225 g (8 oz) granulated sugar
2 tablespoons golden syrup
Pinch of salt
5 tablespoons water
25 g (1 oz) unsalted butter
½ teaspoon vanilla essence

Serves 4–6

Break the chocolate into small pieces. Combine the chocolate, sugar, syrup, salt and water and heat slowly until the chocolate has melted and the sugar dissolved. Bring to the boil, stirring continuously, and cook over a high heat for 10–15 minutes until a few drops of the liquid dropped into a cup of cold water will form a soft ball.

Remove the sauce from the heat and beat in the butter and vanilla essence. Serve hot.

Soft Fruit Sauce

150 ml (¼ pint) water
225 g (8 oz) granulated sugar
1 tablespoon cornflour
300 ml (½ pint) fruit purée
2 tablespoons lemon juice

Serves 4–6

Use strawberries, raspberries, blackcurrants, redcurrants or tinned fruit to make a quick, delicious sauce for fruit ice-creams or sorbets. If sweetened tinned fruit is used the amount of sugar should be adjusted accordingly.

Heat the water until boiling. Mix together the sugar and cornflour, blend in the boiling water and boil over a high heat, stirring continuously, for five minutes until thick and smooth. Cool and mix in the fruit purée and lemon juice.

This sauce will keep well if stored in a sealed container in the refrigerator.

Raspberry Sauce for Ice-Cream

225 g (8 oz) raspberries
1 tablespoon lemon juice
175 g (6 oz) sugar
2 teaspoons cornflour
(2 or more tablespoons brandy)

Serves 4–6

Very popular with children. Leave out the brandy if this is to be purely a children's pudding; perhaps increase the quantity for a more sophisticated sauce. The sauce can also be turned into a jelly.

Combine the raspberries, lemon juice and sugar in a saucepan and cook slowly for about ten minutes until the fruit is soft. Press through a sieve or through a fine food mill to extract the pips. Mix the cornflour with the brandy or with two tablespoons of water until smooth, add to the fruit purée and cook over a low heat, stirring continuously, until the sauce is thickened, clear and shiny. Serve hot or cold.

To make a delicious jelly double the quantities and add a teaspoon of gelatine dissolved in a little water to each pint of fruit purée. Pour into a flat mould and leave to set in the refrigerator. Turn out, mask with sweetened whipped cream and decorate with a few whole berries.

Loganberries can be used in exactly the same way but will need a little more sugar.

Quick Raspberry Sauce

225 g (8 oz) frozen raspberries
2 teaspoons lemon juice
75 g (3 oz) sugar
Finely grated rind of 1 orange
2 tablespoons water

Serves 4–6

Serve over ice-cream or fresh peeled and lightly poached peaches.

Combine all the ingredients in a saucepan and heat gently until the raspberries are soft. Stir well to break up the berries and serve either hot or cold.

For a clear sauce press through a sieve and discard the pips and orange rind.

Pastry, Scones and Cakes

Pastry plays a major role in many of the classic dishes of the Western world and there are all kinds to suit different cookery requirements. In this section I have included the basic pastry recipes, plus a few unusual ones, together with some of the most popular recipes I have published on scones and cakes. There are not many items in the cake section for the simple reason that I try to steer clear of too much starch being eternally figure-conscious and also because there are so many basic cookery books on the market which give a wealth of recipes and ideas for tea-time eating.

Basic Pointers for Good Pastry Making

The inexperienced cook is liable to quail at the thought of trying to make pastry and may become depressed by stories of how good pastry cooks are born not made. The most important rule about good pastry making is that it is a matter of practice more than anything else; the more you make it the more efficient you become and the better your pastry will be. So if your first attempts are not a hundred per cent successful do not despair.

The lightness of pastry depends on the number of particles of air trapped in the dough which expand during cooking lightening the pastry. Using ingredients which are well chilled, using your hands lightly and rolling the pastry as little as possible all helps to keep the air in. Use plain flour for almost all pastry. Self-raising flour is usually only used for making a suet crust.

Butter provides a good rich flavour, margarine helps make it crisp, and lard gives a lighter but less well flavoured pastry. The higher the proportion of fat the more luscious and crisp your pastry will be but it will also be more difficult to handle.

Make sure all your ingredients are well chilled (it even helps to chill the flour and the bowl you use as well as the fat, water and any other ingredients).

Roll pastry on as cold a surface as possible. The best is a slab of marble, which can be bought from good kitchen shops (or you can buy a piece of marble or slate quite cheaply from a monumental mason). Pastry should always be rolled away from you and never back and forth, which tends to make it shrink during the cooking time.

If you use the pastry as soon as it is made (and if you use cold ingredients) it is not necessary to chill it before rolling out and, in fact, over-chilling can toughen the dough and make it hard to handle; but do chill the pastry before baking as this helps to prevent shrinkage in the oven. Many recipes demand pastry cases that are 'baked blind' (cases are baked until partially cooked or crisp before the filling is added). This method is usually used for fruit flans, sweet pastry dishes and some savoury tartlets but, in my opinion, it is often well worth while baking pastry cases for a short time before adding almost any filling as it prevents the filling seeping into the case and the pastry becoming soggy. Roll out your pastry thinly, line your case and then prick the base lightly with a fork.

Chill or freeze the case before baking, line it with foil and fill it with dried beans or metal beans which can be bought from kitchenware shops. Bake the very cold case in a hot oven (220°C, 425°F, Reg. 7) for ten minutes, remove the beans and foil, press down any bubbles with your fingertips and return the case to the oven for 3–10 minutes until the desired crispness is reached. Leave the case to cool in the tin before filling.

Finally, for the lightest and most delicious pastry ever, for both savoury and sweet dishes, add a teaspoon of sherry or brandy in the place of some of the ice-cold water used to bind the dough–the effect is magical.

Note : Most pastry can be made in the new food processors. Put the flour in the bowl, add the chilled fat cut into small pieces and process until the mixture is reduced to coarse breadcrumbs. With the motor switched on, pour enough ice-cold water in through the feed tube to make the dough bind and begin to form a ball around the centre of the bowl. You will find that less liquid than usual will be required; do not overprocess.

The dough can be rolled out immediately and will need a really well floured board and roller.

Pâte Brisée

450 g (1 lb) plain flour
Pinch salt
(1 tablespoon castor sugar for sweet pastry)
225 g (8 oz) butter, well chilled
50 g (2 oz) lard, well chilled
1 egg beaten with enough ice-cold water to
  make 225 ml (8 fl oz)

A French pastry that is ideal for those pre-baked cases which are used for fruit or savoury dishes. Large or small cases can be frozen and used to make quick desserts by filling them with fresh or lightly stewed fruit and a well reduced fruit glaze or melted apricot or redcurrant jelly. Savoury first courses can be produced by filling the baked cases with pâté, a fresh or smoked fish mousse or cooked vegetables in a well seasoned mayonnaise.

This quantity is enough for two 25 cm (10 in) pie cases. Any not used can be refrigerated.

Sieve the flour into a bowl with the salt (and sugar if a sweet pastry is required). Cut the butter and lard into small squares. Cut the chopped fats into the flour (use an electric mixer or two sharp knives) until the mixture is the consistency of fine breadcrumbs. Add the liquid a little at a time, working the dough with the fingertips until it is smooth, firm and slightly elastic (the amount of liquid required will depend on temperature and on climatic conditions). Roll out the dough on a really well floured board and follow the instructions for baking cases blind (on p. 256.)

Quiche Pastry

175 g (6 oz) plain flour
Pinch salt
75 g (3 oz) butter, chilled
1 small egg
Iced water

A rich pastry for making savoury quiches. (Please read notes on lightly pre-baking cases on p. 256.) This quantity is enough for one 20–23 cm (8–9 in) case.

Sieve the flour and salt. Add the butter, in small pieces, and cut it into the flour using two sharp knives until the mixture resembles coarse breadcrumbs. Add the egg and knead the dough with the fingertips, adding a little ice-cold water if necessary, handling the dough as little and as lightly as possible until it is smooth, firm and elastic.

Roll out the dough immediately (or wrap it in a clean cloth and refrigerate for at least 30 minutes before rolling out) on a well floured board, using a well floured roller–the thinner the pastry is the crisper it will turn out.

To line the case, dust the rolled out pastry lightly with flour, fold it in half and place it half over the case. Unfold the pastry, press it firmly into the bottom and sides of the case and trim the edges. Chill or freeze before filling and baking.

Flaky Pastry

100 g (4 oz) butter, chilled
50 g (2 oz) vegetable fat, chilled
225 g (8 oz) plain flour
$\frac{1}{2}$ teaspoon salt
1 teaspoon lemon juice
Scant $\frac{1}{4}$ pint ice cold water

A rich but light pastry to use as the topping for both savoury and sweet pies. I use this for meat patties as well, as it is lighter than a shortcrust and absorbs some of the delicious flavours of the fillings.

Finely chop and mix the butter and vegetable fat and divide into four equal quantities. Sieve the flour and salt into a bowl. Add one portion of the fats and rub them into the flour with fingertips until the mixture resembles fine breadcrumbs. Add the lemon juice and mix in enough ice-cold water to make a firm dough. Turn on to a floured board and knead lightly until smooth. Wrap the pastry in a clean cloth and chill in the refrigerator for 15 minutes before rolling out.

Roll out the pastry to a rectangle about 6 mm ($\frac{1}{4}$ in) thick and lightly mark into three even portions. Cover two of the portions with one-third of the remaining fats dotting it evenly over the surface of the pastry. Fold over the piece that has not been covered with fat and then fold the remaining piece on top. Press the edges firmly together and roll out the pastry again to its original size. Wrap in a cloth and refrigerate for 15 minutes.

Repeat the folding and rolling process twice more using half the remaining fat each time and chilling the pastry between each process and before the final rolling.

Basic Shortcrust Pastry

450 g (1 lb) plain flour
1 teaspoon salt
75 g (3 oz) vegetable fat, chilled
150 g (5 oz) butter, chilled
Ice-cold water to mix

Probably one of the most widely used pastries: it can be used for sweet or savoury pies, piecrusts or tarts. The crust should be light and crisp and, as it does not include an egg, it is not too rich. The mixed flour and fats can be made in bulk and stored in a sealed bag in the refrigerator to use as required.

Sift the flour and salt into a bowl, add the fats cut into small pieces and then cut the fats into the flour using two knives. Rub the fats into the flour using your fingertips until the mixture resembles coarse breadcrumbs. Using a fork mix in enough ice-cold water (you will probably need little more than a tablespoon) to make a stiff dough. Turn on to a floured board and knead lightly until smooth.

Roll out the pastry on a well floured board to a thickness of 3–6 mm ($\frac{1}{8}$–$\frac{1}{4}$ in).

Variations:
Cheese Pastry: Substitute 1 oz finely grated mixed Cheddar and Parmesan cheese for 1 oz lard.
Savoury Pastry: Season with salt and pepper and mix a few mixed herbs into the flour.
Sweet Pastry: Add 1 tablespoon castor sugar to the flour and 1 teaspoon lemon juice to the iced water.

Almond Pastry

2 egg whites
Pinch salt
Drop almond essence
100 g (4 oz) castor sugar
175 g (6 oz) ground almonds
50 g (2 oz) plain flour
Flour

A delicious, crisp, almond-flavoured pastry to use for sweet fillings.

Beat the egg whites with the salt until stiff. Add the almond essence and sugar, and the almonds and flour and mix lightly with the fingers until a firm stiff dough is formed. Generously flour a board and rolling pin and roll out the dough to 3 mm ($\frac{1}{8}$ in) thickness, cut into circles of 7·5 cm (3 in) diameter and line well-greased tartlet tins. Line with foil, fill with dried beans and bake in a moderate oven (180°C, 350°F, Reg. 4) for 10 minutes. Remove foil and beans and continue to bake for a further 5 minutes until crisp and golden brown. Leave to cool before filling with strawberries or raspberries mixed into stiffly whipped cream and flavoured with a little castor sugar and a few drops of vanilla essence.

Basic Choux Pastry

300 ml (½ pint) water
70 g (2½ oz) butter
200 g (7 oz) plain flour
4 large eggs

Choux pastry and those gloriously sophisticated examples of its use (eclairs, profiteroles, cream and savoury puffs) is a dough the inexperienced cook believes to be difficult and arduous to make. In fact this is a pastry that even a real beginner can make with every hope of success. Without an electric mixer or food processor it does require hard work, as you beat the eggs into the flour paste to give the lightness and puffiness that is the essence of this pastry, but as long as that is done properly the rest is plain sailing. Cooked choux pastry freezes well and is useful to have in your freezer for quickly-made dishes, both sweet and savoury.

Combine the water and butter in a saucepan and heat until the butter has melted. Bring to a fast boil, remove from the stove, and add the flour all at once. Beat vigorously with a wooden spoon until the mixture becomes smooth and forms a ball which comes cleanly away from the side of the pan.

Beat the eggs with a rotary whisk until smooth. Add to the paste, a little at a time, beating continuously until each addition has been absorbed and the mixture is no longer slippery–the final result should be light and elastic and a small quantity pulled on the end of a spoon should stand erect.

Below are suggestions for various shapes and variations of choux pastry cases. To cook them, bake in a pre-heated oven (200°C, 400°F, Reg. 6) for 10 minutes. Reduce the heat to 180°C (350°F, Reg. 4) and continue to cook for a further 15–40 minutes depending on size (the cooked shells should be well risen and a uniform golden yellow; they should feel light and sound hollow when tapped on the bottom). Turn off the oven and leave the shells, with the door open, to dry off for 10 minutes before removing and cooling on a wire rack.

Choux Pastry Variations:
Cream Puffs

Add 1 tablespoon castor sugar to the water and butter. Squeeze the paste through a large nozzle on to an oiled baking sheet holding the forcing bag still and pressing the paste out firmly to form cabbage-like rounds about 5 cm (2 in) across. Cook as above, cool, cut a slit half-way through the puffs and pull out any soft dough from the centre. Fill with sweetened whipped cream or vanilla custard (during the strawberry season insert a large ripe berry into the centre of the filling) and dust with a little icing sugar.

Profiteroles

Push neat rounds of paste from a dessertspoon on to a lightly oiled baking sheet and cook as above. Split half way through the centre and fill the shells with whipped cream or ice cream. Pile on to a serving dish and pour over a chocolate sauce just before serving.

Chocolate Eclairs

Pipe the paste through a plain 1 cm ($\frac{1}{2}$ in) nozzle into 8 cm (3 in) lengths on to a lightly oiled baking sheet and bake as above. Cool, split half-way through the centre and remove any soft paste from the inside.

Fill the eclairs with whipped cream sweetened with a little castor sugar and flavoured with a drop or two of vanilla essence. Coat the tops with chocolate glacé icing made by breaking 100 g (4 oz) plain or milk chocolate into a small bowl, melting it slowly over a saucepan of hot water and thinning it slightly with $\frac{1}{2}$ teaspoon mixed water and vegetable oil. Spread the icing over the eclairs while it is still warm and before it begins to set firm again.

Savoury Cases

Add a little salt and white pepper, a pinch of cayenne and 1 tablespoon finely grated Parmesan cheese to the basic mixture, and shape and cook in the same way as profiteroles. Fill with a savoury hot or cold mixture (the puffs with hot fillings should be re-heated in a moderate oven before serving). I fill my cold savoury puffs with a chopped ratatouille, a finely chopped chicken salad mixture, cooked flaked fish in mayonnaise, devilled ham, cream cheese with chopped capers and gherkins, prawns in mayonnaise, or pâté. Hot fillings can be based on chicken or fish in a white sauce, fish or shellfish in a cheese sauce or finely chopped kidneys in a wine sauce. The shells can be sprinkled with a little extra grated cheese and a fine sprinkling of paprika or cayenne before re-heating, and make excellent first courses or light luncheon dishes.

Canapés

Make mini-puffs by using the paste from a teaspoon and follow the ideas for Savoury Cases above.

Choux Paste Puffs for Soup

An excellent garnish can be made by adding some grated cheese and cayenne pepper or a little curry powder to the basic paste and forming very small mounds on your lightly oiled baking sheet. Five or six of the savoury puffs can be floated (at the last minute) on top of each serving of soup and any left over can be frozen.

Banana Bread

100 g (4 oz) butter or margarine
225 g (8 oz) castor sugar
3 eggs
3 ripe bananas
275 g (10 oz) plain flour
1 teaspoon baking powder dissolved in 3
    teaspoons cold water
50 g (2 oz) chopped blanched almonds

Cream the butter with the sugar. Beat the eggs and mash the bananas. Mix eggs and bananas into the creamed ingredients, add the flour, baking powder mixture and chopped almonds, and mix well. Put into a well-oiled loaf tin and bake in a moderate oven (180°C, 350°F, Reg. 4) for one hour or until a skewer inserted into the bread comes out clean.

Turn onto a rack and leave to cool. Banana bread can be spread with butter and jam.

Easter Fruit Cake

150 g (5 oz) softened butter
150 g (5 oz) lard
100 g (4 oz) castor sugar
75 g (3 oz) dark brown sugar
5 eggs, beaten
350 g (12 oz) self-raising flour
350 g (12 oz) raisins
50 g (2 oz) glacé cherries
75 g (3 oz) walnuts
Grated orange rind
75 g (3 oz) ground almonds

Quantities are for two cakes

Cream the butter and lard with sugar until smooth and fluffy. Beat the eggs into the fat and sugar. Gradually mix in the flour. Add the raisins, cherries, walnuts, orange rind and ground almonds and mix well. Turn into two well-oiled and floured 26·5 cm (10½ in) by 9 cm (3½ in) loaf tins and bake in a very moderate oven (160°C, 325°F, Reg. 3) for about one hour until a skewer plunged into the centre of the cake comes out clean. Turn out on to wire racks and store, when cool, in air-tight tins.

An Old-fashioned Raised Pie

1 boiled chicken
175 g (6 oz) streaky bacon
2 tablespoons finely chopped parsley
2 teaspoons mace
Salt and freshly ground black pepper
400 g (14 oz) can artichoke hearts
1 onion
225 g (8 oz) mushrooms
25 g (1 oz) butter
175 g (6 oz) tongue or ham
225 g (8 oz) lard
1 teaspoon salt
150 ml (¼ pint) half milk and half water
450 g (1 lb) plain flour
4 hard-boiled eggs, thickly sliced
175 g (6 oz) liver pâté
750 ml (1¼ pints) good jellied stock
1 egg, beaten

Provides 12 generous portions

Remove the breasts from the chicken and cut the meat into thin strips. Mince the remaining chicken with the bacon, add the parsley, season with mace, salt and pepper and mix well. Drain and slice the artichoke hearts. Peel and finely chop the onion and thinly slice the mushrooms. Melt the butter, add the onion and cook until transparent, add the mushrooms and cook them for three minutes. Cut the tongue or ham into thin strips.

Combine the lard, teaspoon salt, milk and water in a saucepan and heat until the lard has melted and the mixture comes to the boil. Put the flour into a basin, make a well in the centre and pour in the hot liquid. Stir with a wooden spoon then knead until the dough is smooth. Leave for eight minutes, cut off a third for the lid and roll out the rest on a well-floured board into a circle about 1 cm (½ in) thick. Place the circle into a 23 cm (9 in) diameter (about 6·5 cm (2½ in) deep) cake tin with a removable bottom and press it gently into the bottom and sides of the tin making sure there are no breaks in the dough. Press half the minced ingredients into the bottom of the case, cover with layers of sliced hard-boiled eggs, onion and mushrooms and the strips of chicken and tongue, seasoning the layers with salt, pepper and mace. Press the remaining ingredients on top and finally cover with a layer of pâté cut into thin slices (ingredients can be mounded). Pour in enough stock to moisten the ingredients and cover with a lid made from remaining pastry, dampening the edges and pressing them firmly together (it is very important that nothing should be able to leak out).

Chill in a refrigerator for at least an hour then carefully push the pie out of the tin from the bottom leaving it on the base of the cake tin. Make a round hole 2 cm (¾ in) wide in the centre of the pie and decorate with pastry leaves made from any remaining pastry. Brush the top and sides with beaten egg and bake in a moderately hot oven (200°C, 400°F, Reg. 6) for 20 minutes. Then lower the oven to 150°C (300°F, Reg. 2) and continue to cook for a further 40 minutes, covering the top with damp greaseproof paper if it begins to get too brown.

Remove from the oven and pour as much warm stock through the central hole as the pie will absorb. Leave to cool and chill in a refrigerator for at least four hours before cutting.

Serve the pie with Cumberland sauce.

Cornish Splits

50 g (2 oz) fresh yeast
1 teaspoon sugar
300 ml (½ pint) warm water
1·3 kilo (3 lb) flour
150 ml (¼ pint) milk
225 g (8 oz) butter
50 g (2 oz) lard
1 teaspoon salt

Delicious with clotted cream and home-made strawberry jam.

Put the yeast in a basin with the sugar, add the warm water and one tablespoon of flour. Cover with a cloth and leave to rise in a warm place.

Put the milk, butter and lard in a pan to get warm. Warm the flour and put into a large mixing bowl. Make a well in the middle and pour in the milk and fat and the yeast mixture. Add the salt, mix all into a soft dough and leave to rise in a warm place for about one hour until doubled in bulk.

When well risen knead the dough and place on a baking tray in small rounds; leave to rise again. Bake in a moderate oven (180°C, 350°F, Reg. 4). While still hot rub over with a slightly buttered paper to give them a gloss. Put them all on a warm blanket or cloth and fold it lightly over them. This makes the outside soft instead of crisp.

Orange Almond Flapjacks

100 g (4 oz) golden syrup
75 g (3 oz) butter
50 g (2 oz) soft brown sugar
175 g (6 oz) rolled oats
50 g (2 oz) finely chopped or nibbed almonds
Grated rind of 2 oranges

Flapjacks have always been among my favourite tea-time treats, and they couldn't be easier to make which is fortunate as they are so popular they disappear like magic into hungry mouths. In this recipe I have added variety by including some chopped nuts and orange peel.

Combine the syrup and butter in a saucepan and heat gently until the butter melts. Mix in the sugar, cook for a further two minutes and stir in the oats, nuts and orange rind.

Pour the mixture into a well-greased tin measuring about 28 × 18 cm (11 × 7 in) and press down firmly with the back of a wooden spoon.

Bake in a moderate oven (180°C, 350°F, Reg. 4) for 30 minutes until firm and golden brown. Remove from the oven and cut while still hot into neat finger slices about 2·5 cm (1 in) wide. Cool in the tin and turn out when hard.

Sweet Sultana Scones

225 g (8 oz) plain flour
2½ teaspoons baking powder
40 g (1½ oz) sugar
40 g (1½ oz) butter
50 g (2 oz) sultanas
150 ml (¼ pint) milk
1 small egg

Sieve the flour, baking powder and sugar into a bowl. Add the butter cut into small pieces and rub it into the dry ingredients until the mixture resembles coarse breadcrumbs. Stir in the sultanas and mix to a dough with the milk beaten with the egg. Press out the dough on a floured board to a thickness of 1 cm (½ in) and cut into circles with a pastry cutter. Brush the tops with a little extra milk and bake in a hot oven (230°C, 450°F, Reg. 8) for eight minutes until well risen and golden brown. Leave the scones to cool for a few minutes then split them and spread each half generously with butter. Keep warm until they are to be served.

Miscellanea

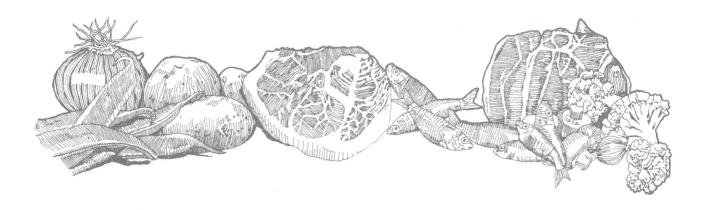

In every cookery book there are a few recipes which do not seem to fit comfortably into any of the major chapters but which have their role in the overall concept of a collection of cookery dishes and ideas. Such recipes have occurred from time to time in my articles for the *Sunday Telegraph* and I have picked out those I felt were really worth including in this book.

They include an egg nogg which is really a remarkable pick-you-up when you feel that the last thing on earth you want to do is to go into the kitchen and start cooking, and some excellent savoury cheese dishes which can be used to make a sensational finale to a dramatic meal or which can be served with fruit as an alternative to a pudding when time is short.

Honeyed Egg Nogg

200 ml (7½ fl oz) hot milk
1 tablespoon honey
2 tablespoons brandy or rum
1 egg

If you feel tired, run-down or just plain exhausted from shopping, have a hot honeyed egg nogg last thing before going to bed. It will make you sleep well and give you strength for the next day. This is also a good drink for anyone suffering from a cold or cough.

Heat the milk with the honey and add the brandy or rum. Beat the egg until foaming, transfer it to a large mug or tumbler, pour over the milk mixture, stirring all the time, and drink at once.

Anchovy Balls

10 anchovy fillets
2 hard-boiled eggs
50 g (2 oz) butter, softened
Few drops Worcestershire sauce
Fresh parsley

Makes about 20

An attractive form of in-between-meal nibbles to serve with drinks or at a buffet party.

Drain off the oil from the anchovies and mash the fillets until smooth. Peel and finely chop the eggs. Combine the eggs and anchovies with the butter, add the Worcestershire sauce and mix well.

Refrigerate until stiff and then form into small balls. Roll in finely chopped parsley before serving.

Moon Mousse

15 g (½ oz) gelatine powder
2 tablespoons warm water
2 egg yolks
150 ml (5 fl oz) double cream
100 g (4 oz) ripe Stilton or blue cheese
2 tablespoons soured cream or yoghurt
Salt, pepper and a few drops Tabasco sauce
3 egg whites, stiffly beaten

Serves 4–6

An unusual way of presenting Stilton or any other type of blue cheese. This can be served as a first course or as a savoury in place of a cheese tray with hot toasted cream crackers or salt biscuits.

Dissolve the gelatine in the warm water. Beat the egg yolks with two tablespoons of the cream, add the dissolved gelatine and mix well. Mash the cheese with the soured cream or yoghurt until smooth. Combine these two mixtures and blend well. Whip the remaining cream until stiff and fold it into the cheese mixture. Refrigerate until the mixture begins to stiffen and set, then season with salt, pepper and Tabasco, fold in the egg whites and turn into a ring mould, lightly oiled. Refrigerate until set firm. Turn out before serving.

To serve as a first course, fill the centre with watercress dipped in a French dressing. To serve as a savoury, sprinkle with a little paprika pepper and accompany with hot salted biscuits.

Potted Stilton

100 g (4 oz) softened butter
225 g (8 oz) Stilton cheese
Salt
¼ teaspoon mace
2 tablespoons port
40 g (1½ oz) clarified butter

Serves 6

Serve in the place of cheese or as a savoury.

Combine the butter with the Stilton and beat with a wooden spoon until smooth. Season with salt and the mace and blend in the port mixing really well. Pack into small jars and pour over the clarified butter. Serve with crisp celery and piping hot cheese crackers.

Note: To clarify butter, heat it until foaming and then strain through muslin.

Camembert or Brie Fritters

1 Camembert or 350 g (12 oz) Brie
1 teaspoon cayenne
1 egg, beaten
3 tablespoons dried breadcrumbs
Fat for deep frying

Serves 4

The next time you buy a Camembert or Brie and have the disappointment of finding it to be well on the unripe side, use it to full advantage by making these finger-shaped, crisply fried savouries which give the cheese a new dimension. Canned Camembert is particularly suitable.

Thinly pare off the rind of the Camembert or Brie and cut the cheese into 4 cm (1½ in) finger-thick lengths. Sprinkle with cayenne. Dip into beaten egg and then into breadcrumbs, leave to dry and then egg and breadcrumb a second time, shaking off excess crumbs.

Fry the Camembert or Brie fritters in very hot deep fat until golden brown and drain at once on kitchen paper. Serve as quickly as possible.

Stuffed Baked Apples ·

4 Bramley apples
75 g (3 oz) sultanas
75 g (3 oz) soft brown sugar
Pinch of nutmeg
12 cloves
70 g (2½ oz) butter

Serves 4

Flavoursome spiced apples which make an unusual and delicious accompaniment for roast chicken or duck, with gammon, sausages and bacon or a whole baked fish such as bass or mullet.

Remove the cores of the apples with an apple corer and slit each one round the middle, using a sharp knife and cutting just through the skin. Finely chop the sultanas and mix them with the sugar and nutmeg. Place the apples in a roasting dish and fill the centres with the spiced mixture and cloves. Melt the butter and pour it into the apple centres, allowing it to overflow the sides. Bake in a moderate oven (190°C, 375°F, Reg. 5) for 30–40 minutes until just tender.

Savoury Butters

Savoury butters are quick and easy to make and can be used instead of a sauce with hamburgers, steaks or grilled chicken. They are a good accompaniment to grilled, poached or baked fish and can also be used as a sandwich filling.

Always use really soft butter for mixing, add the flavouring ingredients, mix well and shape into a roll on a piece of foil. Roll up neatly, chill until firm and cut into thin slices if serving with grilled, poached or baked ingredients. As a sandwich filling the butters need not be chilled.

Anchovy Butter

Cream 100 g (4 oz) unsalted butter with a small can of drained and finely mashed anchovy fillets. Mix well until smooth. This also makes a good alternative to plain butter in egg or tomato sandwiches.

Cheese Butter

100 g (4 oz) butter
75 g (3 oz) finely grated strong cheese, mashed Stilton or blue cheese
¼ teaspoon paprika pepper
1 teaspoon brandy (optional)

Combine all ingredients and mix well until smooth. This makes a delicious sandwich filling with chopped lettuce or watercress.

Parsley Butter

100 g (4 oz) butter
3 tablespoons finely chopped parsley
2 teaspoons lemon juice
White pepper

Combine the first three ingredients, season with a little white pepper and beat until smooth.

Garlic Butter

100 g (4 oz) butter
1–2 cloves garlic

Mash the garlic and mix with softened butter until quite smooth.

Herb Butter

100 g (4 oz) butter
1 tablespoon finely chopped parsley
1 teaspoon lemon juice
1 teaspoon dried mixed herbs

Soften the herbs in lemon juice for 20 minutes. Combine all ingredients and mix well until completely smooth. Leave to stand for the flavours to infuse for about 30 minutes before serving.

Mustard Butter

100 g (4 oz) softened butter
2 tablespoons coarse French mustard with seeds

Combine all ingredients and mix until smooth. A winner for grilled meats and hamburgers.

Smoked Salmon Butter
Pinch of dried dill
1 teaspoon lemon juice
50 g (2 oz) smoked salmon pieces
100 g (4 oz) butter, softened

Expensive but really fabulous as a sandwich filling or to serve with grilled or fried fish. Smoked salmon trimmings can often be bought for much less than slices.

Soak the dill in the lemon juice for 20 minutes to bring out its flavour. Very finely chop or mince the smoked salmon. Combine these ingredients with the butter and mix well until smooth.

Horseradish Butter
100 g (4 oz) butter
3 tablespoons grated horseradish (not horseradish sauce)

Combine the ingredients and mix well until smooth. Good on steaks and delicious with baked potatoes in their jackets.

Cider Butter
100 g (4 oz) unsalted butter
100 g (4 oz) icing sugar
¼ teaspoon ground cinnamon
Grated rind of ½ orange
4 tablespoons dry cider

An inexpensive and milder alternative to brandy butter.

Soften the butter and beat it until soft and creamy. Add the icing sugar and continue to beat until the mixture is light and fluffy (this is best done with an electric mixer if you have one). Add the cinnamon and orange rind and mix well. Gradually blend in the cider, beating after each addition to prevent the sauce separating.

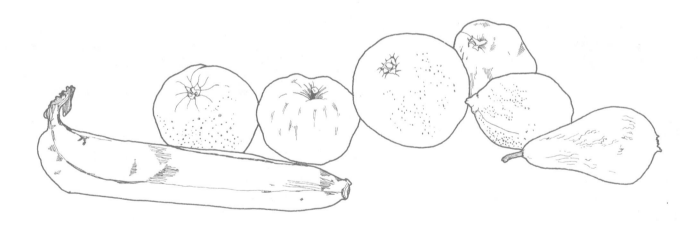

Index